ADVANCE PRAISE FOR
Arrows *in a* Quiver

"A comprehensive and excellent book."
—Cash Ahenakew, Professor of Education,
University of British Columbia

"A useful introduction to Indigenous issues, especially for post-secondary students in Canada." —Jonathan Dewar, co-editor of *Cultivating Canada: Reconciliation through the Lens of Cultural Diversity*

"Focusing on the many relationships between Indigenous peoples and the Crown, James Frideres shows how pervasive colonialism has been on Indigenous Places and Canadian legal system since the first encounters, and into the age of Reconciliation. It is a must-read for non-Indigenous settlers in Canada, and especially for government politicians and lawyers."
—David McNab, co-author of *Canada's First Nations: A History of Founding Peoples from Earliest Times*

"*Arrows in a Quiver* makes a serious advance in state-of-the-art research. Jim Frideres has taken the many disparate—and sometimes conflicting—commentaries on decolonization and situated them in their historical context as shaped by government action/inaction. After having established this historical context, he goes a step further and provides insight into what the path to reconciliation, as called for by the Truth and Reconciliation Commission, necessitates. Situating the historical, political, and social contexts provides understanding into what decolonization and a devolution of governmental power may entail, an understanding which is critical if reconciliation is to be embraced by Indigenous and non-Indigenous Canadians alike."
—Cathy Prowse, Professor of Sociology & Anthropology,
Mount Royal University

"*Arrows in a Quiver* is a remarkable book that is essential reading for all Canadians who want to understand the roots of the ongoing and seemingly intractable relationship of Indigenous Peoples and the state. The author, James Frideres, has devoted his professional life to analysing this critical topic from multiple perspectives and offers crucial insights for possible ways forward."
—Arthur J. Ray, oc, frsc, Professor Emeritus of History, University of British Columbia, and author of *Aboriginal Rights Claims and the Making and Remaking of History*

ARROWS in a QUIVER

INDIGENOUS-CANADIAN RELATIONS FROM CONTACT TO THE COURTS

JAMES FRIDERES

© 2019 University of Regina Press

All rights reserved. No part of this work covered by the copyrights hereon may be reproduced or used in any form or by any means—graphic, electronic, or mechanical—without the prior written permission of the publisher. Any request for photocopying, recording, taping or placement in information storage and retrieval systems of any sort shall be directed in writing to Access Copyright.

Cover design: Duncan Campbell, University of Regina Press
Text design: John van der Woude, JVDW Designs
Copy editor: Dallas Harrison
Proofreader: Kristine Douaud
Indexer: Jenn Harris
Cover art: "Portrait of a One Percenter - Transformation," 2015, private collection, by Lawrence Paul Yuxweliptun. Photo by Heffel Fine Art Auction House.

Library and Archives Canada Cataloguing in Publication

Title: Arrows in a quiver : Indigenous-Canadian relations from contact to the courts / James Frideres.
Names: Frideres, James S., 1943- author.
Description: Includes bibliographical references and index.
Identifiers: Canadiana (print) 20190157615 | Canadiana (ebook) 20190157674 | ISBN 9780889776814 (hardcover) | ISBN 9780889776784 (softcover) | ISBN 9780889776807 (HTML) | ISBN 9780889776791 (PDF)
Subjects: CSH: Native peoples—Canada—Government relations. | CSH: Native peoples—Canada—Politics and government. | CSH: Native peoples—Legal status, laws, etc.—Canada. | CSH: Native peoples—Civil rights—Canada. | CSH: Native peoples—Canada—Social conditions. | LCSH: Canada—Race relations. | LCSH: Canada—Ethnic relations. | LCSH: Decolonization—Canada.
Classification: LCC E92 .F75 2019 | DDC 305.897/071—dc23

10 9 8 7 6 5 4 3 2 1

University of Regina Press, University of Regina
Regina, Saskatchewan, Canada, S4S 0A2
tel: (306) 585-4758 fax: (306) 585-4699

web: www.uofrpress.ca

We acknowledge the support of the Canada Council for the Arts for our publishing program. We acknowledge the financial support of the Government of Canada. / Nous reconnaissons l'appui financier du gouvernement du Canada. This publication was made possible with support from Creative Saskatchewan's Book Publishing Production Grant Program.

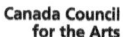  

CONTENTS

Maps and Tables vii
Author's Note ix
Preface xi
Terminology xvii
Timeline of Significant Historical Events xxi

Introduction 1
CHAPTER 1 Indigeneity in Canada 13
CHAPTER 2 Relations between Indigenous and
 Non-Indigenous People 51
CHAPTER 3 Keeping the Land 87
CHAPTER 4 Indigenous Treaties, Métis Scrip, and the
 Manitoba Act 115
CHAPTER 5 Aboriginal Rights 153
CHAPTER 6 The Role of the Courts 185
CHAPTER 7 The Social Organizations of Indigenous Peoples 227
CONCLUSION Reconciliation and Resilience in the Twenty-First
 Century 251

Acknowledgements 277
References 279
Index 305
About the Author 326

MAPS AND TABLES

MAP 1 Tribal Distribution in Canada at Time of Contact 17
MAP 2 Inuit Regional Districts, 2000 31
MAP 3 Métis Areas of Settlement and Hunting, Twentieth Century 33
MAP 4 Historical Treaties 125
MAP 5 Modern Comprehensive Claims 141

TABLE 1.1 Indigenous Identity Population, Canada, 2016 45
TABLE 1.2 Distribution and Percentage of Population Reporting an Indigenous Identity in the Population, Canada, Provinces, and Territories, 2016 46
TABLE 4.1 National Summary of Specific Claims (1973–2017) 145

AUTHOR'S NOTE

When settlers entered what is now Canada, many Indigenous peoples were eliminated by disease, starvation and outright genocide by the state. Those who survived were relegated to the margins of society and had their families, health, spirituality, land, and language taken away or destroyed. Over the years, the state continued these attacks on first peoples.

But now Indigenous peoples and communities are resisting. They are plugging into global and domestic Indigenous advocacy networks, organizing social movements and activist organizations, and participating in the legal and political spheres of Canadian society to combat colonialism and the institutions that have promulgated the marginalization of Indigenous peoples. Community economic development initiatives are emerging from their grassroots, and Indigenous people are taking back control of the education of their young people and preserving their traditional languages.

The emergence of multiple ways in which to resist colonial ideology and action has given Indigenous people an arsenal of arrows to use to confront the state use of genocide, institutional racism, and the promotion of assimilation. These arrows are allowing Indigenous peoples to reclaim what they lost during colonization, re-establish their voice in Canadian society, and achieve equality and justice.

PREFACE

Arrows in a Quiver is written for two audiences: the first is a scholarly one that cuts across academic disciplines, and the second is non-specialists who wish to have a better understanding of how Canada has found itself in such a "messy" situation regarding Indigenous people as we all move further into the twenty-first century. The material in this book provides a context for understanding the current relations between Indigenous people and the government (as well as with non-Indigenous Canadians), and it explains, in clear terms, how the relationship has been dealt with for the past two centuries. It also provides some context for understanding how non-Indigenous people relate to Indigenous people outside the political-legal environment.

When settler colonists took up residence in Canada, and colonial administrators began to govern the land, they operated on the belief that they had the legal rights to remove Indigenous people from their lands, take ownership of those lands, and instill Christian beliefs and capitalist values in all Indigenous people (Ray 2016). Although there were elements of legal pluralism during the nineteenth century, Indigenous sovereignty has always been insecure (Foster, Berger, and Buck 2008). Thus, the settlements made by the government regarding Indigenous people—for instance, the treaties—remain fragile and tenuous.

I also argue in this book that, though colonialism has been destructive regarding Indigenous people's lives, there is some evidence that it is not as intractable as some people would argue (Borrows 2017a).

Through an analysis of court decisions, specifically Supreme Court of Canada rulings, I show how the courts have tried to deal with some of the impacts of settler intrusion. Nevertheless, it is important to note that the court system, like other institutions, is part of the colonial heritage and does not operate outside settler colonialism. My analysis here reveals how inaction by government officials regarding Indigenous issues has been overtaken by the Supreme Court. McHugh (2016) agrees that the intervention of the courts regarding government-Indigenous relations resulted from a political stalemate. The federal government was not supporting or promoting Aboriginal Rights, so Indigenous leaders sought out the courts for the resolution of various issues. As such, court intervention, particularly from 1972 to 1992, and then in the early part of the twenty-first century, has prodded political leaders to address many Indigenous concerns. Once the constitutional conferences were over (1983–87) and it was clear that no further movement by the government was taking place regarding Indigenous issues, First Nations, Métis, and Inuit began to look at section 35 of the *Charter of Rights and Freedoms* as a mechanism by which they could address their concerns. Since then, other sections of the Charter, such as section 15, have been used to address Indigenous concerns.

For years, as McHugh (2016) points out, the major procedure of the courts was to use "common law" to address Indigenous claims. However, the Supreme Court, over time, deemed such a process flawed and began to focus on the "honour of the crown" (moving away from the old philosophy of sole "fiduciary responsibility" espoused by the courts as its core of decision-making) as the strategy by which to deal with a variety of Indigenous claims, including land claims. As such, the involvement of the courts has reduced the footprint of colonial legal architecture and has given some new direction for the near future on the path of relations between Indigenous people and the government (as well as between Indigenous and non-Indigenous people). Nevertheless, Indigenous people continue to resist and adjust to colonial settler strategies that still permeate our institutional orders that have been imposed on them over time (Asch 2014; Barker 2012).

Arrows in a Quiver contributes to the literature on settler colonialism (and Eurocentrism) and specifically on what has been called "explosive colonialism" (Nettelback et al. 2016). It reveals that colonialism is reflected in the many different institutions and individuals that have worked, and continue to work, in parallel and interactively, to dispossess Indigenous Peoples of their cultures, rights, and lands (Graziadei 2009). This European philosophy was reconstructed in Canada by colonial administrators and early settlers to reinforce their views of Indigenous people and to support the emerging capitalist economy as the superior and necessary economic structure. The book demonstrates just how pervasive and dominant settler culture is by revealing how the European worldview (the "ethos") has permeated the institutional orders of Canada and then been implemented through the newly established political and legal processes. As well, the belief in "progress" and science is part of the foundation of this European philosophy adopted by current Canadian leaders in a variety of institutions (e.g., educational, economic, political). This ethos was used in many other ways too, including to develop a definition of the "family," to ensure the importance of "individualism" (versus collectivism), and to support the value of social mobility through individual competition (Monchalin 2016) that many non-Indigenous Canadians hold in high regard.

Arrows in a Quiver also addresses a major concern of Indigenous Peoples, overlooked (or ignored) by the government and many Canadian leaders, through an analysis of how land is central to Indigenous Peoples—their lives, identities, and communities (Alfred 2008, 2013). For Indigenous people, land has a high use value since they are closely tied to the natural world: Mother Earth. It also has a high cultural significance in addition to its subsistence properties. In the end, land, from an Indigenous perspective, is not viewed as a commodity as it is in the non-Indigenous world. In a related discussion, I analyze treaties and similar agreements between Indigenous Peoples and the government of Canada. Finally, I present a clear description of how the political structure of Indigenous Peoples has changed over time and how these changes attempt to deal with the government, themselves, the private sector, and other organizations; I also discuss how the government has dealt with Indigenous organizations.

As Veracini (2013a) and Wolfe (2006) point out, settler colonialism is a structure and not a one-time event. In a settler society, there are many different institutions (e.g., religious, economic, educational, political) and agents that have worked and continue to work in combination to displace and destroy Indigenous cultures (Kelm and Smith 2018). As such, these features have become integrated into settler social structures and acted in an almost invisible manner as the "Western Enlightenment" narrative took hold (Alfred 2009; Corntassel 2008). In addition, as Monchalin (2016, xx) points out, Eurocentric rationality and history, religious bodies, media, and technologies, as well as Western systems of education, became the foundation of settler society in Canada and the institutions that colonial administrators and settlers would put in place. This ethos, and the social-economic-political structures put in place, albeit with changes over time, remain in place today. As policies and practices of settler society were implemented, their influence became pervasive and entrenched, and they continue to diminish the legitimacy of Indigenous Peoples and their cultures today and are integral to carrying out the "logic of elimination" policy entrenched in Canadian society (Kelm and Smith 2018).

I have chosen to engage in a framework of relationality (Henry, Tait, and STR8 UP 2016) in which I had the opportunity to reflect on my space of privilege while writing this book. Through my understanding of how the social space of privilege has promulgated the marginalized position of Indigenous people, I have shared my work with academic colleagues and Indigenous community members to reflect on how my analysis has impacted my conclusions. This process of relational accountability that Henry and colleagues refer to helps all researchers to achieve respect, reciprocity, relevance, and responsibility in carrying out research on Indigenous Peoples.

Finally, I should note that the reference list includes government sources, Indigenous and non-Indigenous scholars, non-Indigenous authors, as well as some popular media outlets. However, the text includes literature from the burgeoning list of Indigenous authors who have contributed to the discussion of Indigenous-government relations. As a result of these new contributions, there is an increasing body of literature that has changed our understanding of the past. Much of it is based upon new oral and archival evidence, but other studies give new interpretations using the same historical records used by previous generations of scholars (Dunbar-Ortiz 2014; Fixico 2013; Richter 2001). To provide the reader with a framework of change in Indigenous-government relations over time, the "Timeline of Significant Historical Events" shows the most significant events. Moreover, it identifies milestones and allows the reader to see how interactions changed over time.

TERMINOLOGY

Below are some basic terms necessary to understand any discussion of Indigenous people in Canada. Although formal and legal documents use the term "Aboriginal," in this book I use the term "Indigenous" in many circumstances because it is more acceptable to Indigenous people in Canada (Younging 2018).

Aboriginal Peoples: The descendants of the original inhabitants of North America. The Canadian Constitution recognizes three groups of Aboriginal Peoples: Indians, Métis, and Inuit. These three distinct groups have unique heritages, languages, cultural practices, and spiritual beliefs.

Aboriginal Rights: Rights that some Indigenous Peoples of Canada hold because of their ancestors' long-standing use and occupancy of the land. The rights of certain Indigenous Peoples to hunt, trap, and fish on ancestral lands are examples of Aboriginal Rights. These rights vary from group to group depending on the customs, practices, and traditions that have formed their distinctive cultures.

Aboriginal self-government: Governments designed, established, and administered by Indigenous Peoples.

Aboriginal Title: A legal term that recognizes an Indigenous interest in the land. It is based upon the long-standing use and occupancy of the land by today's Indigenous Peoples as the descendants of the original inhabitants of Canada.

band: A community of First Nations people living on land set aside by the crown or a community of First Nations people declared to be a band for the purposes of the *Indian Act*.

band council: The governing body of a band established by the dictum of the *Indian Act*. Chiefs and councils are colonial structures imposed on First Nations and are elected, though some are chosen by custom.

Bill C-31: The pre-legislation name of the 1985 *Act to Amend the Indian Act*. This Act eliminated certain discriminatory provisions of the *Indian Act*, including the section that resulted in First Nations women losing their legal status when they married anyone not a Status Indian. Bill C-31 enabled people affected by the discriminatory provisions in the old *Indian Act* to apply to have their status and membership restored.

custom: A traditional Indigenous practice. For example, some Indigenous people sometimes marry or adopt children according to custom rather than Canadian family law. Band councils chosen by "custom" are elected or selected by traditional means rather than the election rules contained in the *Indian Act*.

First Nation: A term that came into common use in the 1970s to replace the term "Indian," which some people found offensive. Although the term "First Nation" is widely used, no legal definition of it exists. Among its uses, the term "First Nations people" refers to "Indian people" in Canada, both Status and Non-Status. Some "Indian" people have also adopted the term "First Nation" to replace the term "Band" in the name of their community.

Indian: People who belong to one of three groups recognized as Aboriginal in the *Constitution Act, 1982*. It specifies that Aboriginal people in Canada consist of Indians, Inuit, and Métis. Indians in Canada are often referred to as Status Indians, Non-Status Indians, and Treaty Indians.

Indian Act: Canadian federal legislation first passed in 1876 and amended several times since. The *Indian Act* sets out certain federal government obligations and regulates the management of reserve lands, money, and other resources. Among its many provisions, the *Indian Act* currently requires the minister of the Department of Indigenous and Northern Affairs Canada to manage certain funds belonging to First Nations and First Nations lands and to approve or disallow First Nations bylaws.

Indian Status: An individual's legal status as an Indian, as defined by the *Indian Act*.

Indigenous: A term now used to refer to "Indians," Métis, and Inuit. It mirrors the constitutional terminology of "Aboriginal Peoples" and is used by Indigenous and Northern Affairs Canada, though legal documents still use the term "Aboriginal."

Innu: Naskapi and Montagnais First Nations Peoples who live in northern Quebec and Labrador.

Inuvialuit: Inuit who live in the western Arctic.

Inuit: Indigenous people in northern Canada who live in Nunavut, Northwest Territories, northern Quebec, and northern Labrador. The word means "people" in the Inuit language (Inuktitut). The singular of Inuit is Inuk.

land claims: In 1973, the federal government recognized two broad classes of claims: comprehensive and specific. Comprehensive claims are based upon the assessment that there might be continuing Aboriginal Rights to lands and natural resources. These claims come up in those parts of Canada where Aboriginal Title has not been dealt with by treaty and other legal means. The claims are called "comprehensive" because of their wide scope. They include land title, fishing and trapping rights, and financial compensation. Specific claims deal with specific grievances that First Nations might have regarding the fulfillment of treaties. Specific claims also cover grievances related to the administration of First Nations lands and assets under the *Indian Act*.

Métis: People of mixed First Nations and European ancestry who identify themselves as Métis, distinct from First Nations, Inuit, and non-Indigenous people. The Métis have a unique culture that draws from their diverse ancestral origins: Scottish, French, Cree, and Anishinaabe.

Métis Nation: The Indigenous people descended from the historical Métis Nation, now comprised of all Métis Nation people; one of the Aboriginal Peoples of Canada as defined in section 35 of the *Constitution Act, 1982*.

Non-Status Indian: A person not registered as an "Indian" under the *Indian Act*. She or he is not listed on the federal roll of individuals listed as Status Indians.

Nunangat: Refers to the four regions (Inuvialuit, Nunavut, Nunavik, Nunatsiavut) in northern Canada that have a majority of Inuit as residents.

Nunavut: The geographical-political territory created in northern Canada on April 1, 1999, when the former Northwest Territories was divided in two. Nunavut means "our land" in Inuktitut. Inuit make up 85 percent of the population of Nunavut. The territory has its own public government.

off reserve: Anything that relates to First Nations—people, services, or objects—but is not located on a reserve.

oral history: Evidence from the spoken words of people who have knowledge of past events and traditions. This type of history is often recorded on tape and then put in writing. It is used in history books and to document claims.

reserve: Land owned by the crown and set aside for the use of a First Nation.

Status Indian: A person registered as an "Indian" under the *Indian Act*, which sets out the requirements for determining who is an "Indian" for the purposes of the *Indian Act*.

surrender: A formal agreement by which a band consents to give up part or all of its rights and interests in a reserve. Reserve lands can be surrendered for sale or for lease, on certain conditions, but only to the crown.

Treaty Indian: A Status Indian who belongs to a First Nation that signed a treaty with the crown.

tribal council: A regional group of First Nations members who work together to represent and/or advocate for common services.

TIMELINE OF SIGNIFICANT HISTORICAL EVENTS

FIRST CONTACT (1100–1550)
Norse explorers
Champlain expedition

EUROPEAN COLONIAL SETTLEMENT/TIMBER CUTTING/INITIAL FUR TRADE (1550–1600)
Emergence of New France, Acadia
Role of voyageurs/missionaries
Logging expansion

EXPANSION OF EUROPEAN SETTLEMENT (1600–1701)
Hudson's Bay Company exclusive monopoly of lands of Hudson Bay watershed, Rupert's Land (1670)
Great Peace Treaty (1701)
Indigenous military alliances with English/French

THE END OF FRENCH COLONIAL EFFORTS (1702–63)
Beginning of Peace and Friendship Treaties
Seven Years War (1756–63)
Royal Proclamation (1763)

ALLIES TO WARDS (1764–1850)

Niagara Treaty (1764)
American Revolution (1776)
Treaty of Paris (1783), Indigenous lands ceded to United States
United Empire Loyalist refugees move to Canada from United States
War of 1812 (Indigenous support for British/colonials against United States)
Territorial sovereignty introduced in 1814 ignoring Indigenous sovereignty and recognizing British sovereignty
Some Indigenous lands taken in Upper Canada
Military control of Indigenous people moved to civilian control (1830)
Crown Lands Protection Act (1839), government made guardian of all crown lands
Douglas Treaties signed (1850–54)
Early Indigenous legislation (1850, 1857)
Robinson-Huron and Robinson-Superior Treaties (1850)

CREATION OF *INDIAN ACT*/ASSIMILATION POLICY (1851–1925)

Indian Lands Act (1860), centralization of control over Indigenous affairs
Transfer of authority over Indigenous affairs to the colonies (1860)
Canadian Confederation (1867) via *British North America Act*
Federal authority over "Indians and lands set aside for Indians"
An Act for the Gradual Enfranchisement of Indians (1869), compulsory enfranchisement for First Nations people
Métis Resistance (1869–70)
Manitoba Act (1870)
North West Mounted Police created (1873), today called Royal Canadian Mounted Police
First consolidated *Indian Act* (1876)
Department of Indian Affairs created (1880)
Establishment of residential schools through amendment of *Indian Act* (1884)
Riel Resistance (1885)
Eleven Numbered Treaties with First Nations (1871–1921)
Indigenous participation in First World War

CHANGING PERSPECTIVES (1926–75)

Natural Resources Transfer Act (1930), control of crown lands to western provinces
Inuit considered responsibility of federal government (but not considered "Indians") (1939)
Indigenous involvement in Second World War
Major changes to *Indian Act* (1951)
First Nations people given right to vote in federal elections (1960)
Creation of National Indian Brotherhood (1961)
Federal White Paper, Indigenous Brown Paper, Citizen Plus (1969–70)
Creation of Native Council of Canada (1971)
Emergence of Inuit Tapiriit Kanatami (1971), national voice for Inuit
Calder case in British Columbia with Nisga'a (1973)
Paulette Caveat case in Northwest Territories (1973)
Native Women's Association of Canada (1974)
First major comprehensive claim, Northern Quebec Land Settlement (1975)

INDIGENOUS CHALLENGES TO GOVERNMENT POLICY (1976–2000)

Declaration of First Nations (1980)
Comprehensive claims policy and specific claims policy amended
Repatriation of Canadian Constitution (1982)
Creation of Assembly of First Nations (1982)
Establishment of Métis National Council (1983)
Inuvialuit Final Agreement (1984)
Paternity rule implemented by Indian and Northern Affairs Canada (1985)
Passage of Bill C-31 (1985)
Inuvialuit Claims Settlement Act (1984)
Oka Crisis (1990)
Congress of Aboriginal Peoples created (1993) for Métis and Non-Status Indians
Aboriginal inherent right policy (1995)

Royal Commission on Aboriginal Peoples (1991–96)
Aboriginal Healing Foundation (1998–2014)
Nunavut created (1999)
Major Supreme Court of Canada decisions, *Guerin* (1984), *Sparrow* (1990), *Delgamuukw* (1997)

CURRENT ISSUES (2001–19)

Powley decision (2003), Métis Right to hunt
Haida Nation decision (2004), government duty to consult with Indigenous Peoples
Residential School Compensation Act (2007)
Federal government apology to Indigenous people (2008)
McIvor case (2009), Ottawa forced to amend *Indian Act*
Truth and Reconciliation Commission (2008–15)
Canada voted against United Nations Declaration on the Rights of Indigenous Peoples (2007)
Canada signed United Nations Declaration on the Rights of Indigenous Peoples (2010)
Supreme Court found federal government failed to meet promises to Métis (2013)
Bill c-3, *Gender Equity in Indian Registration Act* (2011)
Tsilhqot'in decision (2014), First Nation granted title claim in British Columbia
Quebec court finds *Indian Act* discriminates against Indigenous women (*Descheneaux* decision) (2015)
Human Rights Tribunal (2016), Ottawa discriminates against Indigenous children
National Inquiry on Missing and Murdered Aboriginal Women (2016–19)
Daniels decision (2016), Métis and Non-Status Indians within the scope of federal jurisdiction
Ontario Court of Appeal finds "paternity rule" discriminatory against First Nations women (2017)
Bill s-3 to amend *Indian Act*, gender inequity (2017)
Dissolution of Indigenous and Northern Affairs Canada (2018)

Creation of two new departments: Crown-Indigenous Relations and Northern Affairs Canada and Indigenous Services Canada (2018)

Supreme Court decision: the government has no duty to consult with Indigenous Peoples prior to drafting legislation (2018)

INTRODUCTION

"You can't sell what you belong to; you can only share it."
—Elder Fred Kelly, 2015

I begin this book by noting that this is an introduction to Indigenous Peoples (Indian–First Nations, Métis, Inuit) regarding their relationships with the government and thus both directly and indirectly with non-Indigenous people. My focus is on Indigenous-government relations and how the government has controlled the agenda and implemented and interpreted government policy regarding Indigenous people. I also look at how Indigenous people have responded and the actions that they have taken to deal with government policies. In making such an analysis, it is necessary to look at how early settlers and today's Canadian non-Indigenous people have participated in the continuing processes of colonization as well as embarked on some processes of decolonization. In the end, the story told provides a clear understanding of issues such as Aboriginal Rights (including perspectives from both the Western world and the Indigenous world), the importance of land, the role of courts in dealing with Indigenous concerns, and how Indigenous organizations operate as they try to secure a niche for Indigenous Peoples and their communities in Canadian society as they work their way through the maze of settler law (Borrows 2010b). I also reveal how the government has dealt with these organizations over time. Finally, I provide answers to questions that most people ask but cannot easily find answers for (Robertson 2012).

O'Brien (2018) examines the political participation of Indigenous people through using petitions and reveals a new perspective regarding Indigenous political activism. Through petitions, Indigenous people have been able to mobilize communities, subvert authority, and resist colonial oppression. O'Brien finds that this strategy continues to be used and reveals the recognition of prior land ownership while trying to work within the narrative of historical and contemporary notions of justice. Moreover, she shows how Indigenous people have actively tried to influence their quest for self-determination by using petitions. She concludes that the use of petitions historically and contemporarily conveys political meaning, involves power, and rejects colonialism.

Indigenous people are experiencing an unprecedented series of transformations in their relationship with Canada involving issues such as Aboriginal Rights, Aboriginal Title, the duty to consult, the infringement of rights, and the honour of the crown (see *Calder* 1973; *Delgamuukw* 1997; *Haida* 2004; *Sparrow* 1990; and *Tsilhqot'in* 2014). Change in contemporary Indigenous-government relations began in the 1950s and intensified with the creation of modern treaties (comprehensive claims), devolutionary agreements, and substantive rulings of the Supreme Court of Canada (Robertson 2012). Achieving the desired results from these changes continues to be a long-term and demanding prospect for Indigenous people (Asch 2002). Nevertheless, the slow pace of change also reveals the deep influence of Eurocentric thinking and the structures created upon the earlier foundations established by colonial administrators and settlers (Palmater 2015). Nevertheless, these changes also reveal the impacts of resilient, creative, and engaged Indigenous leaders as they deal with the neo-colonialist efforts of today's government (Little Bear 2009).

In recent years, publications focusing on Indigenous issues (and material written by Indigenous authors) have proliferated. Most authors have found that Indigenous people are poor, isolated, in need of better health care, poorly educated, and vastly overrepresented in the incarcerated population (Buckley 1993; Purich 1986; York 1989). Many of these authors proffer solutions to the problems—both short term and long term (Dyck 1991; Ponting 1986). However, more recent works have emphasized the strengths of Indigenous culture as well as the contributions that Indigenous people have made to the development of Canadian society (Alfred and Corntassel 2005; Palmater 2011b; Simpson 2017; Victor 2012). Nevertheless, government officials have deemed these latter analyses and assessments as unimportant or irrelevant as they continue to control and direct the lives of Indigenous people with impunity.

With few exceptions, these publications (both old and new) illuminate that the crown, while seemingly cognizant of the issues facing Indigenous people, has done little to ameliorate their socio-economic situation (MacKinnon 2015). In some cases, the action taken by the government has exacerbated the plight of Indigenous people (Anderson 2014). For example, as Ing (2017) has noted, in 1862 the colonial government refused to inoculate Haida for smallpox, which then decimated village populations. A more recent example is the Sayisi Dene in northern Manitoba, forcibly relocated to an isolated area near Churchill in 1956 by the federal government without consultation, explanation, or adequate planning. The rationale provided after the fact was that the government believed that they were the cause of a steep decline of the caribou herd in the area. The stated rationale proved to be incorrect, and because of the move nearly one-third of the relocated Sayisi-Dene died within a decade. Other examples are when Indian Affairs provides funds for economic activities but does not allow the community to integrate the activities with the local culture (Cornell 2013; McBride 2010). At the same time, the crown continues to argue that it knows best and takes a piecemeal approach to dealing with the issues faced by Indigenous people (Alfred 2009). Overall, crown thinking is embedded in traditional views of how to deal with the "Indigenous problem" (White 2016). It is not visionary, forward looking, or interested in holding a dialogue with Indigenous people on how change might best be achieved (Alvarez 2014). Moreover, it focuses on the "Indigenous problem" as the basis for making decisions—in short, blaming the victim as the source of the problem (Harding 2006).

Today we find that policy makers and government officials seem to be impervious to acknowledging that using past strategies to deal with today's issues will not provide solutions for the future (Benjamin 2014). Time after time, the crown engages in activities that perpetuate the status quo, alienate Indigenous people, and reject the idea that they can govern themselves; the crown is unprepared to engage in major social change in dealing with Indigenous people (Coates 2015; O'Connor et al. 2010). One example that I share with my students is that not a single case has come before the courts in which the federal crown has supported the position of Indigenous people. Barkan (2000) and Regan (2010) note that, even when the process of "reconciliation" is undertaken by the state and involves apology and financial restitution, it turns out to be an inexpensive way of attempting to regain moral legitimacy (de Greiff 2008; Nobles 2008) but does little to achieve reconciliation or address the root cause of the issue. It also allows the state to maintain its hegemonic control and thus redirect people's attention from the issues raised by Indigenous people (Newman 2014).

In Canada, the value of meritocracy is well entrenched in our social philosophy and institutional structures. However, Indigenous people argue that the norms of fair treatment and equality of opportunity (integral components of meritocracy) are not being met (Ketilson 2014). One might hope that Canadians would see this inequity as problematic and of concern. However, both government and non-Indigenous people are sanguine about the status of meritocracy and generally reluctant to attribute the disparity between Indigenous people and non-Indigenous people to "bias" within the social-economic-legal institutional structures of Canadian society (Kelm and Smith 2018; Knowles and Lowery 2012). Why is this? First, the government and most non-Indigenous people see the status quo as legitimate. Second, they claim that there is no problem in protecting their advantaged position in society. Or, as Knowles and Lowery (2012) point out, the government and non-Indigenous people deny inequity because, the greater the importance they place on meritocracy as a norm for distributing valued goods, the less willing they are to see the rule as having been violated. In the end, non-Indigenous people see themselves as possessing merit (e.g., they are talented, hardworking, dedicated) and thus dismiss the claim that socio-economic inequities are based upon white privilege (Gagnon 2014) or result from the nature and structure of the social institutions of Canadian society.

The term "genocide" (physical, social, cultural) in reference to Indigenous people has become so vague and misused that it has been rejected by many Canadians (Woolford 2009). It might be because the term has taken on a mystique that characterizes all actions taken by the government as the pinnacle of evil and thus places representatives who pursued this policy as debasing the social and legal systems in Canada (Girvan 2010). Put another way, Canadians think that such a term is too harsh to characterize how Indigenous people have been treated over the past four centuries (Gray 2011). Others argue that the actions of the government in dealing with Indigenous people were taken in the sense of righteousness and justified in the defence of a communal good (Neu and Therrien 2002). Nevertheless, once the term is introduced into a discussion, many Canadians reject the subsequent arguments.

We know that the individuals who created the laws and policies of Canada regarding Indigenous people rarely showed signs of guilt or remorse (Steckley and Cummins 2008). However, it is clear from Canadian history that colonial administrators and settlers were complicit in the disenfranchisement of Indigenous people, indeed active participants in their removal from the land and later supportive of crown policies of assimilation because they thought that these were appropriate things to do (Foster, Berger, and Buck 2008; Nettelbeck et al. 2016). Settlers did not view their actions as criminal or step back from their opportunities to inflict pain and suffering on Indigenous people since their actions were complicit with existing values and norms as established by themselves, government agencies, and various institutions (e.g., educational, legal). For example, the churches, which controlled the residential schools, had little interest in addressing the cultural concerns of their Indigenous students, for their goal was like that of the crown—to take the "Indian" out of every child and Christianize each one—a policy supported by all administrators, settler colonists, and later Canadian officials (Rutherdale, Abel, and Lackenbauer, 2018).

RESIDENTIAL SCHOOLS

The Jesuit missionaries along with the fur trappers were the first (starting in the early 1600s) to deal with Indigenous people. (For those interested in the specific role of the fur trade and Indigenous relations, see Innis 1999 and Ray 1974, 1982). Later the Anglican Church Missionary Society began to proselytize Indigenous people. For the better part of the nineteenth century, Anglican missionaries worked in eastern Canada and parts of Manitoba and Saskatchewan (Bradford 2012). At the same time, Catholic missionaries and Wesleyan Methodist missionaries were active in working with Indigenous people. Between these two groups, over twenty missions were established across Canada (Huel 1996).

Residential schools were in operation in Canada from 1831 to 1996. These church-supported and -run boarding schools were integrated with federal policy by 1892. As a result, the federal government funded the construction of the schools, but they were operated by church groups. In 1920, the federal government made it mandatory that Indigenous children between the ages of seven and fifteen attend school. Parents who refused to send their children to school were fined or imprisoned, and the children were forcibly sent to residential schools, generally far away from their local communities. By 1931, eighty residential schools were in operation, providing schooling to more than 150,000 children. Given that "Indians" were not "persons" until 1960, they had no legal right to challenge the government, nor could they hire a lawyer to act on their behalf.

In the end, a missionary structure was put in place in northern and western Canada. By the end of the nineteenth century, state-supervised and church-operated schools focusing on Indigenous children were in place. The Davin Report of 1879 outlined a program for developing cooperation between church and state in the arena of education. The first school of this type was the Mohawk (Kanien'keha:ka) institute for boys from the Six Nations in Brantford, Ontario. The federal government operated its own residential schools in 1850, but by 1892 had changed its policy and partnered with churches to run the schools. However, because there were many day schools that Indigenous children could attend, a majority attended them until 1944, when the pattern reversed and more children attended residential schools than day schools (Nettelbeck et al. 2016). Government law stipulated that, if a local school was unavailable to Indigenous children, then the government could force them to attend a residential school.

By the late nineteenth century, a national residential school system was in place and rapidly expanded with several other missionary groups (e.g., Presbyterian). In turn, these religious organizations approached the federal government for operating grants to build and maintain residential schools. The arrangement was supported by politicians convinced that the establishment and operation of the schools would lead to their goal of assimilation (Bradford 2012). Moreover, the cost of operating such schools would be minimal for the state beyond their construction and maintenance. Almost all residential schools were nearly 60 percent less costly to build than provincial schools since inferior materials and construction were used. Moreover, the operating costs would be picked up by the missionary groups and their agencies. Federal changes to the *Indian Act* in the early twentieth century made it even easier for authorities to remove Indigenous children from their homes and place them in residential schools.

INDIGENOUS RESISTANCE

The resistance by Indigenous people to these measures was ineffectual. Given the geographic separation of Indigenous people and their acceptance of the authority of the government, including the RCMP, and supported by their culture that tried to avoid most overt conflict, the massive movement of Indigenous children into the residential school system ensued (Mosby 2013). Despite the lack of overt resistance by Indigenous parents, they engaged in some public conflicts as well as covert actions to evade the placement of their children in residential schools (Ennab 2010). However, any overt sign of resistance was usually met by a show of police force to repress it. Moreover, acts of resistance by Indigenous people were viewed as criminal acts rather than political struggles (Dickason and Calder 2006). Nevertheless, many Indigenous communities submitted petitions and utilized other forms of protest (Alfred 2011). In the end, grievances expressed by Indigenous people regarding the removal of children from families and their placement in schools, sometimes hundreds of miles from their homes, as well as other concerns, were ignored by government authorities (Nettelbeck et al. 2016).

It is also important to realize that engaging in discrimination against and harm of Indigenous people by administrators and settlers was voluntary. As Brannigan (2013) points out, individuals who engage in violence against minority groups often reveal that they were free to refuse to do so and sometimes acted reluctantly, at other times enthusiastically, but they did act without undue pressure or compunction to carry out violence against Indigenous people. Such actions by colonial administrators and settlers were supported by the political and legal institutional orders created during the time of colonization. This process allowed for the "conventionalization" of criminal activities by settlers, businesspeople, and the government (Carson 1979). In this manner, various criminal acts against Indigenous people were taken, and though technically against the law they were resorted to freely. Occasionally, one of the perpetrators would be prosecuted, but few were found guilty, and the punishment, if they were found guilty, was minimal. The lack of sanctions brought against these individuals was the result of many justifications that tended to undermine the severity of the offence and thus minimized the response of the public and legal authorities. No political authorities objected to the policy being carried out, and the public was largely ignorant of the specific policies regarding Indigenous people (Espeland 2001). These actions supported the belief that Indigenous people had full rights as Canadian citizens and were thus subject to British justice (Harring 1998).

As such, there was no moral challenge to the policies carried out by the crown. Some settlers might have noted that the actions of the crown toward Indigenous people were unpleasant, but they justified them by arguing that they were unavoidable. Legal and political authorities noted that the motives of individuals carrying out illegal acts against Indigenous people were not criminal but supported the emerging capitalist economic structure that focused on the creation of individual and national wealth through a productive use of the land and its resources (Nettelbeck et al. 2016). This new philosophy adopted by settlers argued that the value of land was in its ability to generate capital—a basic tenet of capitalism. Thus, it was immoral to allow land to remain in its natural state if it could generate capital through agricultural, mining, logging, or other activities. The absence of objections to the policy of removing Indigenous people from the land and its embeddedness in the legal system of Canada allowed the violence against Indigenous people to be carried out with little restraint (Rutherdale, Abel, and Lackenbauer 2017).

THE EMERGENCE OF NEW NORMS

This ethos began with the establishment of a capitalist economic system and is still in force. For example, as late as 1951, amendments to the *Indian Act* made all provincial laws enforceable on reserves and thus allowed provincial social services to begin apprehending children living in reserve communities. Provincial social services were guaranteed payment for each child apprehended, and the children were routinely "sold" to American adoption agencies for as much as $4,000 per child. By 1953, social services held over 11,000 children. This has not changed, and today they hold over 31,000 children in foster care, of which half are Indigenous children under the age of fourteen (O'Connor et al. 2010; Statistics Canada 2013). This perspective is entrenched in the legal system of Canada even though the impact on Indigenous people continues to be devastating (Graziadei 2009). Today we are left with the legacy of this conventionalization and have used it to blame the victims for their impoverished state in Canadian society.

European settlers in Canada imported colonial legal norms whose validity depended on the legal systems of both France and the United Kingdom (Macklem 2016). Moreover, in the early days of the settlement of Canada, there was little differentiation between law and politics. But, as Macklem (2016) shows, over time law emerged as an autonomous component of Canadian society, and the courts began the process of addressing disputes from this perspective. For example, until the late 1800s, courts viewed treaties as political agreements unenforceable in a court of law. Crown promises were not considered to be legally enforceable through either domestic or international law (Morin 2018).

ORGANIZATION OF THE BOOK

Many of these early actions and structures have long since been conveniently forgotten or glossed over in today's assessment of the place of Indigenous people in Canadian society (Ray 2016). This book will give the reader some insights into how all of this has been dealt with by the government and its institutions. In the prelims, a glossary of terms used in the book will give the reader a good grounding in the definitions used by scholars, political bodies, and Indigenous people themselves.

Chapter 1 begins by outlining the convoluted policies that have been unilaterally imposed by the federal crown regarding who is an Indigenous person as well as the process for resolving disputes. The liability concern of the crown along with gender bias regarding how First Nations women are viewed still underpins many of the policies currently in place (e.g., the *Indian Act*) (Palmater 2015).

Chapter 2 presents a brief history of how this "messy" situation of Indigenous-government relations has emerged over the past two centuries and how it remains a quagmire of processes. The chapter shows how the marginalization of Indigenous people slowly occurred and how it remains embedded in Canadian society. It reveals how colonialization, Eurocentrism, and discrimination ensured that the Indigenous population would not be allowed to participate in the newly developing socio-economic structures.

Chapter 3 reveals how land is integral to Indigenous identity and that much of the conflict today between Indigenous and non-Indigenous people is based upon land issues—a fact that the crown has refused to address for the past two centuries (Corntassel 2012). The crown insists that land is a commodity and nothing more, so dealing with land is an economic concern (Coulthard 2007). Out of this concern for land, treaties and scrip found their way into the politics of land settlement as well as the courts.

Chapter 4 focuses on the meaning of a treaty as well as on how treaties have been viewed by both Indigenous people and the government. The chapter also reveals the process (both historical and contemporary) by which the government "resolves" land claims initiated by Indigenous people (Morin 2018).

Presented in Chapter 5 is a discussion of Aboriginal Rights as dictated by the courts: what they are, how they are defined, and what they mean. Specific case studies illuminate the courts' interpretations of "rights" as well as how such a term is foreign from the perspective of Indigenous people.

From this account, Chapter 6 shows how the courts have taken on the role of setting a vision for how Indigenous people will fit into Canadian society since Parliament has chosen to step back and allow the courts to adjudicate a variety of social and economic issues affecting Indigenous people (Anaya 2014). Although the courts have been reluctant to set the vision for the future, and continually note that Indigenous issues should be settled through negotiations, they have made definite strides in dealing with many Indigenous concerns, such as Aboriginal Rights and Title. Some of these efforts have had the endorsement of Indigenous people, whereas others have drawn their ire. In the end, only Canadian law is available to Indigenous people in pursuing their claims, and the government has been resistant to changing the legal structure.

Chapter 7 focuses on the social and political organizations established by Indigenous people at both national and local levels as they struggle to deal with a foreign organizational and legal system to retain their lands, cultures, languages, and ways of knowing. It also shows how the government has reacted to the actions of Indigenous organizations, including attempts to discredit and/or incorporate them into "mainstream" society. The chapter reveals the different strategies that have been employed by the three subgroups within the Indigenous rubric.

The Conclusion makes some predictions for the twenty-first century and presents scenarios that Canada might enact to deal with Indigenous people. The organization of the material allows the reader to follow a past, present, and future discussion on Indigenous-government relations.

CONCLUSION

Today it seems that the future of Indigenous people does not lie with the political actions of the government, since it is unprepared or unwilling to deal with the issues of high importance confronting them, notwithstanding the pronouncements made by the current Liberal government. The fate of Indigenous people is mired in the past since the government is afraid to take new approaches in dealing with old issues or to accept the wisdom of Indigenous people. Land claims (comprehensive and/or specific) have grown in both number and magnitude, and there is little evidence that the government has taken positive steps to resolve these issues. Today there are nearly 100 comprehensive claims and self-government negotiation tables at various stages, and the number has not decreased over the past decade (AANDC 2015). Negotiations between the crown and Indigenous people still follow the model that the crown is right; if Indigenous people want to negotiate, then they will have to follow the rules set out by the crown with its coercive power. The disbanded Indigenous and Northern Affairs Canada (now divided into two ministries: Indigenous Services Canada and Crown-Indigenous Relations and Northern Affairs Canada) continues to top the list of government departments for money spent on litigation in resisting claims put forward by Indigenous communities. For example, the most recent information shows that in 2012–13 the department spent $106 million litigating Indigenous issues, while Revenue Canada was next at $66 million. A year before, the Department of Aboriginal Affairs and Northern Development Canada spent even more in legal fees. Political leaders in Canada believe that sharing power with Indigenous people will result in a reduction of their current level of power over Indigenous people, and that prospect is not to their liking. Whether this stalemate will be played out through the courts, negotiations, or political and/or conflict activities by Indigenous people remains to be seen.

CHAPTER 1

INDIGENEITY
in CANADA

I begin this chapter by addressing the origins of Indigenous people who reside in what are now known as North and South America. The Western narrative as presented fits nicely within the creation stories of Indigenous people handed down through the generations. I am aware of the issue of appropriation without authorization, and the reader needs to understand the cultural contexts and components of various events. I suggest that the reader consult firsthand retellings of such stories, for example, the Haudenosaunee Sky Woman, Anishinabek, or The Raft (Cree) (Simpson 2008, 2011), as well as other accounts by Indigenous holders of these stories and the knowledge about them. Indigenous stories have contexts that the reader must be aware of, and thus it is important that stories regarding the origins of Indigenous Peoples need to be told by Indigenous Peoples themselves. Nevertheless, their stories, like the stories of Western archaeology and history, reveal many similarities in content and context. However, it is clear to both Western science and Indigenous knowledge that Indigenous Peoples established themselves centuries before European settlers arrived and occupied from time immemorial what is now Canada. I then illustrate how one establishes Indigeneity in Canada. I provide a short prehistory and a contemporary historical review to describe the complex and changing definitions of who is Indigenous (First Nations, Métis, or Inuit). I conclude the chapter with a brief profile of the demography of Indigenous Peoples in Canada.

THE ORIGINS OF INDIGENOUS PEOPLES (PREHISTORY): A WESTERN NARRATIVE

The Western story claims that about 18,000 years ago (the Wisconsin period of the ice age) much of the current continental shelf on the west coast of Canada was exposed as land. At the end of this era, the sea level once again began to rise, and the Bering Strait land bridge between Asia and North America disappeared. The original Beringia theory proposed by Fray José de Acosta in 1589 sowed the seed of an idea that many still believe. He claimed that humans walked over the land/ice bridge between Asia and North America, a distance of about 1,000 kilometres. His evidence was that, since humans first existed in Europe (or so he thought), to get to North America they had to walk there. Subsequent individuals began to build upon this theory by looking at geological and other evidence that they could gather. We know that two major glaciers covered northern North America. The Laurentide glacier stretched from the east coast to the Great Lakes to the Rocky Mountains, and the Cordillera glacier covered the area west of the Rocky Mountains to the Pacific Ocean (Dixon 1999). The Beringia theory posits that, when the two glaciers began to separate east of the Rocky Mountain range, a corridor emerged that allowed people to travel across the Bering Strait and then south in the middle of the continent about 11,000–13,000 years ago (Dixon 1999). A more recent variation of the Beringia theory, called the Beringia standstill hypothesis, has been proposed by Hoffecker, Elias, and O'Rourke (2014). They argue that the land bridge environment supported peoples migrating to North America for perhaps 5,000 to 10,000 years before they completed the trek across it (Hoffecker and Elias 2007). Hence, people went onto the land bridge and remained there for some time before trekking south. Moreover, researchers have found unique DNA common among North American Indigenous Peoples but not linked to peoples in Asia, partially confirming the "standstill" theory and the possibility that earlier migrations came from elsewhere. However, for most of the twentieth century, artifacts from Clovis (13,200 years ago) and Folsom (11,000 years ago), New Mexico, embedded in giant bison, were considered the oldest in North America and supported the Beringia theory.

A more recent alternative explanation of the migration route of first North Americans is that people from Asia skirted the exposed continental shelf (the glacial period had lowered the sea level by well over 100 metres), finding shelter and obtaining some of the necessities of life on shore as they moved south along the shoreline. They moved quickly and in large numbers by boat along the coast, allowing them to survive and establish a base population in what is now northern Canada. They would later continue their migration south (Bumsted, Kuffert, and Cucharme 2011). This theory has been supported by recent discoveries of artifacts on Triquet Island on the BC coast that have been carbon-dated at 14,000 years ago and thus lend credence to the oral history of the Heiltsuk Nation, whose people have lived there since "time immemorial" (Shore 2017). This theory also supports, in a metaphorical sense, some of the creationist versions of life espoused by Indigenous Peoples (e.g., the Sky Woman story of creation, the Cree origin story) (Simpson 2008). Contemporary data reveal that artifacts from human habitation in Canada are between 5,000 and 14,000 years old. The fact that archeologists have found human bones on an island off southern California that are 13,000 years old supports this alternative theory. Again it must be remembered that at the time the western water line of North America was between 100 and 200 metres lower than it is today. In addition, in the Paisley Caves (Oregon), archaeologists have found coprolites (pieces of fossilized dung) over 14,000 years old as well as seeds from desert plants (e.g., parsley) with roots that grow a foot underground, confirming that someone with the know-how and means dug them out. Support for the alternative theory emerged in the late 1990s when a site in Chile called Monte Verde was found to have artifacts ostensibly more than 14,500 years old. Moreover, the

Friedkin site in central Texas reveals human occupation as early as 15,500 years ago (2,500 years before the Clovis people).

Adding to the controversy over historical origins, archaeologists in South America claim to have found stone tools at the Toca da Tira Peia rock shelter in Serra da Capivara in central Brazil dated back 22,000 years. In another area of the same park, archaeologists say that they have found tools and fire pits 50,000 years old. The Pedra Furada site in Brazil also claims to have artifacts somewhere between 19,000 and 30,000 years old. Although the authenticity of these latter claims is yet to be confirmed, they do suggest that the first Americans might have come to South America first, probably by boat from west Africa (Swaminathan 2014).

All of this suggests that humans have lived in the Americas from time immemorial, adding support to the coastline migration theory and the use of boats by which people migrated rather than the singular land movement theory. The coastline migration theory is now considered the more likely migration route of early humans as they travelled by water along the western coastline and approached land when additional food and other resources were needed. Adding to this perspective is the recent find in southern California, where paleontologists unearthed objects suggesting that humans were living in North America well over 100,000 years ago (Holen et al. 2017). Nevertheless, there is evidence that the Beringia movement might well have taken place, albeit later. These archaeological finds support, in many ways, the stories told by Indigenous people about the habitation of North America.

A BRIEF CONTEMPORARY HISTORY

Telling history is based upon perspective (Simpson 2017). Over the years, numerous scholars have traced the history of Indigenous Peoples in Canada (Axtell 1981; Blaut 1993; Dickason 2002; Frideres and Gadacz 2011; Maybury-Lewis, Macdonald, and Maybury-Lewis 2009; Miller 2000, 2009; Moore 2010; Wright 2006) and revealed their long and complex relations with non-Indigenous people. Written Western history begins with the entrance of explorers and settlers into what is now called Canada and the imposition of colonial administrators'

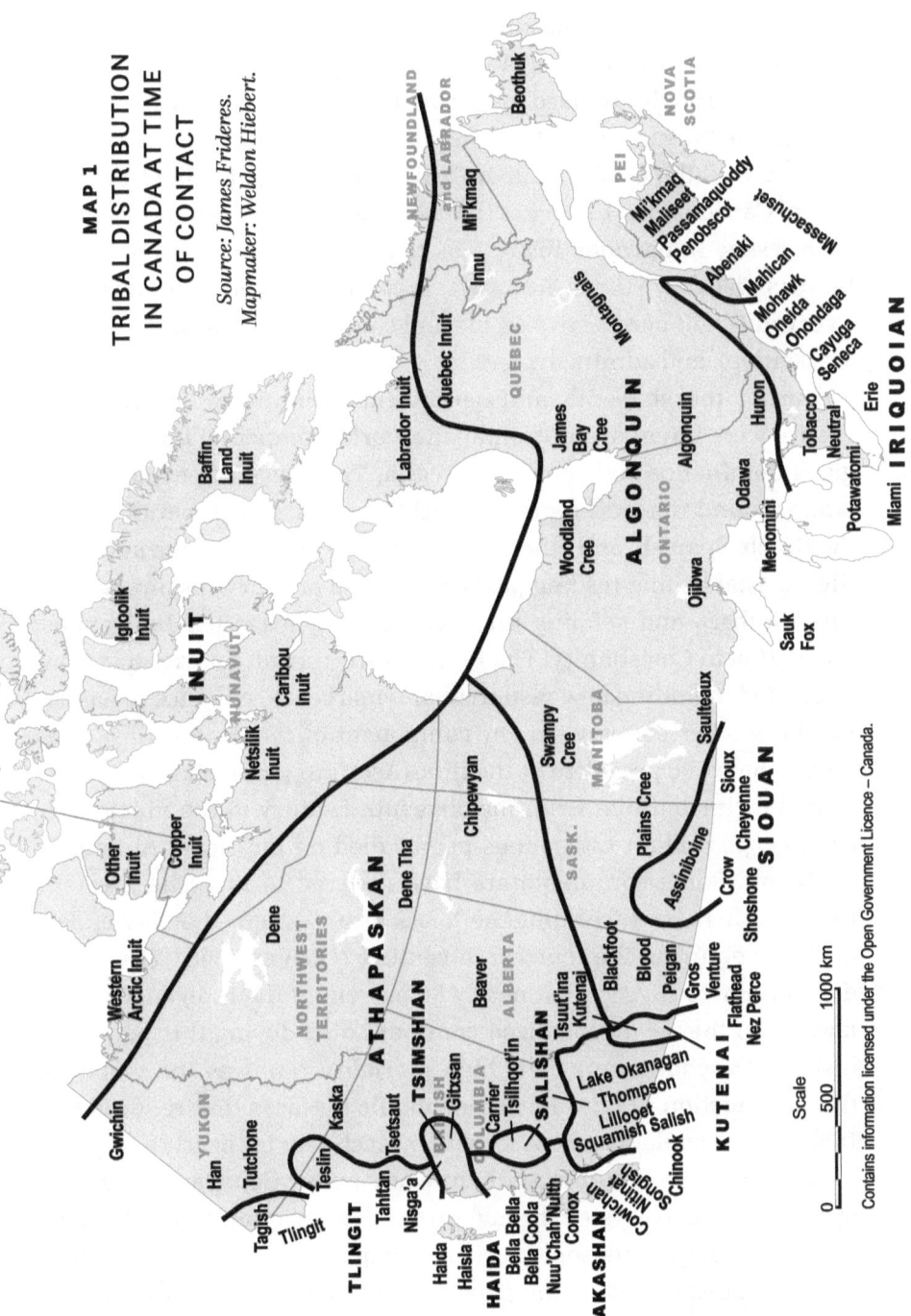

MAP 1
TRIBAL DISTRIBUTION IN CANADA AT TIME OF CONTACT

Source: James Frideres.
Mapmaker: Weldon Hiebert.

and settlers' views of and dealings with the Indigenous population (Cairns 2005; Erickson 2005). Western history takes the view that when Indigenous Peoples refused to give up their cultures, it was a refusal to take up the "advanced civilization" of Western culture and to take on the responsibilities of French or British citizenship. In short, the history of Canada is the history of the colonization of Indigenous Peoples. Conversely, Indigenous history, as told by Indigenous Peoples, has been handed down through stories, ceremonies, and legends. It reveals a very different perspective on life and contact with European explorers, settlers, and administrators.

During the sixteenth and seventeenth centuries, England and France were intent on controlling the world, competing for both religious dominance and economic wealth. They began to explore new lands around the world and in North America. In competition with the Dutch, Spanish, and others, they explored and settled the new continent, establishing trading posts, exploiting primary resources (e.g., furs, timber), and sending missionaries to convert the Indigenous population to Christianity. The French government, for example, was interested in finding new resources and markets to enhance revenues for the mother country—a key component of the mercantilist economic theory so prevalent at the time (Asch 2014) (see Map 1).

It is estimated that from the sixteenth century to the nineteenth century, 90 million Indigenous people died on the North American continent. Some commentators have referred to it as the greatest mortality in history, rivalling the "black death" plague that descended on Europe during the fourteenth century (Dobyns 1966). Historical demographers suggest that nearly 80 percent of the Indigenous population on the newly colonized continent died during this period of history (Daschuk 2013). This high mortality rate was the result of the introduction of chronic and epidemic diseases that reduced the Indigenous population about 1.5 percent each year for nearly a century.

As Europeans began to settle in what is now Canada, they developed a legal-social system brought from the European way of life and based upon legal philosophies such as papal bulls. They were formal proclamations issued by the pope, and many major bulls focused on the confirmation of ownership of land and property. Later some kings and queens from European countries utilized the concept of *terra nullius* to describe a geographical area that had never belonged to any known sovereign state. This concept claimed that sovereignty over the land could be achieved through simple discovery and occupation of it. Thus, a country could claim sovereignty over land on behalf of the "motherland" or "fatherland" if no one was occupying it. Even today many people believe that if others are not making use of the land as the dominant society sees fit (e.g., farming, ranching, resource extraction), it is open and free for the taking.

As Canada continued to receive European immigrants, they built their social, political, and legal systems based upon this concept and myths regarding Indigenous Peoples. As Ray (2016) points out, British settlers argued that the crown gained sovereignty over the land that is now Canada because it had defeated other European powers (e.g., France, Spain). However, they also noted that Aboriginal Title remained in place as a "burden" on the crown's title. This was an acknowledgement that Indigenous Peoples occupied the land before settlers arrived and continued to have the right to occupy and use it until they surrendered it to the crown. British and French laws were brought over to the new land by colonial administrators and over time appropriated by settlers. They fashioned a legal system based upon British and French legal philosophy but designed to fit their new social and geographical environs (Macklem 2016). This legal positivism became the dominant philosophy, whereas Indigenous law was relegated to a series of conventions or moral standards that could be ignored by policy makers, lawyers, and government officials (Ray 2016; Waiser 2018). Over time, this new history convinced colonial administrators and settler Canadians that the social fabric developed was the correct one (Furniss 1999). Today we accept the belief that Canadian "culture" was achieved solely through the efforts of hardworking settlers and dedicated colonial government leaders (Warry 2007). These myths have become maps by which successive generations navigate and make sense of their country. Once the stories are told and retold over time, and embodied in print, they take on a sense of legitimacy, become the "grand narrative," and their veracity is rarely questioned (Aniuk 2018; Fleras 2011).

In short, Eurocentrism is built upon a set of assumptions and beliefs that people accept as true. With the defeat of the French in 1763, the British system of governance became dominant in the new country. After 1815, the ideologies of liberalism, science, and to a certain extent socialism began to take hold in colonial Canada. However, there was a tension between the ideals of universal rights and the conceptualization of moral independence (Nettelbeck et al. 2016). Settlers and British colonial administrators believed that Indigenous Peoples were inferior and in need of improvement (Foster 2018). At the same time, administrators and settlers applied British common law to both themselves and Indigenous people. Because of this ideological implementation, the conflict between the belief in an individual's capacity for improvement (part of the liberal view) and the assessment of Indigenous people as in need of authority and guidance remained solidly in place. As Carey (2008) points out, government leaders and settlers rejected the notion of the inherent sovereignty of Indigenous Peoples because it undermined the imperialist assumptions that underpinned the construction of the modern nation-state. As Foster (2018) points out, causation, collective responsibility, and compensation are the fundamentals of Indigenous law, whereas Western law is composed of fault, individual responsibility, and punishment. Moreover, Indigenous sovereignty would mean that settlers had to recognize the contributions of Indigenous Peoples in building the nation-state. Thus, not recognizing Aboriginal Rights gave precedence to individual citizens over the collective political and cultural aspirations of Indigenous Peoples (Carey 2008, 14).

The beliefs and myths developed in these early years were crucial in terms of how Indigenous people were viewed by colonial administrators as well as settlers themselves. The portrayal of an uncontrolled individual lacking basic "civilized" manners has continued in both media and research today (Hedican 2014). Alfred (2011) and Alfred and Corntassel (2011) refer to this as *"Euroamerican arrogance."* British colonial administrators argued that four strategies—extermination, slavery, isolation, and amalgamation/assimilation—could be used to deal with Indigenous Peoples in various parts of the world depending on the region and the people being colonized. For example, in Australia extermination was the modal response, while in Africa it was slavery.

In Canada, colonial administrators thought that isolation, in conjunction with assimilation, was an appropriate strategy for colonizing Indigenous Peoples. Both strategies were employed over time, though one or the other was used more at various times over the past two centuries. Hence, the development of reserves and policies such as the *Indian Act* aided the strategy of colonization in Canada (Veracini 2013a).

Colonial leaders and settlers followed a technique used during the sixteenth–eighteenth centuries by most exploring nations (Chartrand 2002). For example, a papal document sent by Pope Nicolas V to King Alfonso V of Portugal in 1452 stated that Portugal had the right to attack, conquer, and subjugate Saracens, pagans, and other enemies of Christ wherever they were to be found and "recognized title over any lands and possession gained in these forays" (Gilbert 2006, 5). In 1493, Pope Alexander VI issued the papal bull known as the *Inter caetera divinai*. It approved of Spain's efforts to spread Catholicism in the Americas and stated that lands that had not been discovered by others and not in the possession of any other Christian king or prince would be considered Spanish possessions. Such papal bulls legitimized the taking of lands and resources of all non-Christian peoples and placed Indigenous Peoples under the tutelage and guardianship of Christian nations. These bulls were the origin of the *doctrine of discovery* and the idea of *terra nullius*, which led to the taking of lands and resources. Other European countries agreed with this doctrine and used it as they explored and colonized vast areas of the world.

By the seventeenth century, there was a challenge to the authority of the pope, and with it came the Age of Enlightenment and a precipitous decline of religious authority through the Protestant Reformation. The rise of rationalism also challenged religious authority, and thus new legal and political doctrines were developed to subordinate Indigenous Peoples. For Westerners, a new philosophy emerged, created by Thomas Hobbes and John Locke. Their argument was that there was no such thing as a "natural order" (contrary to Indigenous knowledge), so humans had to take control and establish order and justice in the world. According to their arguments, this was the only way to establish a "civil society," and anyone who objected to it would break the social contract and bring about chaos. Indigenous Peoples were considered part of the original state of nature and thus part of the chaos and war that existed in these societies that prevented the emergence of a civil society. Locke, who basically agreed with Hobbes, thought that the natural order was characterized by people who were solitary, poor, nasty, and brutish. Moreover, these people were in a state of insecurity and dangerous in their "natural state." Both Locke and Hobbes argued that people in this state lacked "positive laws" and needed to be given direction and guidance by those who were "civil." Thus, order had to be established by civilized cultures, and this argument was used to validate European colonization around the world. However, Locke differed from Hobbes in that he argued that land was given to humans in common as a gift from God. So God and natural law were twinned in his argument such that, if social order was to be established, only civilized people who accepted the word of God could achieve it.

Locke also discussed property rights. Although he agreed with Indigenous Peoples that it is a natural human right to preserve oneself by taking things from nature, he argued that land had to be considered the property of people and should be used for their benefit and survival. Hence, an individual acquires property (land) by adding labour to it. This is the essence, of course, of the "theory of value" that colonial administrators and settlers used when colonizing new lands. It meant that an individual was entitled to claim land if he or she engaged in labour to improve it. Finally, Locke argued that productivity would lead to profit because of commerce and colonial exploitation of new lands and resources.

These two philosophers set the stage for the conceptualization of settlers' ideas of property rights and control over lands and resources and fit nicely into the new economic order of capitalism and the values of Western religion. The result of this new ideological view was that "civilized" cultures should colonize all parts of the world to create economic and social development. These views were accepted by colonial administrators and settlers, and over time state control became normalized. Moreover, the rejection of these ideas by people seen as "backward" necessitated help from more "advanced" states. The state thus legitimized the belief that it could tell Indigenous Peoples what they could and could not do, refuse to support their goals, and exclude them from the social-legal-political process (Monchalin 2016). This belief (in various forms) still exists in various government departments (e.g., Indian Affairs, Justice) as they make and implement policy that directly and indirectly affects Indigenous Peoples.

COLONIZATION

Colonization emerged out of the belief that papal claims of authority provided explorers with the right to claim sovereignty over "new lands." Letters of patent were signed by kings and queens to explorers such as John Cabot and Jacques Cartier, and these letters gave these emissaries of kings and queens the right to claim lands considered *terra nullius*. Once it became known that in fact there were "people" inhabiting the lands, this concept was liberally reinterpreted to mean that, if no white and Christian people were living in the area, then it could be considered *terra nullius*. Since Indigenous Peoples living in the new continent were neither Christian nor white, they did not constitute "peoples" who had to be taken into consideration in claiming the lands for the motherland or fatherland.

After 1815, liberalism, socialism, and science were increasingly accepted by people in the Western world. However, in settler societies such as Canada's, there emerged a conflict between the ideals of "universal rights" and "moral independence." This conflict limited the application of universal rights in Canadian society during the initial settler influx. Nevertheless, colonial administrators as well as settlers viewed Indigenous Peoples as non-Christian, inferior, and thus in need of improvement. When they arrive in Canada, settlers (and the subsequent first generation) developed a strong economic relationship with the land and its resources that subsequently supported a Canadian national identity. Thus, it is not surprising that the application of English or French common law was increasingly uniform for Indigenous Peoples in Canada over time (Nettelbeck et al. 2016).

Colonialism continues to exist in Canada regardless of what former Prime Minister Stephen Harper proclaimed publicly—that it is not part of the history of Canada. It is still evident from the actions of Parliament and the decisions of policy makers regarding Indigenous Peoples (Alfred 2013). The colonial history created by the colonial administrators and early settlers has shaped the views of today's government and non-Indigenous people regarding Indigenous people. Canadians today refuse to see themselves as settlers or to recognize their colonial past and hegemony (Tilbury 2000), even though they continue to believe in the values and history established by early colonial administrators and settlers (Nicholl 2004). As Monchalin (2016) argues, places, spaces, and Indigenous cultures have been molded by settler structures and ideologies that try to force them into existing Euro-Canadian institutions without interfering with the goals of capitalism and the goals of Euro-Canadians. Thus, even though the government and citizens have a relationship with Indigenous people in Canada, for the most part it has been ignored or denied (Trees 1998). The relationship is not with actual Indigenous people but between Canadians and the symbols of Indigenous people created by settlers. We know that colonialism continues to be practised in Canada as the state makes policies that undercut the ability of Indigenous people to make decisions and control their lives. Under these conditions, it is easy to deny a relationship with Indigenous people while maintaining a process of marginalizing them (Griffith 2018). As a result, the government continues to tell Indigenous people what they can and cannot do and refuses to support them to achieve their goals. The government continues to apply the dominant Western conception of individualism and materialistic success (Alfred 2008) as a benchmark for assessing the value of the state and its people. However, from the perspective of Indigenous people, the legal and economic systems in Canada are foreign structures that have been imposed on them without the benefit of their input and operate in three different ways: dispossession, dependence, and oppression.

Indigenous Peoples, removed from their land bases and forced to live under Canadian laws, became dependent on a colonial system of governance (Krasowski 2019). Because of the actions of colonial administrators and settlers, Indigenous Peoples became "a problem" for the state, which, backed by a belief in white racial superiority, attempted to solve the "Indian problem" by taking away the lands and destroying the cultures of Indigenous Peoples. As Monchalin (2016) points out, the system was created to produce the results that it has been producing for the past century.

PROCESS AND POLICY IMPLEMENTATION

The federal government has chosen a process by which Indigenous people are incorporated into the dominant order. For example, any political structure in comprehensive settlements approved by the government is consonant with existing Western values and culture. Any processes or values outside this perspective are rejected as unacceptable by the government. These new, modern treaties begin with the assumption that the state has ownership of and control over Indigenous Lands, resources, and politics. Borrows (2013) agrees with Coulthard (2007) and compares the support that American Indigenous people have relative to Canadian Indigenous people. First, he shows that the latter do not plan services for or deliver services to their communities to the same degree as the former. First Nations policy development and delivery in Canada are under federal control through the *Indian Act* created to assimilate First Nations. Borrows goes on to show that the *Indian Act* delegates policy to provincial governments by incorporating provincial laws into federal laws. Since the government controls the political power of First Nations, it does not need to work with them in developing policies or implementing programs. Second, the Canadian government refuses to be clear about the service levels that Indigenous people receive compared with non-Indigenous people. There is considerable evidence showing that financial support for services for Indigenous people is about half of what non-Indigenous people receive. Third, First Nations communities cannot plan and control the delivery of services because the federal government has not created a legal basis to hold those communities accountable.

For example, as Sanderson (2016) points out, there is no legislative basis for the existing funding formula for First Nations communities. The formula applied to any given community is based not upon legislation but upon the policies of the department. On the one hand, policy refers to the government's views regarding the best means for carrying out action designed to achieve its objectives based upon priorities established by a department. It refers to the rules and procedures for how something is done. On the other, legislation is the process of making or enacting laws. However, the size of a community seems to be the predominant criterion in the funding process. Small First Nations communities are funded according to a formula different from that for large ones, and more northern and remote communities have their own funding formula. Moreover, the policies implemented are not transparent. Despite the centrality of funding arrangements in the department, their overall objective is not clear. There is a lack of coherence between programs and the funding authorities that make the arrangements, and there is no clear leadership at headquarters to coordinate the management and implementation of funding arrangements. Responsibility for the design, negotiation, and monitoring of funding arrangements is split between Indigenous Affairs headquarters and the regions as well as across finance, programs, and regional operations. There is no centre of expertise on grants and contributions and no single point of contact for coordination with other federal departments. In addition, Sanderson points out that policy and program officials often are not familiar with the details of funding arrangements, and funding authorities and program terms and conditions can conflict with broader policy objectives or be inconsistent with one another.

Borrows (2013) argues that when a government acts through policy rather than legislation, it maintains a higher level of discretion in carrying out its plans. Canada has not developed any measurable standard of service and thus remains outside the legal claim of unequal service delivery. Borrows (2017b) also argues that since Indigenous people do not have any control over their relationship with non-Indigenous governments, they cannot engage in stable long-term planning. In the end, there is little protection of Indigenous culture by the federal, provincial, and territorial governments, nor is there any ability to develop plans and priorities that meet a community's needs.

DEFINING AN INDIGENOUS PERSON

Historically in Canada, one identified an Indigenous person by his or her language, clothing, phenotypical attributes (e.g., skin pigmentation, and hair colour and texture), and social behaviour, or through a combination of these aspects. However, over time, languages were lost, intermarriages took place, and clothing changed with the fashion of the day, so many of these "markers" are no longer useful in identifying who is Indigenous—Métis, Indian, or Inuit. However, identifying Indigenous people is important because they have specific rights and responsibilities. Unfortunately, the Canadian Constitution does not provide a guide to or operationalization of the defining attributes or how one identifies a Métis, Indian, or Inuit. That has been left up to the courts to decide. Specifically, it has been left up to the Supreme Court of Canada since the decision of any "lesser" court can always be appealed, so the decision rendered is useless or placed on hold until the appeal has been heard and confirmed or denied. However, the decisions of the Supreme Court are final and become law. Only Parliament can deal with a Supreme Court decision by passing a new law that would nullify the decision made by the court. So, in this book, I refer only to how the Supreme Court has ruled on various cases, including how it has defined the three major groups identified in the Constitution.

Although all of us think that we can identify an Indigenous person, it turns out that someone who is Indigenous one day might not be the next day. Or someone who was not Indigenous yesterday finds that today she or he is (Leigh 2009; Sellars 2012). Or, adding to the confusion, it might be that a person who was Indigenous at birth lost that status but later in life once again became Indigenous (LaRocque 2010). Nevertheless, Indigenous people know that they are Indigenous, so that brings us to the question of how the crown defines an Indigenous person. The word *Aboriginal* came into use after 1982 when section 35 of the Constitution defined it. However, many Indigenous people are uncomfortable with that word since it is state defined and imposed. Moreover, it is an English word defined by the government, does not resonate with some communities, and is not a word that Indigenous Peoples have used in the past (Alfred 2009). The word *Indigenous* encompasses a variety of colonized peoples and has been applied globally. For example, the word is used by the United Nations to refer to peoples of long settlement of and connection to Traditional Territories who have been negatively affected by the incursions of industrial economies, displacement, and settlement of their lands by others (Dunbar-Ortiz 2006). Even though the legal structure of Canada uses the term

"Aboriginal" and it is embedded in the Constitution, in this book I use the term "Indigenous" except in instances when it is appropriate to use "Indian," "Métis," or "Inuit" to describe a government department, organization, program, legal decision, or service. In those cases, I use terms such as "Aboriginal Rights" and "Aboriginal Title" to reflect the usage in the Constitution. The reader should note that terminology identifying Indigenous people will continue to change over time.

Today there are two major ways in which Indigeneity is measured by the crown. First, there is the Canadian census, which simply asks the individual if he or she subjectively identifies as an Indigenous person. It then tries to distinguish among the different types (e.g., Inuit, Métis, Non-Status Indian, Status Indian) through a series of follow-up questions. This subjective interpretation allows the individual to decide her or his ethnic identity, just like the census identifies other ethnic affiliations. Second, Indigeneity is measured through the application of some "objective" criteria, such as ancestry, established by the crown (Doxtator 2011). The process by which these criteria are applied varies by Indigenous group and historical period.

INUIT

Historically, people of the North were not called Inuit (a single Inuit is an Inuk). They were referred to as "Eskimos," a term still used in the United States. However, over time, this name gave way in Canada to the current term, now considered a legal term. Just how one becomes Inuit is another example of how the road to identification is long and twisted. Traditionally, Inuit culture allowed individuals to have different names for different social and geographical contexts. This posed a major problem when the Canadian government became involved in the North and wanted to send information or social service benefits to Inuit (Jordan-Fenton and Pokiak-Fenton 2010). So it decided to identify Inuit people by number. Thus, everyone the government considered to be an Inuit at the time was given a small leather disc (*ujamiit*) with a number on it, and that solved the problem for government officials. The original names of Inuit people were replaced with letters and numbers. For example, people living east of the Mackenzie River were called "E's," and those living west of the river were identified as "W's." Then a number was provided on a disc for everyone, so one could then be identified, for example, as E6-234 or W3-677. An individual living east of the Mackenzie River, in a particular area, was identified as person 234. Through this process, a registry of names (numbers) was established by government officials. This registry set the basis for who was an Inuit, and though this method of identification was abandoned later (after 1972), the government had established a base list of people whom the crown considered Inuit.

In 1924, Parliament debated whether to create an Eskimo Act but decided against doing so. However, in that year, a bill was passed to amend the *Indian Act*, assigning responsibility for the Inuit to the Department of Indian Affairs and ensuring that Inuit would be considered Canadian citizens. That amendment was repealed in 1930, and in 1939 the Supreme Court of Canada was asked to adjudicate a case between the province of Quebec and the federal crown. The conflict between the two parties arose over which government should bear the cost of relief rations distributed to "Eskimos" in the Ungava Peninsula of Hudson Bay (Backhouse 2001). The court ruled that "Eskimos" were to be considered "Indians" within the constitutional framework but not subject to the *Indian Act*. What is interesting is that the court requested that all "interested parties" participate in the court case. However, Inuit people were neither consulted nor represented at the hearing or court case. The court, comprised of white men with no cultural knowledge about Inuit, concluded that the Fathers of Confederation must have intended all Indigenous Peoples living in Canada to be considered Indians (Bonesteel 2006). It would not be until the *Indian Act* was amended in 1951 that it explicitly excluded Inuit.

When Nunavut was created in 1999, a new process for identifying Inuit was put in place. The organization Nunavut Tunngavik Incorporated became responsible for enrolling individuals as beneficiaries of the Nunavut Land Claims Agreement, and this became one way (the most important and influential) of determining who is Inuit (Dewar 2009). The process is administered by Nunavut Tunngavik Incorporated through the Enrolment Division of the Department of Human Resources and the Community Enrolment Committees.

Article 35 of the Nunavut Land Claims Agreement requires a designated Inuit organization to oversee the process and to ensure that all eligible Inuit of the Nunavut settlement area are enrolled. A person on the Inuit Enrolment List is entitled to benefit from the Nunavut Land Claims Agreement as long as he or she is alive. Enrolment is guided by the principle that Inuit are best able to define who is an Inuk to benefit from the agreement (Kulchyski 2006). So, though it is not a definitive list of people who consider themselves Inuit, it does indicate those individuals who are beneficiaries.

It is the responsibility of a person enrolled as a Nunavut Inuk to inform the Enrolment Division of Nunavut Tunngavik Incorporated of any change of name, addition of a name, or any error in the spelling of his or her name on the enrolment list or an enrolment card. The Nunavut Land Claims Agreement states that a person must be a Canadian citizen to qualify for enrolment. The agreement also states that a person must be an Inuk per Inuit customs and usages. This criterion is consistent with the recognition in the agreement that Inuit are best able to define who is an Inuk. The enrolment list is updated on an ongoing basis. Other regional areas in the North (e.g., Nunavik) have established similar procedures to ensure that each individual is registered as an Inuk and a beneficiary of the claims negotiated with the federal crown (Fenge and Quassa 2009). One who is not a designated beneficiary probably may claim himself or herself subjectively to be Inuit and would have to take alternative measures to be placed on the registry.

The struggle for an Inuit political voice came to fruition with the creation of the Inuit Relations Secretariat in 2005. This group, housed in Indigenous and Northern Affairs Canada (now part of Crown-Indigenous Relations and Northern Affairs Canada), was established in response to the request from Inuit representatives for a focal point to address Inuit-specific issues within the federal government. The secretariat is an advocate for Inuit concerns within the federal system, supports the development of federal Inuit policy, and works to improve the relevance and effectiveness of existing federal programs and policies that affect Inuit. The Inuit Relations Secretariat also gathers and dispenses resources, information, advice, and expertise on Inuit matters to Inuit across the country (Bonesteel 2006).

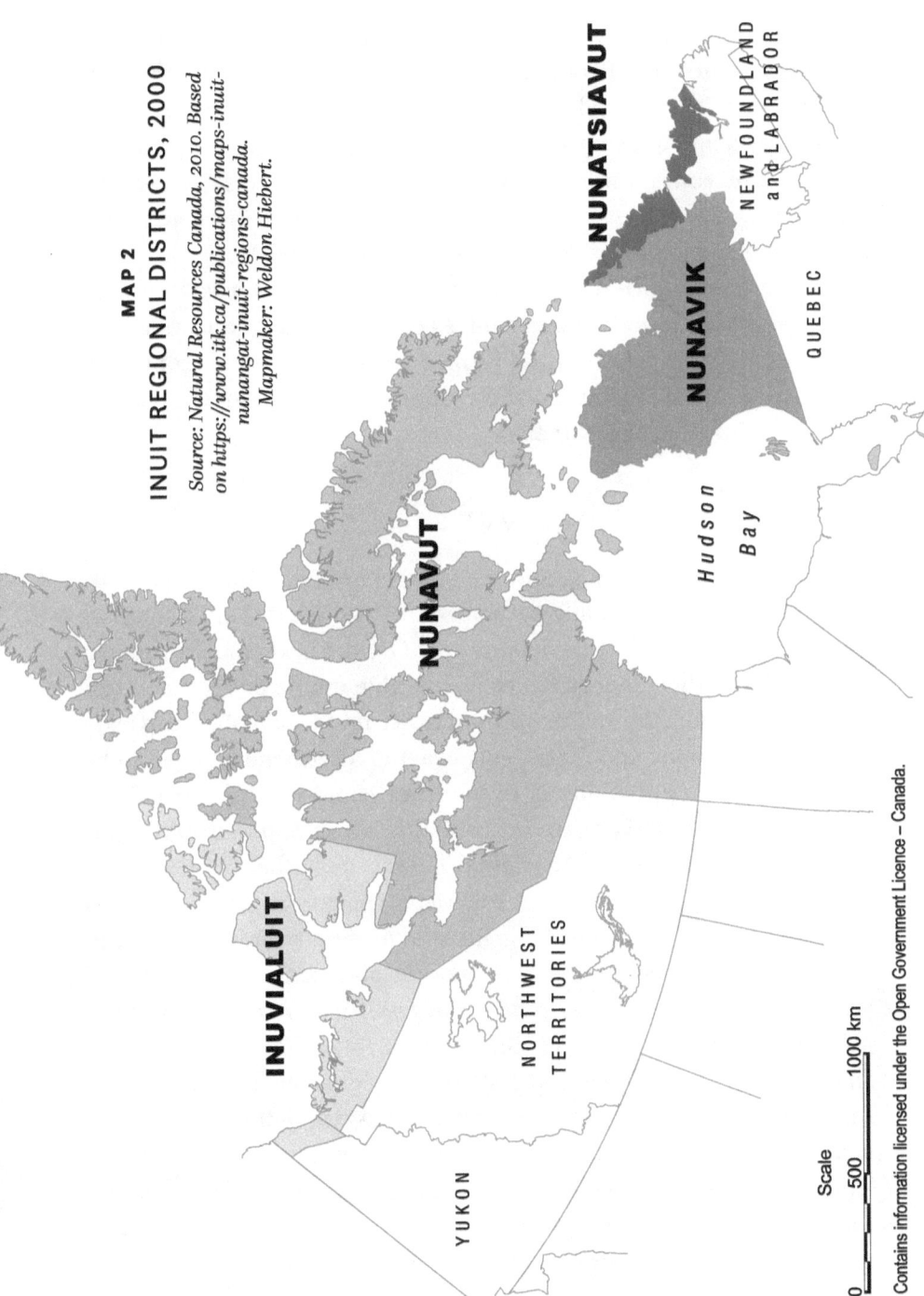

MAP 2
INUIT REGIONAL DISTRICTS, 2000

Source: Natural Resources Canada, 2010. Based on https://www.itk.ca/publications/maps-inuit-nunangat-inuit-regions-canada. Mapmaker: Weldon Hiebert.

Today there are about 65,000 people defined as Inuit. However, as noted above, not all individuals who claim to be Inuit are on the beneficiary "rolls" of the land claims settled with the federal government. Today only about 40,000 Inuit are beneficiaries of these land claims.

Most Inuit communities are in Nunavut, the Northwest Territories, northern Quebec (Nunavik), and Labrador. However, there are some small pockets of Inuit in Edmonton, Winnipeg, and Montreal. Their residence in southern urban centres is a result of prior government policy that sent Inuit to these centres for health and education reasons, and many of them stayed. Nevertheless, nearly 90 percent of all Inuit live in one of the four northern districts of Nunangat: Inuvialuit, Nunavut, Nunavik, and Nunatsiavut (see Map 2).

MÉTIS

The Métis have had a long and disjunctive history with the government of Canada. Originally recognized by the crown, after the Riel Resistance (North-West Resistance) of 1885 the government refused to treat this Indigenous group as a bona fide ethnic or even political or interest group. By 1880, the *Indian Act* had established separate policies for Indians and Métis, encouraging Métis who claimed to be Indians to give up that status so that they could receive scrip. Scrip was provided to Métis on an individual basis as opposed to the collective extinguishment of Aboriginal Title through the treaty process. To extinguish the Aboriginal Title of Métis, the government of Canada awarded a certificate redeemable for land or money (either 160 or 240 acres or dollars, depending on their age and status). Once they received scrip, the government was relieved of any further responsibility to Métis (Kelm and Smith 2018; Smith 2014). Métis (sometimes called "half-breeds") initially were included in the definition of Indian in the *Indian Act*. However, by 1927 the Act was revised with the partial exclusion of Métis, and by 1951 Métis were totally excluded from the Act. In the meantime, the federal crown recognized their existence at an informal level, but by the 1940s it removed them as a legitimate ethnic group and excluded their identification in the census. As Teillet (2013) argues, this collective invisibility was the result of several factors.

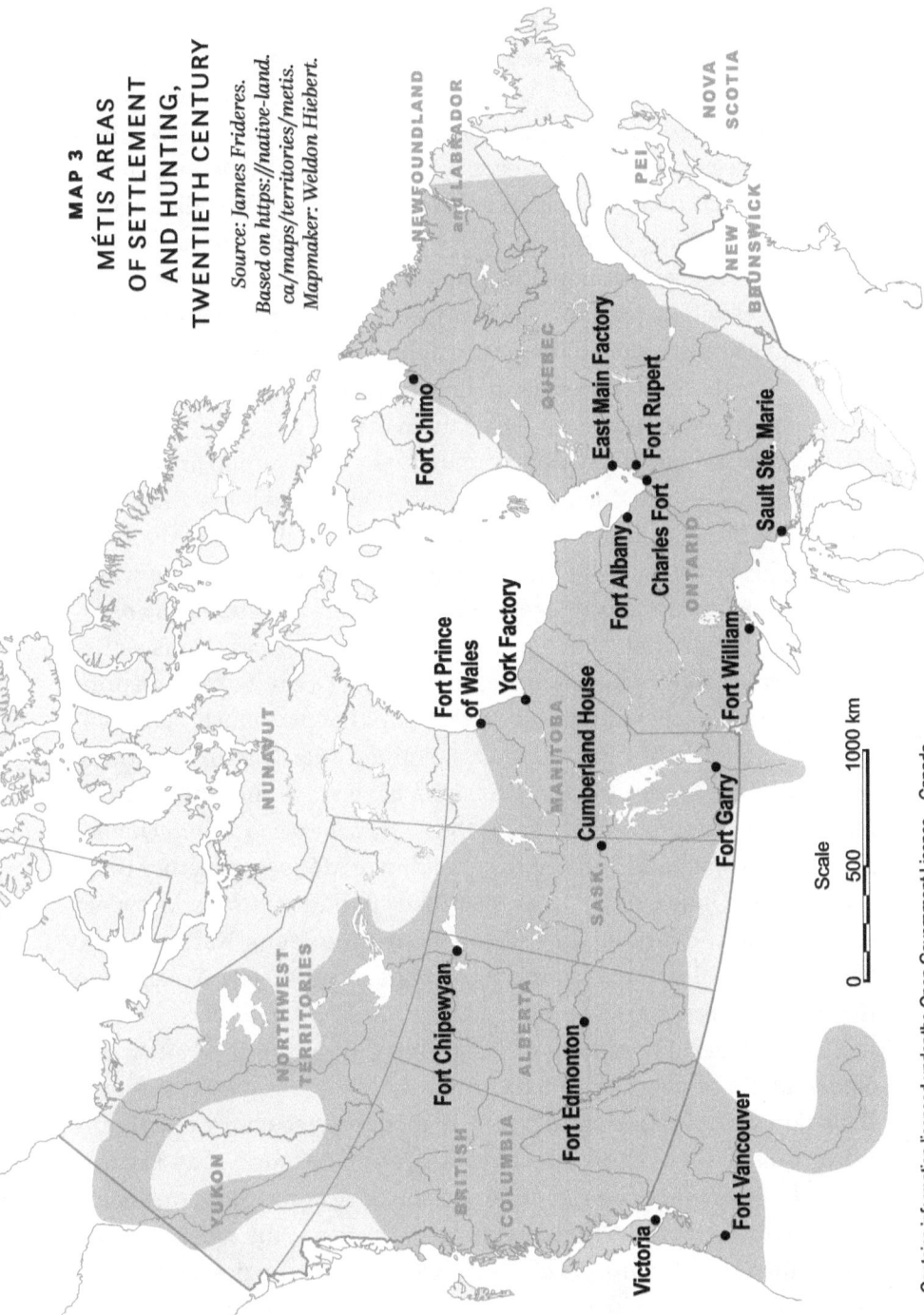

MAP 3
MÉTIS AREAS OF SETTLEMENT AND HUNTING, TWENTIETH CENTURY

Source: James Frideres. Based on https://native-land.ca/maps/territories/metis. Mapmaker: Weldon Hiebert.

First, historically, people had one of two identities to choose from: white or Indian. These limited options arose because no one wanted to acknowledge the existence of a mixed-race people. The crown did not acknowledge Métis as a people, and thus the division between Métis and Indian was not accepted. Second, Métis were not a distinct phenotype (Lawrence 2004), so there was little physiologically to distinguish them from Indians. Culturally, Métis were considered to have insignificant differences compared with Indians or whites—it all depended on their lifestyle. Third, after the Riel Resistance, many Métis were not willing to acknowledge their identity publicly because of the discrimination. Fourth, the high residential mobility of Métis made it difficult to track them down and enumerate them (Teillet 2013).

However, in the 1920s, Alberta feared that Métis would bring political unrest to the province, so it formally recognized them and established ten Métis colonies (now called settlements). Today Alberta is the only province that officially recognizes Métis land bases, of which there are eight, comprising just over half a million hectares and occupied by approximately 8,000 people. The Saskatchewan Métis settlements are no longer in existence, though the Green Lake townships are now the subject of litigation. The group that previously self-identified as Métis in Labrador has determined that it is in fact Inuit. Over time, six separate court decisions have ruled that there are no Métis in New Brunswick. Finally, the *Corneau* case (2015) in Quebec has delivered no judgment on the question of Métis, so whether there are Métis in Quebec is yet undetermined. To date, the only Métis per se in Canada identified by the courts are the Métis Nation of the Northwest, which includes the four western provinces, Yukon, and Northwest Territories (see Map 3).

From a federal perspective, the crown did not until recently recognize Métis as a legal entity or group that had any special status in Canadian society (Macdougall 2010). In fact, as noted above, once Métis were removed from the census as an "ethnic group," they became invisible. However, when the Charlottetown Accord (1992) was being discussed in the context of constitutional reform, the federal crown referred to two definitions of Métis. One was as the descendants of the Red River Métis who received scrip, and the "other" was those who self-identified as Métis. The Royal Commission on Aboriginal Peoples (1996b) also discussed Métis identity. However, it focused on self-identification and culture as the defining characteristics of the Métis. Until recently, the most widely used definitions of a Métis person were (a) anyone of mixed Indian/non-Indian blood who is not a Status Indian, (b) any person who self-identifies as Métis and is accepted by a Métis community, (c) any individual who took or was entitled to take "half-breed" grants under the *Manitoba Act* or *Dominion Lands Act* and his or her descendants, and (d) any descendants of persons excluded because of the "way of life" criterion in the *Indian Act* (Gordon 2009).

So who are the Métis? There appear to be three answers to this question depending on one's perspective:

- the individual/genealogical answer: Métis are individuals with mixed European and Indigenous blood;
- the cultural answer: Métis are a distinct Indigenous People with a unique way of life; and
- the subjective answer: Métis are Indigenous groups who describe themselves as Métis to claim the protection of section 35 of the *Constitution Act, 1982*.

Clearly, this multiplicity of answers is not satisfactory for the crown to develop policy or legislation (Bell 1995). This issue was taken up indirectly by the Supreme Court of Canada regarding the benefits of being Métis. The *Powley* (2003) decision provides a legal definition of people entitled to Métis Rights (Monchalin 2016) but not of identity. Based upon the decision of the Supreme Court, a Métis eligible for benefits is a person who self-identifies as a Métis, is distinct from other Indigenous Peoples, is of historical Métis Nation ancestry, and is accepted by a Métis community. Embedded in this definition are several conditions. First, the individual must have some evidence of an "ancestor" given scrip (either land or money), have resided in some historical Métis Nation community, and now reside in an area encompassed by Traditional Territory occupied by Métis. Nevertheless, in the end, the court accepted the "fact" that Métis were distinct from other Indigenous Peoples.

A recent court case has thrown the entire issue of who is a Métis into limbo. In 2013, the Federal Court (*Daniels v Canada*, 2013 FC 6) ruled that Métis and Non-Status Indians are Indians under section 91(24) of the *Constitution Act, 1867*. This decision clarified the relationship between the crown and the Métis who had brought a claim against the federal government in 1999 by arguing that

1. Métis and Non-Status Indians are Indians under section 91(24) of the *Constitution Act, 1867*;
2. the crown owes to Métis and Non-Status Indians a fiduciary duty as Indigenous Peoples; and
3. Indigenous Peoples have a right to be negotiated with, on a collective basis, in good faith with the crown.

The *Daniels* decision ignored the finding of the Supreme Court that the Métis Nation of the Northwest comprises a distinct Indigenous group and placed Métis into a broader group that includes Non-Status Indians. The Federal Court also ruled that there is no need for any ancestral connection to any group and no need for community acceptance to be identified as Métis. There is also, according to that court decision, no need for any Métis ancestry at all. This means that an individual may self-identify as Métis and be accepted as such for the purposes of federal recognition under section 91(24) of the *Constitution Act, 1867*. Justice Phelan of the Federal Court took a broad approach in *Daniels* in his definition. As such, the decision throws the definition of Métis adopted by the Supreme Court into confusion because the Federal Court defined Métis as a group of Indigenous people who have maintained a strong affinity for their Indigenous heritage without being Status Indians. Thus, under this definition, any individual with some Indigenous ancestry can self-identify as Métis.

However, the Supreme Court ruled earlier that mere self-identification is not enough for the purpose of claiming section 35 constitutional rights. This is because the recognition and affirmation of Aboriginal Rights under section 35 of the *Constitution Act, 1982* apply only to collectives: the Indigenous Peoples of Canada. This means that though an individual may self-identify as Métis, unless he or she can also prove to be a member of a Métis Rights–bearing collective, such an individual likely will not be able to claim that he or she is a Métis and thus section 35 protection (Teillet 2013). The *Daniels* court separated individuals from Indigenous collectives. The case was appealed, and the Federal Court of Appeal agreed with the lower court's decision except for the finding that Non-Status Indians are to be considered Indigenous people. This decision was appealed, and the Supreme Court ruled that Métis and Non-Status Indians are "Indians" under section 91(24), which assigns the exclusive power to pass laws related to "Indians and lands reserved for Indians" to the federal government. At the same time, the court ruled that the crown does not owe a fiduciary duty to Métis and Non-Status Indians. Furthermore, it ruled that Métis and Non-Status Indians do not have the right to be consulted with on a collective basis. The explanation provided by the court was that these two provisions lacked practical utility and would simply restate settled law. The court also noted that the term "Métis" can refer to the historical Métis community in the Red River Settlement or to anyone with mixed European and Indigenous heritage. With these court rulings, the Congress of Aboriginal Peoples and the Métis National Council argue that the federal government must now begin to deal with Métis regarding their support since they now fall within the rubric of section 91(24) of the Constitution.

MÉTIS IDENTIFICATION

In its decision in *Powley* (2003), the Supreme Court did not set out a specific definition of Métis, but it did set out the basic means to identify Métis Rights holders (Anderson 2014). The Supreme Court decision identified three factors crucial to being defined as a Métis Rights holder: self-identification, ancestral connection to the historical Métis community, and community acceptance. In the decision, the term "Métis" refers to distinctive peoples of mixed ancestry who developed their own customs, practices, and traditions. Moreover, Métis have achieved a recognizable group identity separate from First Nations, Inuit, and European ancestors. As such, the term "Métis" does not refer to all individuals of mixed Indigenous and European ancestry.

The Supreme Court pointed out that, though there is no minimum "blood quantum" requirement to be a Métis, Métis Rights holders must provide proof of ancestral connection to a historical Métis community whose collective rights they are exercising. The ancestral connection can be by birth, adoption, or other means. A second condition is that there must be proof of acceptance by a modern Métis community. Membership in a Métis political organization can be relevant, but the membership requirements of the organization and its role in the Métis community must also be put into evidence. The evidence must be verifiable, which means that there must be documented proof and a fair process for community acceptance. Such acceptance is about how the individual has exhibited past and ongoing participation in a shared culture, in the customs and traditions that reveal a Métis community's identity. Other evidence can include participation in community activities and testimony from other community members about a person's connection to the community and its culture. In the end, the court ruled, there must be proof of a solid bond of past and present mutual identification between the person and the other members of the Métis community. What can be understood from this requirement is that, to claim section 35 rights, it is not enough to prove a genealogical connection to a historical Métis community and then join a Métis organization. One must have a "past and ongoing" relationship to the community (Ens 1996) if she or he wishes to be identified and dealt with as Métis. The Supreme Court ruled that there can be many different Métis groups (Ray 2016). After twelve years of litigation, the Federal Court ruled that the federal government has fiduciary responsibilities to Métis, just as it does to Inuit and First Nations, but they are not Indians.

Census data reveal that the number of individuals claiming Métis identity soared nearly 150 percent in Quebec and the Maritimes from 2006 to 2016. As well, many new Métis organizations emerged over the same period. This sudden proliferation of self-reported Métis in eastern Canada has resulted in a divisive debate. Critics argue that there is no distinct Métis identity in eastern Canada and that people of mixed ancestry either integrated into First Nations communities or assimilated with European settlers, unlike the distinct Métis people associated with Louis Riel in western Canada (the Red River Settlement in Manitoba). Others argue that Métis must prove more than a genealogical connection to Indigenous ancestors in order to claim authentic Métis status.

INDIAN (FIRST NATIONS)

Where the term "Indian" came from when referring to the Indigenous population of Canada remains a mystery. Whatever the genesis, it quickly caught on and became the single identifier for the many different Indigenous cultural and linguistic groups in North America at the time of discovery and settlement by Europeans. It was a generic term applied to most Indigenous Peoples residing in southern climes regardless of their geography, culture, or language. It allowed settlers to gloss over the differences among Indigenous Peoples in order to simplify their interactions. All one needed to know was that Indians were pagans, savages (noble in some cases), illiterate, and culturally backward. This assessment applied to all Indigenous Peoples, and thus one acted accordingly.

The names of most Indigenous people were mystifying and seemingly crude, and settlers found it inappropriate that they did not have surnames. So settlers began a process of "renaming" Indigenous people. We find, for example, in certain geographic areas, that Indigenous people were given surnames identical to those of the early settlers in the area. For example, in the Red Sucker Lake community in Alberta, there are many Indigenous people with Harper and McDougall surnames. In other cases, when government representatives distributed treaty payments, instead of writing out the Cree or Anishinaabe names, they randomly assigned the surnames of Canadian government agents to treaty recipients. In this fashion, over the years, Indigenous names, community names, place names, and other geographical identifiers were given Anglo names, and links to Indigenous Peoples and their cultures were rendered invisible. Only in the past two decades have Indigenous people forced the government to rename places, communities, and areas with the original Indigenous names. For example, in 2015, the Northwest Territories approved five name changes: Dehcho (South Slavey), Deho (North Slavey), Grande Riviere (Michif), Kuukpak (Inuvialuktun), and Nagwichoonjik (Gwich'in). In Manitoba, a new name for Lake Winnipeg was approved (Weenipagamiksaguygun); in British Columbia, Canyon City is now called Gitwinksihlkw, and in Alberta the old Gleichen reserve is now called Siksika Nation reserve.

After 1830, the federal crown began to establish a crude registry of First Nations people, and it was mandated when the first comprehensive *Indian Act, 1876* was created. Moreover, the initial *Indian Act* was viewed as a temporary measure, supposed to end in 1901, by which time Indians would have disappeared. Some monitoring was done each year to establish which people were picking up their treaty payments and who had died or was no longer claiming to be an Indian. These first attempts at establishing a registry were unreliable, unsystematic, and subject to considerable discretion by Indian agents. And, in many cases, people were removed from the registry without being informed. Thus, a "black" registry was established by the federal crown without any input from First Nations people. Only in the second half of the twentieth century was a digital registry established that First Nations people could review. The government established a "roll" to use in preparing budgets, establishing policies, and implementing programs defined as its responsibility. Since being on the roll implies a cost to the government, many individuals have been removed from it to reduce the financial liability. The recent *Gehl* case (2017), focusing on gender discrimination, was about the financial liability of the crown.

The early criteria for being on the roll involved phenotype, blood quantum, picking up the annuity payments, and cultural attributes. In the early days, those were sufficient markers of identity for the government to distinguish between who was and who was not an Indian. However, over time, as intermarriages took place and First Nations people were subject to assimilative forces, it became increasingly difficult to use the above criteria. The federal crown therefore attempted to establish a base population and then proceeded to monitor it over time to determine the number of people who could be identified as Indians. This meant of course that genealogy became the key in tracking who was and who was not an Indian. Over time, changes were made to the *Indian Act* as Indian Affairs attempted to refine its ability to identify who was an Indian.

However, as noted above, this meant that each time new criteria were invoked and/or old criteria discarded, the definition of who was an Indian changed. For example, when the process of "enfranchisement" was introduced, an individual could voluntarily or involuntarily have his or her Indian status removed. In the case of voluntary enfranchisement, if an Indian wanted to purchase land, he or she could voluntarily give up his or her Indian status and collect $400 from Indian Affairs, and from then on the federal government would have no responsibility to that person or any descendant. If a First Nations person achieved a university education, he or she would be unilaterally removed from the roll by Ottawa, and any descendant would never be a Status Indian (i.e., involuntary enfranchisement). In other cases, certain rules were placed in the *Indian Act* that affected an individual's Indian status. For example, the "double mother" clause stated that if an individual's mother and grandmother were not Indian, the offspring would be considered Indian only until they turned twenty-one. In other cases, the *Indian Act* stated that if an Indian woman married a non-Indian man, she and her children lost their Indian status. Conversely, if an Indian man married a non-Indian woman, the woman became an Indian and so did their children.

In 1985, changes to the *Indian Act* stated that if an Indian woman could not or would not name the father of her child, it would be assumed that the father was not a Status Indian. For example, in the *Gehl* case (2017), Indian Affairs refused to register Lynn Gehl as an Indian even though she had Indian heritage that went back five generations. Gehl took her case to the courts, and the Ontario Court of Appeal ruled that a woman can have a good reason for not identifying the father beyond the fact that he might not be Indian (e.g., rape, incest, abuse, or simply because the man disavows that the child is his). In the end, the court ruled that the registrar's application of the policy failed to consider the equality-enhancing values and remedial objectives underlying amendments to the *Indian Act* and thus was unreasonable. Consequently, Gehl was awarded section 6.2 legal status, and Indian Affairs enrolled her. However, she has appealed that decision, arguing that she should be a section 6.1(a) Indian. Gehl points out that Indian men who married Non-Status Indian women before 1985 pass 6.1 status to their grandchildren and in many cases to their great-grandchildren if they were born before 1985. This is the case even when their children and grandchildren have children with non-Indians. However, Indian women who married Non-Status Indian men before 1985 can pass 6.2

status on only to their grandchildren, not to their great-grandchildren. Gehl agrees that the 1985 *Indian Act* eliminated some sex discrimination against women, but it also introduced the notion of a "second-generation cut-off rule" that applies only to Indian women and not to the descendants of Indian men. As of 2019, the courts have not ruled on the appeal.

The "status card" for Indians was created by the crown to fit them into the *Indian Act* and thus be able to both enumerate them and regulate their behaviour. Administrative requirements thus trumped reality. For example, as Hankard (2014) points out, the government's definition of an Indian ignores the social relations of First Nations people in which their identities are linked to the land, their particular clan, the First Nation to which they belong, their particular *noswin* (Indian name), who their parents are, where their people come from, and their lineage (Anderson and Innes 2015). In short, for the administrative requirements of the crown, these crucial issues of First Nations identity are irrelevant, and male lineage is the deciding criterion.

One can thus see that the rules and regulations for who is and who is not an Indian have twisted and turned over the decades. Moreover, First Nations people have argued that they have had no say in defining who they are and that unilateral fiats by Indian Affairs have determined their identities. For years, the most egregious sections of the *Indian Act* were denounced by First Nations people, whom the government simply ignored. However, in 1973, the Supreme Court ruled (in *Calder*) that Indians possibly had rights, and this ruling opened the door for a more enlightened perspective of the crown on First Nations people. Then Sandra Lovelace took her case (1977) regarding gender discrimination in the *Indian Act* to the United Nations, which sided with her. The international courts found that the *Indian Act* was indeed discriminatory, so once again it was revised by the passage of Bill C-31 in 1985, and it added over 100,000 people to the official registry of First Nations people. This was followed by another court case (*McIvor* 2007), which found that the revision was still discriminatory, and it was once again revised (Bill C-3). This added another 40,000 people to the registry. In 2015, the Quebec Superior Court ruled (in *Deschenaux v Canada*) that some parts of the *Indian Act* still discriminated against First Nations women and thus gave the federal government until the end of 2017 to make further changes. Parliament then passed Bill s-3 to deal with gender discrimination. The bill leaves in place the sex-based hierarchy between full (6.1(a)) and partial (6.1(c)) status; it also leaves in place the cut-off that bars descendants of women (but not men) born prior to 1951 from eligibility for status. The government removed these discriminatory components in August of 2019.

In the most recent revisions to the *Indian Act*, new criteria were invoked to define who is an Indian. The new rules state that people on the Indian roll prior to 1985 will be called section 6.1(a) Indians. Those people "reinstated" by Bill c-31 and Bill c-3 will be defined as section 6.2 Indians (or in some cases section 6.1(c)). Both are considered registered Indians, and their names are on the registry in Ottawa. Both groups are eligible to participate in various government programs that support First Nations people. What is different, because of the revised *Indian Act*, is that (1) band status is independent of Indian status and now dependent on approval by the Chief and council and that (2) the status of the children of these individuals will differ depending on whether they are section 6.1 or 6.2 Indians—regardless of sex. The new *Indian Act* states that if a section 6.1 Indian marries a section 6.1 Indian, then their children will come under that section. This holds true if a 6.1 Indian marries a 6.2 Indian or if two 6.2 Indians marry and have a child. However, if a 6.1 Indian marries a non-Indian, the children come under 6.2. Finally, if a 6.2 person marries a non-Indian, the children are not considered Indians. Clatworthy (2005) has projected that, with these new changes regarding who is an Indian, the number of Indians will increase until about 2060, and then there will be a precipitous decline until the end of the twenty-first century, when there will be fewer Indians defined by the government than there are today.

As noted above, the government has now divided "Indian status" from "band status," and thus one can be a Status Indian (on the federal roll) but not a registered member of any band. Bill c-31 allows the Chief and council to determine who is a band member. Some bands have opted for rules embedded in the *Indian Act*, whereas others have claimed that band membership is dependent on having one or both parents as Indians. Still others have invoked a blood quantum criterion (father, mother, or both) for determining who is a band member. Doerfler (2015) provides an insightful analysis of how blood quantum is understood by First Nations people and how it relates to their political development. She also reveals how the concept has been debased by government officials. Nevertheless, this means that, depending on the criterion used, many First Nations people living off-reserve might have a say in reserve politics if they become band members.

This brings us to the last term used to define Indigenous people: "First Nations." This term was introduced by the National Indian Brotherhood and the Assembly of First Nations to distinguish themselves from the other two Indigenous groups—Métis and Inuit—as well as other cultural groups in Canada. It is a symbolic term created by these organizations to replace the deprecatory term "Indian." However, it is not a legal term even though it is in common use. Moreover, the current website of Indian Affairs defines a First Nations person as anyone who is a Status or Non-Status Indian. Others use it to refer only to Status or registered Indians. Adding to the confusion is the fact that it is sometimes used to designate a band (e.g., the Siksika First Nation), whereas the media use it to refer to any Indigenous person or group. Nevertheless, the term is solidly entrenched in the vocabulary of Canadians even if its specific definition is unclear.

In summary, Ottawa determines who is an Indian. It controls the registry and sets the criteria for determining who is on the roll. If a person is listed on the roll, he or she is considered an Indian for government purposes. If a person is not on the roll, he or she can petition the government to become an Indian by going through a formal process of application adjudicated by Indian Affairs.

DEMOGRAPHY

To understand the political, social, and economic positions of Indigenous people, it is useful to consider their demographic position in Canadian society. Indigenous people (Indians, Inuit, and Métis) who claimed Indigenous identity in 2018 make up over 1.6 million

Canadians or nearly 5 percent of the Canadian population (see Table 1.1). First Nations (Indians) make up nearly half of the Indigenous population (46 percent), while Métis and Inuit make up about 450,000 and 60,000 respectively.

Table 1.1. Indigenous Identity Population, Canada, 2016

	NUMBER	PERCENT
Total Indigenous identity population	1,673,785	100
First Nations single identity	977,230	61
Registered Indian	637,700	46
First Nations (not registered)	213,900	15
Métis single identity	587,545	32
Inuit single identity	65,025	4
Multiple Indigenous identities	11,400	1
Indigenous identity not identified elsewhere	26,500	2

Source: Statistics Canada (2017).

These figures show an increase of 43 percent for all Indigenous people compared with a 5 percent increase for the non-Indigenous population between 2006 and 2016. During this period, the number of First Nations people increased over 39 percent, and the number of First Nations people without registered Indian status increased by over 60 percent. The Métis population increased by 51 percent, whereas the Inuit population grew only 30 percent. A majority of the First Nations population lives in Ontario and the four western provinces. In the Northwest Territories, Yukon, Manitoba, and Saskatchewan, First Nations people make up the largest shares of the total Indigenous population. Table 1.2 reveals the geographical distribution of the Indigenous population in Canada.

Table 1.2. Distribution and Percentage of Population Reporting Indigenous Identity[a] in Canadian Provinces and Territories, 2016

	PROVINCE/ TERRITORY PERCENT DISTRIBUTION	ESTIMATED PERCENTAGE OF TOTAL PROVINCIAL/ TERRITORIAL POPULATION
Newfoundland and Labrador	2.6	7.1
Prince Edward Island	0.2	1.6
Nova Scotia	2.4	3.7
New Brunswick	1.6	3.1
Quebec	10.1	1.8
Ontario	21.5	2.4
Manitoba	14.0	16.7
Saskatchewan	11.3	15.6
Alberta	15.8	6.2
British Columbia	16.6	5.4
Yukon	0.6	23.1
Northwest Territories	1.5	51.9
Nunavut	2.0	86.3
Total Number	**1,673,785**	**100.0**

a Indigenous identity refers to a person who identifies as First Nations, Métis, or Inuk and/or those who are Status Indians and/or have membership in a First Nation or band.
Source: Statistics Canada (2016).

Métis represent 8 percent of the total population of the Northwest Territories, 7 percent of the population in Manitoba, and 5 percent of the population in Saskatchewan. Nearly three-quarters of Inuit in Canada live in Inuit Nunangat, which stretches from Labrador to the

Northwest Territories. Canada's Indigenous Peoples are relatively young: 46.2 percent are under twenty-five (compared to 29.4 percent of the rest of the population); only 5.9 percent are over sixty-five (compared to 14.2 percent of the rest of the population). In Saskatchewan and Manitoba, the median age of First Nations people is just over twenty, half that of the non–First Nations populations in those provinces. About half of the Status Indians in Canada live on a reserve or settlement, though this varies across the country. For example, in Ontario, about 37 percent of First Nations people live on reserves, whereas in Quebec 70 percent do so. There are virtually no reserves in the Northwest Territories. First Nations people who are not Status Indians now make up one-quarter of the total First Nations population in Canada. In fact, in the Maritimes, Non-Status Indians make up about six of ten people who claim to be First Nations.

CONCLUSION

In 1850 and 1851, the first two Acts related to Indigenous Peoples were passed: *An Act for the Protection of Indians in Upper Canada from Imposition, and the Property Occupied or Enjoyed by Them from Trespass and Injury* and the *Act for the Better Protection of the Lands and Property of Indians in Lower Canada*. In 1857, the *Act to Encourage the Gradual Civilization of the Indian Tribes in Canada* was passed, and it introduced the idea of enfranchisement. It stated that if an adult male Indian was free of debt, of good moral character, and could speak fluent English or French, he could give up his Indian status. This person would then be a British citizen, have the right to vote, could claim up to fifty acres of land from his reserve, and obtain—on a one-time basis—a per-capita share of treaty annuities and other disbursements for Indian people. Later, in 1869, a new law was passed: *An Act for the Gradual Enfranchisement of Indians, the Better Management of Indian Affairs, and to Extend the Provisions of the Act 31st Victoria*. This Act added the clause that it was illegal to sell liquor to Indians. It also included the provision that an Indian woman who married a non-Indian man would automatically lose her Indian status (as would their children). Finally, this new Act forbade Indian women from running for Chief or member of council as well as voting for a Chief or a member of council.

The *Gradual Enfranchisement Act* of 1869, for the first time, used a blood quantum requirement for who was and was not an Indian. It stated that the person had to have at least one-quarter Indian blood to be eligible as a Status Indian. Then, when the *Indian Act* was introduced in 1876 and consolidated the many previous Acts regarding First Nations people, it stipulated that no "half-breed" could be an Indian; one had to be "pure" Indian to fall under the *Indian Act*. In this Act was the first formal definition of who was considered an Indian. In addition, the Act created the category of a "Non-Treaty Indian," which focused on people with "Indian blood" who did not belong to any recognized band or treaty group but nevertheless lived an "Indian mode of life." This meant that, even though some individuals were not recognized by the state as Treaty Indians, they were considered Indians and subject to the *Indian Act*.

Canadian government officials in the late nineteenth century and early twentieth century created an Indigenous policy to achieve several major goals. First, they wanted to "civilize" or assimilate all Indigenous people. Second, they wanted to protect Indigenous people until they were sufficiently assimilated so that they did not need ongoing protection or incur special costs. Third, they needed a policy to clear the land of Indigenous people so that settlers could engage in large-scale agricultural activity and natural resource extraction unencumbered. Inherent in this policy was the belief that Indigenous people were impediments to productive national development. Fourth, government officials wanted to control Indigenous people in almost all areas of life from birth to death to achieve assimilation. And fifth, these officials wanted the ability to identify who was Indigenous so that, as paternal protective measures were withdrawn, the legal and financial obligations of the government would decrease. Indigenous people who revealed "success" in assimilation could be "enfranchised" and lose the title of Indian, thus removing them from the strictures of the *Indian Act* and at the same time relieving the federal government of any fiscal or legal liability.

Today the provincial governments have taken issue with any action by the federal government that "downloads" the costs of dealing with

Indigenous people, and for the past century there has been considerable conflict between the two levels of government regarding responsibility for Indigenous people. The result is that Indigenous people get caught in the conflict and are denied support by both levels of government until the conflict is resolved, which sometimes takes many years. All of this has led Guimond (2003) to refer to "fuzzy definitions" and changing identities when referring to Indigenous people.

Over the years, the federal government (and to some extent the provincial governments) have chosen to define Indigeneity in several ways. For instance, the Alberta government has given official recognition to Métis, set aside land for them, and supported educational programs related to them. Conversely, in Ontario there is no recognition of Métis. Who exactly is First Nations is another complex issue, for the federal government has used many different criteria in defining this category. Over the years, approximately 125 criteria have been used to define a First Nations person. Changes to the criteria have been made by Parliament through changes to the *Indian Act*, though in some cases federal law has changed the criteria. Moreover, though many of these criteria have been unilaterally imposed on First Nations people, sometimes individuals have been given the choice to opt in or out of the category of First Nations.

Today there are different kinds of Indigenous people according to the federal government: Treaty Indians, Status Indians, Non-Treaty Indians, Non-Status Indians, Section 6.1 Indians, Section 6.1(a) or 6.1(c) Indians, Section 6.2 Indians, Métis, and Inuit. What all of these terms have in common is that they have been created unilaterally by the federal government and reflect its concerns about control, coercion, and cost. As we enter the third decade of the twenty-first century, there is little to suggest that this process of categorization will end.

CHAPTER 2

RELATIONS BETWEEN INDIGENOUS *and* NON-INDIGENOUS PEOPLE

In this chapter, I provide a succinct historical assessment of the marginal position of Indigenous people in Canadian society. I discuss key events in the history of Canada that changed the role of Indigenous people from providers to allies to threats to barriers to the development of Canada (Bland 2014). I reveal how a revisionist history provided by settlers permeated the media, the government, and eventually the psyches of individual Canadians, such that policies adopted by the crown ensured a continual marginal existence for Indigenous people while allowing the crown to claim that it was attempting to support them (Simpson and Smith 2014).

THE INDIGENOUS QUESTION

The "Indian problem" has been a topic of conversation for decades, and more recently courts and politicians have been preoccupied with it. How is it that one issue in Canadian society has that kind of interest and resilience? How does such a topic generate that much attention, that much passion, and that much controversy? Or perhaps the question is how come the "Indian problem" is still with us nearly 200 years after Canada developed a policy to deal with Indigenous people? Is it the case that those people refuse (or are unable) to comply with the norms of other Canadians and lead lives like theirs? Or is it the case that the government has dealt with Indigenous people in such a manner that they have been ignored, discriminated against, and marginalized in Canadian society (Jordan-Fenton and Pokiak-Fenton 2010)? Is it the case, as Palmater (2011b) points out, that federal laws and policies have put Indigenous people in their current state of poverty and continue to keep them in that state? Or is it that Indigenous people just decided one day that they would prefer to depend on the crown for their existence and well-being and experience major health issues, die premature deaths from the extreme poverty, and lose their identities (Palmater 2011a, 2015)?

Each of us can give an explanation generally based upon personal experience, from reading a social studies textbook in grade ten to listening to a discussion about a recent article in one of the national newspapers. Suppose that you have no previous contact with Indigenous people. Suppose that you cannot remember the specifics of your social studies textbook. What would fill in the gaps? For most of us, in addition to learning about Indigenous people from our families and friends, we have learned about them from sources such as newspapers, magazines, radio, movies, television, and more recently the internet. These sources seem to be reasonable, and there is no reason to think that they are biased or untrue in any fashion. Or are they?

What is the primary goal of the mass media? Are they interested in providing "the facts and only the facts"? Are they interested in selling copies or TV programs? Are they interested in making money? Do the media have political agendas? How linked are the media with other institutional orders of our country, such as finance, industry, construction, transportation, and oil and gas? In short, are the media unbiased in their presentation of Indigenous people to the public?

We accept that media corporations are interested, first and foremost, in making money. If they do not make money, then they do not continue to exist. However, they also have large holdings in other economic institutions and vice versa. For example, members of the boards of media corporations also sit on boards of energy, transportation, and manufacturing companies. There is a "circulation of elites" at this level, and their power and influence far exceed their immediate corporate affiliations. Integration of the media with other institutional orders creates a formidable influence, and the media can access information from the government and the private sector that promotes their "take" on issues, including Indigenous people. For example, a large energy infrastructure company in North America met with federal representatives, including ministers and staff from the Prime Minister's Office, 368 times over a five-year period. It also lobbied seven provincial governments 458 times.

Economic ideology (today it is neo-liberalism) is an important driver of the behaviour of elites and corporations (Coulthard 2014). As Monchalin (2016) points out, how members of the public view Indigenous people is largely based upon mass media descriptions that characterize them as militant and radical when they try to protect their land and water, or as lazy and dangerous in other social settings (Longstaffe 2017). All of this is linked to the legal structures and processes of Canadian society that elites have established over the years.

Today we also know that in the past many of the books (including their photos) about Indigenous people written by settlers and colonial administrators were fictitious. Much of the material published in the nineteenth century and early twentieth century about Indigenous people was driven by authors and publishers who wanted to sell "copy" and make money. An editorial in the national *Globe and Mail* (April 4, 2017) argued that, when settlers came to Canada, the Indigenous population was "small," implying that settlers had the right to "take the land" since it was not being used properly by the few Indigenous people on it. The editorial went on to say that the settlers came to be farmers and manufacturers and eventually formed a majority of the population, implying that colonialism was not involved and that the process of cultural loss for Indigenous people was inevitable. There was no suggestion that lies and duplicity forced Indigenous Peoples to lose their lands and cultures or that millions of Indigenous people were living in North America at the time of European settlement. Should that not give us pause for concern? Should we not take what the media say with a "grain of salt" (Anderson and Robertson 2015)?

These are not easy questions to answer, but they give us a sense of the complexity of dealing with the media and their corporate affiliates in their portrayal of Indigenous Peoples and issues (Varcoe 2011; Warry 2007). Much of what we think we know about Indigenous people comes from information that flows by us, and we simply reach out, capture, and then utilize the information that we think best fits our pre-existing beliefs and values. It is the easiest and most efficient way to obtain information. Unfortunately, it is not always the most appropriate way to discover "reality." The biggest problem is that we do not always assess the validity and reliability of the information. In fact, many of us would not know how to assess the consistency and/or truthfulness of the messages being passed around (Lawrence 2011).

Many of us resist change and have trouble accepting information that does not fit with our preconceived views about a topic or event. There are strong forces to erase the events of colonial history, as when Prime Minister Stephen Harper stated publicly that colonialism was never practised in Canada. Today the crown identifies protests by Indigenous people, particularly related to land and environmental issues, as illegitimate and even terrorist in some cases. As Monchalin (2016) points out, the public view of Indigenous Peoples is based largely upon mass media descriptions.

For example, a close analysis of the events in Caledonia, Ontario, in 2006 reveals that the media framed Indigenous protesters as criminal, violent, and lawless, whereas non-Indigenous people (including the crown) were viewed as victims. Balfour (2014) points out that the removal of the historical treatment of Indigenous Peoples from an understanding of contemporary resistance is symptomatic of how Canadians view Indigenous protest activities. Moreover, the threat of "terror" is attributed to Indigenous people as a group, whereas settler acts of "terror" are individualized (Flanagan 2009). The colonial history of Indigenous Peoples is also hidden by the media's emphasis on how they continue to be barriers to growth and progress.

We must also deal with the issue of identity (Palmater 2015), which is particularly important for Indigenous Peoples (Warry 2007). When I ask people about their ethnic identity, most quickly respond that they are Canadian, Irish Canadian, or Sudanese, reflecting their self-defined single or hyphenated ethnic identity. Few times in your life will you be challenged about the legitimacy of such an identity, and it is virtually unheard of for someone to tell you that you are not Canadian or Irish Canadian and then go on to define you as German. Under most circumstances, your self-identification is accepted by others as legitimate and respected as such (Brewer 2010). The identities of Indigenous people, however, have been contested for the past two centuries (Palmater 2011b). Which ethnic group has been told by a government department that they are not who they claim to be and in fact will have their identity defined by the government? This issue is paramount for Indigenous people as they try to navigate Canadian society and find a niche in it for themselves (Lawrence 2012; Shih, Sanchez, and Ho 2010). How did this come about? What are the costs? I now turn to address these questions.

WRITING A HISTORY

History is the description of the past. In this description, we try to identify what occurred (as best as we can reconstruct it) and how it reflects what we understand. Academics agree that history is a mixture of both objective and subjective experiences and interpretations. But the relevant issues here are how history is used by the government and its citizens and which perspective is considered the "right" one—to the rejection of all other interpretations. As Black (2014) notes, disputes about identities and interests that join present and past are important in today's world. Moreover, they cannot be fully understood outside the context of what the government does in presenting this history. As Coates (2018) notes, Indigenous Peoples played active roles in shaping Canadian society; they were not passive pawns manipulated by settlers. History is used to provide an understanding of the past in terms of the beliefs of the present. For Indigenous Peoples, telling their own histories on their own terms is the mortar that binds Indigenous sovereignty and self-determination (Shreve 2017).

Kelm and Smith (2018) argue that, in order to read and think historically, we need to consider five different concepts: change over time (constant changes in government policy), context (understanding the social and political conditions of the day), cause and effect (what led to specific government policies and programs), contingency (of people and their behaviour in certain social conditions), and complexity (looking at different institutional spheres [economic, educational, spiritual]). Thus, as we read historical documents, we will have a better understanding of their meanings. Moreover, Rutherdale, Abel, and Lackenbauer (2018) have shown that recent contributions from emerging literature outside scholarly circles have also provided Indigenous voices that have contributed to Indigenous interpretations of various documents.

INDIGENOUS PEOPLE AS THE "OTHER"

Many people writing history tend to ignore specific political and cultural contexts in which laws are presented, as well as the ideological and linguistic meanings of the terms used in such laws (Griffith 2018). There is a use of *lieux de mémoire* (places of memory) in building the settler history of Canada. For example, the legal profession takes an "on the face of it" interpretation of a public document and then claims a clear cause and effect and concludes that it is the only interpretation. This process fails to capture the context in which the document was prepared and presented. Thus, it often fails to capture the meaning of such a document. In writing a history of Canada, we must understand that terms such as "Indian" and "Eskimo" were created by European explorers and colonists (Kenny 2015) and that, over the years, the terms have taken on different meanings, as dictated by settlers and colonists, including terms such as "savagery," "indolence," and "inferiority" (Lutz 2008). Even the concept of the "noble savage" was rejected by late-nineteenth-century settlers and colonists. The consequence for Indigenous people is that they have vanished as both voice and source. Moreover, until recently, historians and legal experts have spent little time and effort gathering evidence of historical events from a perspective other than that of settler accounts (Anastakis, Kelm, and Morton 2017).

In history, both legally and racially, Indigenous people are generally defined as the other, and as such they are absent from many sources commonly used by policy makers, lawyers, and justices in provincial and/or federal courts. A good example comes from 1884, when band elections (only men could vote) were introduced and traditional leaders were told that they would have no authority in the community (Smith 2014). Trigger (1986) argues that, until the mid-nineteenth century, Indigenous people played important roles in the development of Canadian society. Moreover, their roles—especially their military and environmental skills—were respected by many colonists and administrators. However, as Regan (2010) points out, over time settlers and colonists focused on their own heroic efforts. As a result, the roles of Indigenous people in the development of Canada existed outside the history of Canada. Moreover, the colonial government (and later the Canadian government) would be portrayed as a benevolent peacemaker who met the needs of Indigenous people and brought them closer to civilization.

Today historians recognize that historical, social, and legal contexts must be considered to understand fully the explanations given and the history presented by non-Indigenous people. For example, many of the social and legal institutions of Canada will only consider written materials as useful, valuable, and valid. For these reasons, much of the evidence used in past histories, court proceedings, and political ideologies completely misses the record of Indigenous work through ceremony, story, and language (Kenny 2015). Canadian history and instruction in classrooms throughout Canada have presented students with the dominant society's "grand narrative," which damages the voices of Indigenous people and hampers Indigenous learners' interest in Canadian history (Anuik 2018). For example, Foster (2018) points out that in this grand narrative, when some depredation is perpetrated by Indians against settlers, it appears simply as hostile behaviour motivated by interest or emotion. However, when settlers retaliate by capturing and trying those responsible, they are seen not merely as seeking vengeance or restitution but also as applying settler law.

At the same time, as Canadians go about their daily lives, they become accustomed to "seeing through" Indigenous people. Only when Indigenous people behave in stereotypical ways is there recognition that they exist outside museums, and they then fit the preconceived notions of who they are and what they do. When you see two Indigenous men sleeping on the city bus, you connect with the stereotype. Alternatively, when you come across an Inuit with a PhD, you might be startled. As Coulthard (2014) points out, Indigenous people still find that their cultural expressions require the approval of agents of colonization.

COLONIALISM AND THE "OTHER"

Colonialism is not just a trait of capitalism. Socialist and communist governments have also engaged in it (e.g., China in Tibet, Russia in Georgia). There are two types of colonialism. The first type is referred to as external colonialism and focuses on how parts of the Indigenous world are expropriated by invading forces to build the wealth of incoming colonizers. For example, when the French and English entered what is now Canada, they were interested in exploiting lumber, furs, and other natural resources in the New World and taking them home to their "mother" countries for transformation into ships, clothes, and minerals. However, over time, a second type of colonialism emerged that is called internal (or sometimes settler) colonialism. This type remains within the borders of the state, which uses various modes of control to deal with Indigenous Peoples to ensure that the settler way of life is considered the norm and invalidates all aspects of Indigenous life. In the case of Canada, external colonialism began with the introduction of French and English administrators and then continued once settlers took control of the institutional structures of the newly formed country. Settlers came to Canada intent on remaining in the new land, and they were complicit in establishing settler sovereignty over all modes of life, beginning with land. For example, land taken from Indigenous Peoples allowed settlers to remain, and it became their source of capital (Palmater 2015). In addition, the removal of land from Indigenous Peoples produced major epistemic and ontological disruptions to their ways of life. For settlers, land was defined as property (a commodity), and the relationship with land focused on the ownership of the property. Indigenous communities were destroyed through the implementation of British law and policy adopted by the settlers and then enforced by the state (Tuck and Yang 2012) through treaties and other means. For example, in 1919, the *Indian Act* allowed the superintendent to give mining rights to the private sector even when the band denied them (Smith 2014).

In assessing interactions between settlers and Indigenous Peoples, it is important to understand that, though a "dialogue" between the two parties occurred over the years, it did not imply equity between them. The power imbalance was so great that settlers determined the nature and direction of that dialogue. That power imbalance has continued into the twenty-first century. In fact, Lutz (2008) argues that the imbalance allowed settlers to become dominant and thus led to the dispossession and subordination of Indigenous Peoples over the years. Veracini (2011) identifies two basic attributes of internal/settler colonization. The first attribute he calls "isopolity," a single political community joining separate jurisdictions. The second is "deep colonizing," a situation in which the supersession of colonial practices is entrenched in the operation of the state. In the case of isopolity, British settlers had many of the civil and political rights that they possessed as British subjects in the Old World transferred to them in Canada. It also meant that colonial administrators formally applied external political and legal control over British settler colonists. Over time, as settlers moved toward self-government, this relationship changed in that the enhanced political and legal powers of settlers allowed them to shape their own rules and organizations as well as those of the Indigenous population (deep colonizing). Indigenous people were thus subjected to colonial practices in all aspects of their lives, and settler law allowed for the implementation of policies and programs that led to the elimination of Indigenous people and culture. British law and jurisprudence were carried over to Canada and applied to Indigenous Peoples when they were encountered. At the same time, settlers and their colonial administrators held moral and religious beliefs that convinced them they had the duty to rule over and protect Indigenous Peoples (Nettelbeck et al. 2016).

This inequitable process has two effects. First, it allows the group in power to set the agenda for any discussion. If the dominant group does not wish to discuss some issues, then it simply refuses or ignores the request to have a dialogue on them. Second, the voice of the minority group is lost in history; this is cryptoamnesia, the process by which the minority voice or activity is lost and the dominant group claims voice or creation (Butera, Levine, and Vernet 2009). The issue of isinglass is a good historical example of how Indigenous technology was appropriated by settlers and then claimed as their own, refusing to acknowledge the real origin of such technology. Isinglass is a gelatin product that Indigenous people long ago removed from the bladders of sturgeon, using it for glue and for "fixing" paint on their hides and later canvasses. As it turns out, this has been of great assistance to archaeologists today as they sort through historical artifacts. However, as settlers found out about this substance from Indigenous people, they began to utilize the technology, using isinglass not only as a glue but also as a clarifying agent for making beer and wine. History identifies it as a settler invention, and the agency of Indigenous people in the discovery and use of isinglass was lost.

One might argue that this is a small point, but it clearly identifies the process of cryptoamnesia, and one can find many current issues that have met the same fate. For example, the finding of the courts that the *Indian Act* was discriminatory toward First Nations women has been adroitly handled by the government, erasing the fact that these women have argued this for years. And, in a similar stance, the government argued that Bill C-31 was not discriminatory toward First Nations women. When the government was forced to make changes to Bill C-31 because of a Supreme Court ruling, the explanation presented to Canadians was that the government saw a need for changes and thus made them, thereby obliterating the previous actions and voices of First Nations women such as Mary Two Axe Early and Sandra Lovelace in their quest to make changes to the *Indian Act*.

THE EUROCENTRIC PERSPECTIVE

Early colonizers were convinced that Indigenous people did not engage in labour appropriately. It was not that they did not engage in labour at all; everyone could see that they worked: they hunted, trapped, fished, and provided for the necessities of life for their families and communities. These are activities that require a great deal of effort, time, and skill, and few people would argue to the contrary. Nonetheless, settlers objected that Indigenous people did not work appropriately: that is, they did not work from sunrise to sunset or engage in a specific type of physical labour related to agriculture or forestry. "Idleness is the devil's handmaiden" was the sentiment of the day, and ceremonies such as Potlatches and Sundances that took people away from labour simply did not fit into settlers' ideas about work (McCallum 2015). From the settlers' perspective, Indigenous work was not defined as "good labour," and the "free time" of Indigenous people was viewed with suspicion. Indigenous work would be seen later with outright disdain and defined as inappropriate, illegitimate, and "bad."

INDIGENOUS CLAIMS

Since 1982, numerous court cases have been heard by the Supreme Court of Canada on Indigenous issues. In these cases, lawyers for the crown attempt to prove that Aboriginal Rights have never existed or are less than what the Indigenous group claims. One might argue that this is a game being played out by the two parties, but there are real consequences of these legal contests. Over time, it has been shown that, in the court setting, judges/justices (and crown lawyers) claim that they know Canadian history better than Indigenous Peoples and expert witnesses who participate in the legal battles. After all, the legal authorities took a social studies course in grade eleven, perhaps a couple of history courses at university, and have read popular books on the subject as well as listened to radio programs or watched TV programs on Indigenous Peoples. The result of such obstructionism and ignorance is that these gatekeepers rely on what was taught and learned fifty years ago, on what contemporary pop media portray, and on listening to others equally ignorant of history. If a new perspective is presented by an Indigenous claimant, then it is normally rejected by the judge/justice or crown lawyers since they are convinced that the history they learned through Western ways of knowing is the correct sequence of events and explanatory factors. As Ray (2011) points out, when the first settlers came to Canada, using their own conceptual and historical lenses, they saw mobile, illiterate, and seemingly disorganized Indigenous Peoples. Moreover, they saw the Indigenous population as having no structured commercial enterprises or any interest in engaging in agricultural pursuits. Finally, Indigenous Peoples were viewed as primitive (uncivilized), though some settlers thought that through Christianization and acceptance of settler culture they could come close to being civilized. In the end, it was the "white man's burden" to ensure that Indigenous Peoples became civilized. Nevertheless, these myths were defined as real, and thus the consequences were also real (Woolford 2015).

There has been little acknowledgement that historically Indigenous Peoples had vibrant cultures along with complex governments, political structures, and laws. The fact that Indigenous Peoples engaged in intertribal trading networks extending from the east coast to the west coast is considered preposterous. This Eurocentric view of the world came with the settlers, and the "law of extinguishment" (i.e., the acceptance of *terra nullius*), and other made-up doctrines and tests that served the purposes of the colonial government, have determined the mindsets of most Canadians. For example, in 1727, a memorandum of the Privy Council stated that discovery or occupation could be declared if the land was unoccupied (Culhane 1998). To be sure, the word *unoccupied* was liberally defined by the settlers and the colonial government. And, as noted earlier, this view persists, with a *Globe and Mail* (2017) editorial referring to First Nations people in Canada at the time of settlement as "thinly populated." Although many have claimed that the doctrine of *terra nullius* never applied to Canada, they refuse to identify how Canada acquired its claim over Indigenous Peoples and lands. If *terra nullius* is not the basis for dispossessing Indigenous Peoples, taking away their lands and cultures, then how do we validate Canada's assertion of sovereignty over land and people?

POWER RELATIONS AND MORAL CERTAINTY

The result of exercising the power of the state was that Indigenous Peoples were removed from their lands, marginalized in the economy, and turned into pariahs. Perhaps even more important, they could not obtain any legal protection of their rights and lands. Today the courts demand that, if an Indigenous group wants to exercise a right, they must prove that the right exists and has been in continuous operation since before the arrival of settlers. What is ironic is that the government created and implemented laws over the past two centuries that prevented Indigenous Peoples from continuing some of those activities. Even today Indigenous Peoples find it difficult to obtain legal protections for rights and/or lands that have been lost over the past two centuries. At the same time, as Ray (2011) points out, the legal system in Canada uses history to bury the injustices perpetrated against Indigenous Peoples.

The issue of land rights has re-emerged in British Columbia since no treaties, until recently, were signed with First Nations people there—the exceptions being the small Douglas Treaties on Vancouver Island and the northeastern corner of the province (Treaty Eight). However, the government of British Columbia took the position (until the twenty-first century) that First Nations people had no land rights since they had been transferred to British Columbia when it was established as a province. Furthermore, if there were any periphery rights, they were diminished by the implementation of other pieces of legislation passed by the provincial government over time. Hence, the roles of law and politics regarding First Nations land claims have been disproportionate emerging from these disputes. Nevertheless, the results of these conflicts have reverberated throughout Canada.

Canadian law has also chosen to approach claims and rights through what is called "case law." In this approach, the focus is on a textual reading of the law in place at the time of the claim. The courts often argue that, since we can all read the text of a treaty or law, its meaning is "plain on its face" (Ray 2011). Through a textual reading of the law (e.g., contracts, treaties), the legal system invents its own history. This allows the courts to sift efficiently through the mass of materials sometimes presented by claimants in a land or rights case. It allows the courts to ignore important elements such as context, complexity, causality, contingency, and change over time (Kelm and Smith 2018) in the interpretation of documents. For example, in *Regina v Horseman*, the court had the audacity to theorize (with no evidence) that the drafters of the *Natural Resources Transfer Act* consciously merged and consolidated all of the Treaty Rights (and statutory rights) into the Act and thus dismissed the claims of First Nations people (Ray 2011).

MEANING AND CONTEXT

The manuscripts or records of white fur traders, missionaries, and government officials do "speak for themselves"—but only for themselves (Morin 2018). They comprise one side of an account of a conversation between two cultures (Woolford 2005). They are partial, biased, and fragmentary. Relying exclusively on texts written by non-Indigenous observers—texts that incorporate notions of indolence and dependence into the very definition of an Indigenous person—we hear only one side of a long exchange (Borrows 2017a). It is not surprising, then, that non-Indigenous people tend to reject Indigenous accounts of the past as not true or at best as mythical and thus irrelevant. Moreover, oral history is given less credibility than written records—no matter who wrote them and no matter the contexts. For example, when the Gitxsan-Wet'suet'en land claim came before the courts, "civilization," continuity of culture, and conflict became issues. In this case, the crown argued that only historical documents (written by non-Indigenous people) could be introduced as evidence, and they were documents that said what they meant, meant what they said, and any adult with reasoning ability could understand the meanings of the texts. In short, the crown argued, contextual or historical information about the meanings of the texts was irrelevant and unnecessary.

Others have noted that, given the differences in language, many of the words used in written documents simply would not have been understood by Indigenous Peoples (Leddy 2017). Although most settlers agreed (as do their descendants now) that the intent of the treaties was to take land and other rights from Indigenous Peoples and offer them to settlers, this might not have been the understanding of Indigenous Peoples (Morin 2016). For example, when Alexander Morris was negotiating Treaty Three, he stated that the crown had come to share the land, to give them things, and not to take away their means of livelihood. In these explanations to the Saulteaux group of the Anishinaabe Nation, there is no mention of the word *surrender*. So how could they have fully understood the implications of such a document? Although there is a statement of "yield and surrender" in the long-hand treaty, the evidence suggests that it was never discussed with the Saulteaux during the negotiations (Macdougall 2017). We also know through the transcripts of the negotiations that many clauses and issues were changed after the negotiations, and that oral agreements between the two parties were not included. All treaties were written in English, and there was never a document produced in the appropriate Indigenous language.

Prior to the Seven Years War (1756–63), Indigenous people had fought as allies of the English and French combatants. At the time, Indigenous groups found that "taking sides" was advantageous to them, and they skillfully played their economic and political choices. However, when the English became the dominant force, securing Indigenous support became a paramount issue for the victors. To secure this support (including from those who had sided with the French in the Seven Years War), King George III created the Royal Proclamation of 1763. It was based upon the realities of the time. The military had been disbanded, and many had left its service, while many Indigenous people who had supported the British were waiting for their "rewards," and the ratio of First Nations to settlers was much in favour of First Nations. The proclamation was therefore a pragmatic attempt to appease the Indigenous population. It stated that land not used by settlers would be preserved for the use of Indigenous Peoples and that the federal crown would protect these peoples and their lands. Furthermore, it stated that, if these "Indian lands" were to be purchased, only the crown—not settlers—could do so. Moreover, if the crown were to purchase land, there would be a process by which it would take place, including approval by First Nations to sell their lands to the crown. Although the proclamation would win Indigenous support for the British crown at the time, there was little thought about the future consequences of such a proclamation. Thus, implementation of the Royal Proclamation of 1763 has provided one small ray of hope for First Nations. And, as one might suspect, over the years the crown has been trying to ignore, negate, redefine, repeal, and limit the content of the proclamation.

Later the issue of Aboriginal Rights in terms of land was played out in the famous but long forgotten case *St. Catharines Milling and Lumber Company v Regina* (1888). Although Indigenous Peoples were not represented, let alone knew about the court proceedings, the consequences were real in terms of defining their interest in land. The Privy Council in England (the highest appeal court of Canada at the time) ruled that Indigenous Peoples (specifically the Saulteaux) held only personal (usufructuary) rights to occupy and use the land—at the pleasure of the federal crown—that had not been sold or ceded to settlers. The Privy Council thus ruled that the Saulteaux had surrendered outright their land ownership and that the Province of Ontario owned the land and not the federal government. This decision to define narrowly Aboriginal Rights in terms of land held until late in the twentieth century. Only in the case of *Calder v British Columbia* (1973) would the Nisga'a get a hearing in the courts even though they had tried to exert their land rights since 1881 when they sent a delegation to Victoria and a petition to the queen in London to voice their objections to actions taken by the colonial government regarding their land and rights. To combat such legal challenges, the federal government, in agreement with the provinces, had revised the *Indian Act* in 1927 to bar Indigenous people from raising money or hiring lawyers to represent their land rights. This egregious provision of the *Indian Act* remained in force until 1951, when the government finally removed it.

These little-known historical notes illustrate three points. First, they demonstrate that text is not always "plain on its face" so that all participants understand the meanings of the words in that text. Second, once a text was accepted as having a meaning by the colonial government, it set the foundations for future texts, interpretations, and meanings. Third, they demonstrate that the federal government created its own meanings regardless of what other parties might have thought (Doxtator 2011). The government was then free to implement legislation that prevented Indigenous Peoples' interpretations of those documents to secure their rights. In short, once the government meaning is legitimized, the Indigenous meaning becomes irrelevant.

THE EVOLUTIONARY PROCESS

Historically, most non-Indigenous people viewed culture in an evolutionary sense—starting with primitive "man" and moving toward civilized "man." And, from the perspectives of many settlers and colonial administrators, traditional Indigenous culture was at the "primitive" end of the continuum, whereas settler culture was at the "civilized" end. For example, there was a constant insistence that Indigenous people had little commerce, had no real political structures, and used primitive languages at the time of contact. Ray (2011) and others have conclusively found that traditional Indigenous communities had well-developed economic structures, carried on complex political relations within and outside their communities, and had languages that, though different in form and structure from European languages, were as sophisticated as English or French. The contrast between settler culture, which embodied progress and technological superiority, and Indigenous society, viewed as static and primitive, established a false dichotomy that everyone seems to have accepted without critical evaluation. As a result, there is a tendency to view contemporary Indigenous culture as the "debris" of an idyllic past. With this kind of thinking, Indigenous culture is viewed as being enhanced by settlers' more civilized culture.

THE TRANSFORMATION OF MEANING: CONTACT AND INTERACTION

Anyone who has engaged in cross-cultural communication understands the risk of misunderstanding the meanings of signs and symbols, even when people use the same symbols or words. As individuals move from one culture to another, words and objects are transformed in meaning, and considerable negotiation takes place to ensure the culturally specific meanings of those words and objects (Griffith 2018). Moreover, more complex concepts—such as religion, economy, and crime—have different meanings as one moves from one cultural context to another. An example of different meanings within the English language is the British/Australian saying "Bob's your uncle!" (A loose translation is "There it is.")

The history of relations between Indigenous and non-Indigenous people over the past three centuries is a good example of how exchanges between the two groups have been misinterpreted and labelled in a biased fashion and how a history has been built upon those errors and biases (Morin 2016). The result has been the displacement of Indigenous Peoples from their lands, the loss of control over what were once Indigenous resources, and the marginalization of Indigenous people in Canadian society (Gagnon 2014). Long before Indigenous Peoples and European explorers learned the formal components of each other's language, they developed a system for trading goods. This initial relationship formed the basis for more complex exchanges, eventually developing into treaties and laws. Nevertheless, one of the most important forms of exchange between Indigenous people and settlers focused on the economic system.

As noted earlier, when objects are transformed by the act of exchange, they can take on new meanings. One can imagine what happens when individuals move across cultural divides and into and out of an emerging capitalist economy. Transformational exchange works as a two-way process. Indigenous artifacts and modes of thinking were introduced into the "Canadian" environment, and European goods and modes of thinking were introduced into Indigenous cultures. For example, furs from Canada became markers of status in Europe, as did wool blankets in Indigenous communities. As Lutz (2008) points out, if something as simple as the exchange of an object involves a transformation in meaning, then one can only conjecture about the more complex meanings embedded in the exchange of labour for money.

Indigenous participation in the labour force, or the lack of it, is central to an understanding of settler expansion in Canada and to the debate about what politicians and others have called the "Indian problem." The Indigenous dialogue with capitalism has been complex. In a capitalist society, the workplace is not just a physical place but also the embodiment of a social system based upon private property, individualism, rationalism, and subordination. When Indigenous Peoples have engaged in the capitalist economic system, they have become involved in a social structure in which livelihoods are constantly transformed and reorganized as the changing needs of capital interact with culture.

Thinking about labour as a cross-cultural exchange allows a fresh perspective on relations between Indigenous and non-Indigenous people.

In addition, in the capitalist system is the concept of the "commodity." It invokes the relationship between "exchange value" and "use value." The usefulness of an object or material in society defines its use value, whereas its exchange value is defined as the proportion of its value compared to that of the object or material in exchange. This means that the use value of an object or material is independent of its exchange value. An example is air. In the past, it had high use value but little exchange value. Who wanted to trade air for something else? Water is another example. It traditionally had high use value but little exchange value. However, with the recent pollution of both air and water, they have high use value and high exchange value. People are willing to pay money to obtain clean air and water. In short, they are now commodities, and their exchange value is increasing while their use value has remained constant. Land became a commodity for non-Indigenous people a long time ago and has had high use and exchange value. But for Indigenous people it has high use value (particularly at the level of symbolic/cultural significance) but little exchange value. Hence, there is a great deal of conflict between Indigenous and non-Indigenous people over their conceptualizations of land.

Once capitalism was embraced and became the basis for economic exchange, state structures (e.g., laws and agreements) were put in place to force everyone to adopt capitalism as well as the dominant social, political, and legal activities that facilitated capitalist ideas about land. For example, given that over 95 percent of applications for resource development activities are approved by the government, Indigenous people argue that the predetermined result is approval to support capitalism. They argue that agreements and other "concessions" given to Indigenous people in the development of resources and lands give the illusion of participation in and control over the outcome (Coulthard 2014).

DEFINING HOW THE WORLD OPERATES

From the time of major settler intrusion into Canada, observation of and record keeping on Indigenous people increased, involving new techniques and structures of state monitoring. The *Indian Act*, for example, monitored the behaviour of Indigenous people from birth to death, from bedroom to boardroom. Federal Indian agents stationed on reserves around the country were mandated to report—from the perspective of the state of course—on the cultural "progress" of Indigenous people (Duncan 1913). These reports, in addition, were moralizing judgments about which First Nations individuals were "good" (i.e., working the land and being self-supporting) or "not good" (i.e., participating in ceremonies such as Sundances but showing little interest in paid work). Only after the turn of the twentieth century were agents told to focus on the economic "progress" of First Nations people. The close supervision continued with the implementation of laws that required them to obtain passes from Indian agents if they wanted to leave their reserves. Returning to the reserves meant providing explanations about where they went, what they did, and whom they met. Unsatisfactory answers would result in not being able to obtain a pass in the future. Close supervision was the operative norm of the day (Satzewich 1997).

This process continues. Keith (2015) argues that the state has assumed ownership of and control over the lands and resources of Indigenous Peoples, and this has gone on for the past 200 years uncontested (except by Indigenous Peoples). The state acts in a hegemonic fashion when settlers exercise direct domination through the political and legal structures of civil society. It wields its coercive power when it legally forces Indigenous Peoples, who do not consent either actively or passively, to accept the demands of settlers and their administrative leaders. Thus, today, when the state uses a modern treaty to resolve land issues, it imposes capitalist state values of land and land management on Indigenous Peoples. For example, introduction of the comprehensive claims policy (1986, 1995) was based upon resolving uncertainty and creating a framework for negotiating settlements according to Canadian law. This document clarified the land and resource rights of Indigenous Peoples, the government, and the private sector. The government's argument for the policy was to implement a secure climate for economic and resource development that would benefit Canadians as well as "balance" Indigenous and non-Indigenous interests—all within the context of a capitalist economy. In the end, totalization tries to make everything a reflection of the underlying hegemonic logic (Keith 2015, 52).

A more specific example is when Ottawa was asked to help with the housing needs of the Attawapiskat reserve. The government responded by appointing an outside manager, confiscating the records of the band and Chief, and informing the community that it would have to pay the "audit specialist" $2,500 a day for his work. The funds to pay this specialist were drawn from the community's budget. Only eight months later the courts responded by saying that there was no evidence of fiscal mismanagement, no evidence that band funding had been misappropriated, and no evidence that either the Chief or the band council had engaged in inappropriate behaviour. Indian Affairs has a default prevention and management policy with three levels of intervention. The lowest level is the recipient-managed action plan, which requires Indigenous communities to balance their budgets. The next level is the recipient-appointed adviser, which involves hiring an external accountant to act as co-manager of the band. The highest level is the third-party funding agreement, which involves Indian Affairs appointing a financial manager for the band. Today over 40 percent of First Nations are subject to one of the three levels of intervention. This is extraordinary because all expenditures on reserves are preapproved and reviewed by Indian Affairs. In the case of Attawapiskat, the judgment of the courts was unusual in that they ruled that Indian Affairs had taken inappropriate action and had not resolved the housing crisis. In the end, nothing happened other than the third party continuing to control funding allocation for the band.

Although most Canadians will remember the initial controversy and the charges of "fiscal mismanagement" against the Attawapiskat band, few will know of the subsequent courts' decision. At present, these third-party monitors appointed by the government receive approximately 10 percent of the allocation of funds by Parliament to the bands as payment for their services. In return for this third-party monitoring, Indigenous communities incur the loss of these funds and the loss of control over the remaining funds to an external accounting firm hired by and accountable to the Department of Indian Affairs.

THE WORK WORLD

As pointed out earlier, labour was the core of how early colonists and later Canadians valued themselves (Lutz 2008). Before the Reformation, work was linked to the needs of a person, profit was considered sacrilegious, and businesspeople were considered un-Christian because of their focus on individual wealth accumulation. However, by the sixteenth century, an individual's value was appraised to the extent that the person accepted the "Protestant work ethic." By these new norms, an individual's value was linked to his or her willingness to participate in a certain type of work for long hours, minimize leisure time, and accumulate wealth beyond basic material needs. Not only was this proper behaviour to exhibit, but also, if one was economically successful, it indicated that the person would be "saved" upon death. Because of this fundamental change in norms, businesspeople became stalwarts of the church, leaders of the community, and creators and guardians of policy and ideology. Today Western culture provides the highest status and deference to those individuals most successful in accumulating wealth. The subsequent creation of the "corporation" simply allowed individuals to increase their wealth infinitely without any encumbrances, ignoring community cohesion or support, and (some might add) without any personal liability.

Even though Indigenous Peoples valued both work and leisure time, their type of work was incompatible with the settler "work ethic." Settlers argued that those who chose to avoid certain kinds of labour (e.g., agriculture) and lived by trapping, fishing, and hunting had no reason to complain when their land was taken by settlers who used it in a more "productive" manner for the well-being of both individual and state. Because of such new norms and values, individuals who enhanced the value of the land were considered "worthy" members of society and supported by the state. At the same time, the myth of the "lazy Indian" was derived from this conception of labour, prevalent in settler culture when Canada was being colonized, and it was used to justify the transfer of lands from Indigenous Peoples to the colonial state and then to Canadian settlers and their corporate supporters.

Thus, what constituted appropriate labour became a weapon that settlers used against Indigenous Peoples—defined as lazy and unproductive—because then and only then could settlers justify the displacement of Indigenous Peoples and the occupation of their Traditional Territories. Settlers resorted to the "labour theory of value" espoused by John Locke. The task was now to show how Indigenous people did neither—engage in agricultural pursuits or enhance the value of the land that they used. In doing so, settlers had to overlook the different agricultural practices undertaken by Indigenous people (e.g., the harvesting of wild rice and other agricultural practices) to ensure their definition of the Indigenous world as still in a state of nature. These Indigenous agricultural pursuits were generally ignored or argued as exceptions to the rule. In addition, settlers had to conceptualize the productive activities of Indigenous communities as not involving labour per se, allowing them to declare Canada *terra nullius* and available for the taking. The most expedient way of doing so was to define Indigenous labour as existing outside the economy. This unique and narrow definition of what constituted "real" work and the subsequent actions taken against Indigenous Peoples are at the heart of Canadian history.

For early settlers, labour was the source of all value, and it provided the right to ownership (Lutz 2008). Colonists argued that trapping, fishing, hunting, gathering, and even some domestic farming by Indigenous people did not constitute labour—at least not in a way that met the definition of settler economics. In short, these activities did not remove Indigenous people from their "primitive state of nature." Yet among settlers the same activities, along with manufacturing, were redefined and considered a mix of labour and nature, so they were used to justify making lands, waters, and resources settler property. Thinking about labour as a cross-cultural exchange gives us a new perspective on relations between Indigenous and non-Indigenous people.

MAPPING AND DISPOSSESSION

During the eighteenth century and much of the nineteenth century, settlers and Indigenous Peoples functioned largely independent of each other. However, by the mid-nineteenth century there were increasing conflicts between the two groups, and the colonial government had to take steps to deal with the Indigenous population. The first step in controlling this population was to define it. Various Acts beginning in the 1850s outlined who was an Indigenous person. The consolidation in the *Indian Act* of 1876 formally began to present a biological and cultural definition of an Indigenous person. In addition, the Canadian government regulated the behaviour of First Nations people within a territory (by creating reserves) through the process of "ruling from a distance." This meant that decisions were made in Ottawa with little knowledge of what was happening in the hinterland. This approach allowed politicians and policy makers to remain in Ottawa and dictate principles and programs across the country related to Indigenous people.

Dispossession of First Nations occurred, first, because of settlers' interest in using the land as a base for profit. Second, the government saw this profit-based strategy as useful in winning the support of settlers and as a way of supporting the legitimacy of its laws. Third, a discourse on "civilization" and "savagery" began in which Indigenous people were placed on the continuum at the "primitive" end, thus allowing the government and settlers to treat them differently. Fourth, management of the land would allow the government to control it and make a profit from it. To do so, the creation of maps was crucial.

One of the most useful and thus widely used techniques to legitimize colonial power and authority was topographical mapping. Although mapping has long been used by people occupying land, what was new in developing Canada was the type of mapping used and the subsequent use of the maps. Until the late eighteenth century, governments produced cadastral maps of lands that primarily identified property and government boundaries. Not until 1789 were topographical maps used (such maps show a variety of landmark and landscape information). Indigenous Peoples had employed mental maps of their locales for years, and in some cases they drew topographical maps to indicate specific physical components of the landscape. However, the colonial state used maps not only to produce detailed landscapes (e.g., rivers, valleys, lakes) but also to control people's movements, eliminate Indigenous voices, and reveal a "vacant wilderness" that needed to be settled.

As Canada moved into the late nineteenth century and early twentieth century, it passed laws to deal with the "Indian problem" and organize settlement in an orderly fashion. Reserves were created based upon the new topographical maps. This of course required surveying the country and laying out township grids, which were central to the effectiveness of the survey and remain key to land holding today. For example, baselines and meridians were surveyed first, and townships were numbered in relation to them. East–west lines were called ranges, and north–south lines were called townships. In the end, the survey converted the wilderness into saleable parcels of property (each one is unique) and ensured that ownership of those lands could be identified. Moreover, it meant that purchasing a piece of land would be orderly and simple, and each piece of land would take on a unique identity linked to an individual. Finally, it meant that the government could make money by selling each parcel of land and subsequently taxing the owner.

It was then that the frontier myth was developed. It embodied the notion that westward expansion and the "frontier lifestyle" were central in the development of Canada as a nation. It was viewed as central to the formation of English Canadian identity. This myth, emerging from the settlement of the west, promoted individualism and democracy. It also projected Indigenous Peoples as a barrier to settler expansion and use of the land. It was during the late nineteenth century that Indigenous ownership was redefined as occupancy, driving the concepts of Indigenous stewardship and sovereignty into oblivion. The simultaneous ideology that emerged defining Indigenous Peoples as culturally inferior made it easier to dispossess them of their lands through both legal and extralegal means.

In the end, the establishment of a Cartesian grid of public land produced a map of the country as a "gridded landscape"—which had nothing in common with the mapping used by Indigenous Peoples—endorsed by both the state and settlers. In addition, the settler concept of "rational space" became an overriding component of the mapping of the country. Finally, Indigenous Peoples lost their voices through the obliteration of Indigenous names for landmarks replaced by European names. Thus, any historical importance of Indigenous names for places was lost and could not contribute to Indigenous identity as the land was being settled. For example, Siksika Nation land called

Miistukstakoowa in what is now Banff National Park was unilaterally removed from their control in 1908 by the federal government. In turn, the land was called Castle Mountain and in 1911 integrated into the park. Later it was renamed Eisenhower Mountain but then reverted to Castle Mountain, which it is called today. The Indigenous name of the area is now used only by the Siksika Nation. Only in the twenty-first century have Indigenous Peoples begun to challenge the use of English or French names imposed on their lands and publicly to use traditional Indigenous names (e.g., the Gleichen reserve is now using its Indigenous name Siksika).

Today Indigenous communities are bringing about name changes for communities, lakes, and other landmarks. If a community agrees on a name change, then it approaches the provincial government to enact the change since the "renaming" process has been devolved to the provinces and territories. Each province or territory has its own set of rules and regulations for how a name change can take place. However, Indigenous communities that wish to change a name also have to petition the federal government to recognize the change and formalize it through legal proceedings.

CONTROL AND SUBORDINATION

"Peaceable subordination" refers to strategies used by colonists and colonial states to control Indigenous Peoples and to occupy their lands while not engaging in overt violence against them. When Indigenous Peoples were removed from their lands, the explanation and justification always included the language of incorporation (Lutz 2008). It was argued that Indigenous Peoples would be brought into "civilization" through the actions of the state and its supporting institutions (e.g., churches, schools, the economy). Other settler ideas—such as private property, wage labour, and British justice—helped to support these views. As a result, Canada's marginalization of Indigenous Peoples was seemingly a peaceable process. Although there was little large-scale overt aggression toward them after the nineteenth century, covertly the impact on Indigenous Peoples was near genocide. It was couched in seemingly benign terms of nation building, transitioning into a new order of things with the benefits of civilization, and the rule of settler law.

Over the years, Indigenous Peoples experienced the impacts of laws implicitly and explicitly aimed at limiting their cultures, languages, and economies. Other pieces of legislation, in the process of their application, had similar effects (e.g., the *Natural Resources Transfer Act*). These actions limited the type of work and indeed the kind of life in which Indigenous people could engage. For example, in 1872, the *Act to Amend the Qualification and Registration of Voters* removed the right of Indigenous people to vote in provincial and federal elections. Since they were prohibited from taking up an occupation in law or politics, they were at the legislative mercy of a non-Indigenous minority who used the state apparatus to further marginalize them. Hence, Indigenous people could not represent themselves or elect anyone to represent their concerns, nor could they have a say in who represented them.

Early British settlers supported their home country ideology based upon the principles of liberalism. It is ironic that settler colonists denied Indigenous Peoples the principles of a liberal philosophy. As a way out of this dilemma, settler colonists insisted that peaceable subjugation was required before liberalism could be achieved. The argument was that "in time" Indigenous Peoples would be extended the principles of liberalism. Moreover, it was claimed, peaceful colonization was more "humane" than outright conquest. Nonetheless, the overall goal of peaceful subordination was the subjugation of Indigenous Peoples to the benefit of colonizers. As Lutz (2008) points out, colonizers maintained their dominance over Indigenous Peoples based upon the promise of eventual extension of liberal-democratic institutions to them. However, the preserve-and-destroy aspects of capitalism contributed differently to peaceable subordination (Asch, Borrows, and Tully 2018). This came about because, within a traditional society, there are always opportunities for some individuals to preserve or enhance their power by engaging in capitalist relations even as others are negatively affected by them. Settlers usually found some individuals in the Indigenous community, often elites, who would benefit from, and cooperate with, the new social order. Unknown to the Indigenous people who gave support to capitalism, the privileges gained by cooperation were short-lived. Nevertheless, some individuals in the Indigenous community supported the efforts of the settler state and thus sustained the efforts of the settlers, their institutional structures, and their values. For example, men were given privileges over women in payment for their acquiescence to settler law.

Peaceable subordination can occur through a process referred to as "enframement" (Elsey 2013; Lutz 2008). As Indigenous people enter the wage economy, they participate in a foreign cultural framework. However, the longer they work within this foreign framework, the more their Indigenous framework must adjust. Over the long term, such participation alters the terms of engagement and, ultimately, the traditional cultural frame. There is also a second kind of enframement at work. Because the colonial government and settler colonists held power, many institutional structures were established that directly or indirectly impinged on Indigenous Peoples, such as the declaration in 1849 that British law applied to Canada, the *Indian Act, 1876*, and the *Fisheries Act*. Over time, these frames laid a foundation upon which new settler laws were built. Indigenous Peoples thus found themselves with ever-decreasing physical, cultural, and legal spaces in which to operate.

Despite the shrinking spaces within these frames, the subjugation of Indigenous Peoples was never complete. Indigenous cultures were transformed but not destroyed. Guha (1997) calls this situation—in which Indigenous Peoples are under settler domination and have incorporated some of the Euro-Canadian worldview yet still maintain distinct spiritual, economic, and cultural ideas—domination without hegemony.

As noted above, the new capitalist economy brought by settlers was not always completely rejected by Indigenous Peoples. Some aspects they welcomed and used. Because there were many "strategic congruities" between the values of Indigenous Peoples and those of Europeans, each group could benefit from the other's abilities and desires while pursuing their own agenda. The partial incorporation of Indigenous Peoples into the modern economy did not result in the destruction of their traditional subsistence economies. What emerged, to the benefit of the private sector and to most Canadians, were parallel economies, which allowed for the establishment of a "primary" labour pool (highly educated and skilled) and a "secondary" labour pool (poorly educated and skilled). The latter group can sit idle, at no cost to the private sector (because the state and/or charities support this pool), until they are required to re-enter the labour force.

A NEW PERSPECTIVE: THE MODITIONAL ECONOMY

Today Indigenous people are seen as being caught between a subsistence economy that has not yet disappeared and a modern economy that has not yet arrived. An alternative view put forth by Lutz (2008) is that Indigenous people have chosen to operate in a new economy that encompasses both subsistence and capitalism. In a sense, capitalism has been (partially) incorporated into their traditional subsistence economy and vice versa. Both have been transformed in the process, resulting in a hybrid economy for Indigenous people. They have created a new, distinctive economy out of their available options, choosing independence over capitalism, state support, or solely "living off the land." Lutz (2008) views this economy as a novel and flexible creation responsive to change. It is within this economy, which he termed "moditional," that Indigenous people operate. The moditional economy, with its focus on relationships, chooses or emphasizes different modes as conditions change.

However, most Canadians do not see this new hybrid economy; rather, they see Indigenous people at the beginning of a long process of transitioning from a subsistence economy to a capitalist economy. Their view of change remains linear, and they do not view the Indigenous economy as a hybrid structure incorporating elements of both economies. Indian Affairs has always taken, and continues to take, this approach in developing economic policies and programs for Indigenous people. Even though the Harvard Project (Cornell and Kalt 1992; Lemont 2006) has provided empirical evidence that the linear model of development is inappropriate for Indigenous people, little policy change has emerged from Indian Affairs.

Embedded in the concept of the moditional economy is the key notion that each mode depends on the other. For Indigenous people in Canada, the maintenance of their distinct subsistence economies depended partially on wage labour, just as the expansion of capitalism in Canada depended partially on Indigenous labour. However, in selling their labour, even to enable them to engage more fully in the subsistence economy, Indigenous people became involved in a process that would partially displace their sole reliance on that economy (Lutz 2008). The moditional economy emerged from the partial involvement of Indigenous people in the larger capitalist economy but with limits on the nature and extent of their participation in it. All of this happened as Indigenous people were subordinated through the process of capitalism, Christianization, public education, and close supervision. Nevertheless, many historians and politicians have ignored Indigenous resistance to the wage labour force while investigating its impact on the traditional subsistence economy (Borrows 2018). More startling is that there has been little recognition that the high rates of unemployment and welfare dependence among Indigenous people are a contemporary social issue and not one that existed prior to the twentieth century. Even more importantly, few people realize that the state brought about this marginalization, unemployment, and dependence (McNeil 2018).

The development of a hybrid economy was both imposed on Indigenous people and partially undertaken voluntarily by them. Their entry into the capitalist economy was not easy. For example, Indian agents in 1919 noted that fisheries officers arbitrarily refused to give back fishing licences to Indigenous people who had not fished the year before. The context was that in the previous year there had been high demand for spruce wood for wartime airplane construction, and many Indigenous people who normally fished had logged instead. In rejecting their applications for renewal of their fishing licences, the inspector of fisheries argued that they were likely to go back to fishing as subsistence labour. In addition, Indigenous people were prohibited from having licences to operate the more profitable purse seiners (large boats) on various rivers, and as a result purse seine licences were limited to Métis and settlers.

WORK AND LABOUR

The explorers of North America were followed by the fur traders and then the settlers, accepting and building upon the definitions of Indigenous people outlined by colonial administrators. The stereotypes of being lazy, illiterate, and primitive continued despite evidence that Indigenous people were productive, articulate, and in many ways more civilized than the traders and subsequent settlers. Partially, these stereotypes were reinforced by many Indigenous people because they had little need for European goods (and chose not to trap fur-bearing animals extensively or exclusively) and because they enjoyed periods of diminished labour between food-gathering seasons. Indigenous people also lacked interest in participating fully in the wage economy and thus refused to exchange their subsistence activities for capitalism and its focus on developing a surplus (Lutz 2008). This reluctance reinforced the stereotypes of Indigenous people as "indolent," "backward," and "lazy."

The wage economy introduced them to the norms and values of settler society—individualism, rationalism, and progress—that had emerged from the Enlightenment, the French Revolution, and the Industrial Revolution. Over time, these values were selectively incorporated into Indigenous cultures. Although some elements of capitalism enhanced the subsistence economy, most of the effects were destabilizing. The engagement in wage labour had short-term benefits for Indigenous people, but they quickly realized that it also brought them into a social system that demanded subordination, individualization, and a belief in private property—all foreign values to them. Settlers' values were in opposition to embedded values of subsistence, collective life, and traditional economies. In short, modernity was imposed on Indigenous people's style of living. Individualism challenged the notion of clan or kinship. In other cases, settler rationalism focused on how the environment would be subordinated to human activity. Moreover, settlers' views on the use of resources and progress focused on the future. There was a belief in an endless set of inventions that would occur in the future for the betterment of people. In addition to the extent that wages came to be defined as individual property, this belief supported links among other settler institutions—work, banking, government. Finally, wage labour indirectly privileged the young, strong, and malleable and denigrated the Indigenous belief that Elders were to be privileged (Helin 2008). Although these values were promoted by settlers, many Indigenous people resisted them.

During the nineteenth century, Indigenous people worked seasonally at skilled or well-paid jobs. However, by the twentieth century, they were increasingly confined to an economic niche of low-wage, seasonal labour combined with subsistence activities. For example, they were restricted by a variety of state policies from entering agriculture, education, the hospitality industry, or public works. In short, Indigenous people were limited to taking jobs that no one else wanted in the capitalist economy. Employers, while reluctant to hire Indigenous people as permanent employees, were delighted to have a secondary labour pool that could be called on a few months of the year (e.g., canneries, sugar beet and tobacco harvesting) and then dismissed until the next year. Indigenous people did not choose to be paid low wages and to have access only to the jobs associated with a low socio-economic niche. This position was imposed on them. Nevertheless, seasonal labour did have some advantages for them, allowing them to be free of the capitalist economy for the rest of the year and to pursue their own economic and cultural goals. However, by the late twentieth century, even this niche was disappearing.

In the early labour market niche for Indigenous people, education was of no great advantage, particularly for men. Most of the work open to them did not require higher education, and subsistence activities were valuable contributions to the community and the family economy. Education, for many Indigenous families, meant sending their children to residential schools, which were foreign and often abusive, and the children returned without any knowledge of their traditional language and culture. Moreover, these schools operated at standards well below those of provincial schools (e.g., teacher training, curriculum). As such, the education provided in residential schools was directed toward training for low-skill jobs rather than what was needed to ensure success in the new economy. Today we find that nearly 40 percent of the adult Indigenous population have less than a high school education and are very reluctant to believe educators about the benefits of education for their children.

Indigenous people who wanted to engage in the modern economy also faced barriers in undertaking activities such as agriculture or the commercial fishery. For example, between 1894 and 1911, their right to fish for domestic use was challenged (Lutz 2008). Initially, the federal government made it illegal for Indigenous people to catch fish in traps or weirs that they had used long before Europeans arrived. The argument for limiting their use of traditional techniques was based upon the stereotype that they were so lazy and idle that they fished in a manner so efficient that they did not have to work long hours. Equally important, this activity kept them from working in the canneries as seasonal workers so crucial to the commercial fishery (Lutz 2008).

Through the *Indian Act*, a reserve system was put in place; it resulted in small family groups being brought together into one land area and stopped their seasonal migrations. However, the lands provided for the reserves were insufficient to sustain either agriculture or ranching. In addition, most reserve lands had a lack of potable water. History shows that water rights and services were put in place to deal with Euro-Canadian needs and that the needs of Indigenous people were ignored. Over time, pollution from the activities of settlers resulted in widespread contamination of water used by Indigenous people and the concomitant spread of communicable diseases. Nevertheless, the government redefined the sources of these illnesses brought about by this contamination because Indigenous people were not assimilated into settler society. Most water regulations imposed by the government were designed to support settlers and industry at the expense of Indigenous people.

The *Indian Act* also drastically and arbitrarily limited Indigenous participation in the broader economy. For example, section 71 provided that the minister could operate farms on reserves and purchase and distribute pure seed to Indigenous farmers without charge. This section also allowed the minister to apply profits to extend farming operations on reserves and to make loans considered desirable to promote the "progress" and "development" of the "Indian." The *Indian Act* also allowed the minister to restrict the sale of goods to non-Indigenous people. Section 93 prohibited, without ministerial approval, the removal of minerals, stones, sand, clay, gravel, or trees from a reserve (Sanderson 2016). In 1911, an amendment allowed a municipality to seize portions of a reserve without surrender by the First Nation if they were to be used for railway or road construction or other public works (Smith 2014). The *Indian Act* also allowed judges to move entire reserves away from municipalities without band consent if judges thought that doing so was in the best interests of the municipalities. Illustrating how the *Indian Act* controlled the behaviour of Indigenous people, an amendment in 1920 stipulated that, if an "Indian" wanted to dress in traditional costume off the reserve, he or she needed the permission of the Indian agent (Monchalin 2016).

When Indigenous people entered the labour market, they were forced into a catch-22 position. For example, in some cases employers would not hire them because they were considered to have a "favoured status" since they were "taken care of" by the federal government. This was not the case for non-Indigenous applicants for various jobs. This view was supported by municipal and provincial governments, which argued that Indigenous people did not pay taxes and thus were not entitled to jobs funded by taxpayers. In times of labour shortage, the same employers argued that, since Indigenous people had access to subsistence fishing, hunting, and trapping, non-Indigenous people should be favoured in participating in wage labour (e.g., commercial fishing). When there was a labour surplus, the employers argued that Indigenous people should remain out of the wage labour market because they could continue to live in the subsistence economy and thus had an "unfair advantage" over non-Indigenous workers. These arguments were in addition to the structural and legal barriers that kept Indigenous people from participating fully in Canadian society. Prejudice and discrimination have been prevalent, and employers still argue that Indigenous people are not steady workers or claim that their customers do not want to interact with them (Reading 2013). In other cases, employers argue that their non-Indigenous workers do not want to work alongside Indigenous workers. This is particularly true in restaurants and retail businesses and among unions. In the end, the arguments against involving Indigenous people in the labour market are dictated by both individual discrimination and systemic, institutionalized discrimination (Loppie 2014).

CONCLUSION

As Abdelal and colleagues (2009) point out, the creation of stereotypes alerts us to the fact that the process of categorizing "races" is about establishing boundaries and then codifying through legislation what is appropriate, right, and moral. These social boundaries need to be sustained, so ideas and characteristics of race are constantly being updated and redefined. For example, who is an "Indian" has been redefined by the federal government many times over the past 125 years. Likewise, over the years, new indicators to support the stereotypes of Indigenous people have been invented and selectively applied. Relations today between Indigenous and non-Indigenous people have been derived from early contact experiences, which in turn are products of old histories. These definitions have relied almost exclusively on non-Indigenous observations. Then and now Indigenous Peoples have had little input into the policy and legal processes that have directly and indirectly affected them. As a result, the laws and programs created to address the "Indian problem" are based upon problematic assumptions about Indigenous Peoples made by settlers and the colonial state.

The history of relations between Indigenous and non-Indigenous people reminds us that not all injustices perpetrated against Indigenous Peoples have resulted from recent actions by the government or employers. The injustices stretch back to the initial colonization of Canada. What is extraordinary is that these injustices have been increased over time (Woolford 2005). When encounters between the two groups took place in the sixteenth and seventeenth centuries, settlers and Indigenous Peoples functioned largely independent of each other, and thus the stereotypes and discrimination were more symbolic than real since the groups operated in parallel but independent social realities. In addition, since trade and/or military alliances were paramount during this time, for the most part there was little interest in establishing settler land ownership (Fisher 1977) or in interfering with the Indigenous way of life. However, once settlement increased, this quickly changed. The settlement process required the complete subordination of Indigenous Peoples, and this subordination played an important part in their marginalization. First, it allowed Canadians to see relations between Indigenous and non-Indigenous people identified at a distinct turning point, either at contact or at the beginning of settlement. Second, it described the process and the expansion of a capitalist economy as relatively uniform across space and among Indigenous Peoples. Third, it excluded any discussion of colonialism. And fourth, it excluded Indigenous Peoples from having any influence on history after this turning point. In the end, the colonization of Indigenous Peoples turned them into small communities marginalized from the larger Canadian society. The approach of the government to the "Indian problem" has been and continues to be one of utilizing the three small ds (defer, deflect, deny). Given this approach, little has been done to address the issues created and sustained by the government and the private sector, resulting in the four large Ds (Disease, Disorientation, Discord, Disempowerment) of Indigenous Peoples.

The lack of educational funding, the continued resistance to allowing Indigenous people to participate in the economy, the lack of infrastructure in Indigenous communities, and the chronic underfunding of social services and maintenance of infrastructure all indicate that change is not about to occur quickly. The lack of action reflects the fact that maintaining a secondary labour pool is good for the capitalist economy, and there is little to suggest that the future looks any brighter for the next generation of Indigenous youth—though today institutions such as the Toronto Dominion Foundation have raised the issue. Capitalism overcomes some traditional barriers but not others, so certain elements of traditional society are reinforced while others are transformed or destroyed. However, as Lutz (2008) points out, Indigenous people have been subordinated but not subjugated. He argues that the federal government has been not only unwilling to bring about meaningful changes but also unable to bring Indigenous Peoples under its complete control.

CHAPTER 3

KEEPING *the* LAND

I n this chapter, I identify one of the key concerns of Indigenous Peoples—land—that has been consistently ignored by the crown and non-Indigenous people as they continue their quest to wrestle ownership and control of land away from Indigenous Peoples. I begin by comparing Western and Indigenous ontologies as well as epistemologies, and then I demonstrate that land is an integral part of Indigenous identity (Macdougall 2017). Moreover, from an Indigenous perspective, the land is part of the self, and the self is part of the land. Elsey (2013) refers to this as the "poetics of existence." She claims that the identities of Indigenous Peoples emerge from their experiences with the land. They argue that learning the stories of Elders (in the traditional language) as well as the geographical areas in which these stories are told make one part of the land. First Nations territorial boundaries have existed for thousands of years and were part of a legal system that upheld territorial orders and respected the autonomy of specific First Nations. Acknowledging lands and territorial rights of First Nations across the country now known as Canada existed long before the arrival of settlers. Since everything has a spirit of life (e.g., trees, mountains), it is important that stories are told to all community members. These stories are taught publicly so that they do not change over time. Since everyone in the community knows the story, errors introduced by the storyteller will quickly be identified by others and corrections made. I then discuss the adoption of Western law and the rejection of Indigenous law in dealing with land issues that have generated an ethos of distrust and fear among Indigenous people when dealing with the crown. I show that the continual insistence by Canadians to view land as a commodity engenders anger and resistance among Indigenous people when issues of land are subject to discussion.

LIVING WITH THE LAND

The most significant concern in Indigenous life is linkage with the land. It represents the core of being, and they are concerned about how other people treat the land. The linkage to lands and environments is understood among Indigenous Peoples around the world. For them, it is a spiritual, emotional, mental, and physical relationship between human beings and their surroundings. Spiritual connections to Mother Earth are maintained through ceremonies and acknowledgements of thanksgiving. Indigenous Peoples argue that, as human beings, we are no different from a tree, a plant, an animal, or any other living or non-living spiritual being. There is a common saying among them that "what happens to you and what happens to the Earth happens to us as well." The only difference is that the Creator gave human beings a mind with which to think, with which to make decisions for the betterment of future generations (Jacobs 2014; Lyons 2008).

A major focus for Indigenous Peoples is on stewardship of the land. From a non-Indigenous perspective, concern about the land is based upon its value as a commodity (use and/or exchange value). For example, a pipeline project or development of the tar sands, from an Indigenous perspective, shows little respect for Traditional Territories in terms of either cultural importance or ecological value (Balfour 2014; Vasey 2011). However, before we look at the linkage between the land and Indigenous people, we need to discuss the legal system in Canada, its connection with land issues, and how it differs from an Indigenous legal system. To understand these differences fully, I need to outline the basic components of "Western ways of knowing" and "Indigenous ways of knowing."

ONTOLOGY AND EPISTEMOLOGY

When we use the term "ontology," we are really asking the question "What is your belief about the nature of reality?" If your answer is "Anything that can be determined by your sensory abilities" (e.g., seeing, smelling), then that is the basis of your ontological perspective—a positivistic ontology. If you say that spirits are part of reality, then you have a different ontological basis. These two perspectives differ in terms of what is considered "real." Ontologies are simply assumptions or philosophical premises that structure your reality. Your ontology is nothing more than non-researchable assumptions that you use to interpret what is happening in your life. The term "epistemology" refers to how you know that something is true. How do you come to know something? In a more general fashion, it is a question about how knowledge is obtained, structured, and evaluated.

WESTERN WAYS OF KNOWING

If you accept the Western perspective, you would say that positivism is the dominant ontological paradigm of most Canadians. Positivism claims that the goal of knowledge is simply to describe the phenomena that we experience. We focus on what we can observe and measure; anything beyond that puts us in the realm of a different ontology. Spirits, for instance, are not legitimate topics for building knowledge from the basis of positivism/science. Moreover, positivism operates on the belief in cause and effect. Then, using deductive reasoning, we can test and learn about our theory and in the end explain how the world operates. Embedded in this ontology is a belief in a reality independent of our thinking about phenomena. Positivism, the basis of Western ways of knowing, emerged from the Age of Enlightenment and has several key features:

- It rejects any metaphysical component.
- It focuses on science as a process/product.

- It demands that facts be at the core of knowledge and be measurable, testable, amenable to being confirmed or falsified by empirical observations.
- It rests on the assumption that results are independent of the investigator.
- There is one science of the real world that underlies all scientific disciplines.

This Western way of knowing came from the development of philosophical thinking in Europe during the sixteenth and seventeenth centuries. It was during this time that Descartes and Bacon promoted (much to the dislike of the Catholic Church at the time) the ontological division of "mind from matter" that led to a view of the universe as a mechanical system consisting of separate objects. This view of course allowed Western society to draw a distinction between science and religion or magic. In addition, this ontological perspective allows for the belief that knowledge can be gained by an individual and thus can be owned by either an individual or a corporation. Finally, in Western ways of knowing, the intellect—rational thinking—is used to gain knowledge.

This paradigm has provided a "scientific sanction" that allows societies to manipulate and exploit nature. As Descartes himself noted, science has the goal of dominating and controlling nature. This Cartesian view (Latin for "Descartes duality") of the world and mechanistic consciousness developed by European thinkers became the dominant paradigm of the Western world and continues to have nearly absolute influence on our lives in Canada. Most Canadians are convinced that empirical evidence is the key to knowledge and is superior to any other kind of knowledge.

With these hegemonic changes taking place in Western ways of thinking, Europe entered the Age of Enlightenment or what is sometimes called the Age of Reason. It was a cultural movement in the seventeenth and eighteenth centuries that continued to build upon Cartesian paradigms by focusing on using reason, rather than tradition or faith, to advance knowledge. It promoted science and was opposed to superstition and religion, and over the past 400 years it has been the dominant paradigm in the Western world and certainly in North America.

INDIGENOUS WAYS OF KNOWING

Indigenous Peoples have a very different paradigm (ontology). From their perspective, knowledge is relational and shared with all, including the cosmos, animals, plants, and Mother Earth. Indigenous ways of knowing accept the idea that it is impossible to separate the relationship between the world of matter and the world of spirit. Since every individual element in the world (e.g., rock, plant, person) has its own unique life force, all elements in the world are interconnected. Moreover, individuals must recognize that any action by any element has a reciprocal function. This is the notion that every action has a reaction.

Indigenous ontology does not allow an individual to own knowledge. First, all knowledge comes from the Creator and thus must be shared. When people gain knowledge, they are not only transformed by it but also must assume responsibility for it. Ceremony is one way in which that relationship with knowledge is carried out with respect. The proper performance of ceremony allows the individual to give and gain access to knowledge holders, who in turn allow the knowledge to be transferred from one person to another. Second, Indigenous ways of knowing are focused on the interconnectedness of all elements in existence. Third, Indigenous Peoples approach knowledge through both the senses and intuition. Humans must always ensure that they are "in balance" with the world. And fourth, rather than a focus on some object or idea, the important issue is one's relationship with the idea, concept, or object. In summary, all human experience and knowledge that make up relationships contribute to the overall understanding and interpretation of the world. Relationships are key to understanding the world, and thus all things, animate and inanimate, are relevant in the life of a human. The result of this ontology and epistemology is the creation of what is called Indigenous Traditional Knowledge. This knowledge is defined as the customary ways in which Indigenous Peoples have carried out and continue to carry out specific activities, and it includes new ideas created by Indigenous Peoples that respect their traditions, cultures, and practices (Laidlaw 2019, 606).

ONTOLOGICAL AND EPISTEMOLOGICAL COMPARISONS

These different ontologies are the basis for the different epistemologies of the two ways of knowing. Measuring things is not paramount in Indigenous ways of knowing (as it is in Western ways of knowing). The key in Indigenous ways of knowing is to understand the relations among things and not just to focus on cause and effect. For Indigenous Peoples, the key is to understand the influences on the system. As Newhouse (2004) points out, Indigenous Peoples live in a world of constantly interacting cycles in which nothing is simply a cause or an effect; rather, all factors influence other elements in the world. In the end, Indigenous ways of knowing do not attempt to control the world by analyzing cause and effect but to understand the world as defined by relationships and forces. In summary, Indigenous Peoples think in terms of relationships, responsibility, respect, and reciprocity.

LEGAL SYSTEMS

As can be predicted from the above discussion, Indigenous and Western ways of knowing lead to different institutional structures and legal systems. Thus, it is important that we understand the assumptions of Western and Indigenous ways of knowing and how they shape views of the land. I will focus on the differences in the legal structures of the two cultures and identify the different perspectives on the land and the human relationship with it.

CANADIAN LAW

Canadian law emerged from the Age of Enlightenment, when religion, hereditary rules, and magic were rejected as bases for making decisions. Rational choice, empirical evidence, and logic became the bases for making decisions. And, from that humble beginning, the scientific method spread around the Western world. Law in Canada has evolved over time, but its basic tenets have been derived from European philosophy and specifically British and French jurisprudence. Today it is based upon three assumptions.

The first assumption is that every society needs a legal system to deal with individual or group interactions—the rule of law. Without a legal system, a society would be in chaos and not function in an effective and efficient manner. Thus, norms established by people must be codified into laws that provide guidance for behaviour. Over time, some laws enacted will be dispensed with, and new laws will be introduced as society changes.

The second assumption is that there can only be one legal system in Canada. There is a belief that, with more than one legal system, people will not be able to make or evaluate decisions about how to behave. Having multiple legal systems will again introduce chaos. So the laws are always applicable to everyone under all circumstances. Thus, the principle of "equality" stipulates that all people, no matter their stations in life, are subject to the laws of the land. For example, no rules apply only to the rich and not to the poor.

The third assumption is that individual autonomy exists today. This means that each person can make choices based upon individual reason. The notion is that the individual is free from "coercion" by external sources (e.g., police, politicians, leaders). In carrying out individual choices, the person then strives to achieve the "good life." It is believed that in Canada there is a social structure that allows individuals to make their own choices and that, if the choices are made within the normative structure, the good life will be assured. So, though our legal system does not say what the good life is, it allows the individual to make choices in a manner that does no harm to others (or at least minimizes that harm) and benefits the individual making the choices.

Yet there are limits to choices made by individuals as identified in a variety of documents that Canadians agree to (e.g., the Constitution, *Criminal Code*, *Charter of Rights and Freedoms*, human rights legislation). However, our legal system is based upon the premise that, if the three principles outlined above are followed, individuals can achieve the good life. We see evidence of this when we look at the procedures of criminal law, human rights legislation, and property rights.

These assumptions are embedded in the legal system of Canada and enacted every day. Individuals who make choices that contravene the above principles that we hold so dearly will then be subjected to the law of the land (e.g., punishment for those who break the law). From a Western perspective, law also performs an educative function in alerting others that, if they break it, they will be subject to the same penalties and restrictions. In Canada, the legal system reveals that law is specialized and idealized as separate from and often superior to other social institutions, norms, and cultural beliefs. Yet we should remember that law has been developed and promoted by those who occupy powerful positions in society.

However, as we all know, these are general principles, and their actual implementation differs. The rich are treated better than the poor, for the wealthy make laws that benefit them, and the economy is based upon their ideas of what is correct, moral, and just. But that does not mean that the general principles are not evident in Canadian law.

INDIGENOUS LAW

I begin by noting the difference between "Aboriginal law" and "Indigenous law." On the one hand, Aboriginal law is a body of Canadian law that examines issues related to Indigenous Peoples in Canada. On the other, Indigenous law refers to the legal traditions, customs, and practices of Indigenous Peoples. As stated by Merryman and Perez-Perdomo (2007), Indigenous law is a set of deeply rooted and historically based attitudes toward the nature of law, the organization and operation of a legal system in society, and how law is made, applied, and taught. If we look at the underlying assumptions of Indigenous Peoples regarding law, then we find some similarities to but also differences from Western law. For example, they would agree that individual autonomy exists. However, they would appreciate that external factors (including social structures and spiritual contexts) might have created an environment in which the individual is forced to make certain choices and thus cannot be blamed for violating the law. From an Indigenous perspective, the basic role of law is to maintain good relations between individuals and within communities. This involves all beings, including what Westerners identify as animate and inanimate objects. In short, the legal system adopted by Indigenous Peoples arises from their relationship with the land and all its inhabitants—animate and inanimate. Should the connections be broken or not work well, it is the role of law to correct those disconnections and bring about balance (Borrows 2002).

Indigenous law reflects the basic philosophy of how one can "live well" with the land, other people, and objects. However, unlike Canadian law, Indigenous law is not a separate institution. From an Indigenous perspective, law is found everywhere—in worldviews, languages, values, and teachings. It is implicit, inherent, dramatic, and unwritten in Indigenous cultures. Moreover, Indigenous Peoples focus on restorative justice in dealing with violators, a perspective that the Canadian government strongly resists (Moore 2010). Put in succinct form, Indigenous law expresses a sacred responsibility to protect and maintain the land and everything on it (Webber and Macleod 2010).

Although there was evidence of Indigenous law at the time of the settlement of Canada, over time Canadians have established the primacy of tort law. There was a belief that Indigenous law could not be highly complex and adapted to the conditions in which it operated, and Indigenous Peoples have been ignored or rejected as having any relevance in resolving conflicts. The courts have vacillated between arguing that Indigenous Peoples never had any law and admitting that they did; nevertheless, it has been replaced by Canadian Aboriginal law. For example, the courts do not accept Indigenous law as a normative order that could inform them about title to Indigenous Lands (e.g., the *Tsilhqot'in* decision of 2014). Yet settlers recognized that Indigenous Lands and societies were governed by legal principles, and some court cases (e.g., *R v Van der Peet* [1996]) have noted that "traditional Indigenous law" arose from Indigenous cultures and customs (Foster 2018). Nevertheless, Harland (2017) notes that Indigenous law and legal traditions continue today and remain important to Indigenous communities and identities. He points out that, in *Delgamuukw v British Columbia* (1997), the court ruled that it needed to rely on the perspectives of both common law and Indigenous law, thereby giving equal weight to each (Borrows 2010a).

THE CONFLICT BETWEEN CANADIAN AND INDIGENOUS LAW

Over the years, the crown has questioned the rights of Indigenous Peoples to their Traditional Territories—certainly as *legal* rights—and they continue to be largely ignored. Without legal recognition by the crown, Indigenous Peoples continue to be removed from their lands. Borrows (2005) argues that such action has resulted in the disruption of Indigenous political, economic, and cultural power, and makes it easier for non-Indigenous people to strengthen their claims to Indigenous Lands. He goes on to argue that authorities have created legal theories to support the crown's claim to many Indigenous Lands and to reject any Indigenous claim to ownership. Parliament and provincial legislatures have used versions of these theories to deny rights to lands and resources for Indigenous Peoples. The federal government argues that in "stateless" societies law depends on the sense of duty possessed by the person designated by law to be the enforcer and, if that person is reluctant, on the amount of persuasion brought to bear on him or her by Elders, carriers of the legal tradition (Foster 2018). And, in the *Tsilhqot'in* case (2014), the crown argued that there are rules and customs that govern people's lives, but they do not constitute law as defined by the crown. In the end, causation, collective responsibility, and compensation are the fundamentals of Indigenous law, whereas Western law is composed of fault, individual responsibility, and punishment (Foster 2018).

Do all Indigenous people still have these views? Do urban Indigenous people still have the ontological view discussed above? The answer is a qualified yes. Although some Indigenous people have accepted Western ways of knowing, just because they live in urban centres does not mean that they have given up their ontological and epistemological paradigms. Just because Indigenous people have cars and modern conveniences in their homes does not mean that they cannot have ontologies and epistemologies different from non-Indigenous Canadians. For Indigenous people, their places of residence are not good indicators of their ontological paradigms.

THE EVOLUTION OF LAW

As we can see from the hegemonic force of Western law, Indigenous law continues to be ignored by Canadians as valid. This is particularly true when there is a conflict between Indigenous law and Euro-Canadian law, at which time Euro-Canadian law always wins. In short, as Borrows (2002) points out, crown sovereignty is paramount over any rights that Indigenous people might claim. These principles have been revealed through the operation of Western law for many years.

However, legal thinking and thus decisions change over time as the norms and values of society change. For example, the ruling in the *Syliboy* case (1928) said that the Treaty of 1752 did not give the Mi'kmaq community immunity from the *Crown Lands and Forests Act*. However, this decision was overturned in 1985 in the *R v Simon* case. Thus, three components of law need to be understood when looking at the legal structure of any society. First, legal actors such as judges, police officers, and lawyers are individuals who carry out their actions within a set of social norms and cultural contexts. Thus, their actions sometimes reflect their own changes in thinking. Second, the legal institutions of society reflect social and normative beliefs of the day. How people think today is very different from how people thought 100 years ago. Third, law is influenced and shaped by people and organizations outside the legal structure (e.g., lobbying groups). On the one hand, law, if deemed appropriate, continues unchanged if people see it as a fair and just way to address non-normative behaviour, which legitimizes the social relationships among people, groups, and organizations. On the other, law is contested when concerns arise that it is not working or is not fair or just. We can see how laws regarding women (e.g., historically being considered the chattel of their fathers or husbands), abortion, marijuana, and same-sex marriage have changed over time. So it is important to remember that law changes, and the direction and nature of change are difficult to predict.

Over time, if changes in law occur, processes are developed by which settlements can be reached. For example, some Canadian law is based upon Indigenous jurisprudence. In *Connolly v Woolrich* (1867), the Canadian judicial decision regarding a marriage between a Cree woman and a Scottish man through Cree customs and laws regulating marriage was deemed legal. The court recognized that the territorial rights and laws of the Cree continued in their full force following trade with Europeans. This case is still taught in various law courses and illustrates the recognition of Cree law and government. As late as the 1960s and 1970s, several lower court decisions upheld components of

Indigenous law (Walters 2017b). However, over time, the fundamental basis for recognizing Indigenous law was lost as settlers demanded that governments implement the rule of "one law." And governments were only too happy to do so. In the end, Canadian law refuses to acknowledge Indigenous law and considers it irrelevant and misleading to discuss it in the current legal context. Or, to put it another way, courts define Indigenous law as "tradition," and thus it is discounted as "law." This is particularly true when there is a conflict between Euro-Canadian and Indigenous approaches.

LAW AND THE LAND

I remind Canadians that Indigenous Peoples occupied and lived off the land of what is now called Canada long before the arrival of settlers. We also know from a variety of sources that there were issues regarding land use and resource use among Indigenous Peoples themselves. To deal with these conflicts, they developed organizational structures to ensure peaceful relations with their neighbours and to avoid conflicts. They engaged in a variety of strategies such as treaties, trade deals, negotiations, marriages, conferences, and ceremonial events that allowed for the demarcations of land use. Thus, when settlers arrived in Canada, initial relations between Indigenous and non-Indigenous people followed many of the protocols and values that Indigenous Peoples used previously to create and maintain peace. Among the most important of these values were treaties. However, though Indigenous Peoples saw a connection between the signing of the treaties and the responsibility of the crown, the commissioners who signed the treaties on behalf of the government of Canada had little knowledge of how Indigenous Peoples viewed them—and did not care. Their goal was to obtain lands and resources.

A key difference between the two legal systems is in the understanding of land. It is difficult to comprehend how successive governments and Canadians have not understood the importance of land (place) to Indigenous Peoples. For them, land is a provider, whereas from a Euro-Canadian perspective it is a resource that requires specific management to create profit, and if no profit is forthcoming the land holds little value. Western law allows the owner of land to focus on managing it largely through centralized control. Indigenous Peoples, conversely, see Western legal views of land as estranging people from it, failing to recognize the spiritual connection between people and the land that they occupy. For Indigenous Peoples, the land is not a passive resource from which certain things can be taken. It is not an object to be managed by cutting it up into discrete parts—plants, trees, minerals, rocks, animals, water bodies. The land provides because it is a holistic system in which every part plays a vital role in the survival of the people who reside on it. Learning how to survive on the land is part of respecting it, hunting and fishing in ways that ensure a family's survival and respect the land so that it will continue to provide (Elsey 2013). Land is fundamental to Indigenous identity. It is reflected in the languages, cultures, and spiritual values of all Indigenous Peoples. Indigenous concepts of territory, property, and ecology might differ profoundly from those of other Canadians, but Indigenous Peoples argue that they are no less entitled to respect. Unfortunately, those concepts have not been honoured in the past, though there is some indication that Canadians are now heeding this knowledge (Blackstock 2013; Chisholm 2013; UN Environment 2019).

Over the past 250 years, Indigenous Peoples have been dispossessed of their lands and resources in Canada by colonial governments as well as the Canadian government. As Borrows (2005) points out, land is crucial to the survival of Indigenous Peoples. Its loss haunts their dreams. Its continuing occupation or reoccupation inspires their visions of the future. The relationship with land is seen not solely as a right but equally as a responsibility. Responsibility for the land is more than just seeing the connection in terms of rights. Understanding "first creation"—the importance of the land, the water, and the first peoples—is the foundation of how Indigenous Peoples understand themselves. The understanding of first creation as a gift engenders the responsibility that people feel to look after the land and maintain good relations with it. Indigenous Peoples tend to regard their relationships with the land in terms of an overarching collective responsibility to cherish and protect the Earth as the giver of life (Macklem 2001). As Dussart and Poirier (2017) point out, long after resource development projects are completed or abandoned, Indigenous Peoples continue to claim ancestral ties and responsibilities to the land not understood by the agents of capitalism.

Indigenous Peoples argue that Canadians need to rethink Traditional Territories as the cultural heritage of Indigenous Peoples themselves. For example, in 2017, the Supreme Court of Canada dismissed a spiritual rights claim under the *Charter of Rights and Freedoms* by the Ktunaxa Nation Council of British Columbia. The Ktunaxa were seeking to protect the Grizzly Bear Spirit and the land on which it was situated. The court ruled that the spiritual rights of the Ktunaxa are not protected by section 2(a) of the Charter. The decision held that approval of a ski resort does not interfere with the Ktunaxa's freedom to believe in the Grizzly Bear Spirit or to manifest this belief. As Elsey (2013) indicates, Indigenous Peoples claim ancestral connections to their Traditional Territories, whereas Western ontology does not. Rather, Canadians want Indigenous Peoples to establish their claims to lands from a Eurocentric perspective that includes criteria such as "exclusive use," "fee simple," and "continued occupancy and use." Thus, when Indigenous Peoples approach the Canadian legal system to argue a land claim, the courts insist that they have proof, for example, of exclusive ownership of or control over a geographical region before their right will even be considered.

Indigenous Peoples' oral descriptions of landscapes, sacred areas, and territorial boundaries reveal a mapping of sites used from time immemorial. This mapping is usually demonstrated in the stories of each group but is not considered by the courts as valid evidence. However, as Elsey (2013) and Lewis (2000) note, many of these stories purvey cultural meanings and serve to associate an entire people with surroundings with which, over the centuries, they have become self-identified.

Stories are critical in an oral society, the basis on which information, norms, and laws are passed from one generation to the next (Innes 2013). Suzack (2017) has shown how storytelling is used to discuss issues such as tribal membership, dispossession of Indigenous women from their children, and colonial forms of land dispossession. Recent archaeological finds at the Heiltsuk Nation in British Columbia reinforce the legitimacy of the stories told there and in a way confirm knowledge obtained through Western ways of knowing.

We need to rethink what happened with the Age of Enlightenment as well as how rationalism and liberalism emerged from this movement. Cartesian dualism, with its opposition of subjective and objective, gave Westerners a new focus on the natural world in terms of looking at both the inside and the outside of an individual. This new ontology changed the perception of self, now based upon the differentiation of subject and object defining a separation of humans from all other elements of the world (Elsey 2013). It also brought a distinction between the mind and the body. Westerners compartmentalize experiences and claim that some have no relationship with others. As noted earlier, Indigenous Peoples take a very different position, a holistic ontology. Western ways of knowing have developed complex dualisms—nature versus culture, spirituality versus materiality—that create a new worldview (political, legal, and economic) based upon these ontological assumptions, different from Indigenous ways of knowing.

The different ontologies are best exemplified by how Westerners think about the land. They view its importance almost exclusively in economic terms even if some aesthetic aspects are considered. Even if we argue that the land is important from an aesthetic perspective, underlying this view is that it has exchange value. In fact, Westerners have taken this utilitarian idea even further by arguing that everything in nature can be given a monetary value. The forces of capital and economic gain or loss are primary components of the Western conception of life and specifically the land. To the contrary, Indigenous philosophies are based upon the belief that the land (Mother Earth) was created by a power external to human beings, and having been given the land to live on, individuals have a responsibility to act as stewards of it. Since humans had no hand in the creation of the Earth, they have no right to possess it or dispose of it—ownership of the land by individuals is unnatural and unjust. Moreover, Indigenous cultures have embedded these beliefs into their institutions—political, legal, social, and spiritual (Lewis and Sheppard 2013). Thus, when Indigenous Peoples say that the land is important to them, they are talking not about economic value but about emotional or spiritual attachment and their self-identification with the territory (place).

THE IMPORTANCE OF LAND AND SELF

Indigenous Peoples have a worldview beyond dualistic thinking. They view their environments as parts of their selves, "enfolded" into their bodies as their own experiences (Elsey 2013). Thus, in an Indigenous worldview, the idea of self is focused not on an individual self but on a collective self. This collective self then encompasses all of one's experiences within a given geographical location (place) (Borrows 2019). As the land becomes enfolded into people's experiences, it becomes connected to their self-identities. This worldview confirms that Indigenous identity is a spatial and territorial matter connected to experiences on the land, all within a cultural, linguistic, and geographic niche (Nnaemeka 2017). The identity is specific to a group living in a specific geographical locale rather than being applicable to all Indigenous groups in Canada (Elsey 2013; Lewis 2000). Indigenous Peoples have self-identified with the land for many generations and thus experience it as part of their own existence. As such, Indigenous Peoples live within a world that establishes and sustains spiritual and holistic connections between the people and the land (Borrows 2019). This view is in contrast to the Eurocentric, universal, economic, utilitarian model of the land that encourages private ownership of it.

Elsey (2013) goes on to claim that the linkage between the land and Indigenous Peoples is manifested in their artworks, songs, ceremonies, dances, and stories—all of which comprise their cultures and are expressed through their oral traditions. The many artistic representations of the presence of a self within a territory (space) represent the enfoldment of body and world in stories and ceremonies. It is important to remember that the holistic interactions include animate (humans and animals) and inanimate things (rocks and water). For example, Northwest Coast First Nations' groups exemplify this with the use of masks and totems in their ceremonies. A community's experience is passed from one generation to the next through oral traditions (songs, dances, rituals, speeches, family crests) and gives the community its collective identity.

In Western ways of knowing, the rational perspective excludes the spiritual, oral, and experiential since they are not considered important in terms of generating human knowledge. Nor are they considered significant in the understanding and evaluation of the natural world. For Indigenous Peoples, the criteria of Aboriginal Rights and Title required by Canadian courts during land claims cases do not reflect an authentic Indigenous way of life as it is experienced in Indigenous communities and Traditional Territories. Indigenous Peoples argue that the various stories and ceremonies recorded and passed along orally should be allowed as primary evidence in the resolution of all First Nations land claims (Dewsbury and Cloke 2009). Their argument is that these stories reflect the activities, feelings, and memories of the people within a given place and map out the boundaries of their territory. In summary, Indigenous Peoples find that the Western legal system narrowly defines the importance of land and lacks an understanding of the interrelations of elements of the world and how stewardship should be undertaken (Lewis and Sheppard 2013). Western law, from their perspective, is invasive, inappropriate, and unjust, and it does not deal with the underlying issues related to the land.

THE LAND QUESTION

For nearly two centuries, the federal government argued that the First Nations land question was settled when the Royal Proclamation of 1763 was issued or when the first comprehensive *Indian Act* was established in 1876 or when the treaties were signed. The position of the government has been that crown sovereignty was legislated to supersede Indigenous sovereignty during the period of colonial expansion. The legislation was justified, in part, by the perceived lack of civility among the land's Indigenous inhabitants. The *terra nullius* argument is a good example of the formal rationale used by explorers and settlers to take the land without adequate compensation or negotiation (Borrows 2019). Today part of this philosophy has been retained as a crown bias in the resolution of Indigenous land claims since Indigenous claimants are required to provide proof of having been an organized society within their territory at the time of contact. In short, the argument assumes that precontact Indigenous Peoples lacked social development and that their sovereignty was virtually impossible. The philosophy of the settlers and the colonial government depicted the lands of

Indigenous Peoples as an empty wilderness waiting to be turned into more productive pursuits by the presumably superior civilization of the new arrivals. And, once the land was taken, new laws were implemented to ensure that Indigenous Peoples could not reclaim it.

The conflict between them and the state is best understood when these conditions reflect different interests and aspirations involved in control and use of the land. Throughout the past two centuries, the crown extinguishment of land rights of Indigenous Peoples has occurred in different ways (e.g., scrip, unilateral legislation, creation of reserves). Other strategies—such as treaties, executive proclamations, orders-in-council, litigation, and land claims processes—have also been utilized to achieve the goal of removing Indigenous Peoples from their lands (Joseph 2018). These actions, reflecting similar objectives, have been carried out in different ways and at different times but always with the balance of power in favour of the crown.

As Elsey (2013) notes, the establishment of Canadian law favours a rationalist or atomistic paradigm that stresses exclusive ownership. However, in the Indigenous world, the methods of negotiating and agreeing on differing levels of terrestrial access and use between groups were informal, highly familial, reciprocal, and cyclical as opposed to static and formal. Such patterns are not reflected in the current legal system, which tends to perceive boundaries (for land) as fixed. Moreover, it does not recognize collective ownership unless it fits into the legal entities that Canadian Aboriginal law has created. Indigenous Peoples argue that this shows a denial of both the experiential and the affective affiliations with landscapes with which they are profoundly self-identified. They have cultural legacies based upon oral traditions embedded in traditional forms of knowledge. As a result, they have significant ancestral identities that link with spiritual and experiential meanings of land (Elsey 2013). At the same time, as the Eurocentric model has become more entrenched in Canadian institutions, it renders Indigenous cultures invisible to the Canadian public. For example, the use of settler geographical maps and the process of renaming various sites in English or French render Indigenous concepts of the land invisible and irrelevant.

Today's legal context provides that the rights of Indigenous Peoples must meet criteria established by settlers, the colonial government, and later the Canadian government without consideration of Indigenous law. The current legal system relies on evidence considered appropriate by the Canadian legal system. This means that written material is the core evidence for courts. Requiring written documentation from an oral society has placed Indigenous Peoples at a distinct disadvantage when trying to make their cases. Oral testimony in the courts (for most cases) is unacceptable even though the Supreme Court ruled in the *Delgamuukw* case (1997) that oral evidence is acceptable. Indigenous Peoples argue that the introduction of oral testimonies and stories from Elders could provide the courts with travels on and uses of the land by Indigenous groups. However, these testimonies and stories are generally not parts of court proceedings. Indigenous Peoples argue that these stories are living representations of what people did at specific places, and they speak directly to the question of "authentic dwelling" (Elsey 2013). But this is "anti-rational," according to the courts, and the utilitarian approach used in the justice system is dominant. Economic value and private ownership of the land are paramount and comprise the basis of courts' decisions. Under this conceptualization, forests are "timber stands" and rivers "power projects." None of these interpretations is of quintessential importance in the meaning of land within the Indigenous notion of selfhood.

Indigenous Peoples have a holistic view of self and world as interconnected, and they see the human body as an extended body, including all that it experiences. Thus, the senses are ways in which humans relate to and identify with their world. The boundaries of their experiences become the existence of their selves, the contours of the land, the flora and fauna. For Indigenous Peoples, the meaning of a Traditional Territory in utilitarian terms overlooks its "real" meaning to the particular people. In short, a utilitarian view is considered reductionist, and it removes the land from the people as though it were one of their limbs (Elsey 2013). As noted earlier, Indigenous ways of knowing are holistic and non-compartmentalized and thus speak to the transcendence of subject versus object and to the interrelatedness of human and non-human beings. This long-standing philosophical issue is concerned with the understanding of human experience and differs from the dualistic basis that the world consists of objects perceived or assumed to exist as entities by subjects (observers). But how do subjects relate to objects? As Elsey (2013) points out, enfoldment allows us to conceptualize the unbroken or holistic experience of being between Indigenous Peoples and their Traditional Territories. The holistic perspective can also be described as an "extended body experience" that incorporates the land and humans into one unbroken unity of meaning and being as if into one skin (Elsey 2013). As such, spirituality is shared with other non-human entities and geophysical bodies within a territory. The human experience is connected with features of the landscape such that people are spiritually inseparable from it. This personalization of non-human objects in the Indigenous territorial landscape can be seen, for example, in geological landmarks and stories. Through the stories told, the stones and geological structures are given human characteristics in the same way that certain animals are, and thus ascribed with personhood (Borrows 2019). The Interior Salish People perceive rocks as people who have been transformed into stone and thus give them names. Mountains for prairie people are given special animate properties, talked and prayed to, and addressed by name. For example, mountains are sometimes called "my grandparents." These attributions of personhood to non-human objects represent experiences of enfoldment or imbrication that Indigenous Peoples have with their Traditional Territories and their non-human agents. The sense of living within a shared space, the connectivity of touch, and the overlap of body and world impart spiritual unity between humans and non-humans, which results in the animation of the environment in a spiritual manner.

STORIES, THE LAND, AND COLLECTIVE IDENTITY

Stories establish a people's self-identification with a territory. There are two generic types of stories within Indigenous cultures. First, there are "personal stories" based upon individual observations, and they can evolve over time. Second, there are "creation or teaching stories." The latter type are spiritual and subject to public correction of errors of the storyteller. These spiritual stories are consistent over time. For example, the Cree origin story (*wisacejak*) and the Sky Woman (Haudenosaunee) story of creation have been remarkably resistant to change over the years. This type of story often refers to what was done within a geographical region, such as a watershed or river delta, and tells about the various places on the land that have been special sites of activity. This allows for a body-world overlap at a meaningful place (e.g., fishing, berry picking), and these geographical areas become social and human places described through stories (Redmond 1996). In turn, these sites become parts of a people's cultural memory. The stories of travels of prehuman ancestors and deities set out the significant subsistence grounds (e.g., fishing sites, hunting areas). They furnish the people with a cultural map that allows the enfoldment of body and world in a non-dualistic sense (Elsey 2013). In the stories, each sacred place or landmark is referred to with statements such as "it all happened right over there on that very place," then described according to its physical characteristics. Moreover, these stories connect past to present and thus allow a connection to ancestors. As a result, the land is mapped on either an epic or a folkloric scale, and it is a primary aspect of the collective selfhood and identity of the people (Borrows 2019). Through the oral tradition, the land and a people's actions on it are built into the cultural memory and identity of the region (Redmond 1996), then passed along through the ancestral stories commonly involving both human and non-human agents of a shared landscape.

The experience of being and doing speaks to a people's living on the land collectively and to its having a spiritual value as well as a community personality in both aesthetic and moral terms (Elsey 2013). For example, the story of a given event in a First Nations community allows people to link themselves with the land in a meaningful way. This provides an ancestral connection because it ties people together on the land as part of a collective system. For example, a story can express the collective enfoldment of people and land with the animals and inanimate objects as a totality. Thus, because the land is the repository of social and spiritual meanings, and records people's actual journeys and life experiences, it is reasonable to claim that the land is in the people as much as the people are on the land (Elsey 2013).

For Indigenous Peoples, the land is more than a geographical location, a spatial marker, or a piece of property. It is the source of knowledge, as evident in the visual representations of Inuit, Métis, and First Nations. So land and place comprise the foundation, expression, and context of Indigenous knowledge. It is embedded within the concept of the land and ecologies regarding it. It is through relationships with and experiences of both land and place that knowing and learning occur and in turn inform Indigenous identity (Hare 2018). Place is multidimensional and implies history, memory, and ceremony, and this connection is made through stories. Place is permeated with meaning and encompasses the spiritual and emotional sensibilities of Indigenous Peoples (Cajete 1994). Without this connection to the land, they are in a state of nihilism and lack identity.

Indigenous Peoples have created and maintained their worlds by passing along oral representations of ancestral travels dating back to early times and of living within a shared landscape. The stories shared speak to how Indigenous identity within a territory occurs. The stories, in turn, offer local orderings of the world as well as individuals' possibilities for the future. These stories are useful because they show how the territory of a people becomes personalized within narratives that depict their collective life story (Elsey 2013). A story establishes the regional context of a people's social and environmental interactions and provides the foundation for their territorial self-identification.

THE LAND AND THE FUTURE

Indigenous Peoples regard their Traditional Territories as sacred and integral to their cultures and identities. They want to continue to live on territories that have provided them with life-giving resources for hundreds of years. Yet, over time the crown (both federal and provincial) has claimed ownership and occupation of these territories through the establishment of treaties and other means. As Wilkes and Ibrahim (2013) note, each time the crown claims more land, it leads to potential conflict. Indigenous Peoples wish to remain one with their lands and resources in order to preserve their ancient relationships. Over the years, they have resisted, in many ways, the power of the crown to take away the lands that they once occupied and on which they acted as stewards (Wilkes 2004). Today Indigenous Peoples believe that their traditional occupation confirms their right to present occupation. They also argue that settlers and their colonial governments unjustly took over their Traditional Territories and that the Canadian legal system has sanctioned that activity. These actions have affected the identities of Indigenous people and diminished their respect for Canadian law. Borrows (2005) claims that the abuse of Canadian law, when applied to Indigenous Peoples, creates a desire for change and focuses their efforts on reoccupation of lands long taken away. They have attempted to use different strategies to help Canadians recognize and understand their continuing connection to lands and resources in Canada.

CONFLICT OVER THE LAND

One way in which Indigenous Peoples have tried to maintain their lands is through the continued occupation or reoccupation of significant sites, using occupations, blockades, and various forms of civil disobedience to prevent non-Indigenous people from occupying their lands. These actions have created heightened tensions and conflicts between the two sides. The activities have disrupted Canadians' access to government offices, roads, and in some cases homes. More radical forms of resistance involving violence by Indigenous Peoples generally occur only if other avenues of relief have been exhausted (e.g., Oka, Ipperwash, Caledonia). These conflicts continue to involve Indigenous and non-Indigenous people in attempts to settle ownership, occupancy, use, and stewardship of lands in Canada.

As noted by the Royal Commission on Aboriginal Peoples, they have lost much of their Traditional Territories in Canada, and this lack of a sustainable land base, linked with non-recognition by the government, is a major source of tension in relations between Indigenous and non-Indigenous people. Today the former have taken steps to resist further encroachments on their lands. Because of their close linkage with the land, they argue that certain amounts of land are needed for their cultures to survive. In short, Indigenous Peoples are fighting for a way of life that makes up their psyches. In addition, they are resisting further diminishment of their land base because of their intimate feelings for the land as well as how it has been lost. An example of the process is presented in Box 1.

BOX 1
CONFLICT OVER SACRED LAND

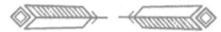

The Lil'wat Nation is located 160 kilometres north of Vancouver with over 2,000 community members living within its territory on ten reserves (2,930 hectares) near Pemberton. British Columbia claims that it owns the land in the Pemberton Valley, even though it is the Traditional Territory of the Lil'wat Nation. The Lil'wat have lived on this land for thousands of years, and back in 1911 the Lillooet (St'at'imc) community claimed that they were the rightful owners of this territory.

According to the Lil'wat Nation, when settlers came to Canada, they used and occupied Lil'wat lands and resources without their consent. There were no treaties or agreements that gave others rights to the territory. Nevertheless, gold seekers flooded the area in the late 1850s, and those who stayed engaged in farming, logging, and commerce.

Over the past 150 years, roads and railways have penetrated the Lil'wat Traditional Territory. In 1947, a provincial highway was built in the area, with a portion running through what is now the Mount Currie Indian Reserve. The province claims that it holds title to all of the land in the region, whereas the Mount Currie Band claims that much of the land is part of the reserve. The conflict focuses on non-Indigenous people's lack of recognition of Lil'wat land use, occupation, and title, leading to non-Indigenous people's occupation of the land and displacement of Lil'wat in their own territory.

After years of trying to settle the claim, the Lil'wat set up a roadblock in 1990 to protest clear-cut logging and other activities that they said were destroying the land. The province obtained an injunction against the roadblock, and sixty-three Lil'wat people were charged and imprisoned for refusing to recognize or obey the injunction. Most of the protesters refused to recognize the jurisdiction of the court; nevertheless, it rejected their arguments. In

February 1991, the Lil'wat blocked another road to prevent logging. The protesters stated that the location of the roadblock was an ancient burial site. Each conflict resulted in a provincial government decision to allow further resource development on lands that the Lil'wat Nation viewed as its own. The Lil'wat were not successful in stopping development, and resource extraction continued unabated within their territory. The legal system used by the province and resource developers was successful in dealing with the conflicts only by issuing injunctions and arresting protesters. Although some semblance of peace was restored by the legal system, Canadian law did not successfully resolve the dispute.

In 2008, after many years of more protest and legal wrangling, British Columbia and the Lil'wat Nation signed a land-use agreement that encompasses about 800,000 hectares. In the agreement, the province and the Lil'wat agreed to create six new conservancies, double the size of a provincial park, and establish over 200,000 hectares of wildlife zones and nearly 50,000 hectares of cultural management areas. They also created new environmentally sensitive areas and old-growth management areas that addressed the concerns of the Lil'wat Nation about logging in old growth, rare ecosystems, and ecosystems that support traditional and cultural uses by the Lil'wat. The agreement will also protect sixty "spirited ground areas" that encompass villages, archaeological sites, spiritual places, and other traditional-use areas. In the end, as the Lil'wat Nation gains more control of its lands and resources, greater economic opportunities are emerging, such as an independent power plant and a forestry partnership, that respect the values of the Lil'wat people and fit with the Lil'wat Nation's vision. Today the Lil'wat Nation continues to move toward the goal of self-determination, creating economic and educational opportunities for the community.

As Borrows (2002) points out, conflict over land occurs for at least two reasons. First, it emerges because of historical and contemporary political actions taken by the government that relate to the loss of Indigenous Lands. Second, conflict emerges because of the feelings of

Indigenous Peoples regarding the underlying circumstances of their loss of land and culture. Unfortunately, the resolution of disputes over land by governments and courts has focused on only one of the elements of Euro-Canadian law ("written facts") and has not been attentive to the spiritual and psychological connections of Indigenous Peoples with the land.

CONCLUSION

Today Indigenous Peoples want Canadians to acknowledge and affirm their stewardship of the land. They want people to recognize that they have regard for more than the physical landscape and to understand how they interact holistically with the Earth. At the same time, they want Canadians to appreciate Indigenous values, norms, customs, and laws operative in their communities that govern land and resource use. These aspects have taught Indigenous Peoples how to take from the land while respecting interaction and interdependence with other humans as well as the non-human world. There have been few safeguards throughout Canadian history to protect the rights and freedoms of Indigenous Peoples. Their collective and individual lives have been susceptible to government interference (e.g., suppression of Indigenous institutions, denial of land, forced taking of children, negation of rights of religious freedom, association, due process, and equality). In short, Indigenous Peoples want Canadians to value their ecological understanding of the environment and its organisms and their relationships. Indigenous Peoples argue that their lands have been reduced to such an extent that their maintenance of these relationships is threatened. This situation has led them to try forcefully to take back lands that they regard as being rightfully theirs (Borrows 2005).

These concerns have been raised over the past century as Indigenous Peoples have identified unjust and inequitable allocations of land. The Royal Commission on Aboriginal Peoples (1996a, 4) argued that this loss of land is not simply a historical event and demonstrated that the reserve or community land base of First Nations has shrunk by almost two-thirds since Confederation. Moreover, any reserve resources that existed at the time of their creation have now largely vanished. As

Stevenson (2013) argues, the legal system promotes a sense of non-urgency in maintaining a land base for First Nations while it presents a sense of urgency for non-Indigenous people. For example, when extended land negotiations take place between First Nations and the government, the latter might establish new third-party interests in the land being negotiated. It might lease the land, provide timber licences for it, or allow oil and gas development on it while negotiations are ongoing. This is problematic because, when the negotiations are finally settled, these interim agreements take precedence over the rights included in the final agreement.

Although the oral tradition is considered inappropriate by Euro-Canadian law for expressing jurisprudence, from an Indigenous perspective it is the way to teach law to family and community. Indigenous Peoples believe that they have a duty to protect, look after, and keep their lands. They have a sacred duty to look after the Creator's gift of the land. Their cultures express the responsibility inherent in the communal connection to the land as well as their duty to maintain that connection. Use of and connection with the Traditional Territory is crucial to the people despite their seemingly sedentary lifestyle in small communities. In summary, the exclusion of Indigenous Peoples from Canadian democracy has been partially a result of law that has ignored and purposely undermined their institutions and ideas.

CHAPTER 4

TREATIES *in* CANADA
First Nations Treaties, Métis Scrip, and the *Manitoba Act*

Beginning with the myth of *terra nullius*, I focus in this chapter on how treaties were part of the subordination of Indigenous Peoples used by settlers, the colonial government, and later the federal crown. I review the historical contexts in which treaties were created, discuss the contents of the Peace and Friendship as well as the Numbered Treaties, and show how they extinguished Aboriginal Rights, relegated Indigenous Peoples to peripheral participants in building Canadian society, and cleared the land for settlement. Overall, as Jai (2017) points out, there were three periods in which treaties were established. Each period reflects what she calls the "bargaining power dynamics" in relations between First Nations and the crown. In the first period (from contact to the late 1700s), the number of Indigenous people and settlers was equal, and thus had relatively equal bargaining power. However, the second period (from the late 1700s to 1950) saw a dramatic decrease in the Indigenous population with a commensurate decrease in bargaining power. The third period (from 1950 to today) reveals an increase in Indigenous population and a commensurate increase in bargaining power. The relative changes in bargaining power, Jai argues, allowed for more favourable terms for Indigenous Peoples in the early Peace and Friendship Treaties and the current comprehensive claims agreements. I also discuss how the treaties disenfranchised Indigenous Peoples through their illegal enforcement and then the subsequent refusal to meet the conditions outlined in the treaties. As Moore (2010) points out, the Numbered Treaties do not reflect a sense of fairness or a just basis for intercommunal relations, and the courts have recognized that the crown has not honoured them.

I then analyze the treatment of Métis and how they were systematically removed from their land base, and not for another 100 years would the Supreme Court look at how the crown acted in concert with land barons to remove Métis in order to promote settler development. I also discuss the courts' assessment of the *Manitoba Act* and how it is now viewed as a treaty requiring the crown to fulfill its obligations to Indigenous Peoples. Finally, I analyze the modern-day treaties (comprehensive claims), their distinguishing features, and the extent to which they have evolved since the early 1970s.

DISCOVERING CANADA

When explorers and settlers first came to Canada, they found Indigenous Peoples living on the land yet defined it as *terra nullius*, allowing them to declare their sovereignty over it and impose French and English jurisprudence. Many people would argue that this was not the basis of establishing sovereignty, yet they provide no plausible alternative explanation of how Indigenous Peoples were disenfranchised. Claiming the land by "right of discovery" drew from international law developed by and for the benefit of European colonial powers (Borrows 2019; Ray 2016). For example, as the newcomers attempted to engage with the Indigenous Peoples, general rules were established to facilitate it. Starting in 1701 in what would eventually become Canada, the British crown established Peace and Friendship Treaties to encourage peaceful relations between First Nations and fur traders as well as immigrant settlers. Over time, the type of treaty between First Nations and the British crown (and later Canada) varied. The original Peace and

Friendship Treaties were signed to ensure that each party could engage in its own way of life without worrying that one group would interfere with the other. Under these treaties, First Nations could keep their hunting, trapping, and fishing rights, and settlers would not disrupt their way of life. In return, settlers would engage in various economic pursuits (e.g., logging, mining, and agriculture) that did not impinge on the lives of Indigenous Peoples. For example, the Treaty of 1752 between the Mi'kmaq and the British, still considered to be valid and operating, worked initially because there was an abundance of land and few people competing for it and its resources.

Later, as European settlements grew, increasing conflicts between the British and French emerged and took precedence over the concerns of First Nations. With the defeat of the French in 1763, the British had to deal with the First Nations that had participated on one side or the other in the various conflicts over the years. The British drafted the Royal Proclamation of 1763, which stated that First Nations held the rights to the land (a large area with vague boundaries) and that there had to be negotiations with the crown if Traditional Territory was to be used or purchased by the crown. However, it was clear that the land could only be sold (surrendered) to the crown, and the proclamation said nothing about compensation or benefits for First Nations. A year later the Niagara Treaty (a Peace and Friendship Treaty) established the principles of how the British and First Nations would relate to each other (Ariss and Cutfeet 2012).

Later, when William Robinson was sent to deal with First Nations' complaints about intrusions of settlers looking for minerals on their lands, a new era in relations between Indigenous and non-Indigenous people emerged. The copper discoveries in the Great Lakes area in the 1840s and the government's desire to exploit these resources led to the appointment of Robinson to deal with First Nations. He met with the Anishinaabe leaders, and the first treaties were established in Ontario (the Robinson-Superior and Robinson-Huron Treaties of 1850). These treaties offered annuities (annual payments) to First Nations for their surrendered lands. In addition, there were a few provisions for the establishment of reserves; explicit rights to hunt, fish, and trap; and lump sum payments with nominal yearly rents for the lands. These early treaties were concluded in trust, and the government assumed responsibility for disposing of the First Nations lands surrendered. Robinson also agreed to discuss land issues with the Métis, but he did not have a mandate from the colonial government to do so. Instead, he assured the Métis that he would bring their concerns to the government. Although Robinson did present a report on Métis land concerns, the government ignored it. Nevertheless, in 1875 a "half-breed adhesion" was signed between the government and the Anishinaabe First Nation, the only such adhesion to any treaty (Treaty Three) in Canada.

These early treaties provided the government with a template that would be used by Robinson's successors when imposing the Numbered Treaties on First Nations, and they would forever change the social and legal landscapes of Canada. In 1870, Canada claimed sovereignty over Rupert's Land but with an agreement that it would protect the interests of the First Nations there. Later treaties were intended to recognize First Nations' interests in the land, to provide compensation to them, and to establish an orderly transition of land ownership from one group to another. The treaties also established the rules of the relationship between First Nations and the government once lands were transferred (Daniel 1981). The Numbered Treaties reflected the government's desire for brief, simple, and uniform content for all lands surrendered. Regarding any change to a treaty requested by a First Nation, the commissioners responded by claiming that the "Great Mother" (the queen) had not given them permission to change it. Moreover, the treaties avoided discussing the nature or extent of Aboriginal Rights regarding land since the government took the position that First Nations had no such rights. Finally, no treaty was ever brought to Parliament for ratification; rather, each one was approved by an order-in-council (a notice of an administrative decision issued by the governor general of Canada). Orders-in-council originate with the cabinet and are approved by the governor general. The responsible minister of the crown then makes a recommendation, and the minister reads out "batches" of orders-in-council drafted by the government in front of the governor general, who then approves them. They then become law. As a result of the treaties, the government of Canada received millions of acres of land "surrendered" by First Nations; in return, only 0.32 percent of Canada's landmass was set aside for reserves.

None of the Numbered Treaties was substantially revised (to include oral promises made by government officials) after negotiations with First Nations leaders. Moreover, none of the treaties was ever translated into a First Nations language so that the people could more fully understand the documents that their leaders had signed. As such, all of the Numbered Treaties reflect a high degree of similarity, though some differences are noticeable (e.g., Treaty Six included a "medicine chest"). In other cases, early treaties provided for 160 acres of land per family (later increased to 640 acres in some treaties) and annuities and gratuities of three dollars per person. Annuities for ceded land rights first appeared in a treaty in 1818 and thereafter became routine. There was also an agreement to place a school on reserve land. Finally, in negotiating the treaties, many agreements were oral (since Indigenous people could not read English or French). Although some oral agreements were given formal recognition by an order-in-council as part of the formal written treaty, overall they were not recognized by the government when the treaties were signed.

WHAT IS A TREATY?

Over the years, treaties have been interpreted in several ways. Some people view them as agreements between two or more sovereign nations. Most First Nations accept this interpretation when they refer to the various treaties with the federal government. Ariss and Cutfeet (2012) claim that, when the treaties were signed, First Nations were understood by the crown as peoples with the rights of sovereignty. Henderson (1997) argues that treaties between First Nations and the crown are basic constitutional documents even though they have been ignored throughout most of Canada's history. Nevertheless, the use of treaties by First Nations reflected their understanding of their general meaning. Henderson argues that treaties from the perspective of First Nations are grants of certain rights to settlers.

As Teillet (2013) argues, over the next two centuries treaties were signed to define and limit the rights of First Nations and to ensure settlers' rights to use and enjoy lands that First Nations had traditionally occupied and controlled. The British crown used this process with many different First Nations across the country. Teillet goes on to argue that there can be no doubt that a treaty was an international agreement between the British crown and the several distinct and independent First Nations across Canada.

The Canadian government, however, has not interpreted the treaties in the same way. Many lawyers and politicians argue that each historical treaty between the crown and First Nations contained provisions considered binding at the time. However, they go on to argue that the force of these agreements no longer holds given that the legal, social, political, and economic issues of the day have changed.

Treaties have also been interpreted as contracts between two parties. There is some legal support for this interpretation, though the courts have not been asked to rule on this question. Finally, treaties can be viewed as pieces of legislation. This is certainly how the Supreme Court of Canada has interpreted the *Manitoba Act*—as a legal means to establish an orderly relationship between First Nations and settlers and thus equivalent to a treaty (Henderson 2009). In other cases, for example the Mi'kmaq Treaty of 1752, the County Court judged it to be nothing more than an "agreement" between the Mi'kmaq and the British governor since the court determined that neither party had the right to sign a treaty (*R v Syliboy* 1928). In 1985, the Supreme Court overturned the *Syliboy* decision and vindicated the rights of Syliboy.

Supreme Court decisions since 1982 have confirmed the basic understanding that the treaties were nation-to-nation agreements signed with the consent of First Nations. However, the treaties were focused on land and as such did not deal with many other aspects of the relationship between the crown and First Nations. Regardless of the interpretation, the courts have viewed treaties as enforceable obligations, requiring the federal government in large part to live up to those obligations; indeed, both section 25 of the *Charter of Rights and Freedoms* and section 35 in Part 2 of the *Constitution Act* (1982) enshrine "existing" Treaty Rights. The inclusion of Treaty Rights in section 35 of the Constitution confirms the original constitutional status of the treaties (Borrows 2010a).

Thus, in a more general sense, treaties are legal arrangements between First Nations and the government of Canada. Moreover, they confer benefits on successors even though at times it is difficult to identify those successors. In attempting to build a cohesive set of laws, the Supreme Court identified several issues that must be settled to claim that a document is a treaty. The following elements characterize a treaty as defined by the court:

1. The content must reveal the continuous exercise of a right in the past and at present.
2. The content must provide the reasons that the crown made a commitment.
3. The content must explain the prevailing situation at the time the document was signed.
4. The content must provide evidence of relations of mutual respect between the negotiators.
5. The content must determine the subsequent conduct of the parties.

The Supreme Court ruled that, if ambiguity remains after reviewing the above criteria, one could look at extrinsic evidence such as information on what went on when the document was signed, the historical context, and the subsequent conduct of the parties that signed the document. As noted earlier, the Supreme Court initially interpreted treaties in favour of, and for the benefit of, Indigenous Peoples as part of the "honour of the crown" as well as fiduciary duty (see the *Van der Peet* decision of 1996). Moreover, the court's reasoning extends to the Peace and Friendship Treaties of the eighteenth century, as shown by the *Marshall* decision in 1999.

Yet many Canadians believe that treaties between First Nations and the crown are no more than outdated agreements (contracts). They argue that treaties are not relevant in today's world, nor are they enforceable. However, in several Supreme Court decisions concerning treaties and Treaty Rights, the court regards them as agreements *sui generis* (unique) and still binding on both parties. In 1998, the federal government announced a new program through its policy *Gathering*

Strength—Canada's Aboriginal Action Plan to deal with the issue of treaties. This was an attempt to resolve many outstanding claims (including treaty claims), increase the efficiency of the process, and create more certainty in land ownership. However, more than two decades later, the policy has done little to achieve these aims, and a large backlog of treaty claims remains unresolved.

THE HISTORICAL CONTEXTS OF THE TREATIES

The earliest agreements between First Nations and the government, called Peace and Friendship Treaties, were reached primarily in the Maritimes. They did not involve specific land transfers or surrenders, annuities, trading rights, or the establishment of reserves, and they did not talk about hunting and fishing rights or compensation for rights limited or taken away. Rather, they dealt with military and political relations. A good example of a Peace and Friendship Treaty is the one signed between the Mi'kmaq and the governor of Nova Scotia in 1760–61. After the Peace and Friendship Treaties were signed, the colonial government and then the Canadian government moved to more formal treaties, and thus the Numbered Treaties were signed well into the twentieth century.

However, when the crown negotiated the Numbered Treaties, it primarily saw them as territorial cessions. First Nations involved in signing the Numbered Treaties, conversely, thought that they were sharing the land, not surrendering it, and that the government was assuming broader trusteeship as part of the treaty process. Even though the two parties signed the treaties, it is clear that they had different conceptions of what they were signing (see Box 2).

BOX 2

TWO VIEWS OF TREATIES

Even though the two parties attended the same meetings, listened to the same speeches, and signed the same piece of paper, it is clear that they had different conceptions of what they were agreeing to. This difference was reflected in the ontological bases of the two parties as well as in their understandings of the language used in the treaties. Today the parties agree that First Nations exchanged some of their interests in land for some payments and promises made by the crown. However, the specifics of this exchange remain unclear.

THE GOVERNMENT VIEW

The government needed to clear the land of First Nations so that settlement, agricultural and resource development, and a national railway could be achieved. From this perspective, the government viewed the treaties as surrenders of all lands that were final and without exception. Since it was believed at the time that Indigenous Peoples had no rights, from the perspective of the government the treaties were full surrenders of Aboriginal Rights and Titles regarding land. Nevertheless, the Numbered Treaties had provisions for the care of First Nations in time of need, the allocation of lands for reserves, and the continuance of traditional subsistence activities. However, from the perspective of the government, treaties were the essential first step in doing away with "Indianness" and assimilating "Indians" into the fold of mainstream Canadian society.

THE INDIGENOUS VIEW

The ontological view of Indigenous Peoples is that the land is sacred, given to them by the Creator as a gift. They are therefore the stewards of the land and its resources and must ensure the care of all things animate and inanimate on the land. The land is not to be privately held or used to exploit its resources to bring benefit to an individual. Indigenous Peoples also regard the land and the plants and animals on it as a sacred trust to protect for future (seven) generations. Indigenous Peoples strongly deny that the treaties obligate the government to fulfill only the terms that appear in the written documents. They uniformly insist that the written versions must be taken together with the words (oral commitments) spoken by the government's agents during the negotiations. In addition, their view of the treaties is that they established a special relationship with the crown, which would ensure that their ways of life would continue in the future. The treaties allowed settlers to use the land for agriculture for subsistence, but First Nations did not see the treaties as transferring "title" to land to individuals. They did not see the treaties as relinquishing their sovereignty or agreeing to assimilate into mainstream society. Moreover, Indigenous Peoples see the treaties as negotiated agreements that built specific and reliable relationships (Coyle 2017).

The federal government decided to negotiate treaties with First Nations largely because its agents foresaw violence against European settlers if treaties were not established. However, this perception was not based upon specific threats by First Nations, which simply wanted to carry out direct negotiations with the government to establish their rights and possible compensation for the lands that they occupied prior to European settlement. The commissioners, appointed by the government to negotiate treaties with the First Nations, were inexperienced and unfamiliar with First Nations customs. Hence, most drew on the experiences of Hudson's Bay Company employees in their dealings with Indigenous people (an exploitive and coercive relationship) as the starting point of a negotiation.

After the first treaty was signed, neither the government nor First Nations attempted to find alternative means to deal with "Indian claims." Government officials based future treaties upon prior ones, and First Nations insisted on terms received by those who had signed earlier treaties. However, as Daschuk (2013) points out, because of extreme hardship (famine and disease) in many First Nations at the time of early treaty negotiations, government officials found that First Nations were in weak positions to negotiate the terms of treaties. Crown representatives thus exploited this condition to force them to "take treaty" by promising that in times of famine and epidemic the government would take care of them (McCallum 2017). The signing of Treaty Four is a good example of how famine played an important part in the First Nations' signing of this document. Daschuk (2013) claims that, when Treaty Four was negotiated, it was during a time of famine for First Nations. Instead of supplying rations to starving people, the

TREATIES IN CANADA · 125

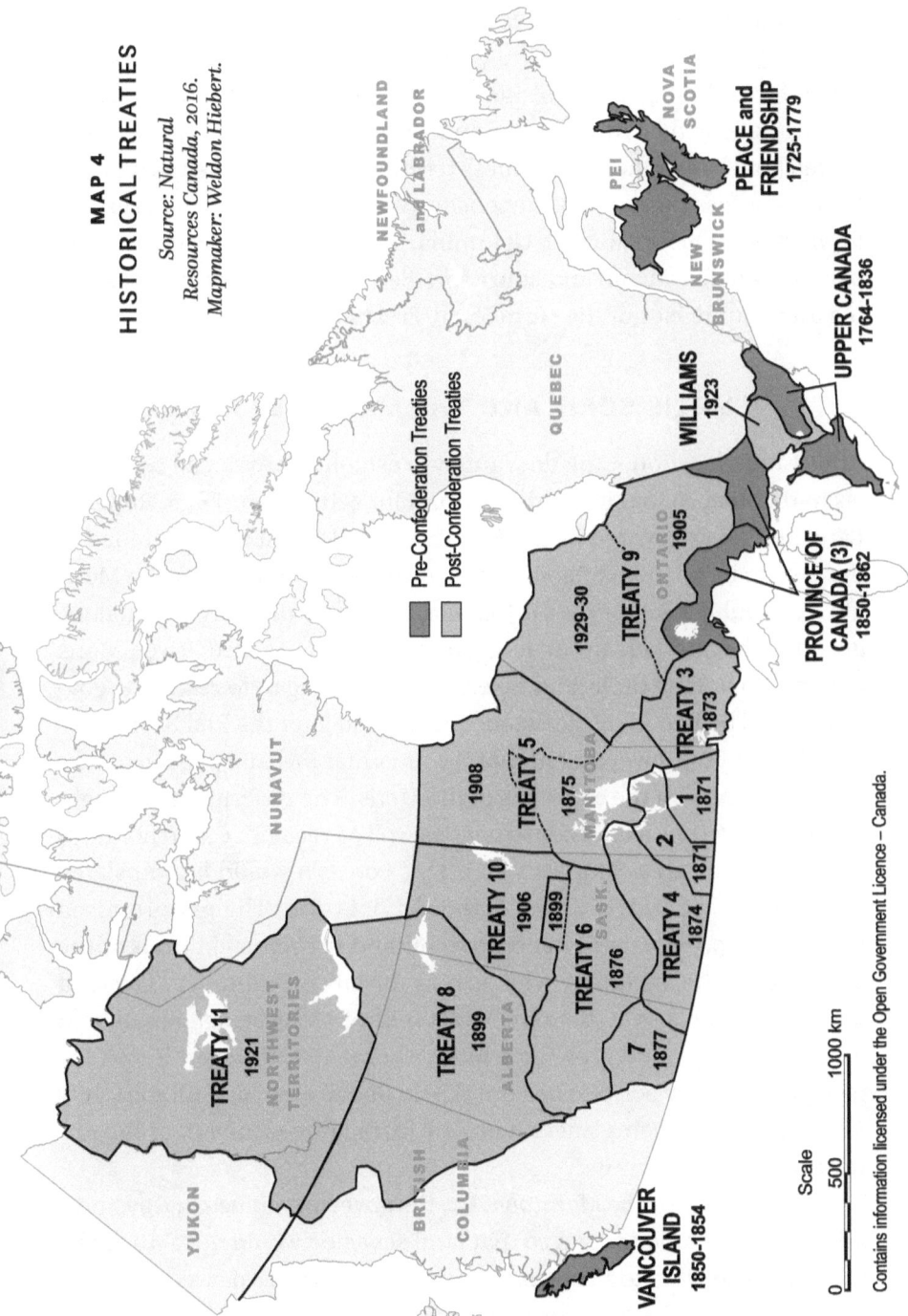

MAP 4
HISTORICAL TREATIES
Source: Natural Resources Canada, 2016.
Mapmaker: Weldon Hiebert.

government used the hunger as a means of coercing them into signing the treaty. Moreover, the crown was unapologetic for using this strategy to force First Nations to sign treaties and accept reserves deemed appropriate by the crown. In the end, eleven Numbered Treaties were signed (and later adhesions to these treaties would be signed) with First Nations across the country that encompass nearly all of Canada except for northern Quebec, British Columbia, the Northwest Territories, and parts of Newfoundland and Labrador. (See Map 4 for the times of signing and boundaries of the Numbered Treaties.)

MÉTIS SCRIP AND THE *MANITOBA ACT*

After Confederation, Canada wanted to establish provincial boundaries in the west so that it could open land for settlement. Thus, Rupert's Land and areas covered by the Red River Settlement were included in the area to be opened for settlement. As noted by Ray (2016), the Métis have a troubled history with Canada. They are the only Indigenous group to have taken up arms against Canada. As Red River Métis objected to having their land taken away, they began to resist the government. The Red River Resistance (1869) and later the Riel Resistance (1885) taught the government that it was vulnerable and needed to take action to deal with the concerns of the Métis. The government thought it best to negotiate a land settlement as well as recognize land holdings of Métis in the area (Moffett 1982). This concern would be translated into sections 31 and 32 of the *Manitoba Act, 1870*. The Act promised to set aside 5,565 square kilometres of land for 7,000 children of the Red River Métis, including what is now the city of Winnipeg. The land deal was made to overcome the resistance of Métis struggling to hold on to their land amid growing white settlements. However, it took fifteen years for the scrip to be completely distributed, and all the while Métis faced increasing encroachment from large numbers of incoming settlers.

After passage of the *Manitoba Act*, the government began a systematic process of amending it so that land set aside would not actually be allotted. From 1873 to 1884, eleven amendments were passed, referred to as the Manitoba Supplementary Provisions. Nearly half of these amendments altered substantive portions of the original Act. The effect of these amendments was the dispersal of the original Métis in Manitoba. Only about 20 percent of the claimants received and made use of their land allotments. A similar percentage of riverlot occupants obtained patents and remained on the lands that they occupied in 1870. Over half of the potential recipients were denied their lands through several political and legal manoeuvres by the government (Sawchuk, Sawchuk, and Ferguson 1981).

The allocation of land (or money) to Métis was through the process of scrip. Scrip is a certificate giving the holder the right to receive payment later in the form of cash, goods, or land (Milne 1995). This process differed from the treaties with First Nations in that it involved grants to *individuals*. For almost forty years (1885–1923), there was a series of scrip allotments to individual Métis. Each time a new part of the prairie provinces or the Mackenzie Valley was ceded by First Nations, persons of mixed blood who did not participate were allocated scrip redeemable in land or money (Flanagan 1991).

Initially, land was set aside for the Red River Métis, but administrative mismanagement resulted in much of it never being distributed. Two successive allotments were never made, and the third and fourth allotments were not completed until 1880. The lands provided were divided randomly among eligible Métis children living in the area. At the same time, the government of Manitoba was working with speculators who acquired the Métis children's land after enactment of the *Manitoba Act*. In addition to the administrative bungling, the government of Canada underestimated the number of Métis children eligible for land allocations. The "allotment" provided for Métis children by 1885 (fifteen years after the *Manitoba Act*) was in the form of cash scrip since most of the land was no longer available. The value of the scrip was based upon 1870 prices, but the value of the land had increased substantially between 1870 and 1885, so the Métis children who received this cash scrip were not able to purchase the same amount of land (240 acres) as the Métis children who had received their scrip earlier.

The Manitoba Métis Federation (now called the Manitoba Métis) launched a suit against the government nearly forty years ago. It argued that implementation of the *Manitoba Act* represented a breach of the crown's fiduciary obligations to the Métis. It claimed that the crown had failed to implement the Act in a manner consistent with its honour and that other legislation passed by the Manitoba government was *ultra vires*—outside its mandate—and negatively affected Métis Rights. During this period of litigation, several scholars and consultants were hired to act as historical experts for the federal Department of Justice. After reviewing the historical materials, they argued that the federal government had fulfilled the land provisions of the *Manitoba Act*. These were important contributions to the earlier case that the Manitoba Métis Federation brought to the Manitoba Court. The consultants served as witnesses for Alberta, Manitoba, and Canada in litigation involving Aboriginal Rights and land claims, providing testimony on the Numbered Treaties and the administration of federal programs for Métis and First Nations in western Canada, and concluded that the crown had legally carried out its duties according to the *Manitoba Act*.

The Métis concerns would be indirectly addressed in the decision in *Blais* in 2003 (focused on whether a Métis was an "Indian" under the *Natural Resources Transfer Act*—the answer was no). The *Manitoba Métis Federation* case (2013) upheld the action by the government in the nineteenth-century distribution of land and scrip in extinguishing Métis land rights in Manitoba. In 2010, the Manitoba Court of Appeal upheld the lower court ruling that the government had not violated its duty to Red River Métis. In this decision, the judge dismissed the Métis claim, arguing that by passage of the *Manitoba Act* the government had no requirement to uphold the honour of the crown, nor did it have any fiduciary duty to the Métis. Government lawyers also countered that the Métis lawsuit had been filed far too long after the land deal, so the doctrine of laches (see below) had been violated, and that Ottawa had not actually violated its side of the agreement.

The trial judge agreed and found that, since the Manitoba legislation passed regarding scrip was constitutional, the claim was barred by the doctrine of laches. Laches is based upon the legal notion that "equity aids the vigilant, not those who slumber on their rights" (MacNeil 2018). In short, if one does not pursue a case within a reasonable time, then the defendant can argue that too much time has passed and that he or she will be in a disadvantaged position. Thus, the case was dismissed.

Finally, the judge found that the Manitoba Métis Federation could not bring a claim against the government since that had to be undertaken by individual plaintiffs. This ruling was appealed to the five-member Manitoba Court of Appeal, which upheld the trial court decision and dismissed the appeal.

The Manitoba Métis Federation then appealed to the Supreme Court of Canada, and the appeal was accepted in 2011. This appeal was based upon the issue of Indigenous law, fiduciary duty, crown law, and the honour of the crown. Issues of civil procedure (e.g., parties, standing, public interest standing) were also involved in the court case. However, the Métis did not seek damages but simply asked the Supreme Court to declare that Canada had failed to fulfill its constitutional obligation to the Métis and their children. The claim was for declaratory relief as opposed to damages. It was based upon the Canadian government's agreeing in 1870 to provide Métis children with 1.4 million acres of land and to recognize existing Métis landholdings.

Until the *Powley* decision in 2003, the Canadian government had never established a process by which Métis claims could be adjudicated. Métis must still resort to the courts to clarify issues of rights. The Supreme Court ruled that the federation should be granted standing since it was representing the collective Métis interest in coming before the court. The Supreme Court also found that, though there was no fiduciary duty of the government, the Métis were entitled to argue that the federal crown had failed to act with diligence in implementing the land grant provision set out in section 31 of the *Manitoba Act*—hence there had been a breach of the honour of the crown flowing from section 31 of the *Constitution Act*. In reviewing the appeal, the court also found that the purpose of the *Manitoba Act* was to provide Métis children with a "headstart" in dealing with white settlers about to enter the area. The court noted that the crown did not just engage in "occasional" negligence but also made consistent mistakes and succumbed to inaction for a decade and thus made section 31 of the *Manitoba Act* ineffective and irrelevant. And, because of the increase in the value of land from 1870 to 1885, the court found that the scrip received by Métis children in 1885 represented a value much less than 240 acres of land. Finally, the court said that the honour of the crown is not bound by the law of limitations, and thus the case could move forward. Because Canada continued to claim that there was nothing wrong with how it had enacted the *Manitoba Act*, and given that the Métis were in a distinct subordinate position in terms of power, the case would be considered.

In the end, the Supreme Court found that the *Manitoba Act* established a constitutional obligation to the Métis of Manitoba and provided Métis children with land. The justices went on to say that the provincial government had acted with persistent inattention and failed to act diligently, adding that it could and should have done better. Finally, the court noted that, as long as the issue remains unresolved, the goal of reconciliation and constitutional harmony, recognized in section 35 of the *Charter of Rights and Freedoms* and underlying section 31 of the *Manitoba Act*, remains unachieved. The court found that the *Manitoba Act*, in principle, was just another treaty. In its ruling, it did not order any specific action that the government had to take to remedy the situation. However, it did suggest that land claim negotiations and other forms of compensation will now have to proceed. The decision could allow the Métis to negotiate a claim to vast tracts of land in Manitoba, including present-day Winnipeg, though some representatives of the Manitoba Métis Federation noted that land was not the main issue in this case and that practical considerations would not allow this to happen.

Now that the Supreme Court has ruled, the ramifications of its decision will be felt by Canadians across the country. The Métis of Canada now want to achieve reconciliation with the crown, which has already occurred with other Indigenous Peoples in Canada. After the ruling, the federal Liberal government issued a statement saying that it was reviewing the decision. However, the Conservative government of Stephen Harper (2006–15) subsequently argued that the decision simply meant that the government needed to continue working to improve the lives of Métis across Canada.

THE MÉTIS IN CANADA

Over time, distinct Métis communities were established along the fur trade routes and include the three prairie provinces as well as parts of British Columbia, Ontario, and the Northwest Territories. These communities are referred to as Métis Nation Homeland, and the Métis in them have pursued strategies to maintain a distinct culture, tradition, and language. In many areas across Canada, the Métis existed in positions of political and economic power during the colonial and early provincial governments. In addition, some Métis (e.g., the Red River settlement in Manitoba and the Fort St. John area in British Columbia) were recognized by the federal government as having Métis Rights (1858). However, after 1884, federal troops in the Red River area engaged in a "reign of terror" that led to an exodus of Métis to Saskatchewan, northern Alberta, and British Columbia. In other places, discrimination against the Métis forced them to go underground with their identity. With the decline of the fur trade, the end of the bison hunt, and the insistence by the government that Métis was not a legitimate ethnic identification and had no rights, the label was soon regarded as illegitimate and phased out of government terminology and legal recognition. The Métis were not viewed as a distinct group and thus were not identified as having any special rights. They were considered a subjective social category that people used to identify themselves.

Nevertheless, over the years, the resilience of the Métis has resulted in the emergence of both provincial organizations (e.g., Métis Nation of British Columbia, Métis Nation-Saskatchewan, Métis Nation of Ontario) and federal organizations (e.g., the Métis National Council representing Métis of northwest Canada, the Métis Nation of Canada representing Indigenous people not recognized by the Métis National Council). In addition, the *Powley* (2003) and *Daniels* (2016) court decisions added to the legitimacy of Métis Rights and identity. Alberta chose to treat the Métis as a distinct social entity and thus established legislation to deal with them.

THE MÉTIS IN ALBERTA

With the passage of the *Natural Resources Transfer Act* (1930), the Alberta government thought that it had to deal with the Métis. Moreover, the politicians of the day claimed that the Métis had high rates of respiratory and venereal diseases that threatened the non-Indigenous population and that some action had to be taken to deal with the threat. In short, they pathologized the Métis as a people who needed help (Moffett 1982). The issue of Métis Rights regarding land was dealt with through the recommendations of the Ewing Commission that resulted in the *Métis Population Betterment Act* (1938). In addressing these concerns, the Ewing Commission was influenced by four assumptions that led to a focus on perceived social needs rather than legal rights: (1) Métis claims to Aboriginal Title had been dealt with through the allocation of scrip; (2) the Métis and Non-Status Indians were the responsibility of the province; (3) the Métis in Alberta were asserting needs, not rights; and (4) the response by the province needed to involve land allocation (Healey 2013).

Under the *Métis Population Betterment Act*, the lands allocated to the Métis could not be alienated without the consent of the settlement councils, requiring a majority of settlement members and the crown. In this Act, the settlement lands were granted, through letters patent, to the Métis General Council in fee simple title with all of the ownership rights and obligations associated with fee simple title. Under the legislation, the provincial crown also reserved specific user rights such as the diversion of water, access to crown infrastructure, and the right to manage highways (Healey 2013). An important protection for the settlements exists under the Act that prevents the crown from expropriating any of the land without the consent of the Métis General Council. In addition, the General Council's title to the land is constitutionally protected under the *Constitution of Alberta Amendment Act, 1990*. Earlier Peter Lougheed, then the premier, restructured the relationship between the province and one group of Métis in it. He wanted a made-in-Alberta solution to Métis self-reliance and introduced Resolution 18 in 1982, which led to the Métis Settlements Accord (1990). This accord led to the creation of four pieces of legislation in Alberta that established land ownership rights (fee simple ownership of 1.28 million acres) and a reorganized form of governance for the Métis in the eight Alberta settlements. The Alberta government agreed to pay $310 million over seventeen years. Thus, the Métis of Alberta have a permanent land base under Métis settlements legislation.

In 2017, the Métis National Council signed the Canada–Métis Nation Accord with the federal government that fosters a government-to-government relationship. The accord is based upon the legal premise established by the Supreme Court confirming that the crown is in a fiduciary relationship with the Métis as a distinct people and that there is unfinished business of reconciliation with the Métis regarding Canadian sovereignty. The accord states that the Métis agree to meet with federal policy makers and hold one meeting each year with the prime minister. It also provides for the Métis to have semiannual meetings with key cabinet ministers, including the minister of Indigenous affairs, as well as quarterly meetings with various assistant deputy ministers on issues of concern to the Métis. Policy priorities will be established at these meetings and result from joint Métis-government initiatives.

I now turn to those areas of Canada not "treatied out" through the Numbered Treaties or those negotiated before that time but being dealt with in a different manner.

CONTEMPORARY TREATIES

COMPREHENSIVE AND SPECIFIC LAND CLAIMS

In 1973, the federal government revised its policy on Indigenous Peoples' claims (specifically those involving First Nations) and divided them into two broad classes: comprehensive and specific. Comprehensive claims have a wide scope and are based upon the recognition of continuing Aboriginal Rights to lands and natural resources. These claims emerged in places in Canada where Aboriginal Title was not previously dealt with by treaty or some other means (e.g., British Columbia, northern Quebec, Northwest Territories). Specific claims deal with narrower claims of First Nations related to treaties or other legislative provisions by governments that have had deleterious effects on them. These specific claims focus on Canada's obligations embodied in treaties or on how the government has managed the assets of First Nations. For example, a specific claim could focus on the failure of the government to provide services as promised in a treaty or on the improper handling by the government of First Nations Traditional Territories. Another type of claim is referred to as "other" since it does not meet the strict criteria of the above two programs but nonetheless has a legal basis. Several of these special claims have been accepted by Canada as requiring resolution through negotiation (Canada 2007). For example, Treaty Land Entitlement is a process by which land can be added to an existing reserve when the original allocation of land in a treaty was not fulfilled. These "add-on" lands do not have to be contiguous with the existing reserve, and in fact there are over twenty urban reserves within municipal boundaries (e.g., Saskatoon, Winnipeg). However, for these lands to be considered officially part of an existing reserve, the minister of Indian affairs must approve a lengthy legal process initiated by the band.

POLICY EVOLUTION

Prior to 1970, the Department of Indian Affairs, along with the Department of Justice and the Treasury Board, ruled on all Indigenous land claims. These decisions were made behind closed doors and were thus neither transparent nor public. Moreover, government officials were reluctant (as they continue to be) to develop procedures to deal with Indigenous land claims not controlled by the federal government. Nevertheless, the Pearson government (1963–68) brought to Parliament an *Act to Provide for the Disposition of Indian Claims*. It was an innovative and forward-looking piece of legislation that would create an independent commission to deal with Indigenous land claims. However, it died on the order paper and was never revived by subsequent governments. In 1969, the first Indian commissioner (1969–77) was established. However, First Nations opposition to the activities of the commissioner led to the demise of the agency. During its eight years of operation, the commissioner was unable to bring about a resolution to land claims since the mandate did not include an examination of Aboriginal Rights.

By the late 1970s, it became clear to the courts that the process of adjudicating Indigenous land claims placed Indian Affairs in a conflict of interest, and changes were implemented. In 1973, the Office of Native Claims was established to deal with both specific and comprehensive land claims. This move was a reaction, of course, to the famous *Calder v British Columbia (Attorney General)* case (1973), in which the

Supreme Court decided that First Nations did have Aboriginal Rights, not because of the Royal Proclamation of 1763, but because they were in Canada long before settlers arrived.

First Nations were required to submit their claims to the Office of Native Claims, which would solicit the advice of the Department of Justice before deciding to accept or reject the claims. The office stipulated the evidence that claimants had to provide to support their claims if they were to be accepted, and it decided how much funding it would allocate to each claimant. Although the office made the final decision, it did not provide reasons for the decision, nor were appeals allowed. So First Nations saw the process as unfair, biased, and under the total control of the federal government.

By 1981, only a handful of claims submitted to the government had been settled under this process (Flanagan 2019). Subsequently, the government decided not to apply the doctrine of laches in relation to Indigenous land claims—a position that First Nations had argued for the previous forty years. The crown began to carry out negotiations with First Nations that had never "taken treaty."

Comprehensive land claim settlements deal with areas of Canada where claims to Aboriginal Title have not been addressed by treaties or other legal means. (See Box 3 for the key developments regarding Indigenous land claims.) The first of these modern-day treaties was the James Bay and Northern Quebec Agreement signed in 1975. Since that time, the federal government has settled twenty-six comprehensive land claims with First Nations. The claims settled thus far cover 4 million square kilometres of Canadian territory, about the size of the combined countries of Mexico, Venezuela, and Colombia, and the claims were supplemented by capital transfers to First Nations of $2.2 billion. Over 800,000 square kilometres of land has now been given Aboriginal Title and has cost the government nearly $3.5 billion. A great deal of the cost of negotiating a comprehensive claim is also borne by the First Nations claimant. Since the average cost of negotiating a claim is about $25 million, the cost, if the claim is successful, is deducted from the final agreement if the plaintiff has received funding from the government to support its claim. Thus, many claims are not negotiated because the money borrowed from the federal government to mount the claim might exceed the amount of the final judgment. The community would thus be in debt for many years. Either way, the First Nation is disadvantaged in trying to achieve justice for something that it did not initiate (Monchalin 2016).

The government of Canada has agreed to hold an additional seventy negotiations to resolve comprehensive land claims with First Nations and provincial and territorial governments. It is estimated that nearly half of the First Nations population currently involved in the process is in British Columbia, where over fifty comprehensive claims have been accepted for negotiation and where agreement-in-principle negotiations are proceeding at nearly 100 tables.

BOX 3

KEY DEVELOPMENTS ON FIRST NATIONS LAND AND RESOURCE ISSUES

1950–55	The federal government relocated Inuit to experimental colonies in the Arctic Archipelago.
1973	The *Calder* decision. The Supreme Court split on the issue of whether the Aboriginal Title of the Nisga'a had survived into modern times. All justices recognized that Aboriginal Title existed as a concept in Canadian common law, but they differed on the test necessary for its extinguishment.
1973	The government established the Office of Native Claims.
1975	The James Bay and Northern Quebec Agreement. This was the first modern-day treaty, completed with the Grand Council of Cree in Quebec, the Northern Quebec Inuit Association, Hydro-Quebec, and the federal and quebec governments.
1982	*The Constitution Act, 1982*. Existing Aboriginal and Treaty Rights were recognized and affirmed. The federal government reorganized the specific claims process.

1986 — Significant amendments to the federal comprehensive land claims policy were announced following consultations with First Nations. Key changes to the policy included the development of alternatives to blanket extinguishment of Aboriginal Rights.

1990 — The policy of dealing with only six comprehensive land claims at any one time was changed so that there was no limit.

1990 — The *Sioui* case and the Treaty of 1760. The Supreme Court focused on what type of document could be considered a treaty and what kind of interpretation was required to define when a treaty obligation must be fulfilled. The individuals charged with making a fire and camping in Jacques Cartier park in Gatineau argued that they were engaged in customary practices as part of the Treaty of 1760 between the Huron Nation and the crown. The Supreme Court agreed that it was a treaty and that the individuals could continue to practise traditional activities as outlined in the treaty. The Supreme Court also noted that the courts must have a liberal and generous interpretation of treaties. This admonition was heeded in 1999 with the *Marshall* case, in which it was ruled that there was a need for more than a one-sided technical interpretation of a treaty and that the context in which a treaty was signed needed to be considered when interpreting its content.

1990 — The *Sparrow* case. The Supreme Court ruled that the Musqueam Band had an Aboriginal Right to fish for food, social, and ceremonial purposes. The court also found that there was a fiduciary relationship between the crown and First Nations and that section 35 of the *Constitution Act, 1982* must be interpreted with this relationship in mind. The court placed a large burden on the crown to justify any infringement of rights protected by section 35 of the *Charter of Rights and Freedoms*.

1991	The government opened the door to pre-Confederation claims. It also formed an independent advisory body called the Indian Specific Claims Commission.
1993	Establishment of the British Columbia Treaty Commission (BCTC), an independent tripartite commission with the mandate to oversee the negotiation of claims in British Columbia.
1998	The *Delgamuukw* case. The Supreme Court made general pronouncements on the scope and content of Aboriginal Title.
1999	The *Marshall* case. The Supreme Court ruled that there is an implied term in the Treaties of 1760–61 granting Mi'kmaq signatories the right to engage in traditional resource harvesting activities, including for the purpose of sale, to the extent required to provide for a moderate livelihood. The court clarified principles of evidence for the interpretation of First Nations historical treaties.
1999	Nunavut was officially separated from the Northwest Territories and became the third territory in Canada. The area is comprised primarily of Inuit.
2000	The Nisga'a Final Agreement. This was the first time in Canadian history that a land claim settlement and self-government arrangements were negotiated at the same time and given constitutional protection in a treaty.
1975–2012	Twenty-six comprehensive claims were settled in Canada since the announcement of the federal government's claims policy in 1973, the most recent being those of the eight Yukon First Nations, the Nisga'a Agreement, and the Tlicho Agreement.
2010	Canada signed the United Nations Declaration on the Rights of Indigenous Peoples.
2014	The Tsilhqot'in Nations established Aboriginal Title over 1,750 square kilometres of territory in British Columbia.

RECENT GOVERNMENT ACTION ON MODERN LAND CLAIMS

A major reason for the crown to process comprehensive land claims is to come to an agreement with First Nations that will bring about the end of legal ambiguities associated with Aboriginal Rights and Title and establish certainty regarding land and resource ownership—a condition that the government claims is necessary if resource development is to take place (Woolford 2005). The goal is to negotiate modern treaties that provide certainty and clarity of rights to ownership and use of lands and resources for all parties. Governments argue that billions of dollars have been lost by not settling the claims. Moreover, if the claims are settled and certainty is established, then billions of dollars will be invested and thousands of jobs created—some of them for Indigenous people. In short, if economic stability is achieved, then it will create a climate that encourages private investment, leading to increased economic activity, which in turn will lead to new partnerships between Indigenous and non-Indigenous groups and enhanced social and economic positions for Indigenous people. Map 5 identifies the lands thus far dealt with by modern comprehensive claims.

Historically, in land claim settlements the provinces were not involved in negotiations with Indigenous Peoples because the federal crown had negotiated treaties in advance of settler populations and the creation of provincial governments (Hurley 2000). Today most of the lands and natural resources that are the focus of comprehensive claims are under provincial jurisdiction. Provincial and territorial governments are therefore major actors now in the negotiation of settlements of comprehensive land claims. Provinces and territories often have roles because of their involvement in historical events that gave rise to the claims. The federal government has agreed that the provinces and territories must participate in negotiations and contribute to the costs of settlements. Although the federal government has agreed to the tripartite negotiations, it has taken the position that, if the parties cannot come to an agreement, it reserves the right to plead all defenses available to it, including laches and lack of admissible evidence.

The federal government leads the process of establishing cost-sharing arrangements with the relevant province or territory to support the financial settlement of claims and attain certainty. Provincial and territorial governments are also forced to participate in covering the costs of negotiations since they will also benefit from having certainty regarding land and resource ownership. If the claim is not successful, then the federal government absorbs most of the costs.

COMPREHENSIVE CLAIMS

Contemporary land claims have long lists of issues that can be negotiated. For example, they can include issues such as cultural artifacts, financial transfers, fisheries, dispute resolution, forestry, amount of land and its location, subsurface resources, taxation, and water. In addition, self-government is an issue, though its structure and content vary considerably. Comprehensive land claim agreements involve a variety of rights, responsibilities, and benefits such as ownership of lands, harvesting of wild game, involvement in land and resource management, and financial compensation (including resource revenue sharing and economic development projects). Settlements are intended to ensure that the interests of First Nations in resource management and environmental protection are recognized and that claimants share in the benefits of development (Canada 2006).

MODELS OF COMPREHENSIVE CLAIMS

Certainty of ownership and use of lands and resources is a primary goal of the government in negotiating comprehensive land claim settlements. The government and the private sector want clear definitions of the rights and obligations of Indigenous groups regarding comprehensive land claim settlements. In previous treaties, the federal government required First Nations to "cede, release, and surrender" their undefined Aboriginal Rights in exchange for a set of defined Treaty Rights. This model of "extinguishment" has been rejected by most Indigenous groups involved in land claims since they consider it to be unacceptable. Most courts would agree that it does not fit into Aboriginal law in Canada today.

Because Indigenous Peoples reject this model, new strategies to bring about certainty have been developed. They include the "modified

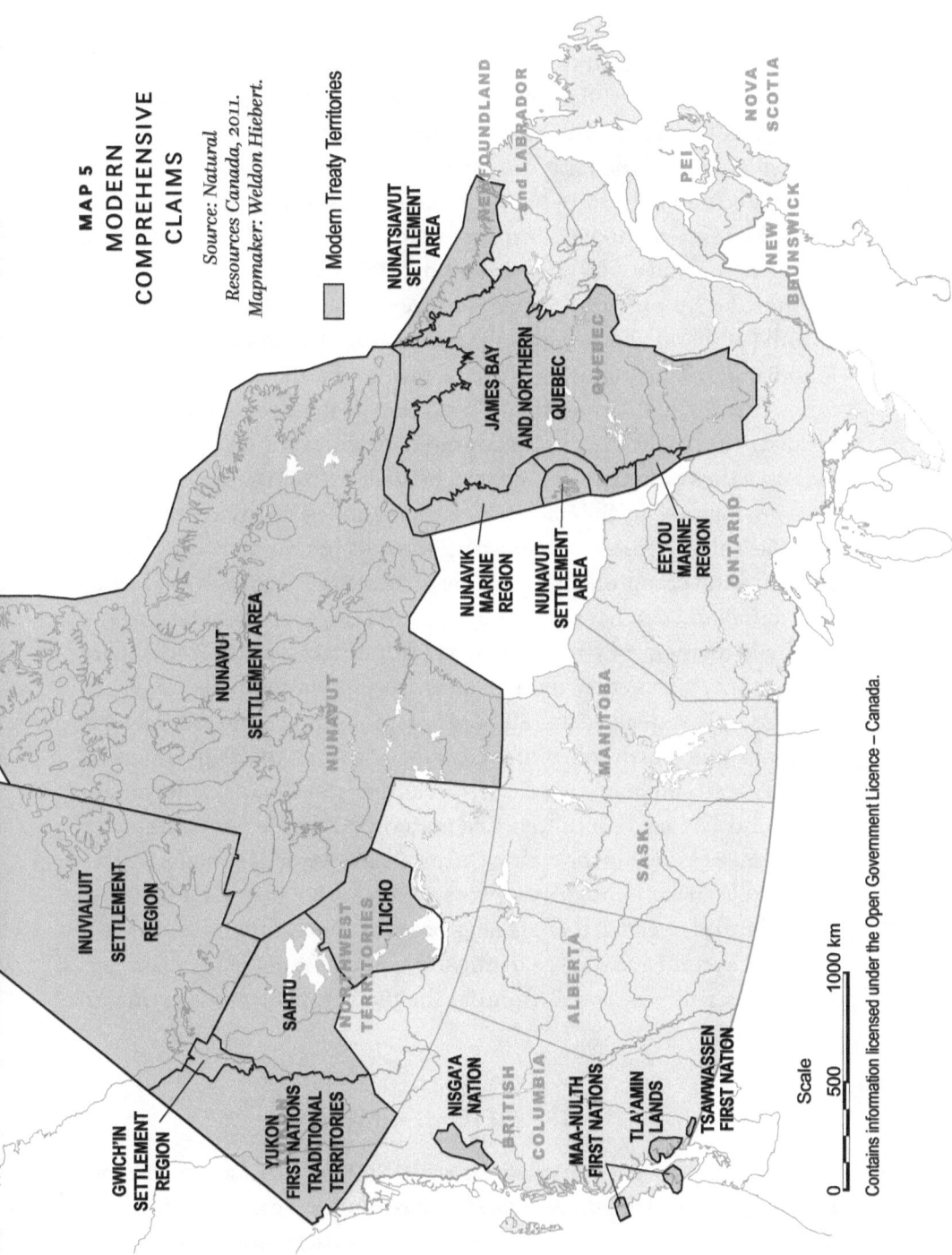

rights model" and the "non-assertion model" as part of the comprehensive agreement. In the former model, Aboriginal Rights are not extinguished but modified and included with the rights articulated and defined in the treaty. In the latter model, Aboriginal Rights are not extinguished, and the First Nation agrees to exercise only those rights articulated and defined in the treaty and to assert no other Aboriginal Right. The second model is implemented in those comprehensive land claims that involve self-government provisions.

After the Numbered Treaties were signed (as well as the adhesions to some of them), there were still vast areas of British Columbia, Newfoundland and Labrador, northern Quebec, and the Northwest Territories that had not "taken treaty," and thus land claims in those areas needed to be resolved. Once the comprehensive claims policy was put in place, a series of settlements was negotiated, such as the James Bay settlement, followed by the Inuvialuit settlement, the Nunavut settlement, and the Yukon settlement (covering most of the territory). However, there are still comprehensive claims to be settled in British Columbia, Newfoundland and Labrador, and parts of the Yukon and Manitoba.

The settlement of comprehensive claims takes, on average, more than twenty-five years, though more recent claims have taken, on average, only sixteen years (Flanagan 2019). Today Crown-Indigenous Relations and Northern Affairs Canada as well as the Department of Justice receive information from the claimant, evaluate the documentation and evidence submitted, and undertake their own investigations of evidence regarding the claim. Only if these two departments believe that the claim has enough evidence supporting it will it move forward. If the claim is rejected, there is no process of appeal other than to enter the court system and engage in litigation. At that time, the government of Canada will remove all funding for the claimant and assume an adversarial position.

SPECIFIC CLAIMS

Specific claims are those made by First Nations that Canada has not fulfilled its lawful obligations as stipulated in treaties. A specific claim must be against the government of Canada and must not be based upon

Aboriginal Rights or Title. In 1982, the federal government outlined its new policy for specific claims in *Outstanding Business: A Native Claims Policy—Specific Claims*. Important amendments were made to the policy in the early 1990s in an attempt to increase the number of resolutions. More importantly, the policy established the Indian Specific Claims Commission (sometimes referred to as the Indian Claims Commission), mandated to review the minister's decisions regarding any rejected claim. The document noted that the government would not accept any claim based upon events prior to Confederation. This policy was in direct conflict with the Supreme Court's decision that pre-Confederation treaties were legitimate and had to be dealt with by Canada. In the end, under this new process, the minister of Indian affairs, acting under a recommendation of the Department of Justice, retained power in deciding which claims were valid. As Ray (2016) points out, the federal government was still in the position of being defendant, judge, and jury regarding First Nations claims. In addition, the specific claims process specifically noted that oral history evidence was not admissible in the court proceedings.

Nevertheless, the Specific Claims Commission carried out its mandate for eighteen years and resolved many outstanding claims. The commission did implement one notable policy in assessing First Nations claims that differentiated it from previous assessments. It became a pioneer in the government regarding the acceptance of oral evidence and giving it equal weight to document evidence when reviewing a claim. When the commission ceased to exist in 2008, it had dealt with nearly 100 claims. The total value of the claims that the commission recommended for negotiation and settled was just over $351 million.

In 2002, Indian and Northern Affairs Canada introduced the *Specific Claims Resolution Act* to address the crown's legal obligations to First Nations. Although duly enacted, the Act was not proclaimed in force. Further changes to the policy were implemented in 2007, and a new policy document, *Justice at Last: Specific Claims Action Plan*, was published. It was intended to ensure impartiality and fairness, greater transparency, faster processing, and better access to mediation. In short, Canada's specific claims policy was established to allow

First Nations to have their claims appropriately addressed by the government through negotiations without having to go to court.

Under this new policy, First Nations can choose to file claims with the independent tribunal that are not accepted for negotiation or have not been resolved through a negotiated settlement agreement within a specified time frame. It was agreed by the then Conservative government that it would not interfere with the processes or decisions of the tribunal. Moreover, a tribunal decision is to be final, and no appeal is allowed. Any future claim based upon the same facts will not be heard by the tribunal (Slade and Lombard 2015). Unfortunately, the Conservative government reneged on its promise to ensure the independence of the tribunal and appealed some of its decisions. Over the years, progress in resolving specific claims has been slow and inconsistent. With the creation of the specific claims policy and the establishment of the tribunal, First Nations have found a greater degree of acceptance by the government and tribunal to take their claims seriously. In addition, the process has become more transparent in that the government can no longer simply deny a claim and consider the issue resolved.

Since 1973, nearly 1,700 specific claims have been brought forward by First Nations claimants (see Table 4.1), but only about one-quarter of the "resolved" cases have been supportive of the claims. In an additional one-third of the cases brought forward, the federal government has been found to have no legal obligation to deal with them. Today the number of cases resolved is increasing, yet the number of new cases brought before the government or tribunal has increased at a rate higher than the number of cases being resolved. From 1974 to 2017, there were 450 specific claim settlements. As a result of these settlements, the federal government paid $4.7 billion. Nearly 45 percent of the 618 First Nations have received at least one settlement (Flanagan 2019). Nevertheless, there are still over 500 specific claims in the federal inventory, 352 claims under assessment, and over 187 claims in negotiation.

TREATY ENTITLEMENTS

In 1973, when the federal government created the Indian Claims Commission to deal with land claims pursued by First Nations across Canada, one solution to the issue was the creation of the Treaty Land

Entitlement process. Provinces have established programs with the federal government to resolve the issue of land claims. For example, in Saskatchewan there was an acknowledgement of "treaty shortfalls" that needed to be addressed. However, it took twenty years of negotiations regarding the Treaty Land Entitlement Framework Agreement before it was signed by Saskatchewan First Nations and the two levels of government (Razack 2002). Today the lands entitled to Indigenous Peoples in Saskatchewan have still not been fully allocated, and now money, in lieu of land, is considered appropriate compensation.

Table 4.1 National Summary of Specific Claims (1973–2017)

IN PROGRESS	
Under Assessment	51
Research	57
Department of Justice Preparing Legal Opinion	68
Legal Opinion Signed	29
In Negotiation	
Active Negotiations	229
Inactive Negotiations	74
Total in Progress	**508**
CONCLUDED	
Settled through Negotiations	450
No Lawful Obligation Found	446
Resolved through Administrative Remedy	39
File Closed	387
OTHER	
Active Litigation	95
Specific Claims Tribunal	78
Total Other	**173**

Source: *Canada (2018)*.

The process of resolving specific claims has been slow and cumbersome. Information from Indian Affairs shows that fewer than half of the specific claims cases are resolved in five years, with another 30 percent taking between six and ten years to resolve. Many specific claims have emerged over time, and thus the backlog continues to increase. Many claims remain in limbo and take more than ten years to be considered by the government. Other claims are rejected by the government with little or no explanation. Because of such inefficiencies, in 1990 a group of Chiefs formed the Chiefs' Committee on Claims and pressured the federal government to act. One recommendation made by the committee was the establishment of an independent Specific Claims Tribunal. The committee's work also brought about the Indian Specific Claims Commission, which reviewed specific claims that had been rejected and issued non-binding reports (Specific Claims Research Centre n.d.). However, thus far, the federal government has taken no action.

A specific claim must be submitted by a First Nations community subject to the alleged grievance. The claim must also concern events that occurred at least fifteen years before submission of the claim, and it cannot be based upon a land claims agreement signed after 1973. A unique clause also stipulates that a specific claim cannot be based upon the delivery or funding for social, health, or correctional services. Finally, the claim cannot be based upon Aboriginal Title or Rights. These latter cases will be dealt with by the courts. In 2011, at least seventy-four claims that qualified for filing with the tribunal were based upon rejection by the minister. Of the 577 claims in the process administered by the Specific Claims Branch, many will be rejected and could then be eligible for filing with the tribunal. Additional claims might become eligible because of the federal government's failure to settle after three years from the date of acceptance. In 2017, the tribunal had seventy-eight claims before it and thirty-five hearings on various claims. Most claims were from British Columbia (thirty-two), whereas Quebec, Saskatchewan, and Alberta made up forty-one cases.

COMPENSATION

First, the compensation for specific claims to be provided to First Nations claimants is only for the losses or damages incurred because of a breach by the federal crown. Second, the compensation will be based upon existing legal principles. Third, if reserve land was taken without proper compensation at the time, then the compensation will be limited to the value of the land at the time that it was taken from the claimant or the amount of damage done—whichever is the case. Fourth, if reserve land was never legally surrendered, then the band shall be compensated by the return of the land or by the current unimproved value of the land. In any settlement of a claim (both comprehensive and specific), the government will take third-party interests into account. It will not accept any settlement that will lead to third parties being dispossessed of lands, nor will compensation be increased for land forcibly taken by the crown. The above criteria are general, and the actual amount that the claimant is offered will depend on the extent to which the claimant can establish a valid claim—the burden of which rests with the claimant. Where it can be justified, a reasonable portion of the costs of negotiation may be added to the compensation paid.

CONCLUSION

It has been estimated that First Nations and the federal government have negotiated approximately 500 treaties over time. Early treaties were generally called Peace and Friendship Treaties, whereas those after 1850 usually involved land cessions. The courts (except for the federal and provincial governments) would agree that treaties between government officials and First Nations were focused on issues of co-occupation and coexistence within a geographical space since most treaties set aside lands for First Nations (Teillet 2013). However, these treaties never specified that First Nations were giving up their rights of sovereignty or self-government.

The government's failure to enforce the contents of treaties and to obstruct outsiders to help First Nations gain federal compliance with those treaties continues today. First Nations were not able to engage the government and to seek recourse from the state for many years. It was only when outsiders were engaged (e.g., the UN Commission on Human Rights) calling for a study of treaties made between First

Nations and Canada that the government changed its relationship of trust with First Nations (Anaya 2014).

Treaty Rights are provisions that specifically appear within the text of a treaty or items that were specifically discussed and agreed to during negotiations of a treaty but might not be specifically mentioned in the treaty document. This issue is hotly contested by the government, which claims that oral agreements are not to be honoured. First Nations argue that it is the responsibility of both parties to observe, acknowledge, and respect their treaty obligations, including oral agreements made at the time of signing the treaty. Moreover, First Nations argue that items not appearing within the treaty continue to exist as Aboriginal Rights. So the lack of discussion during the treaty negotiations regarding the right to self-government, language, ceremony, education, or health care does not mean that they have been relinquished or taken away. The Supreme Court's decisions suggest that only the crown can unilaterally amend treaty agreements and that First Nations have no say in what that amendment might be.

Teillet (2013) argues that, if the negotiating parties saw the necessity of putting something into a treaty, they would have dealt (as is the case with the modern-day treaty-making process) with the land claim agreements that contain many specific provisions. The need to reconsider the treaties, as advocated by First Nations, is apparent from their perspective. However, the reason to re-examine the treaties is not to alter the foundation upon which they were originally entered (i.e., that each party recognized and respected the other's government and ability to enter treaty relations). Rather, the issue of government jurisdiction for specific territories and the need to deal with economic realities comprise the basis upon which the re-examination is advocated (Teillet 2013).

Recently, several First Nations in Manitoba, Saskatchewan, and Alberta have indicated their intention to challenge the legitimacy of the treaty-making process and of the *Natural Resources Transfer Act* that followed it. It appears that the challenge is premised on the view that the Numbered Treaties were not land cession agreements. This argument claims that, notwithstanding the written versions of the treaties, the actual understanding of the First Nations signatories was that the land was to be shared with—not ceded to—settlers. The legal position advanced is that all subsequent government actions have been inconsistent with this definition of the situation and thus constitute an infringement of Aboriginal or Treaty Rights. This would include passage of the Natural Resources Transfer Agreements and extend to all judicial decisions made on the assumption of the legitimacy of those agreements. This position is partially based upon the Supreme Court's decision in *Horseman* (1990), in which Justice Cory, speaking for the majority of the court, addressed the question of the legitimacy of the *Natural Resources Transfer Act*. In addressing the extinguishment of the commercial right to hunt (in the agreements), he said that it was imposed without consultation and thus might be open to challenge.

The goal of the federal government continues to be twofold. It seeks first to assimilate Indigenous people and second to establish certainty and finality when it settles a claim. For the government, settlement of a claim must achieve complete and final redress. First Nations claimants must therefore provide the government with a release and an indemnity with respect to the claim, and they might be required to provide a surrender, end litigation, or take other steps so that the claim cannot be reopened at some time in the future.

In the process of dealing with Indigenous claims, Indian Affairs is not the only department involved. The Departments of Finance, the Environment, and Justice must also be consulted by Indian Affairs to secure consensus on any negotiated settlement between the government and the First Nations claimant (Diabo 2012). Moreover, sometimes Indian Affairs is prepared to settle a claim only to have it rejected by other "affected" departments since they can veto the negotiated settlement. In addition, the prime minister, the Prime Minister's Office, and the Department of Finance wield power in the outcomes of negotiations. As Dewar (2009) indicates, the prime minister can unilaterally alter the mandate, delay the process, or even end the process. In addition, provincial governments have substantial influence on the process and are ultimately under the control of their premiers. As the federal government has mandated that provincial governments be involved in land claims located in their provinces, this is an additional hurdle for

First Nations claimants since provincial governments have demonstrated their reluctance to approve land claims because, if settled, they would have impacts on provincial lands, powers, and jurisdiction (Alcantara 2013).

Indigenous Peoples have argued that the federal government has assumed, since the arrival of explorers and settlers in Canada, that Indigenous Peoples are culturally backward and need to be assimilated into mainstream society. This imperative has been part of the government's way of thinking about them. This settler assumption of superiority was embedded in the process of treaty making. The signing of a treaty is an act of recognition of the need for mutual respect and consent, but this was not the case when Canadian settlers dealt with Indigenous Peoples. The treaties (sometimes negotiated) offered to them were generally unfair, and communities unwilling to sign treaties as offered were coerced into signing them because of illness, starvation, or some other calamity. As such, the treaties do not exhibit a sense of fairness or a just basis for intercommunal relations (Moore 2010).

Once the treaties were in place, they were systematically ignored or violated, and the Canadian government's idea of superiority provided a reason for abrogating them. The relationship between First Nations and the government has a long history of "broken promises." Indigenous Peoples have taken the stance that the concept of justice embodies the idea of fair treatment, which has not characterized the treaty process. They also argue that these policies are not the results of just one government; rather, there has been a long history of abuses and injustices enacted by governments since the eighteenth century. Thus, the problem is not simply the actions of several different governments or the specific administration of Indigenous Peoples but the result of something endemic to the state order. For example, some scholars have argued that prior to the *Calder* decision there was no law regarding Aboriginal Rights to land (see *Ross River Dena Council* 2002). However, other scholars, such as McNeil (2017), claim that the common law and documents such as the Royal Proclamation of 1763 and the Rupert's Land Order of 1870 acknowledge the land rights of Indigenous Peoples.

One can ask whether the treaties have been successful in resolving competing claims for lands. Jai (2017) notes that there are three criteria to assess whether an agreement is successful. First, an agreement is successful if all parties to it have similar understandings of what was agreed. Second, a successful agreement includes all of the key terms within the document. And third, a successful agreement addresses the key underlying interests of the signatories. When applied to the Numbered Treaties, these criteria are not evident in the written texts. Nevertheless, First Nations want the government to address these issues and to make substantive changes to correct the inequalities and injustices embedded in the system of Canadian governance. Finally, the Supreme Court has ruled that, while First Nations, for all purposes, would be the exclusive owners of their lands, interjurisdictional immunity would not apply to Aboriginal Title lands. This was explicitly noted in the *Tsilhqot'in Nation* case (2014) as well as in the *Grassy Narrows First Nation* case (2014). This means that Aboriginal Rights can be constrained by both federal and provincial governments. Moreover, in the *Grassy Narrows First Nation* case, the court ruled that Ontario, without involving the federal government, could "take up" land from Treaty Three as long as it consulted the First Nations community and accommodated it appropriately (McNeil 2016). Nevertheless, the Supreme Court has noted that a policy of reconciliation requires that equal weight be placed on common law and the Indigenous perspective (Imai 2019). Looking at Treaty Rights has generally focused on who has the correct history. However, as Morin (2018) argues, the treaties involved two parties (the government and Indigenous Peoples) seeking to conclude agreements, and their reasons and intentions for reaching agreements were different. As such, the treaties reveal the interactions of different cultures and worldviews and are understood differently depending on the ethos. The Supreme Court has therefore ruled that treaties with Indigenous Peoples should be liberally construed; if there is ambiguity in the treaty document, then it should be resolved in favour of Indigenous Peoples to ensure the integrity and honour of the crown.

CHAPTER 5

ABORIGINAL RIGHTS

Almost from the time of the first explorers of Canada, there was a belief that Indigenous Peoples had no rights. Subsequent court decisions, crown policies, and laws enacted by colonial administrators and settlers built upon this belief. As Canada entered the twentieth century, the laws regarding Indigenous Peoples built upon these beliefs and British jurisprudence. In this chapter, I review how this belief emerged, was sustained, and only recently has been challenged by the Supreme Court of Canada. I will show that the subsequent repatriation of the Canadian Constitution provided Indigenous Peoples with a platform for challenging some of the current limitations on Aboriginal Rights. I end the chapter with a detailed discussion on how the courts have defined Aboriginal Rights, the conditions for limiting or extinguishing those rights, and how these decisions have created a new vision of the place of Indigenous Peoples in Canadian society.

THE CONSTITUTIONAL CONTEXT

I begin the discussion of Aboriginal Rights by putting the issue in its proper context. Canadians have a Constitution by which they agree to abide. It is what is called written "fundamental law" and sets out the nature of the government, the basic principles of how the government operates, and the basis of the laws of the country. However, people tend to forget that there is also an "unwritten" side to the Constitution, the components of which are are called "conventions." They are the customary ways in which the government does things over the years. Although we do not always think about conventions, they are just as important as the written Constitution. However, they are vague in content, difficult to interpret, and hard to deal with. For example, when Prime Minister Pierre Trudeau wanted unilaterally to repatriate the Constitution, he was told by the Supreme Court that from a written constitutional perspective he could do so. However, there was a convention that required him to consult with the provinces. (Remember that repatriation means repealing a provision of a British Act requiring that all Canadian constitutional changes be carried out in Britain). Nevertheless, in the end, many of the components of the current Canadian Constitution are still British legal documents, and the current Constitution still contains most of the Acts that made up the Canadian Constitution, 1867 (though some Acts, such as the *Dominion Lands Act*, were removed). Hence, many legal and political questions need to be addressed to sort out the relationship between Indigenous Peoples and the crown regarding their rights vis-à-vis the Constitution.

Many Canadians argue that until 1995 the federal government acted in accordance with the Constitution. However, when Prime Minister Brian Mulroney unilaterally declared that year that First Nations had the inherent Aboriginal Right to self-government, his critics argued that this violated the Constitution. Their argument was that, since Canada is a constitutional monarchy, sovereignty is held only by the federal crown. Sovereign powers are controlled and distributed by the Constitution and operate based upon constitutional law. Thus, if the federal government is sovereign, then how can a lesser government have any right to self-government? This can happen if the federal crown distributes certain powers to lesser governments (e.g., provincial governments). However, since the Constitution distributes all legislative jurisdiction to Parliament, and since Parliament has delegated some jurisdiction to provincial legislatures, this division of power is both exclusive and exhaustive; there are no "leftover" self-government issues to be taken up by another level of government (i.e., First Nations, municipalities). Yet, if the federal government wants to delegate rights to Indigenous Peoples, provinces, or municipalities, then doing so is possible, but it underscores the idea that there is no such thing as an inherent Aboriginal Right to self-government within the Constitution. Moreover, the Supreme Court has reiterated in several cases that the federal crown alone has sovereignty over all aspects of life. It can, of course, delegate some of these responsibilities to "lesser" governments. However, inherent Indigenous self-government has now been accepted by the federal government for twenty-five years, and thus it might qualify as a convention.

CHANGING VIEWS OF ABORIGINAL RIGHTS

Aboriginal Rights have evolved since the Royal Proclamation of 1763. The government of Canada argued for years that Aboriginal Rights and Title were the sole result of the Royal Proclamation, despite Indigenous communities recognizing and affirming other sources of sovereignty. Neither Parliament nor the Supreme Court seems to have any appetite to definitively spell out what Aboriginal Rights are, but it is clear that they are unwilling to accept their meaning from an Indigenous perspective.

It is important to realize that over time many different actors engage in the process of enacting and enforcing laws. Since the time of Confederation, some of these individuals changed their perspectives and actions regarding law. Canadian law was introduced in Rupert's Land, where the Hudson's Bay Company carried out its business. In the Charter of 1670 given to the company, it was proclaimed that all people who were not subjects of some other country would now be subject to the law of England. Nevertheless, the Hudson's Bay Company, in some circumstances, accepted Indigenous law (e.g., domestic concerns of Indigenous Peoples such as cultural customs). For example, Indigenous activities such as gambling, drinking, prostitution, and sports on the Sabbath were not really prosecuted. Moral issues were not pursued, but if theft or homicide were involved, the full force of British law was brought to bear. The Hudson's Bay Company established the

General Quarterly Court of Assiniboia (at Winnipeg in 1836), and it held jurisdiction over all activities (except capital offences, though even they were sometimes ignored). This court continued until 1872. In 1873, the North West Mounted Police was formed and dealt with issues outside the boundaries of Rupert's Land. The Criminal Code of Canada was enacted a decade later, and Indigenous Peoples fell under its jurisdiction. British law regarding gender was also imposed on Indigenous Peoples. As a result, Indigenous women were considered chattel; no longer could they separate from their husbands, hold communal property, and participate in band affairs, and they could not benefit from their matrilineal or bilateral rules of descent and inheritance (Nettelback et al. 2016, 147). These changes were sometimes based upon personal beliefs, but many of them reflected the changing norms of society. For example, unions were illegal in Canada at the turn of the twentieth century, and it was well into the century before this law was changed. Discrimination against minorities and women was legal at one time, but as the norms of society changed so did the laws. Laws are shaped by a variety of domestic and international influences, and laws themselves produce social change and legitimize behaviour over time. Hence, laws regarding Indigenous Peoples are also influenced by many different events as the social norms of society change and in turn influence the role of laws in society.

From the perspective of Indigenous Peoples, rights were given to them by the Creator, and in turn they agreed to be stewards of the land and everything on the Earth. For First Nations, the Royal Proclamation simply affirmed their Aboriginal Rights and Title. From their perspective, Aboriginal Rights are inherent and collective and include many activities (e.g., education, self-government, land ownership). Nevertheless, in its decision in *Behn v Moulton Contracting Ltd*, the Supreme Court stated explicitly that Aboriginal Rights, though collective in nature, can have individual aspects (Allodi-Ross 2017, 149).

The government of Canada argues that Aboriginal Rights, including those regarding land (and also jurisdiction to govern the land), lie within the jurisdiction of Parliament. For example, the crown argues that Aboriginal Title is nothing more than a "property right" and a "burden on the crown." It claims that First Nations have no ownership of the land and that Aboriginal Rights are nothing more than common law rights that can be restricted by government legislation any time that it meets the criteria outlined in the Supreme Court's rules regarding extinguishing Aboriginal Rights. This is reflected in the fact that individuals living on reserves cannot have fee simple ownership of a piece of land. However, the *Indian Act* does provide for individual property rights. A band council can grant a "certificate of possession" (replacing a "certificate of location") for a piece of land to an individual (usually a male individual) for an indeterminate period, but the certificate can be cancelled for many reasons. In short, the council creates an individual interest in a parcel of land so that one can build on it and improve it, but the land can also be removed from one's use by the council for any reason. The new certificate of possession has been issued to about 44,000 people, while an additional 10,000 people hold a certificate of location. Certificates of possession can only be transferred to another member of the same First Nation or to the band government after approval by the minister of Indian affairs (Alcantara 2003; Flanagan 2019).

Complicating this definition is that Aboriginal Rights regarding land have three unique dimensions compared to fee simple title:

1. First Nations Lands can be surrendered only to the crown.
2. Aboriginal Title arises from the prior occupation of Canada by Indigenous Peoples.
3. Aboriginal Title is held communally, which distinguishes it from normal proprietary (fee simple) interests.

Until recently, the federal government took the position that all Aboriginal Rights were extinguished by Canadian law (implicitly or explicitly). However, after the withdrawal of the ill-fated White Paper of 1969 (in which the Liberal government attempted to do away with the legal status of "Indians"), a new awareness of "Indigeneity" emerged among Indigenous Peoples across Canada. With the subsequent *Calder* decision in 1973, a growing political consciousness emerged among Indigenous communities. In addition, many other Canadians showed their support for Aboriginal Rights and demonstrated clearly to the government that more attention needed to be paid to those rights.

By the late 1970s, political awareness among First Nations focused on their desire to make constitutional changes regarding Indigenous issues. As the federal Liberals first introduced their suggested changes to the Constitution in the 1970s, there was a glimmer of hope among Indigenous Peoples that finally their concerns would be addressed. However, by the early 1980s, the provincial governments rejected the proposed changes, so the federal government decided to "go it alone."

The revised 1980 federal proposal for constitutional change totally omitted any reference to Indigenous Peoples or the issues that they had raised earlier. This "critical incident" brought Indigenous Peoples from across Canada to unite in a single cause. In addition, churches, women's organizations, and other non-governmental organizations gave their support to First Nations and the need to address their issues via the Constitution. In a last-minute change of heart, Peter Lougheed, then premier of Alberta, offered a compromise: Aboriginal and Treaty Rights would be reinstated in the proposed *Constitution Act* along with the word *existing* placed before *rights* and *treaties*. The revised *Constitution Act* was approved, and Aboriginal and Treaty Rights are now embedded in the Canadian Constitution, 1982. It fundamentally changed how Canadians viewed the legal rights of Indigenous Peoples since they were now given constitutional recognition. Section 35 in particular has become a major component of the Indigenous fight to obtain their lands and rights, though sections 2, 15, and 25 also have implications for Aboriginal Rights.

When the Nisga'a sued the BC government in 1967, they argued that they had the Aboriginal Right (Title) to their land. Until that time, lower courts had denied the existence of Aboriginal Title and argued that the existence of Aboriginal Rights was derived from colonial law. The Supreme Court ruled in *Calder* in 1973 that Aboriginal Title had existed at the time of the Royal Proclamation and that such a right existed outside colonial law. Nevertheless, British Columbia refused to acknowledge Aboriginal Rights (Title to lands) until 1990, nearly a quarter of a century after the Supreme Court ruling.

In 1980 (prior to repatriation of the Constitution), the Baker Lake Inuit went to court to seek a decision that a tract of land belonged to them. In short, they were trying to establish whether Inuit held

Aboriginal Title to a parcel of land. In its decision, the Supreme Court developed what would be called the "Baker Lake Test." The court identified criteria to be taken into consideration in an Indigenous claim to establish an Aboriginal Right, in this case Aboriginal Title to land. The criteria included (1) that the ancestors of the claimant group were part of an organized society and that the group be part of one in the present, (2) that the group had exclusive occupation of a specified territory to which they claimed Aboriginal Title, and (3) that they could prove that, at the time of contact with Europeans, their ancestors occupied the specific tract of land that they were claiming. This groundbreaking decision was the first contemporary attempt by the Supreme Court to develop criteria for establishing Aboriginal Rights.

Prior to 1982, Aboriginal Rights (e.g., Treaty Rights, Title) were subject to unilateral federal modification or extinguishment. However, under the new *Constitution Act*, this is no longer possible. Under the *Charter of Rights and Freedoms*, Aboriginal and Treaty Rights are not defined since it was the intention of the Supreme Court that further litigation would clarify those rights. Since repatriation of the Constitution, the Supreme Court has clarified some aspects of Aboriginal and Treaty Rights, though much more delineation is required before it is clear which rights are secure. Section 35 of the Constitution does much more, however, than just protect Aboriginal and Treaty Rights from legislative interference; it has changed the relationship between the crown and Indigenous Peoples.

The courts have also dealt with the issue of infringement or extinguishment of a right. Thus far, the Supreme Court has ruled that, for a Charter right to be limited or extinguished, two criteria must be met:

1. The legislation in question must be sufficiently important to supersede a constitutional right.
2. The limitations imposed on a right must be reasonable and justified using a "proportionality" test:
    a. the legislation or other action by the government must be designed to achieve the desired objective;
    b. the action by the government must impair rights as little as possible; and

c. the proportionality between the effects of the measures and the objectives desired must be of sufficient importance. (See the *Sparrow* [1990] and *Gladstone* [1996] decisions for further details.)

Moreover, the court ruled that, if the legislation imposes undue hardship or denies the holder of the right the preferred means of exercising it, then the legislation is inappropriate.

A SHORT HISTORY OF ABORIGINAL RIGHTS

To understand the concept of Aboriginal Rights fully and how it is now an integral part of Canadian law, it is useful to review various documents prepared by the government of Canada since they provide historical context for where we are at today. Some of the more salient documents demonstrate the changing relationship between Indigenous Peoples and the government.

THE ROYAL PROCLAMATION, 1763

This proclamation was issued by King George III following the British conquest of New France and the signing of the Treaty of Paris ending the Seven Years War. Under this proclamation, First Nations have collective legal rights derived from their prior occupation of their Traditional Territories (subject to colonial and then Canadian sovereignty). It also makes explicit that the federal crown has a unique fiduciary relationship with First Nations that creates a duty to act honourably in any dealing with them. Finally, it acknowledges that First Nations are a legally distinct group from other Canadians. The proclamation represents the federal crown's formal recognition of First Nations interest (Aboriginal Right) in land and the protection of such interests from third parties. Moreover, the proclamation confirms the existence of Aboriginal Title; it does not create it. It also stipulates that First Nations Lands can only be obtained by (transferred to) the federal crown if the First Nations agree to the surrender of such lands. The Royal Proclamation is still considered an important legal document by the courts.

THE *CONSTITUTION ACT, 1867*

A century later Canada emerged as its own state and created its own *British North America Act*, 1867, which would serve as its formal Constitution. At the time, the Fathers of Confederation divided the country into two domains: federal and provincial. Section 91(24) of that Act says that the primary responsibility for "Indians and Indian land" is assumed by the federal government. Moreover, the provinces cannot legislate or infringe on certain matters, such as First Nations status. However, they can incidentally affect First Nations when exercising their section 92 powers. Over time, responsibilities to First Nations have been allocated to various federal ministries, such as Agriculture, Industry, and today Crown-Indigenous Relations and Northern Affairs Canada and Indigenous Services Canada. The *British North America Act* also says that any lands subject to unextinguished Aboriginal Title are section 91(24) lands. Finally, it says that the constitutional authority for the federal government to act does not translate into a "duty to act." For example, the federal government is "responsible" for Inuit, yet it chose not to implement specific legislation regarding them as it did for First Nations. Over the years, the federal and provincial governments have been in conflict over who has financial jurisdiction over Indigenous Peoples. Today urban Indigenous people are the focus of this conflict, and in many cases the jurisdictional wrangles have not been fully resolved.

THE *INDIAN ACT, 1876*

Prior to the *Indian Act*, many pieces of legislation relevant to First Nations were implemented. For example, the *Act for the Better Protection of the Lands and Property of Indians in Lower Canada* and the *Act for the Better Protection of the Indians in Upper Canada from Imposition, and the Property Occupied or Enjoyed by Them from Trespass and Injury* were in force by 1850. Seven years later *An Act for the Gradual Civilization of the Indian Tribes in the Canadas* was passed, and it was followed by the *Management of Indian Lands and Property Act* of 1869. So many different Acts related to First Nations were in force that politicians could not keep track of their contents or be consistent in developing new policies. They thus consolidated the various

Acts that pertained to First Nations into the *Indian Act, 1876*. For the first time, there was a single document that outlined the duties and responsibilities of the federal government regarding First Nations. Over the years, numerous amendments have been made, though the Act of today is remarkably like the original one. (See Box 4 for examples of amendments to the Act.)

BOX 4

AMENDMENTS TO THE *INDIAN ACT* IN THE TWENTIETH CENTURY

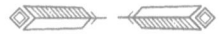

In 1880, Indigenous Peoples were prohibited from selling agricultural products without the consent of the Indian agent. More amendments were made early in the twentieth century. In 1905, the Act allowed Indigenous people to be removed from reserves (and the lands) next to or partially within a town having more than 8,000 people. By 1918, the land on a reserve could be leased to non-Indigenous people if the superintendent general thought that the lease could contribute to the market economy. A 1920 amendment to the Indian Act noted that First Nations had to get permission from the Indian agent if they wanted to appear in traditional dress outside the reserve. It also stated that discretional enfranchisement of all First Nations people would be determined by a board of examination established by the Department of Indian Affairs. Further revisions to the *Indian Act* also permitted Indian Affairs to do away with hereditary leadership and to invoke elections. In 1930, an amendment included a clause restricting the sale of wild animals and furs by First Nations people. By 1936, amendments allowed the Indian agent to participate in band council voting and cast a deciding vote if there was a tie. Moreover, the enfranchisement component of the Act remained and stipulated that any Indigenous person who received a university degree or became a lawyer, doctor, or clergyman would no longer be a Status Indian. In 1951, many of these egregious components of the *Indian Act* were removed, though it still determined who was an "Indian." In this revision, the "double mother" rule altered this determination. Then in 1985 the government changed the criteria for who is an "Indian" and can have her or his name on the roll. It allowed for nearly 100,000 people to become "Indians" overnight. In 1989, Sharon McIvor, an Indigenous woman, launched her sex equality challenge to the *Indian Act*, suing the federal government under section 15 of the Charter. In 2007, the BC Supreme Court ruled in favour of McIvor and forced the federal government to amend the *Indian Act* again regarding its definition of who is an "Indian." However, this decision was challenged (*McIvor v Canada* 2009), and the BC Court of Appeal narrowed the scope of who could be included in the registration and left it to Parliament to decide how to fix the problem of sex discrimination. A further appeal by McIvor to the Supreme Court of Canada was not accepted.

ST. CATHARINES MILLING AND LUMBER COMPANY v THE QUEEN (1888)

This case became the "gold standard" that courts used in subsequent cases regarding Aboriginal Rights and Title. The decision regarded the division of legislative powers and property rights under the *Constitution Act, 1867*. The case began after Canada negotiated Treaty Three with the Anishinaabe (1873) and argued that it was entitled, under the treaty and section 91(24) of the *Constitution Act, 1867*, to administer treaty lands. The crown issued a federal permit to a private company to cut timber on the land designated as part of Treaty Three. However, that permit was challenged by Ontario, which argued that control over lands and resources belonged to it and that federal permits to cut timber were invalid. Ontario claimed that section 91(24) of the *British North America Act* extended only to lands set aside as reserves.

The Privy Council (the highest court at the time in Canada) ruled that Parliament had authority over lands set aside for reserves. However, it ruled that, after land was set aside for the Anishinaabe under Treaty Three, the remaining land was under the control of the province. The federal government had no property rights, nor did the treaty show that the Anishinaabe were intended to have any beneficial interest in timber revenues. The Privy Council also said that its decision kept the Anishinaabe from obtaining any beneficial interest in lands and resources outside the reserve established under the treaty. Nevertheless, the Privy Council ruled that under Treaty Three the Anishinaabe ceded and released the territory in dispute in order that it might be opened for settlement or other purposes. Thus, it was taken as "fact" that the British crown had title to and sovereignty over the Traditional Territory of the Anishinaabe even before the treaty was signed. Under this ruling, Aboriginal Title was described not as a constitutional right but as a "burden" on the underlying crown title, whose existence was dependent on the goodwill of the sovereign.

In *St. Catharines Milling*, the Privy Council ruled that the benefit of these surrenders by First Nations was not to the federal government but to the provinces and that the lands fell to the provinces under section 109 of the *Constitution Act, 1867*. Not only was the federal government saddled with the financial obligations incurred in establishing the treaties, but also it could not seek reimbursement from the provinces. In addition, the federal government lost its legal capability to deliver to First Nations the promised reserves because now it was necessary to secure provincial cooperation, and of course the provinces often refused to release certain lands for reserves. In the end, Ontario was successful in protecting lumber, mining, and other natural resource interests since Ottawa chose not to deal with the issue any further. Meanwhile, many First Nations went without reserves and experienced social and economic disintegration since it was accepted that they had no Aboriginal Title to land. It took a series of federal and provincial agreements, culminating in 1924 in the *Indian Lands Act*, to solve the problems created by this decision.

The Privy Council also ruled that First Nations did not have sovereignty over or Aboriginal Title to lands, though individuals did have personal and usufructuary rights (e.g., the right to occupy and use crown land that was unoccupied). However, even those rights were dependent on the goodwill of the crown. Although the federal government lost the *St. Catharines Milling* case, it is amazing that, after the decision, it did not change its procedures for negotiating with First

Nations. Instead of requiring and obtaining enforceable legal obligations or equivalents from the provinces before these surrenders, or at least before transfers of lands to the provinces, Ottawa persisted in the same old strategy of establishing treaties.

THE *NATURAL RESOURCES TRANSFER ACT, 1930*

The western provinces had long chafed knowing that the eastern provinces held control over lands and natural resources and that this control had been given the force of law by the *St. Catharines Milling* case in 1888. After considerable debate and tension, in 1930 the federal government agreed to transfer ownership of natural resources to the four western provinces. Although there are some specific differences in the agreements with these provinces, overall they are very similar. For example, British Columbia had surrendered certain portions of its natural resources and crown lands to the federal government when it had entered Confederation in 1871, and it wanted to re-establish its control. After implementation of the agreements, the British Parliament passed the *Constitution Act, 1930* to ratify the agreements, thereby entrenching them in the Constitution. Today, however, there are unresolved issues in the Atlantic provinces and Quebec in dealing with unextinguished Aboriginal Title to land regarding their ability to manage lands and resources subject to claims of Aboriginal Title since these are federal lands.

THE *INDIAN ACT, 1951*

For much of the first part of the twentieth century, major issues of the rights of First Nations remained in the background of federal policy and legislation (even though there were many changes to the *Indian Act*). After the Second World War, the situation came to a head in 1951 when the federal government made major changes to the Act to deal with both domestic and international pressures.

At the end of the war, a series of events had a liberating effect on First Nations, which began the modern-day challenge to establish their Aboriginal Rights. Since as many as 20,000 Indigenous people served in the military during the Second World War, they experienced for the first time temporary escape from the control of various domestic laws (e.g., the *Indian Act*). Moreover, they experienced a modicum of "equality" while in the military, albeit not at the level that Indigenous soldiers were equal to non-Indigenous soldiers. Nevertheless, there was more equality and freedom from discrimination than they had experienced back in Canada (Harrison 1985).

In addition, after returning home from the war, Indigenous soldiers discovered that payments to their dependants while they were overseas, as well as their own benefits as veterans on their return, were not equal to those that non-Indigenous people received. It was at this time that Indigenous activism was born (Dobbin 1981). Although Canadians grudgingly accepted that Indigenous soldiers had served Canada well, they argued that Indigenous people were "wards" of the government and thus would receive other compensation that would make up the difference between what was paid to non-Indigenous and Indigenous military personnel. So neither Veterans Affairs nor Indian Affairs took any action to deal with the inequity. Moreover, Indigenous men returning to Canada found themselves unable to obtain jobs because of discrimination and stereotypes attributed to them; in some cases, they found themselves involuntarily enfranchised.

Other international atrocities (e.g., the Holocaust) were placed on the political agendas of countries, and thus the birth of Aboriginal Rights began. All of this must be juxtaposed with the content of the *Indian Act, 1951*. From the initial Act of 1876 to the 1950s, the powers of Indian Affairs and Indian agents on reserves grew exponentially. Over time, Indian agents gained more and more control over deciding who would be "enfranchised," and thus they could remove people from the reserve (and/or the roll)—which they did with great regularity. "Troublemakers" as well as those who had obtained advanced educational credits were unilaterally removed from the roll. In many cases, the agents acted as justices of the peace, making judgments on criminal matters. They managed the money for the band and sometimes for individuals. Under the *Indian Act*, the "pass" system was implemented ostensibly to limit the opportunities for Indigenous people to meet and organize outside reserves. It also limited parents' ability to visit their children attending residential schools. Moreover, Indigenous people could not sell agricultural products or furs without a licence issued by Indian Affairs. All of these measures of control in the *Indian Act* contributed to the origins of marginality and poverty on the reserves.

Thus, when the *Indian Act* was revised in 1951, while much of the Act remained in place, there were some major changes. For example, the pass system was removed, and the *Tamanawas* dances (west coast First Nations ceremonies and initiation rituals), Sundances, and Potlatches were no longer considered illegal. The new Act also removed the clause that made it illegal for any lawyer/barrister to assist a band with land issues. Finally, under the new Act, provincial voting rights were implemented. These changes brought about massive structural, legal, and social changes for Indigenous people and provoked the modern emergence of Indigenous activism.

THE 1969 WHITE PAPER

In 1969, the federal Liberal government introduced the White Paper that would have done away with the legal concept of an "Indian." Although a coalition of Indigenous, human rights, civil rights, and religious organizations was successful in forcing the government to abandon the legislation, for the next twenty years successive governments attempted to introduce variants of it in disguised forms. As Harold Cardinal, an outspoken First Nations political activist, noted at the time, Indigenous people had a stake in building Canada and would no longer tolerate the "white man" telling them what they could and could not do (Cardinal 1969). Subsequent Indigenous position documents (e.g., the "Brown Paper," *Wabung*, the "Red Paper") made it clear that Indigenous Peoples had their own views regarding their roles in building Canada. In the end, the government withdrew the proposed legislation, though some of the principles are still part of the mandate of Crown-Indigenous Relations and Northern Affairs Canada as well as Indigenous Services Canada.

THE *CONSTITUTION ACT, 1982* AND THE *CHARTER OF RIGHTS AND FREEDOMS*

A decade would pass after the White Paper was published before any further substantive changes were made regarding Indigenous issues. Then, in 1982, repatriation of the *Constitution Act, 1867* was approved, and the *Charter of Rights and Freedoms* became part of the new *Constitution Act, 1982*. The Charter acknowledges the existence of Indigenous Peoples, affirms their existing Aboriginal or Treaty Rights prior to 1982, and establishes that Aboriginal Rights are legally enforceable, recognized by Canadian common law. Several other Acts are part of the Constitution, for example the *Manitoba Act, 1870*, which sets out, in principle, the basic operations of Canadian society and its government, as does the Royal Proclamation of 1763. These Acts are thus part of the Constitution and as such supersede other federal or provincial legislation if it conflicts with a provision in the Constitution. The *Constitution Act, 1982* has become the scale by which the federal government's behaviour toward Indigenous Peoples is assessed by Canadians.

However, this means that the *Constitution Act, 1982* is only as respectful of human rights as the government and citizens of the day. The *Charter of Rights and Freedoms* constitutes the first section of the Constitution. Aboriginal Rights are specifically addressed in Part II of the Constitution, specifically in section 35, though other sections might be important in deciding Aboriginal Rights in the future. However, section 35 has become the most widely used and thus far has yielded the most change in relations between Indigenous and non-Indigenous people. To illustrate the applicability of these sections, I provide the relevant components of the Constitution.

Section 2 begins thus:

> 2. Everyone has the following fundamental freedoms:
> (a) freedom of conscience and religion; (b) freedom of thought, belief, opinion and expression, including freedom of the press and other media of communication; (c) freedom of peaceful assembly; and (d) freedom of association.

These freedoms apply to each Canadian and all levels of government. These rights have roots in the Canadian Bill of Rights.

Section 15 states that

> 15(1) Every individual is equal before and under the law and has the right to the equal protection and equal benefit of the law without discrimination....

15(2) Subsection (1) does not preclude any law, program or activity that has as its object the amelioration of conditions of disadvantaged individuals or groups including those that are disadvantaged because of race, national or ethnic origin....

Thus, section 15 provides that all individuals are equal before and under the law and have the right to equal protection, and the equality rights do not prevent laws, programs, or activities designed to assist disadvantaged individuals or groups.

Section 25 permits the courts to balance such rights with the rights of Indigenous people:

25. The guarantee in this Charter of certain rights and freedoms shall not be construed so as to abrogate or derogate from any aboriginal, treaty or other rights and freedoms that pertain to the aboriginal people of Canada including:
   a. Any rights or freedoms that have been recognized by the Royal Proclamation of October 7, 1763 and
   b. Any rights or freedoms that now exist by way of land claims agreements or may be so acquired.

Section 28 states that, "notwithstanding anything in this Charter, the rights and freedoms referred to in it are guaranteed equally to male and female persons."

Finally, section 35 states that

(1) The existing aboriginal and treaty rights of the aboriginal peoples of Canada are hereby recognized and affirmed.
(2) In this Act, "aboriginal peoples of Canada" include Indian, Inuit and Métis people of Canada.
(3) In subsection (1), it says that treaty rights include rights that now exist by way of land claims agreements or may be so acquired.

The significance of the new Constitution is that Canada acknowledges that these rights emerge from the traditions of Indigenous Peoples prior to the arrival of Europeans. In addition, the Charter recognizes that Aboriginal Rights are collective in that an Indigenous community holds them even if they are enjoyed by individuals (e.g., hunting rights). Finally, the Constitution recognizes Treaty Rights. It also notes that, whether the treaties are Peace and Friendship Treaties, Numbered Treaties, or modern claims agreements, the contents of most of those treaties are legally binding.

The Charter guarantees political rights to all Canadian citizens and ensures that the civil rights of everyone are acknowledged. Prior to the Charter, Canada implemented a Canadian Bill of Rights in 1960. However, it was a federal statute and not a constitutional document. As such, it was limited in scope, easily amended by Parliament, and had no application to provincial laws. The new *Constitution Act, 1982* changed all of that. The Charter and section 35 represent major changes in Canadian law. In terms of Indigenous relations, the federal and provincial governments acknowledge that Aboriginal Rights exist, and they must justify infringements or extinguishments of Aboriginal Rights.

Repatriation of the Constitution and introduction of the Charter have fundamentally changed how Canada deals with Indigenous Peoples. Moreover, once the constitutional changes were fully understood by Indigenous communities, they began to challenge actions taken by the government of Canada toward them. This challenge has led to considerable involvement by the courts in trying to assess the propriety of government actions as well as how to right the injustices that Indigenous Peoples feel have been perpetrated in the past.

The intervention of the courts in government-Indigenous relations was also the result of a political stalemate. The federal government was not promoting Aboriginal Rights, so Indigenous Peoples looked to the courts for resolution of various issues. Court interventions from 1972 to 1992 influenced political leaders to deal with many Indigenous issues raised by Indigenous groups. For example, land claims became important in the early years. *Calder* (1973) was the first major shift in federal policy on First Nations land claims. In addition, there were strong and persistent scholarly attempts to persuade the courts to reassess their views on a variety of Indigenous issues. However, as McHugh (2015) points out, for most of the 1980s the constitutional conferences among Indigenous Peoples, provincial governments, and the federal government diverted interest from Aboriginal Rights and specifically section 35 as a way of resolving Indigenous issues. However, once the conferences were over and no new decisions or policies emerged from them, First Nations began to look at section 35 as a strategy to move forward on resolving issues.

For years, the courts used common law to try to resolve First Nations land claims. However, the Supreme Court recognized that common law was inappropriate to resolve many Indigenous claims. It moved away from this approach and now focuses on the "honour of the crown" and "the duty to consult" as the strategies to deal with land claims. Property rights law is now on its way out as a means of settling claims (McHugh 2015). The questions now facing Canadians are, What is an Aboriginal Right? What are the criteria for establishing an Aboriginal Right? The courts have been active in trying to establish criteria to verify an Aboriginal Right. In the beginning, the focus was on First Nations and Inuit and their rights, but more recently Métis and Non-Status Indians also have been acknowledged as having specific rights. I now turn to the criteria for establishing an Aboriginal Right as defined by the Supreme Court of Canada. To be sure, not all Indigenous Peoples find this method of determining Aboriginal Rights proper or legitimate.

ABORIGINAL RIGHTS (FIRST NATIONS AND INUIT)

As noted earlier, the *Calder* case (1973) would open "Pandora's box" and establish that Indigenous Peoples do have some "rights" beyond those of non-Indigenous people. When the Charter was implemented a decade later, it gave further legitimacy to the claims of Indigenous Peoples, and though politicians did not address the issues the courts were thrust into their midst.

However, it was not until 1984 (the *Guerin* case) that Aboriginal Rights were defined by the courts as *sui generis* (meaning unique), and the courts agreed that using general property tort law is inappropriate when dealing with Indigenous property cases. Then, five years later, the *Sparrow* case (1990) ruled that Aboriginal Rights were protected, and those rights can be extinguished only with First Nations consent.

Sparrow was the first decision of the Supreme Court to interpret section 35(1). Prior to this case, lower courts had offered a range of conflicting views on its nature and scope. But the Supreme Court ruling also said that there was never any doubt that sovereignty and legislative powers underlying title were vested in the crown. The court also held that Aboriginal Title is a communally held right regarding land. Aboriginal Title confers the right of exclusive occupation and use of land for a variety of activities. Since that time, there has been a constitutional obligation of the government to consult with First Nations when exercising authority in ways that might interfere with Aboriginal or Treaty Rights (Macklem and Sanderson 2016, 1). In 1997, the *Delgamuukw* decision added clarity in the trial involving the Gitxsan and Wet'suwet'en regarding Aboriginal Rights and Title. However, the court ruled that Aboriginal Rights may be infringed (some might say diminished) by the government, but there must be good reasons for such action, and compensation must follow.

The *Van der Peet* test (1996) devised by the Supreme Court assumed that Aboriginal Rights are shaped entirely by factors specific to each First Nations community. Moreover, the court believed that they are specific rights rather than generic rights. However, over time, the court has rethought its earlier decision in three ways. First, it has relaxed its exclusive focus on specific rights and recognizes the existence of generic rights—uniform rights that operate at an abstract level and reflect broader normative considerations. Second, the court recognizes that the date of European contact is not the appropriate reference point in all contexts. Third, the court has placed a greater emphasis on the need for Aboriginal Rights to be defined by negotiations between the parties (Slattery 2016). By the end of 2014, the Supreme Court had made numerous pronouncements regarding Aboriginal Rights, and for the first time in Canadian history a First Nation was given title to a large section of south-central British Columbia (*Tsilhqot'in Nation v British Columbia* 2014) under a robust definition of Aboriginal Title.

Thus far, two generic rights have been recognized by the courts: Aboriginal Title and the Aboriginal Right of cultural integrity. In situations in which the crown has assumed discretionary control over specific First Nations interests, the honour of the crown gives rise to fiduciary duties that require the crown to act in a First Nation's best interests in exercising its discretion (Slattery 2016). Specific rights are concrete instances of generic rights. For example, the right to receive honourable treatment by the crown is a high level of abstraction, but from that right might flow intermediate and specific rights (Slattery 2016).

Overall, the Supreme Court has defined an Aboriginal Right as an element of a custom, practice, or traditional activity integral to the culture of a First Nation claiming a "right" not extinguished prior to 1982. The court has developed a protocol for assessing an Aboriginal Rights claim. However, it must be reiterated that Aboriginal Rights are considered communal rights and not individual rights even though all of the court cases are identified as an individual versus the government. However, individuals may carry out those rights if they belong to an Indigenous community that existed historically. So the courts have ruled that these rights are grounded in the activities of a historical Indigenous group.

When an Indigenous claimant brings a case (claiming a right) to the court, it first determines whether there is an existing Aboriginal Right. To do so, the court considers five elements of the claim. The first element is one of the most important in that the claimant must ensure that the "right" in question is identified precisely. The characterization must be specific since it is well known that the Supreme Court has consistently rejected Aboriginal Rights claims not clearly specified. An example is gambling. A claimant might argue that gambling is an Aboriginal Right. But this claim would probably be too general, and the court would likely dismiss the case. Alternatively, if the right being claimed is to establish and operate a casino (high stakes) under Indigenous law, then this would be an acceptable claim because of its specificity. The court would then assess this characterization by considering the nature of the government regulation, statute, or action affecting that right. The Indigenous claimant might argue that the Criminal Code of Canada negates the Aboriginal Right to operate a casino according to Indigenous law.

Having addressed this issue and finding the rights claim reasonable, the court considers the second element, establishing the geographical location of the right. Here the court would ask whether the claimed Aboriginal Right is site specific. The claimant must now present evidence on where and how the traditional activity took place. In short, did high-stakes gambling take place in specific Indigenous communities, and how was gambling practised in those communities? The claimant would have to specify the location where gambling occurred in terms of a community, region, and province. Again, the degree of clarity and specificity in the claim determine whether the court would move forward.

The third element to be investigated by the court is that of time. Here the Indigenous claimant must provide evidence that the traditional practice of high-stakes gambling existed prior to contact with settlers. The nature of the evidence might vary, but in most cases oral testimony is not accepted by the court as "evidence." However, the *Delgamuukw* case (1997) opened the possibility that oral evidence could be used to substantiate a claim.

Continuity is the fourth element that the Supreme Court considers to establish the validity of an Aboriginal Right. This element focuses on whether the applicant can demonstrate that the activity claimed as an Aboriginal Right was practised historically and is still being practised. The court has argued that the doctrine of Aboriginal Rights is based upon a commitment to protect Indigenous practices that were important historically—something that was not done in the past. Thus, the court attempts to establish whether high-stakes gambling was part of the traditional culture of a specific community and whether it is still practised today (i.e., continuity). Over time, the court has relaxed its definition of continuity, and the activity undertaken today does not have to be an exact mirror of what took place in historical times. Nevertheless, there must be enough "overlap" of the activities to qualify as continuity.

The fifth element is that the activity must be "integral to distinctive culture." Originally, the court claimed that the activity had to be "distinct," but this was subsequently clarified to mean "distinctive." The claimant must prove that the asserted right was an "integral" component of the culture of the precontact Indigenous community. In *R v Van der Peet* (1996), the Supreme Court ruled thus:

To satisfy the integral to a distinctive culture test the Aboriginal Claimant must do more than demonstrate that a practice, tradition or custom was an aspect of, or took place in, the Aboriginal society of which he or she is a part. The claimant must demonstrate that the practice, tradition or custom was a central and significant part of the society's distinctive culture.

He or she must demonstrate that the practice, tradition or custom was one of the things which made the culture of the society distinctive—that it was one of the things that truly made the society what it was. (para 69)

In the example of high-stakes gambling, the case of *R v Pamajewon* (1996) is instructive. In this case, the First Nations communities of Shawanaga and Eagle Lake had passed initiatives that allowed for such gambling to take place on their reserves subject to Indigenous law. Since the government claimed that the laws were not valid under the *Indian Act* and violated the federal Criminal Code, several First Nations people were convicted of illegal gaming activities. However, the claimants argued in court that they had the right to operate casinos (high-stakes gambling) and regulate their activities on reserves because they had an Aboriginal Right to manage the use of their reserve lands. In response, the Supreme Court said that this claim was too vague to address. In fact, the court took the unusual step of redefining the claim of Aboriginal Right and stated that the appellant's claim was that section 35(1) "recognizes and affirms the rights of the Shawanaga and Eagle Lake First Nations to participate in, and regulate, gambling activities on their respective reserve lands" (4). Nevertheless, it found that the characterization of the right was not specific enough to rule on it. The court went on to say that, even if the claim was specific enough (as redefined), the right to deal with high-stakes gambling was never part of the Indigenous culture of the claimants and thus rejected their claim. The Supreme Court ruled that the right to self-government, if it exists, is subject to what it defined as "reasonable limitations," but the right to high-stakes gambling was beyond a reasonable activity in the traditional First Nations communities that brought the claim to the court.

LIMITATIONS ON ABORIGINAL RIGHTS

As noted above, the first question that courts must answer is whether there is an Aboriginal Right as the claimants argue. The government of Canada argues that it has the responsibility to act in a manner that honours the crown regarding Indigenous Peoples, and the courts have ruled that the relationship between the crown and Indigenous Peoples is that of trust. It is not to be an adversarial relationship. The crown thus recognizes and affirms the concept of Aboriginal Rights as defined in the historical context of Indigenous-crown relations. Therefore, the crown has the duty to work with Indigenous Peoples to develop regulations that do not diminish or invalidate Aboriginal Rights. If, following the process outlined above, the courts determine that there is an Aboriginal Right, they must then answer the following questions if they are about to take some action that diminishes or extinguishes that right:

- Has the Aboriginal Right been extinguished? If so, how?
- Does the legislation in question interfere with an existing Aboriginal Right? If so,
    a. Is the limitation reasonable?
    b. Does the limitation impose an undue hardship?
    c. Does the regulation deny to the holders of the right their preferred means of exercising that right?
- Can that infringement be justified?
    - Is the legislation in question of sufficient import to warrant an infringement of a constitutional right?
    - The limitations imposed must be reasonably and demonstrably justified using a "proportionality" test that involves the following.
        - The measure must be designed to achieve the desired object.
        - The measure must impair rights as little as possible.
        - The proportionality between the effects of the measures and the objectives desired must be of sufficient importance.

The court begins by asking whether there is a *prima facie* infringement of that right. If the legislation enacted denies the Indigenous holder of his or her right of preferred means of exercising that right, then the court would rule that the legislation is invalid. In addition, if the law imposes undue hardship on the right holder, then the court would rule against the law. (See Box 5 for how government circumvented this rule.)

In summary, the Supreme Court has ruled that the doctrine of Aboriginal Rights exists and is recognized because, at the time of contact with settlers, Indigenous Peoples were living in Canada in well-organized communities and as distinctive cultures. Moreover, the Supreme Court has ruled that section 35 of the Constitution should be interpreted in a purposive way and that the courts' rulings on treaties and statutes related to First Nations should be liberally construed and doubtful expressions resolved in favour of First Nations. This interpretation began in 1951 when the *Indian Act* was amended so that provincial laws of general application were subject to treaties. This meant that individuals charged with violations of provincial laws could raise Treaty Rights (promises) in defence of their actions. For example, in *R v White and Bob* (1965), the Supreme Court considered this defence and ruled that treaties should be interpreted broadly in favour of Indigenous Peoples and in a manner that upholds the honour of the crown (Coyle 2005). However, this ruling was not revisited until the Supreme Court decision in 1983 in *The Queen v Nowegijick*, one year after repatriation of the Constitution.

BOX 5

TAXES AND TREATY INTERPRETATION

Gene Nowegijick was a Status Indian living on a reserve, employed by an Indigenous corporation having its head and administrative offices on the reserve, and paid at the head office. However, the actual work was done off the reserve. Nowegijick claimed that his personal income was exempt from taxation through section 87 of the *Indian Act*. The court ruled that no Indigenous person should be subject to taxation for personal property on a reserve. And, since income is personal property, taxable income is equally personal property. Thus, the effect of section 87 of the *Indian Act* is not only to exempt direct taxation on property but also to exempt Indigenous people from taxation.

If the statute contains language that can reasonably be construed to confer a tax exemption, then it is to be favoured over a more technical interpretation that might be available to deny the exemption. Consequently, if the employer is on the reserve, then anyone who works for that employer earns tax-free personal income. However, this decision was unilaterally changed in 1993 by Revenue Canada. Under the amendments, the condition that an employer is situated on a reserve is not sufficient to warrant a tax exemption for someone working for that employer. It is a necessary but not a sufficient factor. Today the tax exemption on personal income for First Nations people applies only to the following situations:

- employment income for duties performed entirely on the reserve;
- employment income for duties performed entirely off the reserve but where the employer and the First Nations person reside on the reserve;
- employment income for duties most of which are performed on the reserve and either the employer or the First Nations person resides on the reserve;
- unemployment or pension income; and
- employment income (prorated) from duties performed both on and off the reserve.

MÉTIS RIGHTS

As noted earlier, the term "Métis" in section 35 of the Constitution does not encompass all individuals with a mixed Indigenous and European heritage; rather, it refers to distinctive peoples who, in addition to their mixed ancestry, developed their own customs, language, ways of life, and recognizable group identities separate from their First Nations or Inuit and European forebears. The Métis were not considered a distinct or legal group by either the government or the courts after 1885 until late in the twentieth century. However, an anomaly exists in Alberta, where Métis were given both recognition and legal standing beginning in 1938 on the recommendations of the Ewing Commission. Alberta passed the *Métis Population Betterment Act*, which set aside "colonies" (now called settlements) for Métis. In doing so, Alberta became the first and only province in Canada to enact legislation specific to Métis and to give them legal standing before the courts. In all other provincial jurisdictions (with some exceptions in Saskatchewan), the Métis are not recognized as a distinct Indigenous group. Canada gave people two choices: they could be either "Indian" or "non-Indian."

Then in 1993 two Métis were charged with hunting moose out of season and possessing game. The defendants argued that they had Métis Rights to hunt for domestic purposes. Ten years later, after several appeals by the federal government, the case was decided by the Supreme Court, which recognized and affirmed that Métis were a distinct Indigenous People with existing rights. These rights were protected by section 35 of the *Constitution Act, 1982*.

The court went on to offer its guidance on how one could be defined as a Métis Rights holder. It ruled that the appropriate way to define Métis Rights in section 35 is to modify the test used to define the Aboriginal Rights of First Nations (the *Van der Peet* test). The Métis test is now called the *Powley* test, from the case in 2003 in which the Supreme Court established criteria to ascertain whether a person claiming to be a Métis would have certain hunting rights. The test is set out in several parts. First, the courts require that the claimant identify himself or herself as a Métis and that this claim be recognized by a Métis community. There must also be a clear and precise characterization of the right being claimed. Second, the individual must be able to demonstrate that she or he is part of a historical Métis community with a distinctive collective identity that resided in the same geographic area and shared common traditions. Third, this community must still be in existence and show how it is a continuation of the same historical Métis community. Fourth, there must be some verifiable process that identifies specific individuals of the Métis community—a kind of census of the community. Fifth, the individual must show that the community to which he or she is attached existed before it came under the effective control and influence of European laws and customs. Sixth, the Métis claimant must demonstrate that the right being claimed is integral to her or his distinctive culture. Seventh, the Métis claimant must show that the right being claimed reveals a continuity between the historical practice and the contemporary right; although the activity might not be an exact replica of past behaviour, there must be sufficient evidence to show a connection. Eighth, the right being claimed cannot have been extinguished; before 1982, this could have occurred by legislation passed unilaterally by the government or by agreement with an Indigenous People.

As noted earlier, the courts have ruled that no right is absolute, and this is as true for Métis Rights as for any other group rights. This means that Métis Rights can be limited (infringed) for various reasons. If an infringement is found to have occurred, then the government might be able to justify its action. Finally, the court ruled that the crown had to justify any infringement of Métis Rights, but the crown could not totally remove a right such as hunting. The question remains whether continual infringement or diminishment of Aboriginal Rights over time effectively eliminates them.

One might have expected the Supreme Court to invoke a similar recommendation for a generous application of Métis Rights following the *Powley* (2003) decision as it did for Aboriginal Rights following the *Van der Peet* (1996) decision. However, a liberal application of the *Powley* principles has been resisted. Instead, most provinces have insisted that the Métis must prove the existence of an individual Métis Rights–bearing community in court before they will apply the *Powley* test. In Saskatchewan, the Métis have been to court twice since *Powley* in the cases of *Laviolette* (2005) and *Belhumeur* (2007), and only after those two cases were successful did the Saskatchewan government agree to negotiate with the Métis toward a province-wide agreement that recognizes Métis harvesting rights in the province. In Manitoba, the provincial government agreed to negotiate a settlement only after *Goodon* (2008) and *Beer* (2012) went in favour of the Métis (Teillet 2013). The Métis Nation of Alberta signed a framework agreement in 2017 with the provincial government stipulating that they will work together on a nation-to-nation basis. It also identifies Métis harvesting rights and the socio-economic well-being of the more than 30,000 members of the Métis Nation of Alberta.

All of this is now back in the courts since Justice Phelan (2013) ruled that Métis and Non-Status Indians are in fact Indians. This was followed by the *Daniels* case (2016), in which Métis Rights were acknowledged in Manitoba. Notably, the definition provided above is used to determine whether a Métis has certain rights and is not a definition of who is a Métis. The latter definition has yet to be decided. *Daniels* focused on who was a federal responsibility under section 91(24) of the Constitution, and in the end the Supreme Court ruled that Métis and Non-Status Indians are the responsibility of the federal government. However, the court did not outline which specific benefits the Métis would gain from this new status. It opined that the Métis and the federal government would negotiate the specific benefits in the future. As a first step, the two groups need to define (independent of rights) who is a Métis.

MÉTIS AND NON-STATUS INDIANS

In 1982, a split occurred between the organizations that represented Métis and Non-Status Indians. The Métis National Council was created and represents the Métis in the three prairie provinces. The council argues that legal Métis are those who meet two conditions: (1) they must be accepted by the larger Métis community, and (2) they can trace their ancestry to someone who has lived in the historical Métis homeland. This homeland includes the three prairie provinces, though it can extend into parts of Ontario, British Columbia, and the Northwest Territories. This definition is contested by the Congress of Aboriginal Peoples that represents First Nations people living off reserve, Non-Status Indians, and Métis because, according to the Métis National Council, no one east of Manitoba could be a Métis. In addition, the congress argues, there is no formal, precise definition of the boundaries of the historical Métis homeland. At present, the legal definition of a Métis remains undetermined. A similar condition exists for people who consider themselves Non-Status Indians.

INDIGENOUS REACTIONS

Although the courts have acknowledged the existence of Aboriginal Rights, Indigenous Peoples have noted several concerns in the approach of the courts in determining those rights. First, the criteria for assessing whether an Aboriginal Right exists have been constructed by non-Indigenous people who accept Aboriginal law as well as tort law. No consultation with Indigenous Peoples on what might be appropriate criteria has taken place, and the courts have unilaterally imposed their definitions. Second, some of the criteria imposed are inappropriate. For example, the criterion of continuity flies in the face of cultural change and government action. In the past, government action has prevented Indigenous Peoples from practising certain aspects of their cultures. Third, the notion of continuity assumes an invariant culture over time when it is well documented that cultures change over time; this is sometimes called the "frozen" cultural model (Walters 2017a). Thus, to hold a culture to a condition of "no change over time" is inappropriate and simply wrong. Indigenous Peoples also argue that it is not for non-Indigenous people to tell them what is integral to their cultures. In fact, they challenge the courts to identify the criteria for what constitutes "integral" for any community.

CONCLUSION

The federal crown has not given unambiguous recognition of Aboriginal Rights to issues such as ownership of land. As such, Aboriginal Title is usually restricted and independent of self-government. Neither provincial nor federal governments have succeeded in reaching comprehensive political and/or legal accommodations with Indigenous Peoples with regard to their rights. Aboriginal Title and sovereignty are at the heart of historical and unending resistances, protests, and claims made by Indigenous Peoples.

The issue of Aboriginal Rights is new for Canadians, and it has changed the relationship between Indigenous and non-Indigenous people forever. In the early days, there was no differentiation between law and politics. However, over time, Macklem (2016) argues, law emerged as an autonomous and powerful sphere of society. The courts began to address the legal consequences of treaties. Until the late nineteenth century, the courts defined treaties as political agreements unenforceable in a court of law. Because colonial countries viewed Indigenous Peoples as uncivilized and dependent, they concluded that crown promises were not legally enforceable under either international or domestic law. Eventually, though, treaties became viewed as a kind of contract. As such, their terms were subject to the exercise of unilateral legislative authority. Thus, prior to 1982, Parliament could (and did) unilaterally regulate or extinguish existing Treaty Rights. Moreover, these rights were interpreted by the courts using non-Indigenous legal norms and values (Macklem 2016) and according to the written texts accepted by the government.

At present, Parliament chooses not to engage with the issue of Aboriginal Rights and lets the courts sort out the details. This approach places the government in a good position in that, if a court's decision is not popular, the government can claim that it did not make the decision. Moreover, the general population can express its dislike of certain decisions by castigating the courts. Conversely, if a decision is popular, the government can bask in the wisdom of the court. From the perspective of the courts (particularly the Supreme Court), they have been reluctant participants in resolving conflicts between Indigenous Peoples and the government regarding Aboriginal Rights. Many times the courts have noted that they do not have the expertise required to make decisions of this nature, but since Parliament refuses to make decisions they have cautiously entered the arena. Moreover, the courts have never consulted with Indigenous Peoples with regard to their definitions of rights. The Supreme Court is now in the process of making major decisions regarding Aboriginal Rights and setting a vision for Canada regarding those rights.

Nearly all First Nations communities have experienced significant changes stemming from contact with settlers and incorporation into the state. These transformations continue today as these communities affirm their persistence and express their legal, cultural, and political rights. Ideologies vary from community to community, and their intensity varies, but they are evident in almost every Indigenous community (Kroskrity and Field 2009).

CHAPTER 6

THE ROLE *of the* COURTS

The role of the courts in Canada in dealing with Indigenous issues is a recent phenomenon. Since repatriation of the Constitution, Indigenous Peoples have found that several sections of the *Charter of Rights and Freedoms* have provided them with entries into the courts with the goal of resolving some long-standing issues (e.g., Aboriginal Rights and Title). In this chapter, I address how the courts have become involved in dealing with Indigenous issues. I also show how the courts have evolved over time regarding their views on Indigenous issues. I review some of the major Supreme Court of Canada decisions regarding Indigenous claims and reveal how these decisions have created a new vision of how Canadians will need to interact with Indigenous Peoples in the future. I show that, from issues of fiduciary responsibility, trust, honour of the crown, and duty to consult, the Supreme Court has given the federal crown instructions on how negotiations should be carried out, how treaties should be interpreted, and how claims should be identified as Aboriginal Rights. Given the nature of this book, it is not possible to provide details of the various Supreme Court decisions, and I refer readers to specific cases if they are interested in the details.

PARLIAMENT VERSUS THE COURTS

Over the past three decades, court decisions have helped Canadians to understand better the boundaries of Aboriginal Rights, the contents of treaties, and how these rights relate to non-Indigenous Canadians. For example, the *Badger* case (1996) demonstrated that a treaty is not to be considered a political agreement or a contract. A treaty is now to be considered as having formal constitutional status, and the substance of the treaty must be determined in a way consistent with an Indigenous understanding of it. However, the courts have also made it abundantly clear that they are not the only institution that needs to address Aboriginal Rights. They argue that the crown must take steps to address and resolve Indigenous issues (Reilly 2014) so that they never enter the court system. Over the past decade, the federal crown has chosen to step aside from making tough political decisions regarding Indigenous concerns and claims and has allowed the courts to make decisions, which are then announced to the public (Gallagher 2012). The courts have thus come under considerable scrutiny as well as criticism by the crown and by some Canadians for setting a vision for Canada and making the rules regarding Indigenous people, particularly when they differ from the crown's agenda or run counter to the principles of capitalism. However, the courts have done so partially because of inaction by Parliament.

My focus here is on the decisions made by the Supreme Court of Canada. These decisions are not appealable and provide a vision of and direction for the rights and responsibilities of Canadians regarding Indigenous issues with which they deal. However, the Supreme Court has stated that it decides many cases individually, and thus no single case sets a precedent for future cases that might appear before the courts. Nevertheless, the Supreme Court has taken on many Indigenous cases over the past three decades, reflecting its willingness to commit to addressing Indigenous issues. Although the Supreme Court has ruled on numerous cases over the past thirty years, less than 7 percent of all the constitutional cases ruled on have focused on Aboriginal Rights. Nevertheless, this is more than were ruled on in the previous 100 years. A review of the Supreme Court cases reveals that well over 80 percent of those dealing with Aboriginal Rights have been "fact specific" and considered "guides" for the lower courts to use in deciding cases. Since 1982, Supreme Court decisions have informed Canada's understanding of the nature of section 35 of the Constitution. The court also stated that the purpose of section 35 is reconciliation of the pre-existence of Indigenous societies with the assertion of sovereignty of the crown and that negotiations represent the best approach to achieving reconciliation.

The involvement of the courts regarding Aboriginal Rights has a short but important history. The colonial administration pursued a process of litigation that shaped the rules of evidence that could be used in the courts. For example, the "hearsay rule" made it virtually impossible for Indigenous people and their legal supporters to bring forward cases based upon oral historical evidence. This rule is still generally enforced by the courts and restricts witnesses to present evidence from first-hand observation. It means that presenting historical evidence passed down orally by Indigenous leaders or Elders is unacceptable to the courts. Most judges are reluctant to accept the fact that Elders are the authorities on their histories and cultures. Ray (2016) also notes that this rule has limited the inferences that "experts" appearing in the court can draw from accounts in documentary records. Finally, even if non-written documentary evidence is accepted by the courts, the judge has the responsibility to decide how much weight will be given to the information compared to written documentary evidence. Most judges do not give much credence to hearsay evidence in deciding on the disposition of the case. However, it was not until 1997, when the Supreme Court ruled in the trial involving the Gitxsan and Wet'suet'en, that oral evidence was given some weight.

The new era of court proceedings begins with the historic *Calder v British Columbia (Attorney General)* decision (1973). In this case, Aboriginal Rights and Title were at the centre of the legal issue. Calder represented the Nisga'a Nation, which claimed Aboriginal Title to its Traditional Territory and argued that this title had not been extinguished by the crown since the territory in question had not been the subject of any treaty. When the Supreme Court made its decision, it was news to everyone. The court rejected the earlier decision by the

Privy Council that the Royal Proclamation of 1763 was the sole source of Aboriginal Title. It also rejected parts of the ruling in the *St. Catharines Milling and Lumber* case of 1888. Nevertheless, the court was split, with three justices ruling that Aboriginal Rights and Title existed, three ruling that they had been extinguished, and one deciding that the case was inappropriate for the Supreme Court to rule on and thus sided with those justices who did not support the concept of Aboriginal Rights and Title. This last justice said that the Nisga'a had not sought permission from the BC crown to proceed to sue the government, so he found in favour of the crown—not based upon the merits of the case but because of the process. As such, the court ruled four-three against the Nisga'a. Nevertheless, it demonstrated that there were substantive reasons for thinking that Aboriginal Rights to land did exist, and thus a new era in relations between Indigenous and non-Indigenous people emerged. From a legal point of view, the case affirmed that Aboriginal Rights (including to land) might exist and are not solely dependent on treaties, the crown, or legislative enactments for their existence. The Supreme Court ruled that the rights flowed from Indigenous Peoples' occupancy and use of their Traditional Territories.

Indigenous Peoples appreciate the role that the courts have played in dealing with the many issues and concerns that they have expressed. However, this has meant that the process of definition, evidence, and testimony is now in the legal arena, reflecting Canada's historical reliance on British or French jurisprudence. Monchalin (2016, 234) points out that, though at first glance the negotiating stance of the federal government looks like a positive step, it reveals that the government created these processes to expedite its own priorities, derived from a self-serving agenda rooted in colonialism. The singular focus on the "legal" aspects of a case has meant the subsequent diminishment of other concerns raised by Indigenous Peoples in the resolution of these cases. For example, collective harm is not considered an issue that the courts will address, and any reference to Indigenous law has been dismissed as unimportant or irrelevant. The focus on tort law has frustrated many Indigenous people, who prefer using "restorative justice."

Other limitations of the current legal system mean that the relationship between Indigenous Peoples and the land is dealt with strictly in terms of Canadian Aboriginal law and capitalist ideology. For example, in such a system, land is a commodity that can be individually (or corporately) owned, and its value is determined from a "value added" perspective, not by the collective or psychological attachment of Indigenous Peoples to their Traditional Territories. Remember that the development of a commodity refers to the relationship between exchange and use value (Coulthard 2014; Keith 2015). The usefulness of an object or material defines its value in pragmatic terms. This way of thinking about land is foreign to most Indigenous people, for whom land is not a commodity but has spiritual value and little exchange value. Land is part of the identities of Indigenous Peoples, and its spiritual and identity components are independent of exchange value. Land has use value in that it is part of the ceremonies and rituals carried out by Indigenous Peoples, and thus its maintenance is important. In the end, Indigenous Peoples are forced to accept land as a commodity even though they differ in their understanding of it. Conflict over land thus ensues between the two parties. Coulthard (2014) argues that traditional land-based practices known as "grounded normativity" comprise a critical component of what it means to be Indigenous. Grounded normativity conceptualizes land as a relationship with Indigenous Peoples based upon their obligations to it. It is a reciprocal relationship involving all aspects of Indigenous life. This relationship, in turn, provides the basis for resistance to further dispossession by contemporary colonialism through the Indigenous resurgence movement (Alfred and Corntassel 2005). Finally, Newman (2016) argues that the doctrine of the duty to consult keeps consultations with Indigenous communities in the hands of the government rather than under constant judicial supervision or the control of Indigenous Peoples.

CONSTITUTIONAL ARGUMENTS

The Constitution is considered the supreme law of the country, and as section 52 of the Constitution states, any law inconsistent with the provisions of the Constitution has no force or effect. Yet there is no direct remedy for breaches of constitutional rights. In other words, if the Supreme Court of Canada finds a law in breach of the Constitution, it can only say that the law in question has no effect and that the government should stop using it. Section 52 of the Constitution does not allow the court to punish or otherwise bring action against the agent who breaches the Constitution. If an individual wants to pursue restitution of the breach, then she or he must go to section 24 of the *Charter of Rights and Freedoms*, which allows one to apply to the courts for punishment or compensation. However, the "notwithstanding clause," section 33 of the Charter, mediates the impact of a breach. Currently, section 33 does not apply to the Aboriginal Rights stated in Part II of the Constitution.

Since introduction of the Charter, the courts have dealt with many Indigenous issues. Overall, the types of cases can be placed into five categories: Aboriginal Rights, Treaty Rights, duty to consult (honour of the crown), jurisdictional issues, and residual issues. I will illustrate how the courts have dealt with each of these issues.

ABORIGINAL RIGHTS

How have the courts justified their decisions regarding Aboriginal Rights? *R v Sparrow* (1990) was the first case that the Supreme Court of Canada dealt with regarding Aboriginal Rights after repatriation of the Constitution and introduction of the Charter. In this case, the court also addressed whether an Aboriginal Right had been extinguished.

The case involved fishing in British Columbia by a First Nations person. Ronald Sparrow, using an "Indian Food" fishing licence that his band (Musqueam) had obtained under the *Fisheries Act*, was charged with violating the content of the Act. The government claimed that he was using a net larger than that allowed under the Act. Sparrow argued that his First Nations community had been fishing in the Fraser River for over 1,500 years and that salmon was an integral part of their daily diet and traditional culture. He argued that his community had an Aboriginal Right to fish in the river and that the *Fisheries Act* contravened that right. Moreover, since the Musqueam had been doing this for so long, the continuity and place criteria were met since he was claiming an Aboriginal Right only for his community.

At the trial, the crown argued that Sparrow, by using a net larger than was acceptable to the provincial game laws, was catching more fish than he or his family could eat in the foreseeable future. The crown also argued that many other bands, commercial fishers, and recreational fishers used the river to catch salmon. The crown's expert witness claimed that an average Indigenous person could eat 100 salmon a year and that the net size prescribed under the *Fisheries Act* would allow him to catch that number. The larger size of net used by Sparrow would allow him to catch well beyond 100 salmon. Finally, the prosecution noted that Sparrow's First Nations community had never signed a treaty with the government, and thus any Aboriginal Right that he might have had before repatriation of the Constitution had been extinguished by both federal and provincial legislation.

At his initial trial, Sparrow was found guilty. The trial judge accepted the argument by the prosecution that federal and provincial legislation implicitly extinguished any Aboriginal Right that Sparrow might have had regarding fishing. The case was appealed to the BC County Court, which upheld the trial judge's decision. The case then went to the BC Court of Appeal, which found that the trial judge's findings of facts were insufficient to lead to an acquittal. Its decision was appealed and cross-appealed. However, the BC Court of Appeal noted that extinguishment by regulation (or implicit extinguishment) cannot be used as evidence that a right has been extinguished. Moreover, it ruled that, if First Nations did not have a special right regarding the fishery, then why did the *Fisheries Act* make specific mention of them and limit the size of their nets? If all of their fishing rights had been extinguished, they should be treated just like all other people catching fish. The court also noted that, even though the First Nations community had not signed a treaty, the *Charter of Rights and Freedoms* applied. It noted that section 35(1) of the Constitution should be read to include both a Treaty and an Aboriginal Right to fish. However, it found that the defence had not provided appropriate evidence, so the court sent the case back for a new trial with explicit instructions to the trial judge not to consider the regulations in his or her decision-making. Both parties appealed the decision, and eventually the case was taken up by the Supreme Court.

After hearing the case, the Supreme Court came to a unanimous decision. It ruled that the facts of the case met all of the criteria outlined in the *Baker Lake* decision (1979) to establish an Aboriginal Right. The court went on to say that the *Fisheries Act* itself was valid since its objective was to conserve the fish stock but not to regulate an Indigenous person's behaviour per se. It asserted that the argument that an average Indigenous person eats 100 salmon a year and thus should be limited to that number was invalid. That argument, the court said, regulated First Nations people's eating behaviour and had nothing to do with the conservation goals of the *Fisheries Act*. Since the Act was a conservation issue, the Charter did not apply.

The Supreme Court went on to rule that section 35(1) applied to Aboriginal Rights in existence when the Constitution was repatriated; it did not revive extinguished rights. It also ruled that both levels of government had failed to prove that the First Nations community's Aboriginal Right to fish had been extinguished. The court noted that section 35(1) does not promise immunity from government regulations in contemporary society, but it does hold the crown to a substantive promise. The government is required to justify any legislation that has a negative effect on any Aboriginal Right protected under the Constitution. The Supreme Court thus found Sparrow not guilty. In addition, it addressed the issue of the infringement of Aboriginal Rights that had complicated the establishment of those rights.

In a later case, *Van der Peet* (1996), the Supreme Court used the initial ruling in *Baker Lake* (1979) to outline formally the criteria for establishing an Aboriginal Right. *Van der Peet* dealt with a member of the Sto:lo First Nation. She was selling salmon caught under a legally held Native Food fish licence. The trial judge found Dorothy Van der Peet guilty, though a summary appeal judge overturned this decision. However, the British Columbia Court of Appeal agreed with the trial judge, and thus the case was sent to and accepted by the Supreme Court. It ruled that the Aboriginal Right to fish was limited to using the fish caught for food and not for commercial selling. The commercialization of food was the deciding issue for the Supreme Court in rejecting the claim of an Aboriginal Right to sell legally obtained fish. Nevertheless, one of the dissenting justices noted that this logic was flawed and warranted a closer look, particularly if the food legally obtained was then sold in order to obtain other food.

In a less famous case, *Mitchell v Minister of National Revenue* (2001), Michael Mitchell, a Status Indian, was bringing personal goods into Canada from the United States (e.g., Bibles, motor oil, food items, and blankets). When he attempted to enter Canada with his goods, the customs officer said that he had to pay duty. Mitchell objected by claiming that he had an Aboriginal Right to bring things across the border and that Revenue Canada was violating that right by imposing a duty on his personal goods. The court asked whether the goods declared were "crucial, distinct and unique to the Mohawks of Akwesasne, Quebec," where Mitchell lived (para 4). It was unclear which Aboriginal Right Mitchell was claiming, and the court found that the claim was too vague. It also said that the goods being brought in were not "integral" to Mohawk (also known as Kanien'keha:ka) culture (e.g., motor oil, Bibles) and thus ruled that Revenue Canada could impose a duty on them.

Having made this ruling, the Supreme Court noted that section 35 of the Charter should not be rendered illusory by imposing an impossible burden of proof on those claiming Aboriginal Rights. The court explained that a flexible approach was necessary to deal with such rights. Specifically, it noted that in trying to ascertain the boundaries of an Aboriginal Right, the courts would apply the rules established by *Van der Peet*.

In turn, Indigenous Peoples have argued that the criteria imposed by the courts to establish Aboriginal Rights are unrealistic and inappropriate. First, they point out that after contact settlers, the colonial government, and subsequent Canadian governments emphasized the assimilation of Indigenous Peoples. Thus, the criterion of "continuity" cannot be met in some cases since the government ensured that Indigenous cultures and traditions were destroyed. Second, they point out that it is impossible to identify "integral" components of a culture. They argue that each component of a culture is integral because each makes up a "node" in the entire cultural configuration. Thus, the criteria imposed on Indigenous Peoples to establish Aboriginal Rights are inappropriate and fictionalize Indigenous cultures by attempting to identify a "pure" Indigenous individual or culture. They also argue that the reliance on settler law (tort) to make decisions excludes any reliance on Indigenous law, perspective, or interest. Indigenous Peoples argue that Canada's legal system contradicts the Royal Proclamation of 1763 and the Treaty of Niagara (sometimes referred to as the Covenant Chain) negotiated in the mid-eighteenth century.

A decade after *Van der Peet*, two additional cases, *R v Sappier* (2006) and *R v Gray* (2006), once again addressed the issue of Aboriginal Rights. These cases involved First Nations people cutting timber for their personal use without a timber licence. Dale Sappier and Darrell Gray were charged with unlawful cutting and possession of crown timber under New Brunswick's *Crown Lands and Forests Act*. The defendants were Maliseet and Mi'kmaq, and they admitted to cutting and possessing crown timber. However, they argued that they had an Aboriginal Right to harvest timber for personal use (building a house). Gray had cut down a maple tree on crown land, intending to use the wood to make his own furniture and flooring. Both defendants were acquitted at trial. On appeal, the Supreme Court of Canada unanimously agreed with the New Brunswick Court of Appeal and ruled that the two First Nations individuals had successfully demonstrated an Aboriginal Right to harvest timber for domestic purposes. The Supreme Court said that this action reflected an Aboriginal Right since it was a domestic activity "central" to the culture of the group. However, it once again ruled that the activity did not involve commercial wood cutting or selling.

Infringement of Aboriginal Rights

Aboriginal Rights used to be considered integral to fiduciary law. In 1984, the Supreme Court of Canada argued that the government had a fiduciary relationship with First Nations and had to act in their best interests. This fiduciary relationship was unique and trust-like. More recently, the courts have extended the fiduciary relationship to include "the duty to consult," which emerges from the principle of the "honour of the crown." The duty to consult is triggered when (1) the crown has knowledge of or anticipates an Aboriginal Right, (2) there is contemplated crown action regarding an Aboriginal Right, or (3) the contemplated action might adversely affect an Aboriginal Right. Moreover, the crown argues that the duty to consult is not to address past harms but to mediate their current effects. As Bryant (2016, 223) states, "if the relationship between governments and Indigenous people in Canada is truly one belonging to the law of equity, then the Crown is without a doubt the most notorious miscreant of legal entity known to fiduciary law."

In the *Sparrow* (1990) decision, the Supreme Court went on to establish the *Sparrow* test, which outlines what might justify an infringement of an Aboriginal Right. The duty to consult is distinct from the issue of infringement. The court stated that an infringement of Aboriginal Rights might be justified if it serves a valid legislative objective. For example, the conservation of natural resources would be paramount in developing legislation in which Indigenous interests might be subordinate to it if infringement is as minimal as possible to achieve the desired result and if fair compensation is provided.

If the Supreme Court decides that there has been a breach of the Charter or Constitution, then it can only issue a "stop and desist" order. A new twist is that the court has ruled that the onus of proving a prima facie infringement of Aboriginal Rights is on the individual or group challenging the legislation. In short, if a breach of the Charter is alleged, then one must prove it. The Department of Justice wrote a legal opinion for the government of Canada regarding this issue, but it refuses to make it public, and thus it remains confidential and its contents unknown. In summary, the *Sparrow* (1990) decision confirmed that Aboriginal Rights are not absolute and can be infringed if the government can legally justify doing so. Moreover, the court did not outline what would qualify as adequate consultation or compensation regarding infringement of rights. Outstanding questions about "adequate consultation with First Nations" eventually will have to be answered by the Supreme Court to establish criteria. However, the court also stated that these Aboriginal Rights are not inherent rights of Indigenous Peoples. This raises the issue of "piecemeal infringement" and the cumulative effects of continuing infringements of Aboriginal Rights since the criteria do not address the issue of cumulative effects that might result in eventual extinguishment of those rights.

A continuing issue faced by the federal government and Indigenous Peoples concerns how to interpret the legislation passed by the crown to decide whether it affected Aboriginal Rights held prior to the repatriated Constitution. The Supreme Court developed criteria for courts to consider the implications of section 35(1) regarding the infringement or extinguishment of Aboriginal Rights. However, it is the role of the crown to justify the infringement or extinguishment of an Aboriginal Right. Moreover, there must be concrete proof of the infringement or extinguishment. The court also noted that only Parliament has the power to extinguish unilaterally Aboriginal Rights and that it must demonstrate the need for extinguishment as well as have a clear and transparent plan to do so. However, the courts are not prepared to invoke the principles of the UN Declaration of the Rights of Indigenous Peoples to deal with Aboriginal Rights. Thus far, the courts have viewed this document as "aspirational" and not part of accommodation or reconciliation to be dealt with by them.

TREATY RIGHTS

Three different types of treaties have been negotiated between First Nations and the colonial government and then the Canadian government. The Peace and Friendship Treaties were agreements between First Nations and the colonial government. Later the Numbered Treaties were established between the Canadian government and First Nations. Finally, there are modern treaties called comprehensive land claims. In terms of how the courts have ruled on issues involving treaties, Treaty Rights can be divided into two periods: pre-1982 and post-1982.

Pre-1982 Treaty Rights

Historically, First Nations established treaties among themselves. For example, the Great Law of Peace of 1451 led to the formation of the Haudenosaunee Confederacy. Treaties between First Nations and colonial governments date back to the early 1600s. However, when settlers negotiated treaties with First Nations, they imported colonial laws whose validity depended ultimately on the legal systems of France and the United Kingdom. The notion of crown title is based upon fictional ideas developed in feudal times to legitimate the landholdings in England by treating the crown as the original occupant and others as holding title by way of grants from the crown. These early treaties sometimes exchanged the use of land for money as a one-time payment or an annuity (e.g., the Robinson Treaties of 1850). In these early treaties, Borrows (2002) argues, First Nations were active participants in establishing their contents, and they had their own powers and interests in the negotiations.

As an example, the Treaty of Niagara (1764) affirmed the Royal Proclamation of 1763, and in turn it was ratified by twenty-four different First Nations and nearly 2,000 participants. The result was the Two-Row Wampum Belt (*Kamien'Kehaka Kaswentha*) that codified the nation-to-nation relationship between the colonial government and First Nations. It established the principle that one nation would not be superior to another, and it represented a negotiated peace based upon the coexistence of power. It also symbolized that one nation would not interfere with the autonomy of the other nations. In 1665, there was another peace treaty between the French crown and four First Nations (the Haudenosaunee Confederacy). The text of the treaty acknowledges the First Nations' continuing title to their Traditional Territories as well as certain territorial rights of the French crown. The central thrust of these early treaties was peaceful coexistence. Some of these treaties also included one-time payments for use of the land by settlers. Others went beyond payment and set aside some land that would be used only by the Anishinaabe so as not to affect their lifestyle and economy at the time. The British did not continue to "take treaty" with First Nations in the Maritimes and Quebec because they argued that they had obtained the land from the French and therefore recognized only French ownership of it and not First Nations' claims to it—even though the French had never properly acquired the land from the First Nations in the first place.

The negotiation of Treaty Three reveals both the written and the oral difficulties in communication between the parties. The treaty was negotiated between the Saulteaux and the government of Canada. The written record was the result of the work of Joseph Nolin (a Métis), who had been hired by the Saulteaux to ensure that a written transcript would be available after the treaty was signed.

As treaties continued to be completed between settlers and First Nations, lands were set aside for First Nations by the colonial government, and the Canadian government later continued to do likewise. The reserves were small areas that settlers did not want, though over time some reserves were abolished when settlers needed the lands. For example, the Papaschase and Michel First Nations no longer have reserves near Edmonton because their lands were taken by the federal government based upon the argument that they did not need it. The Salish near the Kitsilano area in Vancouver, as well as the Fort St. John Beaver Band in British Columbia, were dispossessed of their lands through unilateral decisions of the federal government.

The crown no longer regarded a treaty as necessarily linked to its sovereignty over Traditional Territories, and over time the treaty process was a way for the crown to facilitate the relocation and assimilation of Indigenous Peoples. And, though the early treaties suggested a nation-to-nation relationship, the crown did not regard treaties as creating legal rights enforceable in a court of law. Instead, it viewed them as evidence of ongoing relationships, rights, and obligations not from the treaty itself but from the relationship formalized by it (Duthu 2013; Macklem 2016). Over time, though, the crown once again changed its rationale for completing treaties and argued that they were simply "contracts" between First Nations and the government.

One of the first cases involving a Treaty Right in Canadian law was *Syliboy* (1928). A Mi'kmaq man was charged with and found guilty of having illegal possession of furs. The plaintiff argued that, under the Treaty of 1752 between the British and the Mi'kmaq, the Mi'kmaq were allowed to hunt and trap at any time. However, the Provincial Court ruled that this was not a real treaty since it had not been made between legally constituted parties. Moreover, the individual charged was not a direct descendant of the Mi'kmaq who had signed the treaty. Finally, the court ruled, since Indigenous people were not yet fully defined as citizens, it was doubtful that "savages" could be signatories to a treaty. The case was never appealed, and the trial court decision still stands. Almost fifty years later the Supreme Court overturned the decision, and he received a posthumous pardon and an apology from the government of Nova Scotia ninety years after his conviction.

Three and a half decades later, in 1965, the Supreme Court decided the *White and Bob* case. The crown appealed a decision by the trial court in the acquittal of two First Nations men of possessing six deer carcasses during the closed hunting season without valid and subsisting permits under the British Columbia *Game Act*. The defendants argued that an agreement between their ancestors, members of the Saalequun community, and Governor James Douglas, dated December 23, 1854, gave them the right to hunt for food on the land in question and that, as First Nations people, they possessed the Aboriginal Right to hunt for food on unoccupied land within their ancient hunting grounds.

The court ruled that, even though the document filed (defined by the defendants as a treaty) was not signed by Douglas in his capacity as governor, it was nevertheless a treaty, and the two accused men were entitled to the benefit of the exception in section 88 of the *Indian Act*. It also decided that the Aboriginal Right of the Nanaimo First Nation communities to hunt on unoccupied land, confirmed to them by the Royal Proclamation of 1763, had never been extinguished and was still in full force. Thus, the accused men were acquitted. The appeal was dismissed, and because a valid treaty existed covering the hunting rights of the accused the provisions of the provincial *Game Act* did not apply.

After the 1973 *Calder* case, the federal government created a special office called the Office of Native Claims (ONC). Through this office, Indigenous people could submit two types of claims: comprehensive and specific. Within the ONC, the specific claims branch had the dual role of reviewing claims and representing the government if it went to negotiations. In 1982, the government introduced a new policy, but the ONC continued to evaluate claims and accepted or rejected them. In addition, provincial governments set up special units to deal with land claims. By 1991, the new Indian Claims Commission (also known as the Indian Specific Claims Commission) was created, and its mandate was to examine First Nations claims independently, provide mediation if necessary, and offer support to First Nations people to obtain fair settlements. Six commissioners reviewed specific claims rejected by the government and issued non-binding decisions. Thus, the commission had no real power in that it could only provide suggestions and advice, and nothing that it said or did was legally binding.

Specific Claims

For the next two decades, the Indian Claims Commission called for a new independent body to deal with specific claims. It would not be until 2008 that the *Specific Claims Tribunal Act* came into existence, and the Indian Claims Commission was phased out one year later. The tribunal created under the Act is a federal government–Indigenous structure that hears and resolves specific claims. Its goal is to speed up the specific claims process as well as to deal with a backlog of cases. It is also to ensure "certainty" of the claims so that developments can move forward unencumbered by lingering doubts.

There are four ways in which a First Nation can make a claim with the tribunal. First, it can do so if the claim has not been accepted for negotiation. Second, it can do so if the government has not informed a claimant about the status of the claim within three years of its filing. Third, if the parties agree, the claim can move to the tribunal at any stage of negotiation. And fourth, if after three years of negotiation a final settlement has not been reached, the First Nation can make a claim with the tribunal. It was established by the existing superior court judges, and they have established the Specific Claims Tribunal Rules of Practice and Procedures, which outline the process of submitting a claim, processing it, and making a final ruling. They appoint six judges to make up the tribunal, and as of 2018 they had dealt with 132 cases and had another seventy-four waiting to be heard.

Comprehensive Claims

At the same time, comprehensive claims were mounting up. Previously, the Departments of Justice and Indian Affairs determined whether a land claim was valid, and then the two departments along with other federal agencies determined the outcome. Comprehensive claims were limited to six active cases at any time. In addition, the negotiations culminated in a "blanket extinguishment" of all Aboriginal Rights once an agreement was reached. In 1990, the case limit was scrapped, but the government policy still insisted that the negotiations would result in clear and long-lasting definitions of rights to lands and resources (i.e., certainty).

When a comprehensive claim is accepted, the federal government appoints a team of negotiators, lawyers, and others to negotiate with the claimant. Other levels of government (e.g., provincial, municipal) also participate in the negotiations with claimants. Indigenous claimants first provide a statement of claim and then wait for the team to accept or reject the claim. If the claim is accepted, the process moves forward. If it is rejected, the claimant either accepts the verdict or moves the process into the courts, and litigation begins.

If a claim is accepted as valid, the government team assesses whether there is the likelihood of a settlement soon. If so, then the claim is given priority, and the team begins negotiations. If the claim is not deemed resolvable quickly, little attention is given to it, and it can languish for many years before serious negotiations take place. However, once the team agrees to move forward with the claim, the negotiators construct a "framework agreement" in which there is an explicit statement on the substantive content of the agreement regarding the basis of the claim. If negotiations continue to move forward, an agreement in principle is signed, though at this point there is nothing legally binding on either party. The last phase of the negotiations involves the "final agreement," in which formal ratification and the passing of all necessary legislation are undertaken to make the agreement conclusive and legally binding.

The government has imposed some conditions on when negotiations take place that have added to the complexity and the length of time for completion. For example, if claimants seem to be reluctant to move from an agreement in principle to a final agreement, the government usually stops all loans to them until they agree to the conditions outlined in the interim agreement. In other cases, the government will refuse to move forward with claims if the claimants make claims that the negotiators are unwilling to entertain. The new federal policy on comprehensive land claims has deleted the term "surrender" and replaced it with the term "certainty."

In many cases involving Treaty Rights, the court decisions have not been in favour of First Nations, nor have they been appealed. The lack of appeals has been the result of laws that have prohibited First Nations people from suing the government, lacking money to sustain an appeal, not understanding the consequences of the court's decision, or not having detailed substantive information on why the court rejected the claim to a Treaty Right. However, most of the court cases that took place prior to 1982 reflected a belief that First Nations had no rights and that the government was acting legally regarding First Nations claims for Treaty Rights.

In summary, prior to 1982, the Departments of Indian Affairs and Justice decided whether a land claim was valid and, if so, how it would be resolved. There was no appeal process, so First Nations had little recourse if decisions were not in their favour. All of this would change when section 35 was introduced in the Constitution, and it would have profound effects on Treaty Rights. Section 35 states that such rights can no longer be unilaterally modified or extinguished by the federal crown. The crown must now justify laws that diminish or interfere with existing Treaty Rights.

POST-1982 TREATY RIGHTS

Treaties have been considered legal arrangements that establish how the government can settle outstanding disputes over lands and resources with First Nations. They also legally define the rights and responsibilities in the relationship between the federal government and First Nations. Modern treaties, now called comprehensive claim settlements, continue this process but add certain dimensions: certainty, self-determination, and reconciliation. Despite the legal recognition of Aboriginal Rights, modern treaties continue to have the same objectives as the Numbered Treaties—a homogenized process for all settlements, a refusal to accept sovereignty, and a minimization of land claims. Self-government is now sometimes interwoven with comprehensive claims, and in several recent cases First Nations have negotiated self-government clauses in their agreements. However, a new element is now part of treaty negotiations, that of "certainty and clarity of the right to ownership and use of land and resources" (INAC 1986, 9). For the government and the private sector, certainty is a central issue in capitalism, and neither wishes to leave it for discussion in the future. Moreover, the private sector has impressed on the government that, before financial investments can be made, certainty must be established. A secondary goal of these modern treaties is to establish the boundaries of rights and responsibilities regarding the jurisdiction of First Nations. Today the federal government argues that those boundaries are limited to matters in First Nations communities (e.g., language, unique culture).

Keith (2015) argues that modern treaties do not achieve safeguards for First Nations cultures or ways of life, nor do they help First Nations to protect their political and economic ways of life or the directions that they wish to take with them. By imposing non-Indigenous economic and political structures regarding lands and land management processes on First Nations, modern treaties are just as controlling as the Numbered Treaties and do not protect First Nations and their ways of life (Borrows 2019; Coulthard 2014).

Modern treaties including both land claims and self-government agreements are legal arrangements that propose to settle any outstanding disputes over lands and legally defined rights. For the government of Canada, the purpose of the modern treaty process is to define the limits of rights and jurisdictions that Indigenous groups have in relation to matters internal to their communities, integral to their unique cultures and identities, and with respect to their relationships with lands and resources. Negotiations in the past three decades appear to be the same as those for the Numbered Treaties; First Nations have been expected to give up large tracts of land and their Aboriginal Rights in exchange for a small fraction of their Traditional Territories and a narrowly defined set of rights. In the end, modern treaties do little to protect Indigenous ways of life and in fact erode them. They do so by entrenching non-Indigenous economic and political conceptions of land and its management. The interpretation of Coulthard (2014) is that modern treaties reproduce colonial state power and find new strategies by which to assimilate Indigenous people into the dominant culture. He goes on to argue that modern treaties reflect the values of Western logic and embody and perpetuate Western cultural values.

After repatriation of the Constitution, the courts found that they were dealing with a new set of laws. For example, in dealing with treaties, the Supreme Court of Canada has indicated that the rules of evidence need to be relaxed and that information on the context in which a treaty was signed can be considered. This is a major change from the normal rules of "on the face" evidence used in other legal cases. In *R v Marshall* (1999), the court noted that "even in the context of a treaty document that purports to contain all of the terms, this court has made clear in recent cases that extrinsic evidence of the historical and cultural context of a treaty may be received even absent any ambiguity on the face of the treaty" (para 11). This case involved a Mi'kmaq (Donald Marshall) found guilty of selling eels without a licence, fishing without a licence, and fishing during a closed season with illegal nets under the federal *Fisheries Act*. The plaintiff argued that under the treaties of 1760–61 the Mi'kmaq had the right to catch and sell fish. The Supreme Court ruled that the texts of the treaties reflected an agreement that the Mi'kmaq could fish. Thus, the plaintiff was found not guilty.

In 2005, the Supreme Court ruled on two related cases: *R v Marshall* and *R v Bernard*. In the former case, thirty-five Mi'kmaq were charged with cutting timber on crown land without a licence. In the latter case, a Mi'kmaq was charged with unlawful possession of timber that he was transporting to a sawmill. In both cases, the accused argued that they did not need provincial authorization because they had a Treaty Right to harvest timber on crown land for commercial purposes. The court reviewed the 1760 and 1761 treaties signed by the British and Mi'kmaq and defined the "truckhouse" (a trading house used by First Nations) clauses in the treaties as a right to trade at the truckhouse but not a right to harvest the traded goods. The court also found that the evidence presented did not support the conclusion that logging formed an integral part of Mi'kmaq traditional culture and identity. In the end, the court ruled against the Mi'kmaq and upheld both trial courts' convictions.

Although each case of determining Aboriginal Rights is place specific, these rulings (plus those involving the *Natural Resources Transfer Act*) have implications for First Nations that want to use Aboriginal Rights to create business opportunities for Indigenous Peoples. The court has ruled that, when considering a treaty, it must acknowledge the context in which it was negotiated, concluded, and committed to in writing.

In the cases of *R v Simon* (1985) and *R v Sioui* (1990), the Supreme Court noted that treaty terms must be assessed generously in favour of First Nations. Furthermore, any ambiguities in the language of the treaty should be settled in favour of the Indigenous signatories. The court also ruled that any limitation that restricts an Aboriginal Right in a treaty must be narrowly interpreted. These rulings also noted that the treaties were never translated into Indigenous languages so that the Indigenous groups could see written versions of them. The pronouncement was based upon the fact that treaty texts were written by the crown's representatives. In addition, in many cases Indigenous Peoples were not able to read English.

In a more recent case, the Williams Treaty of 1923 claim was settled in 2018 through negotiations involving seven First Nations (both Mississauga and Chippewa), the Ontario government, and the federal government. This settlement focused on the fact that the harvesting rights of First Nations were not protected in the treaty. Moreover, the lands provided for the various First Nations communities were not appropriate. The settlement provided for an apology from the governments, $1.11 billion in payment, and 11,000 acres to be added to each existing reserve.

The courts have noted on occasion that the written treaty texts differ markedly from the oral promises made by crown representatives. Historians have pointed this out for many years, and Treaty Three is a good example because we have archival evidence of the process of treaty signing. When Treaty Three was being negotiated by the crown, the treaty commissioners made many oral promises in response to Anishinaabe demands. However, many of these promises were not included in the written treaty text, such as the promise that Indigenous people would be exempt from military conscription and the promise that minerals found on the reserve would be sold only with Anishinaabe consent. In this case, these oral promises were left out of the written text because the commissioners had brought with them a text compiled from failed treaty negotiations the year before, as noted in a ledger by one of the commissioners. Thus, the text did not reflect the new concessions made by the commissioners. As one can imagine, once the signed treaty was brought back to Ottawa, no one there was inclined to rewrite it and take it back to the Anishinaabe for final signing. Nevertheless, the treaty remains in effect, even though there is ample archival evidence to show that it does not reflect what was agreed to by the parties.

The Natural Resources Transfer Agreement, 1930

In 1930, the Natural Resources Transfer Agreement (now part of the Constitution) between the western provinces and the federal government modified Treaties Six, Seven, and Eight by extinguishing the Treaty Right to hunt commercially but expanding the geographical areas in which First Nations had the Treaty Right to hunt for food. In the *Badger* (1996) decision, the judges found that the Natural Resources Transfer Agreement limits the geographical area where Treaty Indians could hunt for food. (See Box 6 for an example of how the court resolved the issue.)

BOX 6

R v BADGER (1996)

Three First Nations men were hunting for food on privately owned lands within the Traditional Territory surrendered by Treaty Eight (which covers a large tract of northern Alberta and a small area of northwestern British Columbia). Each man was charged with an offence under the *Wildlife Act*. Wayne Badger was hunting on scrub land near a run-down but occupied house, Leroy Kiyawasew was hunting on a posted, snow-covered field that had been harvested that fall, and Ernest Ominayak was hunting on uncleared muskeg. All three were convicted in the Provincial Court in Alberta. They unsuccessfully appealed their summary convictions, first to the Court of Queen's Bench and then to the Court of Appeal, challenging the constitutionality of the Act as it might affect them as Cree with status under Treaty Eight. The constitutional issues to be decided were (1) whether Status Indians under Treaty Eight have the right to hunt for food on privately owned land within the Traditional Territory surrendered under that treaty, and (2) whether or not the hunting rights set out in that treaty were extinguished or modified by the *Natural Resources Transfer Act*.

The Supreme Court agreed that the Act is the dominant statement of the law, trumping the provisions of Treaty Eight. The decision was that the geographical limitation on the hunting right should be based upon a concept of visible incompatible land use. The court presented several historical references, including historians' accounts of oral history from Treaty Eight Elders, to confirm that visible incompatible land use was the historically appropriate test. The court decided that Badger and Kiyawasew were hunting in locations where they did not have a Treaty Right to hunt and that Ominayak was hunting where he did have a Treaty Right to hunt.

It appears that the judicial statement in *Badger* (1996) is the final word on this matter. However, one of the dissenting justices wrote that this did not mean that in the 1990s Indigenous people were to be precluded from selling their meat and fish to buy other items necessary for their own sustenance and that of their children. She went on to say that, if the purpose of their hunting is either to consume the meat or to exchange or sell it to support themselves and their families, then there was no reason why this should be precluded by any common-sense interpretation of the words *for food*. It will be a question of fact in each case, of course, whether a sale is made for the purpose of sustenance or commerce. The courts have ruled that the areas in which First Nations people can hunt, trap, and fish are all unoccupied crown lands and any other lands to which they might have a right of access. However, that is not a general right of access; it is limited to access for the purpose of hunting, fishing, or trapping for food.

In *R v Horseman* (1990), the Supreme Court of Canada agreed that Treaty Eight was understood by the First Nations that had signed it as having conferred a right to hunt bison and exchange the products of the hunt for resale. In the case of Bert Horseman, he was hunting moose when a grizzly bear attacked him. He shot and killed the bear in self-defence and proceeded to prepare the meat and hide. He was charged with unauthorized hunting contrary to Alberta's *Wildlife Act*.

The trial judge found him not guilty, and the Supreme Court upheld his acquittal and said that the *Wildlife Act* was applicable to First Nations people only if they engaged in sport or commercial hunting, not domestic hunting. Later Horseman sold the hide of the bear, and again he was charged with violating the *Wildlife Act*. This case was also considered by the Supreme Court (1991). Horseman argued that he was within the rights granted to him under Treaty Eight when he sold the hide of a bear that he had killed while unlicensed. He argued that he was not subject to the statutory provisions that regulated trafficking in wildlife. The court held that, though the original Treaty Right included hunting for the purpose of commerce, that right had been extinguished by the *Natural Resources Transfer Act*, which limits the right to hunting for food only. The court found that the sale of the bear hide constituted a commercial transaction. As a result, it was no longer a right protected by Treaty Eight as amended by the Natural Resources Transfer Agreement.

The court said that the *Natural Resources Transfer Act* clearly intended to extinguish the Treaty Right to hunt commercially. Since the clause applies equally to hunting, trapping, and fishing, any Treaty Right to fish, hunt, or trap for commercial purposes has been completely extinguished.

The prosecution in this case argued that the *Natural Resources Transfer Act* extinguished and replaced the terms of Treaty Eight. The Supreme Court rejected this interpretation and said that the government had to go back and look at the content of Treaty Eight and not use the *Natural Resources Transfer Act* as the basis for interpretation. In short, the court ruled that a treaty cannot be extinguished without the consent of the First Nations involved, even though its decision was in direct opposition to this admonition.

One of the most up-to-date cases regarding Aboriginal Title is *Delgamuukw* (1997). This case was initiated by the Gitxsan and Wet'suwet'en Chiefs who sought to affirm their Aboriginal Title to about 60,000 square kilometres in northwestern British Columbia. Justice McEachern of the BC Supreme Court heard the case and ruled that the Gitxsan and Wet'suwet'en (earlier known as the Broman Lake and Bulkley River Carrier [Dakelh] Bands) failed in all of their claims.

Moreover, he rejected most of the oral testimony and most of the expert witnesses, claiming that only the historical documents provided by both sides were acceptable and "plain on the face," and thus he could read and interpret the documents as well as the "experts." His overall assessment was that written documents were the only thing that could be brought into the court as evidence and that context and oral testimony were inappropriate and irrelevant to the case. McEachern ruled that Aboriginal Title as well as the Aboriginal Right to self-government had been extinguished a century earlier and thus were not "existing" rights under section 35(1) of the Constitution. The province insisted that all Aboriginal Rights to land in British Columbia had been extinguished by the colonial government before the province became part of Canada in 1871 and that any remnants had been extinguished by provincial law. McEachern ruled that Aboriginal Rights in general existed at "the pleasure of the crown" and could thus be extinguished whenever the crown clearly stated that intention. (In the Court of Appeal, the province changed its position to argue that Aboriginal Rights to land had not been extinguished.) The Gitxsan and Wet'suwet'en argued that, though the crown had underlying title to the lands under review, their claims to the lands constituted a burden on that title. In addition, they claimed unspecified Aboriginal Rights to use the land and also sought compensation for other lost lands and resources.

The BC Court of Appeal issued its reasons why it was prepared to accept some of the First Nations' arguments but not all of them. The court ruled that the Gitxsan and Wet'suwet'en had unextinguished Aboriginal Rights other than a right of ownership or property. The court also referred the scope, contents, and consequences of these rights of occupancy and use back to the trial judge for a decision. At the same time, the court was explicit in its admonition to the parties (the federal and provincial governments on one side and the Gitxsan and Wet'suwet'en on the other) that they resolve their differences through a process of negotiation and consultation. All other aspects of the claim were rejected by the Court of Appeal. This decision was also appealed, but before it was accepted by the Supreme Court of Canada the two parties attempted to negotiate a settlement. However, by early 1996, the province suspended negotiations, claiming that the two parties had fundamental differences regarding Aboriginal Rights. As such, the case proceeded to the Supreme Court.

That court accepted the case, reviewed it, ruled that it was unable to consider the merits of the case, and sent it back to the lower court for a new trial. It noted that the two individual claims from the two parties had been amalgamated into two communal claims but not formally amended when brought to the Supreme Court. The justices also found that the "characterization" of Aboriginal Title brought by the plaintiffs was too broad and the province's definition too narrow. The Supreme Court identified other technical aspects that precluded its ability to render a decision, but basically the justices noted that the case had been improperly framed by the lawyers who had filed it, and thus it could not decide anything.

However, like the Court of Appeal, the Supreme Court explicitly encouraged the two parties to sit down and negotiate a settlement. It noted that the crown has a moral and legal duty to negotiate in good faith (the honour of the crown). Importantly, the Supreme Court noted that oral testimony was admissible in a court of law and had an important role to play in an Aboriginal Rights claim. Rather than continue with the litigation in the court, the British Columbia Treaty Commission helped to form a tripartite Treaty Commission Agreement that would govern further negotiations between the two parties. A Reconciliation Agreement between the BC government and the Gitxsan and Wet'suwet'en was signed, and further discussions began. However, the negotiations were still not completed as of 2019.

In the case of Aboriginal Title, the courts have ruled that First Nations must satisfy a three-stage test. This test is like establishing an Aboriginal Right, but because land is the focus there are some differences. The first stage of claiming Aboriginal Title is that the land under dispute must have been occupied by the ancestors of the claimants prior to British sovereignty. In establishing this "fact," the courts have been clear that a regular pattern of hunting or fishing in a specific area is not sufficient to establish Aboriginal Title, though the *Tsilhqot'in Nation* case (2014) did deviate from that condition. Nevertheless, even regular seasonal use of specific lands (rivers) might not be sufficient to support this criterion. However, if the evidence supports the first stage, the second stage is to establish evidence that the occupation of land occurred prior to British sovereignty—the continuity criterion. The third stage requires that the claimants demonstrate that occupation of the land by their ancestors was exclusive. The courts have stated that the claimants must offer proof that the First Nations group had the intention and/or the capacity to retain exclusive control over the use of that land even though it might have been used occasionally by other groups. The courts have also noted that the constitutional question of a First Nations community's territorial sovereignty is legitimate and outstanding. However, the Supreme Court has not yet been presented with a case in which it would have to deal with this constitutional issue.

DUTY TO CONSULT (HONOUR OF THE CROWN)

The idea of consultation emerges from the notion of the honour of the crown and has its roots in the Royal Proclamation of 1763. Until recently, the courts' decision regarding Aboriginal Title was based upon a fiduciary responsibility held by the crown. More recent cases have involved the duty of the government (federal, provincial, or territorial) to consult with First Nations when development projects are proposed and might have impacts on Aboriginal and Treaty Rights or Title. Court rulings generally have been clear, and provincial governments have taken (or are about to take) action to ensure that the duty to consult is fulfilled. Most provincial governments have established policies and processes by which they communicate and negotiate with Indigenous Peoples regarding real or potential impacts on their rights. The federal government also has taken steps to ensure that all federal departments have policies for establishing consultations with Indigenous Peoples when required. This does not mean, though, that all development projects must carry out such consultations.

The crown's duty to consult with and accommodate Indigenous Peoples emerges from Canadian law saying that all people in Canada should be dealt with by the crown in a fair and reasonable manner and in accordance with common law. Indigenous Peoples have an additional source for this duty in section 35(1) of the Constitution, which specifies the honour of the crown and describes how the crown is to carry out its duty to consult with them and, if necessary, accommodate their interests (Laidlaw and Passelac-Ross 2014). The overall goal of the duty to consult is to reconcile the rights of Indigenous Peoples with those of the crown. The Supreme Court has noted that there is a low threshold for invoking the duty to consult. For example, the court has ruled that the duty exists when the crown is considering carrying out activities that might adversely affect Aboriginal Title (e.g., Treaty Rights). However, the extent of consultation required will depend on the nature of the proposed development and its real or potential impacts on Aboriginal Rights. As a result, some projects might require only minimal consultation, whereas others will require extensive consultation. In most jurisdictions, the policies on consultation and accommodation also apply to any proposed provincial development project. Most provinces also have extensive "trigger lists" that include strategic decisions and major documents outlining the consultation process.

The first case in the Supreme Court focusing on the duty to consult was *Haida Nation v British Columbia (Minister of Forests)* (2004). The Haida Nation argued that the crown did not consult with Indigenous Peoples regarding the transfer of a tree farm licence from MacMillan Bloedel to Weyerhaeuser. First Nations leaders claimed that in doing so the minister of forestry exceeded his jurisdiction and that the result negatively affected their rights. The BC Supreme Court dismissed the case. However, the BC Court of Appeal allowed it and ruled that both the crown and Weyerhaeuser had a duty to consult with the Haida Nation. This decision was eventually appealed to the Supreme Court.

That court ruled that the crown had a duty to consult First Nations but that a third party did not. It subsequently dismissed the case against Weyerhaeuser but found the crown irresponsible for not carrying out its duty to consult. For the first time, the Supreme Court also laid out the rules of proportionality. It noted that the scope of the duty to consult is proportionate to a preliminary assessment of the strength of the case supporting the existence of the Aboriginal Right or Title and the potential of a serious adverse effect on that right or title.

In *Mikisew Cree First Nation v Minister of Canadian Heritage* (2005), which followed *Haida Nation* (2004), the Supreme Court confirmed that the duty of the crown is to consult and accommodate First Nations when making land and resource decisions that might negatively affect their Treaty Rights or Aboriginal Title. The Mikisew Reserve is located within Treaty Eight territory in northern Alberta in Wood Buffalo National Park. In 2000, the federal government approved a winter road through the reserve without consulting the residents. After the Mikisew protested, the road alignment was modified (but again without consultation) to track around the boundary of the reserve. The total area of the road corridor was approximately twenty-three square kilometres. The Mikisew's objection to the road went beyond the direct impact of closure to hunting and trapping in the area covered by the winter road; the Mikisew also argued that it would have an adverse impact on their traditional lifestyle, central to their culture. The Federal Court ruled that the minister's approval would be retracted, and a rare interlocutory injunction was given. There was a breach of the honour of the crown (some would say fiduciary duty) to consult, even though the court recognized that, under the terms of Treaty Eight, it was agreed that from time to time some of the surrendered land over which the Mikisew had hunting, trapping, and fishing rights would be "taken up" for other purposes (e.g., a road). However, the court noted that this agreement did not mean that the crown did not have to act honourably. It also remarked that the proposed road was not a permanent road, so the duty to consult was at the lower end of the spectrum of consultation. Nevertheless, the crown was still required to provide adequate notice and information to the claimants before construction began. The court ruled that the government had to engage directly with the Mikisew and respond to their concerns. The crown had simply provided the Mikisew with a written notice and began construction. The court thus set aside the road approval on the basis that the crown had not adequately consulted with the Mikisew.

A third case, *Taku River Tlingit First Nation v British Columbia (Project Assessment Director)* (2004), involved a mining company in British Columbia that wanted to build a road to a mine that would cross through the Tlingits' claimed Traditional Territory. Before the road was built, the BC government carried out an environmental assessment, and as a result the minister of energy approved the project. Both the lower court and the BC Court of Appeal found in favour of the Tlingit. However, when the Supreme Court ruled on the case, it found that the BC government had indeed consulted with the Tlingit and denied the appeal. Thus, the road went ahead. The court noted that, though the Tlingit had made a case of violation of their rights and the road could negatively affect their claim and rights, the crown had fulfilled its duty to consult with them and thus satisfied the honour of the crown. The court did not comment on the need to accommodate the Tlingit concerns.

Alberta: The Outlier

In Alberta, there is little discussion about the duty to consult. The province has a very different interpretation of the rulings issued by the Supreme Court. The government of Alberta first released a consultation policy in 2005, which was an attempt to meet the new obligations to consult and accommodate Indigenous Peoples regarding development projects. Then in 2013 the government revised its initial document and introduced the *Government of Alberta's Policy on Consultation with First Nations on Land and Natural Resource Management*. This policy is a set of principles that identifies, in general terms, how the Alberta government anticipates consultation will occur. The specific consultation process will be defined by each of the departmental *Consultation Guidelines* in relation to specific activities such as exploration, resource extraction, and management of forests, fish, and wildlife (Laidlaw and Passelac-Ross 2014).

The policy of consultation and accommodation developed by Alberta attempts to reconcile Aboriginal and Treaty Rights and traditional uses of the land with the government's mandate to exploit crown lands and resources. However, leasing and licensing of mineral rights are not considered subject to consultation in Alberta. The most recent document prepared by the Alberta government outlines its duty to consult with First Nations where land management and natural resource development can adversely affect their rights. These consultations will be held before the crown decides on any management or development project. In carrying out these consultations, the province will provide relevant information to First Nations and allow a reasonable time for them to review the proposals. In turn, First Nations have a duty to respond in a timely and reasonable manner. Accommodation will be assessed on a case-by-case basis and applied when appropriate. In addition, proponents of development projects must act in accordance with the government of Alberta's *Corporate Guidelines for First Nations Consultation Activities*. Finally, the duty to consult, according to Alberta, does not give First Nations communities a veto over crown decisions.

First Nations have objected to the Alberta policy for several reasons. They argue that it was not a negotiated agreement but unilaterally imposed by the ruling Conservative government. In fact, they point out that the *Aboriginal Consultation Levy Act* was passed before there was any public consultation (the Act has since been repealed). When Alberta implemented the *Land-Use Framework* and regional plans in 2012, there was no consultation with First Nations. Their leaders argue that Alberta does not understand the Numbered Treaties and has not honoured their contents. For example, they point out that the government continually insists on the need to "balance" Aboriginal Rights with the interests of the broader public and corporate rights (Passelac-Ross and Potes 2007). This seems to be the result of a misinterpretation of the *Badger* case (1996), in which the minority opinion was that Treaty Rights to hunt, fish, and trap are restricted to domestic food use and should not interfere in commercial enterprises, thus ensuring a balance. First Nations leaders also argue that Alberta views the duty to consult as just one more hurdle to jump over to implement a project.

First Nations point out that the Alberta policy is not law but only a guideline. As such, it is not subject to legal enforcement and varies considerably in how proponents and the government interpret it. For example, the *Government of Alberta's Guidelines on Consultation with First Nations on Land and Natural Resource Development (Consultation Guidelines)* do not outline a specific process for determining how First Nations issues are to be incorporated into the Environmental Impact Assessment process. In addition, many First Nations leaders have disagreed with the substance of the policy, and the Alberta Assembly of Grand Chiefs has unanimously rejected it. The Chiefs take the position that the provincial government has adopted a policy without adequate consultation with and consent of First Nations affected by it. Furthermore, the policy does not acknowledge the government's legal obligation to protect and accommodate the rights of First Nations, nor does it refer to the ultimate purpose of reconciliation, which, in the view of the Supreme Court of Canada, the consultation process is designed to achieve. This last issue was recently dealt with by the court, which ruled that the Alberta government did not have to consult with Indigenous Peoples as it was drafting the policy. The court argued that doing so would be an extreme burden on the government and that, if the policy or legislation adversely affected Aboriginal Rights, then the issue could be taken to the courts to resolve.

Alberta views its role as "managing" the consultation process and, when deemed necessary, consulting directly with First Nations. The policy states that consultation will occur in two ways: (1) through general consultation and relationship building, and (2) through project-specific consultation. General consultation is intended to build relationships by increasing the flow of information between parties and will occur, for instance, through information-sharing sessions (Passelac-Ross and Potes 2007). Project-specific consultation can occur between the government and First Nations on major projects. However, in most cases, the policy anticipates that the project proponent will engage directly with the First Nations community affected. Although the province understands that third parties do not have a duty to consult with and accommodate the rights of First Nations, it has, for all practical purposes, required the proponents of various projects to consult with First Nations before the provincial government engages in consultation. Once that has happened, the government informs the third party whether the consultation and accommodation are sufficient.

More importantly, Passelac-Ross and Potes (2007) argue that, by assuming the position of neutral broker, the Alberta crown disregards its overarching obligation to respect and protect the constitutional rights of Indigenous Peoples by delegating it to industry. In doing so, the provincial government fails to acknowledge that, according to judicial doctrine, the crown, not industry, is the duty holder. It is the honour of the crown that is at stake (Passelac-Ross and Potes 2007). First Nations leaders in Alberta therefore argue that the Alberta government does not take the obligation to consult and accommodate seriously. Moreover, accommodation requires that the proponent of a project amend its initial proposal substantively to address the legitimate concerns of the First Nations communities potentially affected by the project. The probability of major development projects adversely affecting Aboriginal Rights is high, so the scope of substantive accommodation measures must be broad. This includes the possibility of rejecting the proposed project if the risk of a de facto extinguishment (or infringement) of Aboriginal Rights is likely. Although the duty to consult does not imply a veto power by First Nations, the overarching obligation to protect constitutional rights prevents the crown from making decisions that might lead to the extinguishment of these rights in practice (Laidlaw and Passelac-Ross 2014). However, data from Alberta reveal that 98 percent of all major resource development projects are approved, and this suggests that the approval process is one-sided, though one might argue that resource development proponents are careful in their submissions to meet the honour of the crown. Recent changes in Alberta have restricted who can "intervene" at various hearings regarding major project developments. Thus, opponents of a project, unless they are "directly" affected, are not granted intervenor status at the hearings. Conversely, the Canadian Petroleum Association argues that, though the acceptance rate is high, it does not reflect the "conditions" that the energy regulator places on the developments before they can proceed.

Nevertheless, the scope of consultation and accommodation is severely curtailed by the Alberta government's interpretation of the rulings of the Supreme Court of Canada. No other provincial government has made this interpretation. The Indigenous organizations of Alberta have criticized the limiting definition of their rights and traditional uses that the province has adopted in its policy. Such a unilateral definition of Aboriginal Rights and uses significantly reduces the scope of negotiations, to the detriment of the supposed beneficiaries of the duty to consult (Passelac-Ross and Potes 2007). Nothing in the rulings by the Supreme Court suggests that the crown has the authority unilaterally to define or limit rights. In fact, the Supreme Court explicitly noted that it wanted to prevent such actions by tempering crown power with the duty to consult and accommodate. Finally, the Alberta approach provides no clear criteria for substantive accommodation. Although the provincial government retains the responsibility to determine whether project proponent–led consultation has been adequate, there is no indication of how adequacy is assessed. This favours the kind of unstructured decision-making that the Supreme Court criticized (Passelac-Ross and Potes 2007).

JURISDICTIONAL ISSUES

There are cases in which there is dispute among the parties over who has legal authority over issues. Sometimes the dispute is between the federal and provincial governments, whereas at other times it is between Indigenous Peoples and the government or between Indigenous groups themselves. Historically, the *St. Catharines Milling and Lumber Company* case (1888) was the most important case regarding jurisdiction in Canada. The Privy Council went further and claimed that the sole source of Aboriginal Title was based upon the Royal Proclamation of 1763. This decision put to rest the issue of Aboriginal Title until 1973 with *Calder v British Columbia (Attorney General)*.

In the *Campbell v British Columbia* (2000) BC Supreme Court decision, the opponents of First Nations self-government argued that, once the federal and provincial governments were established, all legislative powers had been distributed, and thus there was no room for First Nations self-government. The court disagreed and noted that legislative powers had not been exhaustively distributed, and thus, if British Columbia and the Nisga'a wanted to define the inherent jurisdiction of the Nisga'a, they were welcome to do so. Justice Williamson went on to argue that First Nations communities had decision-making authority over how Aboriginal Rights (which have been affirmed) can be exercised. However, those rights remain to be determined (McNeil 2007, 2013).

RESIDUAL ISSUES

In this section, I focus on concerns of Indigenous Peoples not covered in the previous sections, specifically the issue of trust, fiduciary concerns, as well as Aboriginal Title.

Prior to 1950, the term "trust" was used to characterize the relationship between the federal crown and First Nations, considered "wards" of the federal government. However, over time, the term took on a different legal definition in property and corporate law, and as such it is no longer used to characterize the relationship between the federal crown and Indigenous Peoples. Instead, the term "fiduciary" was created. Fiduciary obligations emerge when the trustee has the right to exercise discretion in decision-making. It is like the relationship between lawyer and client or parent and child. In addition, a fiduciary relationship exists when the trustee can unilaterally exercise that power or discretion and affect the beneficiary's interests. Finally, if the beneficiary is vulnerable to the agent holding the power, then the relationship is considered fiduciary. In the end, it means that a trustee has an obligation to act in a selfless manner on behalf of the beneficiary.

This issue emerged in the case of *Guerin v The Queen* (1984). The case involved the surrender of reserve land to the federal crown as noted in the *Indian Act* (sections 37–41). This occurred because First Nations do not own their lands (fee simple) and can only surrender them to the crown. Following is an example of how First Nations can dispose of lands through the process identified in the *Indian Act*. It also reveals the thinking of the Supreme Court regarding fiduciary responsibility to First Nations carried by the crown.

The Musqueam Band surrendered a parcel of reserve land in 1957 to the federal crown upon the request of the crown. It asked the Musqueam to lease reserve land to the government for a period of seventy-five years. At the time of the surrender, the terms and conditions of the lease were not part of the surrender but were discussed between federal officials and Musqueam leaders. When the land was leased to a third party (a golf and country club), the terms agreed to with the crown were not as favourable as those originally agreed to by the Musqueam. Moreover, the Musqueam did not give the crown the right unilaterally to change the terms and conditions of the lease. Indeed, the crown withheld information from both the Musqueam and an appraiser assessing the adequacy of the proposed rent. Until recently, the federal government had a policy of "non-disclosure" to the beneficiary First Nation, and it was unilaterally imposed until 1972. Nevertheless, after the surrender, the Musqueam requested a copy of the lease in 1958, but the crown did not provide them with a copy until 1970. Upon seeing the terms of the lease, the Musqueam brought an action against the crown for breach of trust.

The crown's first defense was that the Musqueam could not sue the crown since they were the agent of trust. The court decided otherwise. The trial judge found the crown in breach of trust and found in favour of the Musqueam, awarded $10 million. This decision was appealed, and the Federal Court of Appeal overturned this judgment on the basis that the crown's trust was not enforceable. It ruled that the obligations of the crown to the Musqueam were of the nature of a "political trust" (which could not be subjected to legal judgment), and thus the crown had considerable discretion in the final terms of the lease that would be in the best interests of the Musqueam. Eventually, the case went to the Supreme Court. It concurred with the trial judge's ruling and noted that the breach of trust by the crown resulted in a much higher compensation than that of a simple case of fraud. The legal import of the case was that the concept of the fiduciary trust relationship was born, and until recently it has been considered commonplace in the courts when dealing with Indigenous-crown relations. Today the duty to consult and the honour of the crown are more important considerations in the framework of legal decision-making regarding First Nations, though the fiduciary relationship remains an important legal issue for Indigenous-crown relations.

ABORIGINAL TITLE AND THE COURTS: A CASE STUDY

Aboriginal Title is a property right to land not held in fee simple but considered by the Supreme Court of Canada as a *sui generis* (unique) interest in the land. This conceptualization includes the right to use the land for cultural and economic purposes; the land is held communally and can be transferred only to the crown.

The Tsilhqot'in Nation consists of six bands in central British Columbia and has long been in an adversarial relationship with the BC government regarding logging practices within their Traditional Territories. In 2007, after five years of court proceedings, the BC Supreme Court ruled that Aboriginal Title can exist to a specific land area of the Traditional Territory if the case has been presented properly. This was the first time in Canadian history that Aboriginal Title to a broad area was recognized by a court. In 2012, the BC Court of Appeal overturned the lower court decision and ruled that Aboriginal Title can exist only to specific, traditionally occupied, sites (e.g., camps, villages). The case was appealed to the Supreme Court of Canada, which ruled on it in 2014 (150 years after the Tsilhqot'in Nation first objected to external resource development in its Traditional Territory). The court found that Aboriginal Title applies to a broader range of Traditional Territory. The court found that, even though the Tsilhqot'in were semi-nomadic, they controlled and protected a broad geographic area. As such, they met the tests of occupation and continuity of living on and using the land, and their control was exclusive to the broader area.

The Supreme Court declared Aboriginal Title to nearly 2,000 square kilometres of the claim area in British Columbia. This decision showed that Aboriginal Title is not limited to the intensive use of small areas of land over long periods of time. The court found that Aboriginal Title extended to all of the land that a First Nations community regularly and exclusively used. Moreover, the Tsilhqot'in continued to hold Aboriginal Rights to hunt, trap, fish, and trade anywhere in the claim area.

The Supreme Court also established that Aboriginal Title includes the benefits associated with the land as well as the right to both use it and profit from it. Nevertheless, the court ruled that Aboriginal Title is not absolute, so development can take place on the land if one of two conditions is met. First, development of the land can proceed if the First Nation gives consent to it; second, development can proceed if the crown can make a case that it is in the national interest and meets its fiduciary duty to the First Nation. Finally, the court noted that provincial law still applies to these lands.

CONCLUSION

Indigenous Peoples have found that using the courts to resolve conflicts with the crown is both time consuming and expensive. Moreover, it is unclear whether their claims will be validated or rejected. In short, from an Indigenous perspective, the courts have proven to be unreliable forums for resolving Indigenous claims (Belanger 2014). Moreover, having a claim rejected at the lower court level is less risky since generally it can be appealed, but once the issue is decided by the Supreme Court the decision is final and irrevocable.

Several cases are currently in the system and await decisions that will have far-reaching implications for both Indigenous and non-Indigenous people. For example, *Chartrand v The Queen*, which began in 2014, focuses on tax relief for elected officials who work for Métis bodies that provide government functions. As of 2019, the case has yet to be resolved. In other cases focusing on Métis (e.g., *Peavine Métis Settlement v Alberta* [2007]), the focus is on the duty to consult with Métis and the fiduciary duty of the crown. The Métis are now drawing on the courts to decide their claims.

Nevertheless, the courts reflect Western law and are reluctant to allow alternative forms of evidence or law to be introduced. This of course reflects the "one law" doctrine that settlers and colonial officials agreed to many decades ago. Western (tort) law narrows the issues to be dealt with by the courts and how they are decided. In other cases, government agencies unilaterally and arbitrarily changed the rules for Indigenous Peoples without the benefit of court wisdom in doing so (e.g., Revenue Canada and taxes). The Supreme Court has recognized the uniqueness of Indigenous grievances (e.g., land claims), and it has tried to incorporate that uniqueness into tort law—some would argue with little success. So Canadian Aboriginal law remains foreign and hostile to the goals of Indigenous Peoples in trying to resolve their claims.

In fact, the courts have been complicit with Parliament in ensuring that Aboriginal Rights are not well served. For example, Borrows (2017a) points out that, when Parliament unilaterally revised the *Indian Act* and passed what is now section 88, it forced First Nations to abide by all general laws within a province. In short, it made First Nations subject to provincial laws contrary to the Royal Proclamation of 1763 and the Treaty of Niagara of 1764. And, as Borrows (2017a) argues, this change limits Indigenous political power and provides disincentives for the federal government to work with Indigenous Peoples to develop legislation that recognizes Treaty Rights. In *Cardinal v Attorney General of Alberta* (1974), the Supreme Court of Canada held that First Nations lands are not free from provincial control. Borrows goes on to say that this case and *R v Dick* (1985) show that the courts reject the spirit of the Royal Proclamation and the Treaty of Niagara in that Indigenous people cannot claim immunity from provincial laws because of their legal status as such.

More recently, the Supreme Court's rulings in *Grassy Narrows First Nation v Ontario (Natural Resources)* (2014) and *Tsilhqot'in Nation v British Columbia* (2014) have also diminished the rights of Indigenous Peoples. In both cases, the court provided for and increased the presence of the province regarding resource development and Indigenous people. In the *Tsilhqot'in Nation* case, the court explicitly noted that general provincial laws apply to Indigenous people even if there is no legislative intervention. Borrows (2017a) also notes that the court held that interjurisdictional immunity would not apply when there is an application of provincial laws to Aboriginal Title lands. In the *Grassy Narrows* case, the court ruled that Ontario can take up land within Treaty Three without any consideration of the federal government and its requirements. In other words, as Borrows (2017b) points out, federalism does not protect Indigenous Peoples to any significant degree, and this has been supported by the Supreme Court decisions.

As Ray (2016) points out, the courts face two fundamental and conflicting challenges when dealing with Aboriginal Rights and Title. They must deal with the claims of Indigenous Peoples who have been dispossessed through the process of colonization. This means that the courts must deal with the grievances and come to a resolution regarding the claims. At the same time, the courts must make a disposition of the claim in such a way that it does not disrupt the existing social order (e.g., remove third parties from land areas, develop policies for Indigenous people that disadvantage non-Indigenous people, provide financial compensation considered excessive). In addition, the courts must demonstrate that the claims presented are dealt with in a rigorous and systematic manner so that, if an Indigenous claim is validated, the public is confident that the claim has had a public and transparent process to support that decision. The courts also operate on the basis that the process must be timely, though this becomes problematic because of the complexity of the claims. Finally, politicians require the courts to bring "certainty" to the resolution of a claim. These conflicting expectations have led the courts to be overly cautious in their approach to the Indigenous claims brought forward. This is particularly true when the courts make rulings in geographical areas outside reserves (Traditional Territories) or outside areas designated by treaty boundaries, or when they deal with jurisdictional issues regarding federal versus provincial obligations (Ray 2016).

Panagos (2017) asserts that the failure of Canada to deal with Aboriginal Rights is the result of the fact that we cannot agree on the definition of the word *Aboriginality*. He argues that the plurality of definitions since 1982 cannot be dealt with in law, and thus the only definition that counts is the one espoused by the Supreme Court. But its definition is radically different from that of Indigenous People, so the court's decisions fail to protect Indigenous interests and in fact threaten them. The Supreme Court implicitly uses a kind of "frozen rights" or "citizen plus" definition of Aboriginality—a collective identity defined by its relation to the state. This version of Aboriginality can only apply to instances when the identity-based interests are compatible with the citizen-state conception (Chartrand 2018). As noted by Panagos (2017), the use of section 35 of the *Charter of Rights and Freedoms* only protects rights to "a way of life" that reinforces a dominant-subordinate relationship between the Canadian and Indigenous communities. It should come as no surprise, he argues, when the government justifies its infringement of Aboriginal Rights for a major pipeline as "serving the national interest" and then finds that Indigenous people have become indignant and gone to the courts to resolve the infringement. Although there is now talk of a nation-to-nation dialogue, it has yet to be demonstrated by the federal government. Leclair (2006) agrees with Panagos and argues that the government needs to take a new approach in addressing Aboriginal Rights. He suggests that "federal constitutionalism" is the correct approach. It would open the door to recognizing Indigenous people as actors in the construction of Canadian federalism. With this approach, there would be recognition that Canadians have a shared and divergent national experience, and Indigenous people would achieve some autonomy.

There is some hope that the courts will begin to reconsider the claims of Indigenous people regarding their rights. For example, since repatriation of the Constitution, the Supreme Court has argued that the assumption of section 35 of the Constitution is reconciliation of the pre-existence of Indigenous societies with the assertion of the sovereignty of the crown. Moreover, the Supreme Court continues to hold that negotiations between the crown and Indigenous Peoples represent the best approach to achieving reconciliation. Nevertheless, Borrows (2017b) claims that these latest court decisions have plunged Canada into a more discriminatory and colonial state. He openly argues against asking Indigenous Peoples to reconcile themselves with the operation of colonialism, and he suggests that it is necessary to focus on Indigenous law in constructing remedies for eroded settler-Indigenous relations. Although Borrows is somewhat pessimistic about the future of Aboriginal Rights, he has hope that there will be change in the views of the Supreme Court that will support Indigenous claims through an evolution of interpretation of the Constitution.

CHAPTER 7

THE SOCIAL ORGANIZATIONS *of* INDIGENOUS PEOPLES

In this chapter, I focus on both the internal and the external organizational structures that have shaped the lives of Indigenous Peoples as well as how their communications with external agents were formed and sustained. I look at both local and national organizational structures of Indigenous Peoples in the twenty-first century. This portrait of First Nations, Métis, and Inuit organizations will allow the reader to understand more fully how Indigenous Peoples organize politically as well as to acknowledge the pervasiveness of politics in their communities and lives. I show how history, external agencies, and internal community debates perpetuate Indigenous social organizations. Indigenous Peoples and their organizations have pointed out that the government of Canada has assumed, following the ethos of its predecessors, that Indigenous Peoples are culturally backward and need to be assimilated into mainstream society. Such thinking continues to be integral to the government's attitude toward them.

GOVERNMENT IDEOLOGIES

Euro-Canadian assumptions of superiority are embedded in the structure and process of the legal and economic systems of Canada, which in turn create the environment in which communication takes place. For example, the signing of a treaty is a recognition of the need for mutual respect and consent; although this might have been the case at the time of signing the first Peace and Friendship Treaties, it was not the case later when the Numbered Treaties were signed, nor is it the case in the more recent comprehensive claim agreements. The language of the treaties was always English, structured to meet the goals of the settlers and the crown, and if First Nations communities were unwilling to sign them as offered they were often coerced into doing so (Daschuk 2013). In other cases, refusal to sign a treaty meant that the government would simply ignore the Indigenous group and treat them as though they did not exist. This policy still exists when the crown deals with Indigenous Peoples and their claims (Alcantara 2013).

For example, for many years the Inuit were considered an encumbrance on the crown assigned to it by the Supreme Court. As Rutherdale (2018) points out, a combination of neglect, parsimony, and colonizing discourse characterized the federal government's activities regarding the Inuit. The result was that consideration of the rights and/or claims of the Inuit was as minimal as possible. In the case of the Métis, after the *Manitoba Act*, the federal government refused to acknowledge their existence (Alberta being the exception) as a people and thus took no action to deal with them until the Constitution of 1982 and the *Powley* decision of 2003 forced it to negotiate.

INDIGENOUS GOALS

The primary goal of Indigenous Peoples is to achieve self-determination. Moreover, they wish the government to make substantive changes to address the systemic inequalities and injustices that are embedded in Canadian institutions and have operated for many decades. Indigenous organizations argue that the current state, in some respects, is not legitimate, and until it makes substantive changes to address unjust systemic policies and laws Indigenous self-government and self-determination continue to be viable alternatives.

Indigenous organizations are also faced with the issue of how to deal with the human rights abuses that Indigenous Peoples have experienced over the past two centuries. Indigenous groups have argued for the creation of a "restorative justice" system to be implemented to deal with historical and contemporary injustices. The government strongly resists such a move. In other cases, Indigenous organizations have argued that "liberal constitutionalism" needs to be implemented. Moore (2010) argues that it involves a "pre-commitment" to resisting certain undesirable propensities of the state. The government would have to design various laws and policies to prevent mainstream institutions from engaging in discriminatory and unjust activities regarding Indigenous people. For example, Canadians have built in safeguards for free speech because they understand that sometimes the dominant group is inclined to attack minority views. In this respect, many Indigenous organizations have tried to get the government to think about extending that constitutional tradition to include Aboriginal Rights since Indigenous Peoples have long histories of being victims of the state. In short, their goal is to build structural and legal protections for Indigenous Peoples to keep them from being subjected to future injustices. Indigenous Peoples argue that a legitimate political authority cannot result from the unjust usurpation of a previously existing legitimate authority (Moore 2010). Other Indigenous organizations have non-political missions to foster business relations, build capacity in Indigenous communities, and develop other business opportunities (e.g., Aboriginal Business Service Network Society, Council for the Advancement of Native Development Officers, National Aboriginal Forestry Association).

INDIGENOUS SOCIAL ORGANIZATIONS

To deal with local, regional, and national issues regarding the Canadian government's treatment of Indigenous Peoples, they have created unique social organizations to deal with the institutions that control the agendas of political and economic activities of the country. Over the years, Indigenous Peoples have established hundreds of organizations to deal with their defined injustices or concerns, but many of these organizations have been impeded or changed by government policy (Frideres and Gadacz 2011). In the past, Indigenous organizations were under-resourced (in both finance and social capital) and multifaceted, and they lacked a coherent focus, all the while defined as illegitimate or irrelevant by the government. In some cases, the organizations have been defined as terrorist or subversive, and an increase in their surveillance and policing has occurred. In a case study of government scrutiny of Indigenous organizations, Crosby and Monaghan (2018) reveal that CSIS and the RCMP have defined some Indigenous organizations as dangerous and, when possible, neutralized their activities. Well over 300 Indigenous activists in various Indigenous organizations were identified in 2014–15 as potential national security threats (Project Sitka).

Some of the people in those organizations were identified by government officials and police as extremists, criminals, or militants who promoted violence and thus were viewed by Canadians as irresponsible and illegitimate leaders. Other members found that, once the "crisis" was over, the organization tended to dissolve. Yet several organizations have focused their activities, developed socially cohesive organizational structures, retained financial bases, and remained intact until their long-term goals have been achieved. Today we see cohesive, pan-Canadian Indigenous organizations such as the Assembly of First Nations, the Congress of Aboriginal Peoples, the Métis National Council, the Inuit Tapiriit Kanatami, and the Native Women's Association of Canada. In addition, each year numerous local Indigenous organizations are created to focus on some specific objective of importance (e.g., the BC Aboriginal Network on Disability Society, Métis Culture and Heritage Resource Centre, First Peoples Development). Equally noticeable is that many of these organizations fade into extinction within a year or two. These temporary organizations—which lack cohesion, expertise, and funding—mean that their effectiveness in bringing about change is low, and even their educative function is limited.

EXTERNAL ORGANIZATIONAL STRUCTURE

Since the time of contact, the colonial government (and later the federal government) has made promises that Indigenous Peoples would share the resources of the country. These promises shaped the initial and later relationships between the government and Indigenous Peoples. However, the government subsequently enacted exclusionary policies and appropriated the resources of Indigenous Peoples for others. Indigenous Peoples still live with dysfunctional, ineffectual, and institutionalized relationships that stigmatize them. Since non-Indigenous people have been unable to appreciate their own identities, they assume that this must also be true for Indigenous Peoples. Even when subgroups such as the Québécois argue that they comprise a "state" and have their own identity, they refuse to accept the argument that Indigenous Peoples also have distinct identities. Somehow they rationalize that, while they are unique in Confederation, Indigenous Peoples are not.

The actions of Indigenous Peoples across the country vary in terms of approach, process, and strategy. Although all aspire to self-determination, the path to achieving it differs across communities. Some communities argue that self-government is the pathway to self-determination, whereas others argue that economic development will lead to self-determination. Some are supportive of allowing First Nations to manage their reserve lands; others are not. Some are in favour of allowing urban Indigenous people to participate fully in the affairs of the reserve; others are not. Some bands have invoked "blood quantum" as a criterion for band membership, whereas others have used different criteria. Some organizations claim to represent all Métis, whereas others are more regionally focused. Major ideological and practical differences exist among the many Indigenous communities across Canada. But equally evident is that the government treats Indigenous Peoples as a homogeneous group—though agreeing (on paper) that there are differences among Inuit, First Nations, and Métis without clarifying those differences. Some Indigenous communities are well organized, prosperous, and clear in their goals for the future, whereas others do not have these attributes. Finally, some Indigenous communities are more active in Canadian politics than others. Why do we find these differences? What has happened to bring about this lack of unanimity that weakens their positions when dealing with the government?

Most people give simplistic answers, saying that the time of contact or the geography of the country has brought about these differences. Others naively claim that the extent of assimilation of each Indigenous community has brought about this diversity. Finally, others argue that the communities have different natural resources to develop and that this explains the variety of ideological positions evident across the country (e.g., some communities have access to oil and gas, others to different forms of fishing). Research carried out by the Harvard Project has clearly dispelled that argument. Moreover, few point out that the impacts of different levels of colonization on communities have brought about the differences. My argument is much more sanguine. First, there have been cultural and linguistic differences among Indigenous groups since time immemorial. Second, the differences among Indigenous communities have emerged over time, partially because the crown has treated them differently. Different ideological forces were operative as the communities were established, and as a result different actions, policies, and programs were implemented by religious orders and the government. Moreover, these communities were differentially subjected to new policies and programs established by the government in its quest to assimilate Indigenous Peoples. The impacts of these government dictates on Indigenous communities have manifested themselves over several generations. We see such diversity manifested in non-Indigenous communities across Canada, so there is no reason why we should not expect it to be evident among Indigenous communities. Put another way, the differences among Indigenous communities have resulted in various histories, perspectives, ideologies, and levels of integration. Hence, we should recognize the differences among Indigenous communities and perhaps agree that they will never be bridged, nor do they need to be. Nevertheless, Indigenous Peoples across the country have many other values and perspectives in common. A lack of trust in the government is one of the most important and common issues among Indigenous Peoples.

DISTRUST OF THE GOVERNMENT

Over time, the actions of the government have had two major impacts on Indigenous Peoples. First, they have engendered a lack of trust in the government, whose claims cannot be trusted. Claims both historical and current made by government officials regarding Indigenous Peoples have been found to be untrue, exaggerated, or simply inappropriate. Because of this distrust, Indigenous people view the government with skepticism and cynicism. One can think of only a few times in the history of Canada when Indigenous Peoples were better off once they agreed to a government program or policy. There are abundant examples of when they agreed to a policy only to have the government refuse to implement it (e.g., Jordan's Principle), or implement only part of it, and at times the government has even implemented a very different policy. For example, after the Kelowna Agreement was unanimously accepted in 2005 by the federal government, premiers, and Indigenous leaders, when the Conservatives gained power they refused to honour it. From an Indigenous perspective, most decisions made by the government and the private sector have placed Indigenous Peoples in situations in which their quality of life has decreased. A culture of distrust has thus been sustained in almost every Indigenous community, and this is why it is so difficult for the two parties to reach agreement on almost any issue.

Related to this concern is that Indigenous Peoples are always looking for the "latent" goals embedded in any government pronouncement as well as looking to the future. There is no belief that the manifest content of any policy or program promulgated by the government will lead to the betterment of the lives of Indigenous Peoples. There is only cynicism that the policy or program, which might look good at first, will be to the detriment of Indigenous Peoples as it plays out. For example, the proposed bill to create fee simple ownership of land on a reserve by an Indigenous individual has been rejected. Although Indigenous Peoples agree that the proposed change might be beneficial to some, they argue that it would simply be a way to sell the existing resources and lands of First Nations to the government and private sector so that they can reap the profits. Both trust in and respect for the government have long been eroded, and there seems to be little acknowledgement of this by the government or any attempt to rebuild trust and respect. A recent report by Eyeford (2013) confirms this observation. A further study by the School of Public Policy at the University of Calgary in 2014 found a notable lack of trust in the government among Indigenous Peoples and particularly suspicion about the oil and gas private sector (Moore, Turcotte, and Winter 2014). More than one-third of those interviewed claimed to have zero trust in the private sector. So one can see that it is nearly impossible to carry on a discussion between the two parties that will lead to some concrete action when the level of trust is so low. A similar lack of trust in the government was also evident. Thus, the first attribute of Indigenous communities crucial in understanding how they think and act is lack of trust in and respect for the crown.

The second attribute of any Indigenous community is the existence of a socio-political elite and the pervasiveness of politics in reserve life. This process began when the government first enacted the *Indian Act*. It allowed Indigenous men but not women to become "persons." The men, finding some solace in being acknowledged thus, quickly took to supporting some of the early efforts of the government even though the women in their communities would remain secondary citizens. It also meant that a gendered society would emerge in which men would assume the dominant position in socio-political activities in their communities. This allowed for the emergence of "gender wars" that have troubled Indigenous communities for the past century. This early stratified system also allowed certain families, either through planning or luck, to dominate the economic structure of the community, which in turn gave them political and cultural power. Hence, in any Indigenous community one will find an economic-political elite that controls and gives direction to the affairs of the community. Sometimes the elite will be divided by domain (e.g., economic elite, cultural elite). However, in general, the same families occupy influential positions in the community regarding all of the domains. To be sure, these elites, as in the larger Canadian society, change over time as conditions and politics change—sometimes because of activities by external agents. So the same families over a century might not occupy high-status positions in the community. Nevertheless, these elites, through their actions, determine the ethos of the community and how it will deal with both internal and external agents (e.g., band council members, Indian Affairs representatives, private sector agents, and challenges from the rank and file of the community).

In understanding the actions of sustainable Indigenous organizations more fully, it is useful to examine local and national organizational structures put in place by Indigenous communities as well as how the state relates to these organizations to maintain control and oversight of their actions.

FIRST NATIONS ORGANIZATIONS

LOCAL STRUCTURE

At the time of first contact with settlers, First Nations had developed a sophisticated process of political governance. However, the colonial government refused to acknowledge this structure and process and subsequently created new policies that systematically dismantled existing political structures in Indigenous communities. The government created a political structure called a band and then imposed a municipal style of government on each band, which would be forced to elect a Chief and councillors every two years in a manner prescribed by the *Indian Act*. Some First Nations communities refused to abide by the *Indian Act* and still use a hereditary process for selecting Chiefs and councillors, but they have incurred the wrath of government officials over the years. For those communities abiding by the designs of the government, one councillor is elected for every 100 band members, and the council is responsible for the administration of band affairs (e.g., schools, roads, and other activities internal to the community). However, all decisions are monitored by the minister of Indian affairs and can be overruled at any time. More recently, in modern treaties, self-government has been adopted and gives the band council (or some political structure) more opportunities to manage internal affairs, and in some cases the *Indian Act* no longer applies to the community (e.g., the Nisga'a). But again the minister has the ultimate power in allocating funds and projects for the community. In short, the band council and Chief are administrators and not engaged in governance.

Councillors and Chief, until recently, were voted in by residents of the community. However, in 1999, in *Corbiere v Canada (Minister of Indian and Northern Affairs)*, the Supreme Court found this provision contrary to the equality rights of off-reserve band members under section 15 of the *Charter of Rights and Freedoms*, and thus today any person, on or off reserve, has the right to vote in any public election if a band member (Imai 2007).

Today the legal standing of a band member is not the same as that of a Status Indian. The federal government has "delinked" the two, and thus only it can issue a Status Indian registration to an individual. Thus one can be a Status Indian but not a member of a band. To achieve band status, the individual must be approved by the First Nations community with which the applicant wishes to establish an affiliation. Under the revisions to the *Indian Act*, people legally defined as First Nations can apply to become band members and thus participate in the politics of the community. The government has allowed each First Nations community to develop its own criteria for deciding membership. Some have chosen the criteria outlined in the *Indian Act*, whereas others have chosen more restrictive criteria (e.g., both parents must be Status Indians, blood quantum).

Today Chief and council make a variety of administrative decisions within the dictates of the *Indian Act*. Each decision is implemented through a band council resolution if there is a majority vote in a council meeting. Moreover, the council has the right to make different types of bylaws allowed by the *Indian Act*, but they must be sent to the minister for review and approval. In other actions taken by the band council, there might be community notification and participation before council votes on the actions (Imai 2007), but the *Indian Act* is unclear on this aspect of decision-making. For example, general powers and monetary issues only require the votes of the Chief and council at a meeting. There are thus few procedural requirements for the Chief and council, such as giving notice or getting approval from the electors of the band. Hence, many decisions are made by the Chief and council without community input. In addition, the minister may approve or reject any action taken by the Chief and council without any explanation to anyone. In short, transparency and accountability are lacking in decision-making in First Nations communities by both the Chief and council and the government (Imai 2007). Almost all decisions made by the Chief and council are reviewed by the minister before they become "law." In addition, all financial transactions are approved by Indian Affairs before expenditures are made.

Within the community, many social organizations set the contexts for discussions of other issues. For example, numerous societies focus on spiritual beliefs and practices; establish the roles of men, women, children, and Elders; and ensure that sacred ceremonies are followed (e.g., the Haudenosaunee Green Corn Ceremony, Sundance of the plains First Nations). These local societies or groups interact with the community as well as the band council and influence various decisions.

NATIONAL STRUCTURE

The National Indian Council was established in 1961 to represent Métis and Status and Non-Status Indians. However, the organization had collapsed by 1967, and new Indigenous organizations were founded. That year the National Indian Brotherhood was created as an umbrella group for both provincial and territorial First Nations organizations. Out of this initiative, the "All Chiefs Conference" was conceived, and it was agreed that it would be the singular voice for all First Nations people in Canada. To formalize the governance structure, the Charter of the Assembly of First Nations was created in 1982. Today the Assembly of First Nations (AFN) is the organization representing Status Indians across Canada. In 1985, the AFN established its ideals and actions to be carried out by the organization and publicly communicated them to all First Nations communities. The basic principles of the AFN begin with the belief that First Nations were placed on the Earth by the Creator. The Creator in turn provided them with natural laws to ensure that all entities on the Earth live in harmony. In these natural laws, the Creator provided clearly defined rights and responsibilities, and one of the most important is to take care of Mother Earth. First Nations therefore believe that they must exercise the responsibilities given to them through traditions. They must continue their quest for a better life and the lives of the next seven generations. The AFN argues that the natural laws passed down from the Creator support the recognition of inherent Aboriginal Rights and Title as well as self-determination; the role of First Nations is to exercise their responsibilities to all other entities (living and non-living) and to protect their lands. They also see themselves as advocates to ensure the appropriate implementation of treaties and other agreements made between First Nations communities and the government.

The AFN is structured to take into consideration the diversity of communities, operate as a collective political power, and carry out the aspirations of First Nations. The United Nations is a model of how the assembly is to act. Consensus is the mode of decision-making, but if it cannot be achieved, then a vote of 60 percent of the Chiefs and other representatives of First Nations communities is sufficient to act. The AFN meets once a year, though there may be special sessions convened throughout the year as requested by the national Chief, Confederacy of Nations, or Executive Committee. The AFN has created a charter that outlines the principles on which it will act. In addition, the charter (not unlike the Canadian Constitution) outlines specific actions that the organization will take.

Membership in the AFN is open to all Status Indians in Canada. The organization includes a First Nations-in-Assembly, a Confederacy of Nations, an Executive Committee, a Secretariat, and three Councils of Elders, Women, and Youth. Each component has rights and responsibilities as well as accountability provisions. The First Nations-in-Assembly is made up of all the Chiefs of First Nations communities across the country. It has the right to make decisions on many issues if they are within the mandate of the AFN. When decisions are made, the Executive Committee is instructed to proceed with ratification and to ensure that all First Nations will benefit from the action taken.

The Confederacy of Nations is composed of representatives from each region in Canada. Each region has one representative plus one representative for each 10,000 Status Indians in that region. It operates as the governing body between the meetings of the First Nations-in-Assembly and normally meets on a quarterly basis. It reviews decisions of the assembly, interprets resolutions, and acts when First Nations communities individually or collectively request that action be taken. It also approves and allocates the fiscal resources of the assembly.

The Executive Committee is composed of the national Chief (elected every three years), AFN regional Chiefs (elected by the Chiefs in their regions every three years), and the chair of the Council of Elders.

The Council of Elders is viewed as the keeper of the traditions, values, languages, and histories of First Nations and the guide to the future. Elders are leaders in the community; they speak with honour and wisdom. They are considered teachers and champions and continue to inform forums such as the Chiefs' Assemblies on their experiences, issues, successes, and challenges.

The Council of Women carries out its duties along with the Secretariat to make sure that the concerns of women are taken into consideration when the AFN makes decisions. Its specific goal is to establish a gender-balanced perspective within communities and to honour the rights of First Nations women. It also takes on the responsibility to ensure that cultural teaching and identity occur within the community. Finally, members of the council participate in other committees of the AFN.

The Council of Youth is created from each of the ten AFN regions. Each region appoints two representatives (one male and one female) selected by regional youth councils or regional Chiefs. This council represents youth across the country and addresses issues that affect them (e.g., language, culture, education). The council reports to the AFN as an advisory body on all issues from a youth perspective.

One of the most important roles of the AFN is to monitor government action and ensure that the information presented by the government and the AFN is distributed to all First Nations communities across the country and captures the interest of mainstream media. In reviewing government information, the AFN also provides its interpretation of the documents and, on occasion, detailed commentary. It also has a communications component ensuring that information and commentary are distributed across Canada. The AFN passes resolutions, drafts position papers, and writes reports on timely issues. For example, recently the AFN rejected the government's *First Nations Education Act*, getting the government to redraft the content; the revision was also rejected, and the government did not pursue the proposed legislation. In other cases, the AFN has passed resolutions for the government to carry out (e.g., the Inquiry into Missing and Murdered Indigenous Women and Girls). The AFN brings to the government position papers on First Nations issues that it believes are important. It also responds to government laws, programs, and policies, agreeing or disagreeing with them or pointing out their acceptable and unacceptable elements. The AFN has about thirty current "policy" areas with which it deals, ranging from border crossing, fisheries, and aquatic resource management to international advocacy and activity. The chairs of these policy area committees report back to the First Nations-in-Assembly and to other relevant components of the AFN during the year. Through its research, the AFN prepares resolutions, communicates with appropriate federal/provincial/territorial ministries, and ensures that the information is shared with First Nations communities across Canada.

MÉTIS ORGANIZATIONS

Although there are numerous local, provincial, regional, and national Métis organizations, the local and provincial organizational structures focus on the aspirations and interests of Métis in the community or province. Provincial organizations periodically hold elections, and in some cases Métis Nation provincial community councils have been established. These local councils work with the provincial Métis Nation organization to represent the rights of Métis in the region. In some provinces, regional associations deliver programs and services to their specific geographic areas. Some provincial organizations have established bilateral and tripartite processes with the federal and provincial governments on issues of interest to Métis people and communities in the province. Most provincial associations have developed different portfolios (some are linked to a provincial ministry, and others focus on policy) that focus on issues of importance (e.g., energy, education, housing, economic development).

MÉTIS IN ALBERTA

I focus my discussion of Métis organizations on Alberta because it is the only province that acknowledges the legal existence of Métis and has accepted some responsibility for them. However, in 2002 the Saskatchewan government passed a *Métis Act* that recognized the contributions of Métis in the province and set up a procedure to deal with specific Métis institutions (e.g., the Gabriel Dumont Institute, Métis Nation-Saskatchewan). However, its mandate is to recognize the culture and history of Métis in Saskatchewan, and it allows the Métis Nation to engage in negotiations on capacity building, land, and harvesting for food and other purposes. Similarly, in Manitoba, after three decades of legal wrangling, the provincial government is dealing with the legal consequences of a case brought to the Supreme Court by the Manitoba Métis Federation arguing that the federal crown failed to implement the land grant provisions set out in section 31 of the *Manitoba Act, 1870*. In 2013, the Supreme Court ruled that the federal government did not live up to the conditions of land distribution to Métis. Specific action has yet to be taken regarding this decision.

During the late 1920s and early 1930s, the Alberta government became concerned with the political activities of Métis as well as their marginal status in the province. The Ewing Commission (sometimes referred to as the "Half-Breed Commission") of 1934 was assigned to investigate the plight of Métis in Alberta. It defined a Métis as a person of mixed blood who lived like an "Indian," but it did not include those who had become farmers or did not rely on public assistance. Four years later the province enacted the *Métis Population Betterment Act*, which led to establishing a land base for Métis—initially eleven Métis colonies (now called settlements). However, not until after the *Constitution Act, 1982* was passed did Alberta commence action to deal with contemporary Métis issues. The MacEwan Report (MacEwan 1984) was a result of the government of Alberta's desire to deal with the issue of self-government and the creation of a more regulated land base for Métis in Alberta. The report recommended both self-government and a more secure land base. It dealt with the eight Métis settlements in Alberta that exist today (Randall 2011). By 2000, the *Métis Settlements Act* and the *Constitution of Alberta Amendment Act, 1990* had been placed into legislation. Then, in 2011, the Supreme Court of Canada issued its decision in *Alberta (Aboriginal Affairs and Northern Development) v Cunningham*. The court found that the *Métis Settlements Act, 2000* could limit who could become a member of a

Métis settlement. The court also reaffirmed the central role of Métis in defining who is a Métis and in determining who may benefit from the Act. However, it did not provide any definition of who is a Métis.

MÉTIS SETTLEMENTS ORGANIZATION

Today each settlement in Alberta (in six regions) has a Settlement Council (an incorporated entity). To ensure the effective operation of the various settlements, an administrative and political structure was put in place. The Métis General Council is composed of four elected officers and the settlement councillors, and its primary activity is to implement policies of the provincial government that affect the collective interests of Métis. Under the current structure, the General Council also develops policies on issues that affect Métis ways of life (e.g., forestry, taxation of settlement lands, hunting, trapping, co-management of subsurface resources on settlement lands). In addition, the General Council participates in a variety of commercial activities and engages in financial transactions initiated by the settlement. However, any policy developed by the General Council must first have the approval of six of the eight settlements. Moreover, the provincial minister in charge of the Métis settlements has the right to veto any policy or portion of a policy with no explanation.

Members of the Settlement Council are elected by residents of the settlement, and the powers of the council are like those of a municipality. For example, it can pass a bylaw regarding who can be a resident, deal with health and safety issues, arrange for waste disposal, and regulate businesses that operate in the settlement. The Settlement Council is also expected to implement policies developed by the General Council. People who live in the settlement must meet the membership criteria set out in policies established by the General Council. In addition, each settlement has developed its own dispute resolution strategy called the Métis Settlements Appeal Tribunal. It is a "Métis court" composed of seven people and now has an executive committee as part of its administrative structure. It has a chair and three members appointed by the minister from a list provided by the General Council and three other members appointed by the General Council. Two other administrative structures operate in the Métis settlements. Under the

Métis Settlements Act, there is the Land Access Panel and the Existing Leases and Land Access Panel. These two bodies deal with issues previously dealt with by the Provincial Surface Rights Board. However, if a panel or the tribunal makes a decision that is appealed, the appeal may be taken to the Alberta Court of Appeal.

Several Métis settlements and their surrounding areas are at the centre of future heavy oil extraction. However, the duty to consult with and accommodate (honour of the crown) the settlements is unclear (Teillet 2013). Legal practitioners note that it is incumbent on the province to protect Métis, but Alberta fails to protect the lands surrounding the Métis settlements. This lack of action erodes the purposes of the *Métis Settlements Act*. Courts might favour a broader process of consultation between Métis settlements and provincial governments than what exists today, but this is not in the existing legislation. The courts' discussion of the "distinctive Métis culture, identity and self-governance" might persuade courts that the crown owes a greater duty to consult with the Métis settlements and accommodate their concerns regarding current development (Métis Nation of Alberta 2009).

The *Métis Settlements Act* deals with the identification of Métis as members of the settlements. The criteria for membership are left to each Settlement Council, subject to the terms of the Act. To prove Métis identity under the Act, the person must have Canadian Indigenous ancestry and identify with Métis history and culture.

NATIONAL MÉTIS ORGANIZATION

The National Métis Council has been recognized by the federal government as the representative of Métis in the four western provinces. This organization has established links with federal government agencies and carried out many negotiations with them. In a sense, it has received the "blessing" of the federal government as a legitimate organization that supports the goals of the government. As Belanger (2014) points out, Métis are often viewed as prairie people who emerged from the Red River region in Manitoba. Others argue that there were Métis long before the Red River Colony was founded in 1816. In the 1940s, Métis were defined in terms of blood quantum: one had to be less than one-quarter "Indian" but still have some "Indian blood" to be a Métis.

In 1968, the Canadian Métis Society emerged and was subsequently renamed the Native Council of Canada. During the second half of the twentieth century, prairie Métis associations were part of the Native Council of Canada (now known as the Congress of Aboriginal Peoples). However, its pan-Indigenous approach did not allow Métis to represent themselves effectively, and as a result, in March 1983, Métis separated from the Native Council of Canada to form the Métis National Council, a Métis-specific national representative body, which has since represented Métis nationally and internationally. It receives its mandate and direction from the elected leaders of the organization. At the national level, the council is the overarching voice of Métis. It is composed of five provincial Métis organizations from British Columbia, Alberta, Saskatchewan, Manitoba, and Ontario. Within these provincial organizations are regional councils made up of local or community councils. The Métis National Council has a board of governors made up of the presidents of the provincial associations and the national president. It oversees the everyday activities of the council as well as supports a permanent secretariat in Ottawa.

The Métis National Council governance structures and institutions have changed over time to meet the needs and challenges of Métis. Moreover, provincial authorities have been influenced by the actions of the council. For example, in 2004 the Alberta government amended the *Métis Settlements Act* because of the decision in *Powley* (2003) that gave Métis in Ontario broader harvesting (hunting) rights. Through the Métis Nation Protocol signed by the government of Canada and the Métis National Council in 2008, Métis representative bodies increased their capacity to carry out their mandates as received from their constituents as well as to deliver programs and services. Perhaps most important is their goal of implementing the inherent Métis Right to self-government within Canada.

Complicating all of this is the fractionalization of Métis organizations across the country. For example, the Canadian Métis Council is not affiliated with the Métis National Council. The former is composed of fifty community councils and affiliated organizations across the country. In Quebec, the Nation Métis-Quebec, not affiliated with the Métis National Council, was created to deal with Métis in that province. The Métis Nation of Canada was established in 2009 to deal with Métis not living in the prairie provinces and/or not meeting the criteria established by the Métis National Council, to which it is not linked. Nevertheless, the Métis Nation of Canada is a national organization that represents Indigenous people not recognized by the Métis National Council or other organizations that act as advocates for their rights. Finally, the Congress of Aboriginal Peoples (emerging from the Native Council of Canada, established in 1971) was established in 1993 initially to represent Métis, Non-Status Indians, off-reserve Status Indians, and southern Inuit, and it continues to do so.

The diverse organizational structure of Métis has posed problems for establishing relationships with provincial and federal governments. However, the federal government has singled out the Métis National Council as the primary organization with which it wishes to deal, and it has since signed major accords and framework agreements regarding health, housing, and other issues with this national organization. The government continues to view it as the organization that speaks for all Métis in Canada. For example, in 2005, the federal cabinet met with five Indigenous groups, one of which was the Métis National Council, but it refused to meet with other Métis organizations, including the General Council of the Métis settlements in Alberta, even though it knew that the Métis National Council did not represent the interests of the General Council. The Congress of Aboriginal Peoples is also one of the five major national Indigenous representative organizations recognized by the federal government. Nevertheless, each national organization has worked on specific policies and programs with various provincial and federal government departments in an advocacy role, trying to achieve the aspirations of Métis.

INUIT SOCIAL ORGANIZATIONS

REGIONAL INUIT ORGANIZATIONS

Northern Canada is divided into four regions: Inuvialuit, Nunavut (itself divided into two regions: Kivalliq and Kitikmeot), Nunatsiavut, and Nunavik, all making up Inuit Nunangat, the entire northern area dominated by Inuit. Each regional government has the responsibility for developing its lands and resources as well as preserving Inuit culture and implementing social programs that it or the federal government has developed (Kulchyski 2006). Although each region has some unique governance structures, overall the regions have similar government mandates.

Inuvialuit

The Inuvialuit in northwestern Canada signed the *Western Arctic Claims Settlement Act* with the federal government in 1984, and it is protected under the Constitution in that it cannot be revised by Parliament without the approval of the Inuvialuit. The Inuvialuit Corporate Group, composed of the Inuvialuit Regional Corporation and its subsidiaries, was created after the agreement was in place. Under the agreement, the Inuvialuit Regional Corporation was created to manage the *Western Arctic Claims Settlement Act*. It has also established a system of joint management with the federal government and the northwest territorial government focusing on resource management (e.g., wildlife, fisheries, environment). The overall goal of the Inuvialuit Regional Corporation is to improve the economic and cultural wellness of Inuvialuit by ensuring that the conditions of the *Western Arctic Claims Settlement Act* are implemented along with other pieces of legislation that will have positive impacts on the well-being of Inuvialuit. The mandate of the corporation is to administer the rights and benefits of the Act to all people in the region. After the Inuvialuit Regional Corporation was created, it established subsidiaries such as the Inuvialuit Development Corporation, Investment Corporation, Petroleum Corporation, and Land Corporation. The Inuvialuit Regional Corporation also supports the activities of the Land Administration, Community Development Division, and Inuvialuit Cultural Resource Centre as they carry out their individual mandates.

Each community in this region has a community corporation with elected directors. The directors of the six corporations then elect the chair of the Inuvialuit Regional Corporation. The chairs of each of the community corporations along with the chair of the Inuvialuit Regional Corporation form the Inuvialuit Regional Corporation Board of Directors.

Nunavik

In Nunavik, Inuit have argued for self-government since the 1960s. In 2007, the Inuit of Quebec as well as the federal and provincial governments signed an agreement that created the new regional government of Nunavik, representing all people living in the region. The agreement created an elected assembly of twenty-one people, one from each of the communities in Nunavik. Under this agreement, the Kativik regional government (akin to a municipal government), the Kativik School Board, and the Nunavik Regional Board of Health and Social Services have been amalgamated into one structure that has considerable powers and responsibilities beyond those of a municipal government. The Aboriginal Rights of the Inuit in Nunavik are protected by the Makivik Corporation established under the James Bay and Northern Quebec Agreement (1975) that protects the land claims settlements signed and later amended in 2007. The Makivik Corporation has protected Inuit Rights, including land claims, as well as offshore rights for Inuit in the region. Its operations range from creating large corporations to ensuring appropriate housing for residents to supporting Inuit languages and cultures.

Nunatsiavut

In 1973, the Labrador Inuit Association was created to sustain Inuit culture and improve the well-being of the people. It was not until 2005, though, that the Labrador Inuit began their Nunatsiavut regional government created through the Labrador Inuit Land Claims Agreement. This agreement allowed for self-government provisions; although the Labrador Inuit are part of Labrador and Newfoundland, their local government has authority over areas such as justice, health, culture, education, and community concerns, including the right to make laws based upon their traditions. As such, it operates at two levels: regional and community. At the regional level, there are seven departments, such as Nunatsiavut Affairs, Health, Education, and Land. At the community level, there are five governments responsible for providing residents with appropriate services and programs. The *AngajukKak* (or mayor) of each community government is a representative of the constituency in the Nunatsiavut Assembly. The assembly operates by consensus and is structured in such a way that the political and operational structures of the government are separated. The assembly provides oversight of the region in that it develops policy direction for the government and makes laws. At the operational level, the various departments of the Nunatsiavut government enforce the laws and ensure that the policies are translated into programs and services.

Nunavut

Nunavut was created in 1999 through the Nunavut Land Claims Agreement. Nunavut Tunnagavik Incorporated was established as a private company to ensure that promises in the land claims agreement would be carried out. This new territory has a public government that serves both Inuit and other residents in the region. In fulfilling its mandate, it has established an elected, no-party Legislative Assembly based upon consensus. Residents of Nunavut are referred to as Nunavummiut, and the territory is guided by the belief that its people should be bilingual and bicultural. The political and social organizations of Nunavummiut fall within the framework chosen by other territories. As such, they operate according to a standard set of rules, like any territorial government. The Legislative Assembly of Nunavut has a speaker, a premier, an executive council, and twenty-two members. An advisory council of Elders provides advice on Inuit Traditional Knowledge and its links with the territory's political actions. The commissioner is considered the head of Nunavut, and all laws passed by the Legislative Assembly of Nunavut must receive the assent of the commissioner.

NATIONAL INUIT ORGANIZATIONS

The first national Inuit organization created was the Indian and Eskimo Association formed in the 1960s, which morphed into the Inuit Tapirisat of Canada in 1971. It was an important body that contributed to the creation of the four Inuit regions. As well, it acted as a lobbying agent, pressing the federal government to change its policy on Inuit and their land. Thirty years later it changed its name to Inuit Tapiriit Kanatami, which currently operates for the welfare of Inuit, and its objectives are to ensure the needs and aspirations of Inuit regarding environmental and social issues in northern Canada.

The Inuit Tapiriit Kanatami is organized through a board of directors composed of a president, the elected heads of the four regional Inuit land claims organizations (Inuvialuit Regional Corporation, Nunavut Tunngavik Incorporated, Makivik Corporation, and Nunatsiavut government), the presidents of the Inuit Circumpolar Council of Canada, the National Inuit Youth Council, and the Pauktuutit Inuit Women of Canada. Every three years the president is elected by delegates to the Inuit Tapiriit Kanatami annual general assembly.

CONCLUSION

Although political activism by Indigenous people began after the Second World War, it was the *Calder* case in 1973 (which ruled that Aboriginal Rights existed partially from the Royal Proclamation of 1763 as well as through subsequent government implementation of that decree) that would embolden them to redefine their position in Canadian society. This was followed by repatriation of the Constitution in 1982. Indigenous organizations have not been totally successful in their political efforts, but they have continued to engage in political advocacy and litigation to achieve their places within Canada's parliamentary democracy. In addition to the creation of the five major national Indigenous organizations, other national organizations have emerged to supplement the activities of Indigenous people. The Aboriginal Human Resource Council, Canadian Council for Aboriginal Business, and Indigenous Bar Association have supported the pan-Canadian Indigenous organizations in their quest for a more inclusive Canada.

Independent grassroots movements such as Idle No More have swept across the country in pressing for a new agenda on Indigenous human rights and economic development. These new organizations and their use of social media (Brady and Kelly 2017) reflect the international Aboriginal Rights movement, which demonstrates that Indigenous Peoples around the world share the same marginal existence and lack of protection for their languages, environments, cultures, and human rights. These national and international movements have taken advantage of social media, and the various organizations share their experiences. This movement helped to create the Declaration on the Rights of Indigenous Peoples (2007), which Canada initially refused to sign but eventually did sign three years later. Moreover, the Supreme Court of Canada ruled that Indigenous Peoples are the beneficiaries of their Traditional Territories. It is therefore time to give them that right to decide how to use and manage those lands. This movement has forced Canada to understand more fully the demands of Indigenous Peoples and to develop new ways of accommodating their wishes, something that was not done in the past.

Indigenous organizations support the four epistemological pillars of respect for Indigenous teachings, understanding of their place in creation, knowledge of their purpose in the world, and recognition of how their thoughts and actions affect everyone. As Kelm and Smith (2018, 2) argue, Indigenous organizations are resisting the pressures of the government to eliminate Indigenous Peoples through its power to sever their connections to their Traditional Territories, families, and communities as well as to disrupt Indigenous systems of governance. These organizations are resisting the government's policy of the "logic of elimination." Through the enactment of policies, laws, and programs, the cultures of Indigenous Peoples would cease to exist as Canada enters the twenty-second century. As Kelm and Smith (2018, 29) conclude, the government continues to believe that Indigenous Peoples need to be integrated into neo-colonial society through a shared commitment to capitalism and the ability to govern themselves according to British and French traditions and laws.

CONCLUSION

RECONCILIATION *and* RESILIENCE *in the* TWENTY-FIRST CENTURY

LOOKING TO THE FUTURE

Indigenous community leaders are called on by both governments and members of their own communities to bring about well-being, restore people's health, solve economic problems (in both rural and urban communities), and deal with nepotism and politics—all without the power and commensurate resources to achieve these lofty goals. Over the years, Indigenous leaders have called for the restoration of power, land, and self-respect for Indigenous Peoples. These concerns were clearly enunciated in the Penner Report in 1983 and later in the report of the Royal Commission on Aboriginal Peoples in 1996. However, over two decades later, the recommendations of these reports have been ignored, and no action has been taken to address the issues. Today we have "calls to action" enunciated by the Truth and Reconciliation Commission, and we wait to see whether

Canadians can bring about structural and meaningful changes in the relationship with Indigenous Peoples. Thus far it seems that the educational institutions are the only organizations attempting to address these calls to action, though their actions only touch the periphery of reconciliation in a meaningful manner (Gaudry and Lorenz 2018).

The government continues to play a paternalistic role in its relationship with Indigenous Peoples even though it agrees that they should take on more control over their lives. Yet in the past decade several pieces of legislation have been proposed and/or passed that clearly demonstrate the government is not about to give Indigenous Peoples more control (e.g., *First Nations Education Act, Safe Drinking Water for First Nations Act, First Nations Governance Act, First Nations Land Management Act*). Moreover, until 1995, new federal laws routinely included a "non-derogation" clause that provided some assurance to Indigenous Peoples that new legislation would not be designed to have "unintended" impacts that would reduce the extent of Aboriginal and Treaty Rights. However, since then, the Department of Justice has replaced some of the clear non-derogation language with weaker wording and ostensibly led the way to overturn Parliament's clear intention not to diminish Aboriginal Rights.

A Senate committee discussed this trend and recommended that the federal *Interpretation Act* be amended so that new laws be interpreted to support, rather than diminish, Aboriginal Rights. The Department of Justice has rejected this recommendation. The proposed *Safe Drinking Water for First Nations Act* is a good example of how the legislation diminishes the constitutional and legal status of Aboriginal Rights. The Act specifically states that if Aboriginal Rights conflict with the objective of a law, those rights will not be respected. The new law would negate promises made to First Nations in treaties and the interpretations of those treaties. The Act was developed without consultation with Indigenous Peoples, and it flies in the face of the United Nations Declaration on the Rights of Indigenous Peoples (UNDRIP) that Canada signed.

At the same time, the Conservative government introduced two omnibus bills (C-45 and C-38) that altered nearly 1,000 pieces of legislation regarding the environment, with both direct and indirect effects on Indigenous Peoples. For example, changes to the *Environmental Protection Act* reduced environmental protection regarding regulations, reviews, and consultations. The Act reduced the level of community voting necessary for any First Nations community to surrender its reserve land to pipeline consortiums. When the Conservative government passed Bill C-45, it changed the *Indian Act* regarding the surrender of lands on reserves. Under the new *Indian Act*, if a meeting for the purpose of surrendering or leasing land is held by the band council, then a simple majority of those *attending the meeting* would be sufficient to enact the surrender or lease. Moreover, only the minister of Indian affairs needs to approve it and can call for a band council meeting to vote on the issue. Nevertheless, even the decision of the band council requires the approval of the minister.

Today the Liberal government claims to be committed to reconciliation through a nation-to-nation relationship based upon the acknowledgement of rights, respect, cooperation, and partnership. Nevertheless, if UNDRIP is to be implemented, then it will require a transformation in the relationship between the government and Indigenous Peoples. The government has outlined ten principles as part of the proposed framework for recognizing rights that will initiate the process of decolonization. Moreover, it will review all existing laws and policies within the context of these principles and reflect a commitment to good faith, the rule of law, equity, and respect for human rights. (For a review of these principles, see www.justice.gc.ca/eng/csj-sjc/principles-eng.pdf.) Substantive changes in the relationship between the government and Indigenous Peoples are required, and only time will reveal whether a new relationship based upon equity, trust, and respect for Aboriginal Rights can be implemented (Niezen 2017).

The new relationship will be endemic to the state order, and institutional mandates and relationships will need to be changed (Moore 2010; Webber and Macleod 2010). Indigenous Peoples continue to engage in political activities and conflicts to get the government to make substantive changes in policy as well as to address the inequalities and injustices embedded in the legal and political systems of Canada (Leclair 2000). Indigenous Peoples require that Canada design new laws and policies that will keep mainstream institutions from engaging in discriminatory and unjust activities (Moore 2010). The Department of Indian Affairs does not disclose to the public in either oral or written form its standard operating procedures, aids, directives, and policies. It also refuses to disclose evidence of policies so that they can be adjudicated through the courts. For example, Indigenous organizations argue that the previous Department of Indian Affairs and the Department of Justice developed unreasonable (and mostly unknown) criteria for evidence in establishing paternity. Entering the courtroom, the plaintiff was unaware of the criteria used to adjudicate the particular case. Given these unknowns, some Indigenous organizations argue that the current government is not legitimate; until substantive changes are introduced regarding unjust policies and laws, the state will not be viewed as supportive, and Indigenous self-government is thus seen as a viable alternative (Diabo 2018a).

Some Indigenous communities are in the process of developing self-government strategies, and others are embarking on new economic ventures. Through the *Indian Act, 1876*, the federal government was given control of economic and resource development and land use as Indigenous Peoples became wards of the state. If they tried to engage in economic development, they were handicapped in doing so by the Department of Indian Affairs, which reviewed and approved all actions. Only in recent years has this changed. In some cases, Indigenous Peoples have implemented changes and generated funds. Examples are the Squamish, who are developing major shopping centres; the Osoyoos, who have a winery; the Vuntut Gwitchin (Yukon), who own North Airline and other interests; the Waswanipi Cree (Quebec), who run a silvaculture and timber harvest enterprise; the First Nations Bank of Canada; the Alberta Indian Investment Corporation (Enoch); Peace Hills Trust (Samson Cree); and the Membertou (Nova Scotia) hotel and convention centre.

Nevertheless, the government continues to view historical treaties as outlining the proprietary and governing rights of all parties involved—the federal government, provincial governments, territorial governments, and First Nations communities—and these issues are not part of the framework of rights recognition (Palmater 2018b). Yet it is evident that the treaties are poorly constructed agreements in that they fail to provide details on government involvement, use opaque language, include terms that have multiple meanings, and have clauses rejected by First Nations signatories. Nevertheless, the government has acted from this perspective for the past 200 years and has successfully kept First Nations from negotiating their political and legal rights (Graben and Mehaffey 2017).

Out of this contemporary discontent came social movements such as Idle No More, based upon Indigenous ways of knowing and resistance to the old social order. This includes honouring treaties as well as protecting the land and environment. The overall goal is to create an awareness among all Canadians and to bring collective action against laws and policies that the government has implemented that diminish or extinguish Aboriginal and Treaty Rights. These movements also propose approaches to deal with the conflicts between Indigenous Peoples and non-Indigenous people regarding several issues. Wallace (2013) argues that Indigenous Peoples want to challenge non-Indigenous people to deal with these complex issues involving the environment and resource development and to come to a just settlement. Idle No More participants draw from the work of scholars and activists such as Borrows (2003), Coyle (2005), Lawrence (2004), and Tully (2000), who have presented convincing arguments that the sovereignty of Indigenous Peoples was never surrendered and thus remains inherent, fully alive and operating as best it can in a colonial society.

Indigenous Peoples today are interested in furthering the process of decolonization and reconciliation. For them, Indigenous laws emphasize social harmony, restoring balance and re-establishing peace, rather than retribution or punishment. Their view of justice is based upon relationships with the land, animals, plants, the Creator, and other people (whether offenders or victims). Thus, restoring balance and healing relationships are central issues from Indigenous perspectives (Monchalin 2016). Western law is based upon the separation of land, culture, and governance, whereas in Indigenous cultures they cannot be separated. Indigenous Peoples thus attempt to reclaim power and to extend their authority to relate to the federal authorities in a government-to-government relationship. They also argue that engaging in reconciliation and building a just relationship require recognition by Canadians that the broken agreements need to be addressed. Finally, they believe that the process of reconciliation needs to reflect a specific transformation from ongoing colonial relations to decolonial structures of justice and equity (Wallace 2013). Although the Idle No More movement might be less public today than previously, the movement is still alive and well in First Nations communities across Canada. What will trigger its next public appearance has yet to be determined, but any event might be the spark that creates more sustained and focused activities.

Over the past few years, there were strong pressures from Indigenous organizations to establish an inquiry on missing and murdered Indigenous women and girls, and this had been rejected by the previous Conservative government, arguing that there was no need for such an inquiry. In its attempt to create trust and bring about justice for Indigenous Peoples, the current Liberal government created the Missing and Murdered Indigenous Women and Girls Commission in 2016.

In June 2019, the Commission concluded its three-year investigation. The report *Reclaiming Power and Place* (2019) begins by saying "This report is about deliberate race, identity and gender-based genocide" against Indigenous women and girls. The focus of the report was to propose concrete and sustainable actions to be implemented to prevent situations of violence against Indigenous women, girls, and 2SLGBTQQIA (two-spirited, lesbian, gay, bisexual, transgender, queer, questioning, intersex, asexual) people, and contains more than 200 "calls for justice."

The predominant recommendation is to create a paradigm shift and dismantle colonialism in Canadian society at all levels of government and public institutions. Moreover, these moves are not optional but constitute legal imperatives. For example, the justice system and police services need to acknowledge that the historical and current relationship with Indigenous women and girls is a result of colonialism, racism, and discrimination. The report concludes that all Canadians must bear the responsibility of the atrocities Indigenous women and girls have suffered and deal with it in both the short and long term. On the basis of the report, the government plans to develop and implement a national plan to address violence against Indigenous women and girls.

DECOLONIZATION

Settlers came to Canada intending to remain in the new land, and they were complicit in establishing their sovereignty over all modes of life. Lands taken from Indigenous Peoples allowed settlers to remain and in turn became their sources of capital. In addition, the removal of lands from Indigenous Peoples produced epistemic and ontological disruptions to their ways of life. Settlers defined land as property, and their relationship with it was that of the owner of the property. Indigenous communities were destroyed through the implementation of British law and policy adopted by settlers.

The process of decolonization involves the relinquishing of control by the government. It also means that Indigenous communities can reclaim their authority, which will allow them to carry out their own programs and practices (self-determination). Non-Indigenous people will have to share power with Indigenous Peoples and develop relationships regarding institutional structures. In the past, the power asymmetry of non-Indigenous people over Indigenous Peoples allowed for the normalization of colonial rule (Razack 2002). As Razack goes on to argue, settler society established and maintained its control over Indigenous Peoples through the creation and implementation of a specific ideology. This ideology established a worldview (schema) that created the foundation for laws and ways of doing things. However, it was based upon settler society values, which over time became normalized and the basis for all "common-sense" values of the members of the dominant society. All of the institutions in Canadian society continue to judge one's behaviour in terms of how well his or her actions reflect that ethos. Any knowledge or behaviour that does not fit into this ideology is considered deviant, disqualified, and irrelevant.

In "unmasking" the intent of federal legislation, one uncovers the argument of innocence and the lack of support for Indigenous Peoples. Decolonization is the process by which one sees how unilaterally imposed government policies were used to coerce Indigenous Peoples to give up their cultures but be refused admittance into the culture of the settlers (Razack 2002). It also allows one to see how Indigenous Peoples were dispossessed of their lands and resources as well as their cultures (Wallace 2013). This process of control and coercion continues as the current government extends its tentacles into Indigenous communities.

The early Peace and Friendship Treaties had four components not evident in the later Numbered Treaties. First, these treaties were truly negotiated by both parties and reflected equity in power relationships. Second, the treaties did not involve any surrender of lands. Third, they had an economic component that reflected a trading relationship of mutual benefit. Fourth, they reflected a desire for peaceful relationships between the two parties (Martin-McGuire 1999). When later treaties (post-1800) were signed, they reflected, first, an asymmetrical relationship in which settlers became the dominant power. Second, the economy had changed from the fur trade to timber, agricultural, and mineral exploitation in which Indigenous Peoples were seen as a barrier to development. Third, Indigenous Peoples were no longer seen as valuable since their military skills were no longer required. And fourth, the ideology of "British superiority" began to play an important role in the relationships between settlers and Indigenous Peoples (Innes 2013). Thus, from this time onward, the colonial powers (and later the Canadian government) imposed the contents of the treaties, provided their own interpretations of what the treaties meant, and declared First Nations sovereignty and rights expired. In short, Indigenous Peoples became wards of the state, and that relationship has continued until today. This view Indigenous Peoples have been resisting and attempting to overthrow.

THE COURTS

The role of the courts in relations between Indigenous Peoples and non-Indigenous people has shown a major evolution over the past four decades. Court decisions have placed political officials in positions in which they must negotiate with Indigenous Peoples regarding Aboriginal Rights as well as land claims. Nevertheless, these officials are reluctant to embrace the findings of the courts. Thus, the first strategy for the government in dealing with court decisions has been to appeal, appeal, appeal. This strategy is still exercised by the government when dealing with Indigenous Peoples and has been somewhat successful. First, it emerges from the strong belief that the government position is the correct one. Second, governments have nearly unlimited time, money, and resources with which to argue their cases. Often Indigenous claimants have given up pursuing their claims because they have not had the expertise or the funds to sustain long court battles. Power has its privileges, and this is one that the government exercises on a regular basis. Third, the government can dispose of lands and resources while negotiations are taking place, and those dispositions will supersede any decision made in the subsequent negotiated agreement.

A good example of the extent of control that the government wishes to retain is the case of the Kitselas First Nation. It made a specific claim in 2008 regarding ten acres of land supposed to be given to the Kitselas Indian Reserve years ago. A year later Canada rejected the claim. Subsequently, the Kitselas filed its rejected specific claim with the Specific Claims Tribunal established under the *Specific Claims Tribunal Act* to act as an independent body that would make binding decisions to resolve specific claims rejected for negotiations or when negotiations failed. In 2013, the tribunal found that indeed the ten acres were supposed to be provided to the Kitselas. The tribunal found that the Kitselas First Nation treaty of 1891 had not been fulfilled, and thus the government needed to address the issue. A fiduciary duty existed, the tribunal found, and the crown had breached this duty when it had failed to disclose the exclusion of the acreage—thus not acting in the best interests of the Kitselas. The government responded by applying at the Federal Court of Appeal for a judicial review of the tribunal's decision. Moreover, in this new round of legal wrangling, the Kitselas First Nation would not receive any funding to support its legal efforts. As the Assembly of First Nations noted, the government undermined the stated goals of the tribunal that a fair and timely reconciliation should take place. The legislated authority of the tribunal is now in question, and the issue is whether the tribunal can determine "facts" and deal with questions of law that allow it to make a binding decision in accordance with principles of justice. One year later the Federal Court of Appeal upheld the decision by the tribunal and the specific claim of the Kitselas First Nation. After the decision (2014), the federal government appealed it, and the case is still before the courts.

CANADIAN (ABORIGINAL) LAW

As Coyle (2017) notes, even though treaties were signed with First Nations more than 200 years ago, Canadian law regarding Aboriginal and Treaty Rights and Title remains in its infancy. Over this time, Canadian law dismissed First Nations claims as having no legal standing. It was only when repatriation of the Constitution became a reality in 1982 that this perspective could no longer be considered appropriate. However, since treaties were defined to be *sui generis* (unique) agreements, they did not fall within the boundaries of either international or domestic (tort) law. So there are major gaps in how legal principles are to be dealt with when looking at treaties and Aboriginal Rights. Moreover, Indigenous Peoples argue that a legal system developed by one partner as the "appropriate forum" for resolving claims by the other is hardly the practice of justice.

Legal experts have identified major gaps in Canadian law regarding Aboriginal Rights. Coyle (2017) identifies three major concerns. First, he notes that the courts tend to interpret Indigenous claims such that they are not dramatically different from contracts negotiated by individuals. Second, Canadian Aboriginal law has never acknowledged Indigenous perspectives regarding these claims. For example, First Nations perspectives regarding the "relational" aspect of treaties has never been considered by the courts. Third, Canadian Aboriginal law has not developed a clear remedial principle to guide either the crown or Indigenous Peoples when making treaty claims (Dussart and Poirier 2017).

THE COURTS' PRONOUNCEMENT: NEGOTIATE

Given recent court decisions, the government has found itself forced to negotiate with Indigenous claimants once it has defined the right or claim as "legitimate." This is a daunting process fraught with problems that must be carefully evaluated by the Indigenous claimant. Moreover, not all negotiations culminate in a final agreement, and even if an agreement is reached it might not be what Indigenous Peoples expect. Nevertheless, many negotiations continue, others are cut short, and still others come to successful conclusions (settlements). A settlement does not mean that it is defined as a success by either party, though more often it is not defined thus by the Indigenous claimant. Hence, the residuals of many "successful" negotiations (e.g., those that have led to a final agreement) lead to a sense of distrust, unfairness, and coercion among Indigenous claimants. The Supreme Court, for the past two decades, has argued that Aboriginal Rights are best resolved through political negotiations, and, as Roach (1992) and Walters (2017b) suggest, judicial remedies—such as declarations, suspended declarations of invalidity, and injunctions—should be construed to encourage this political process.

Nevertheless, some factors related to negotiations result in final agreements between the government and Indigenous claimants. Alcantara (2013) has carried out a limited analysis of land claims and identified factors related to the conclusion of a final agreement. He shows that crucial factors in settling a claim are the compatibility of the goals of the negotiating parties (the more closely Indigenous claims fit with government plans, the more likely a final agreement will be signed); the use of non-confrontational tactics in negotiations (the government will resist and use all of its power to discredit the Indigenous claimant if confrontational tactics are used); the degree of Indigenous group cohesiveness (the issue is conflict within the Indigenous community itself, and a lack of political infighting indicates a level of social cohesion); and the government's assessment of whether or not an Indigenous group can carry out an agreement. Moreover, when the government declares the Indigenous community making the claim as only slightly assimilated, there is a perception that the group will not be able to come to the table for a successful final agreement, and thus such claims are put on hold. If the community is identified as not being familiar with Western culture and ways of knowing, and thus unable to bring its people into the mainstream of Canada, then the chances of a successful settlement are very low.

Alcantara (2013) also finds that the Indigenous community's ability to garner resources is an important factor in successfully settling a claim (i.e., the extent of external support that the negotiating parties can gather). Finally, if there are alternative options considered more relevant in dealing with the claim, the government will attempt to resolve it outside the negotiating process. In a claims process, the government takes the proactive position of outlining the negotiating stances for both parties. In short, it circumscribes the nature of the negotiations and sets the boundaries of what is and is not acceptable. A format for the negotiating process is established long before the actual negotiations take place. The process is reminiscent of the Numbered Treaties when the negotiators argued that they could not change the terms of the treaty.

Until recently, these government strategies have been successful in keeping control of the process of negotiation. Today, however, Indigenous people have found that the courts, potentially independent of politics, are venues in which to resolve their claims. The government has had to be more willing to adopt a two-party negotiating stance and accept that Indigenous Peoples have some power in the process. Whether this bodes well for Indigenous claimants in the future has yet to be seen, but preliminary results suggest that it is aiding Indigenous Peoples to negotiate their claims.

Other scholars (Fenge and Quassa 2009) argue that the consistency of a vision projected by Indigenous claimants is a powerful tool in negotiations. Moreover, as one would expect, the pace of negotiations is influenced by the willingness of Indigenous leaders to compromise and accept government proposals. Nevertheless, the extent of resistance to a final agreement might also relate to the offers made to the Indigenous claimants. As we have seen, the "cede, release and surrender" statement in a settlement has been rejected by Indigenous Peoples, and the courts have supported their stance. As Borrows and Coyle (2017) point out, Indigenous leaders argue against asking Indigenous Peoples to accept the tenets of colonialism; they would rather force the government to accept Indigenous law in enhancing settler-Indigenous relations.

Some Indigenous communities have focused on efforts to achieve self-government en route to self-determination. This process can be simpler since it omits the provincial government, and only the federal government and the Indigenous community carry out the negotiations. It allows the Indigenous community to replace the government-imposed political structures and to develop a structure of its own. In doing so, the community creates some powers (unfortunately not important ones). The most important powers that the government allows are related to specific financial transactions. Other powers can include the passing of laws about language, culture, adoption, inheritance and wills, and marriage. All of these powers are normally held by the federal government. It argues that these self-government agreements are powerful instruments for building Indigenous self-determination and necessary for the economic development of Indigenous communities. Yet it is unwilling to cede other powers to these communities that would allow for development and achievement of self-determination (e.g., the authority to budget or spend without ministerial approval, acceptance of Indigenous law). Critics argue that the powers granted to Indigenous communities are nothing more than administrative responsibilities and that the real power still resides with the government (Diabo 2018b). Others note that, by not allowing Indigenous communities to obtain more power, they become more assimilated into Canadian society.

Bilateral, accommodation, and interim agreements can also be reached between the government and Indigenous Peoples. The Carrier (Dakelh) Sekani Tribal Council and Matsqui (Sto:lo) communities in British Columbia used this negotiating strategy. Their argument was that, as the courts reviewed the "facts" and the government refused to negotiate, the natural resource development continued, and First Nations were not able to capture any benefit retroactively. So they thought that they had to work out some strategy to benefit from the resource development while the issues were being settled in court or negotiated. The private sector is willing to participate in these agreements since the outcomes provide certainty. The question is whether the agreements, time-limited as they are, are useful documents: that is, whether they demonstrate that the private sector has accepted the claims, thus strengthening the case when the claimant goes back to court.

Finally, there is the *First Nations Land Management Act*. It was passed in 1999 and created a regime that gives First Nations communities the ability to opt out of the *Indian Act* (regarding land issues) and create their own rules and regulations. But this Act deals only with the land within the reserve and not outside it in a treaty area. There have been nineteen of these cases so far. All that is necessary is that the First Nations community "voluntarily" agree to abide by the

Act and submit a land use plan to Indian Affairs for approval. Then the community must hold a referendum to get approval, and thus land control reverts to the community. This takes about three years to complete. The federal government then has nothing to do with the management of reserve lands, nor does it collect rents or royalties. The First Nations community has the right to negotiate with the private sector to attract investors for a business. Community leaders argue that the problem with this arrangement is that much of the money generated from the business on the reserve leaves it and is not recycled in the community. Nevertheless, it is a new strategy being investigated by many First Nations communities in an attempt to become more economically self-sufficient.

As noted above, Canada has changed its agenda regarding Indigenous Peoples over the past few years. For example, when the United Nations Declaration on the Rights of Indigenous Peoples was passed in 2010, Canada was one of four nations that voted against it. Under Conservative leadership, it argued that the provisions of the declaration would give Indigenous Peoples the right of a veto that would be incompatible with Canadian law. Even though the declaration does not use the term "veto," the government objected to the policy. However, four years later, Canada decided to rescind its veto and voted in favour of the declaration but added that it did not consider the policy binding. The current Liberal government has explicitly taken a reconciliatory approach to dealing with Indigenous Peoples. In 2017, the government formally removed objections to the phrase in the document (Article 10) that Indigenous Peoples have the right to "free, prior and informed consent." The government now agrees with the statement and has made a commitment to develop reconciliatory policies on matters that affect Indigenous Peoples. A private member's bill (C-262) to ensure that the laws of Canada are in harmony with the UNDRIP is now in committee (Senate) and if passed will move back to Parliament for final reading and approval.

This bill deals with how the declaration can be incorporated into Canadian law. It has also raised the issue of the duty to consult with and accommodate Indigenous Peoples when it makes decisions regarding Aboriginal Rights. The Supreme Court of Canada has concluded that, arising from the crown's fiduciary duty, there is a duty of consultation. However, the nature and extent of the consultation will vary depending on the circumstances. When the Supreme Court decided the *Xeni Gwet'in v British Columbia* case (otherwise known as the *Tsilhqot'in Nation* case) in 2014, it stipulated that the land given to the Tsilhqot'in could be interfered with by provincial interests. This decision, of course, limits the content of the UN declaration stipulating that any project that might have a detrimental impact on Indigenous Peoples must allow them to have "free, prior and informed consent." Moreover, the Supreme Court decision in *Mikisew Cree First Nation v Canada (Minister of Canadian Heritage)* (2005) places important limits on the scope of the duty to consult Indigenous Peoples under section 35 of the *Constitution Act, 1982*. However, the court ruled that the duty to consult does not apply to lawmaking. Canada has thus taken a different route than that espoused by the United Nations, and it has raised the thorny issue of the difference between "consent" and "veto," a dilemma yet to be resolved by either Parliament or the courts.

The Supreme Court is also caught in a conundrum over the issue of sovereignty (Beaton 2018). Its pronouncements have referred to de facto rights compared to de jure rights. In other words, how did Canada take on crown sovereignty over lands held by Indigenous Peoples? If the courts have rejected the *terra nullius* and other theories of hierarchical civilization, then on what basis did Canada claim sovereignty? It seems that the *assertion* of sovereignty is the simple answer. Moreover, it seems that the Supreme Court has moved away from a "backward looking" substantive justification of crown sovereignty and toward a "forward looking" procedural legitimation (Beaton 2018). Perhaps it was through the signing of treaties with Indigenous Peoples, but at the time they were not considered "people," so how could they sign treaties? As the Supreme Court attempts to resolve this problem, Canada continues to claim crown sovereignty.

THE TRUTH AND RECONCILIATION COMMISSION

The Truth and Reconciliation Commission was established in 2007 as part of the residential school investigation. Its mandate was to report on the history, purpose, operation, and supervision of Canada's residential schools. The commission's report is based primarily upon the input of over 6,000 residential school survivors, and the commission produced its final report, *Honouring the Truth, Reconciling for the Future*, in 2015, presenting ninety-four "calls to action" covering a wide range of topics (e.g., health, education, justice, sports, language, and culture). This final report was preceded by six additional reports: *Residential Schools* (two parts), *The Inuit and Northern Experience in Residential Schools*, *The Métis Experience*, *Missing Children and Unmarked Burials*, and *The Legacy*.

The first component of the commission was to receive the input of residential school survivors and establish the "truth" of what happened during that 100-year period when Indigenous students were forced to attend residential schools (Angel 2012; Capitaine and Vanthuyne 2017). The second component of the commission was to provide direction for Canada on how it might achieve reconciliation. From the perspective of the commission, reconciliation is the process of establishing and maintaining respectful relationships. As noted in the final report of the commission, part of this process must include repairing damaged trust through apologies as well as providing individual and collective reparations. One of the basic principles of the commission is that all Canadians share responsibility for establishing and maintaining mutually respectful relationships.

The federal government has agreed to work with Indigenous leaders, provincial and territorial leaders, and other key stakeholders to design a national engagement strategy for developing and implementing a national reconciliation framework based upon the ninety-four calls to action. In addition, many of the research documents gathered by the commission will be accessible in the new National Centre for Truth and Reconciliation in Winnipeg. Considerable discussion and legal action have taken place regarding whether the testimonies of participants in the hearings should be made public. Some individuals have given their consent for making public their testimonies, which will be archived and available to the public sometime in the future. The Supreme Court ruled that the testimonies of those who have yet to give their approval (or cannot because of death) will be destroyed rather than provided to the national archives. Before those testimonies are destroyed, they will be held for fifteen years (in confidence), during which time individuals may choose to have them preserved and archived. In addition, all government records on those testimonies and claims will be destroyed. The court ruled that near-absolute confidentiality was part of the process, and thus participants expected privacy when they participated in the closed hearings.

Many institutions (e.g., hospitals, universities) have begun to implement the calls to action. For example, in the field of education, many postsecondary schools have embarked on a strategy of "Indigenization" and are seeking ways to incorporate an Indigenous worldview within the curricula (Gaudry and Lorenz 2018) and structure of postsecondary education. Institutions in the areas of justice and health are likewise attempting to implement various recommendations from the Truth and Reconciliation Commission. Other institutions (e.g., economic, correctional) have yet to respond to the recommendations. The commission is viewed as a catalyst for achieving national awareness of the meaning and potential of reconciliation with an understanding that it will take years to achieve reconciliation.

Even though over the years Indigenous Peoples have been forcibly relocated, blocked from access to their lands and resources, and denied their traditional ways of living, they have exhibited resilience in a number of ways: positive outcomes despite adversity, sustained competence under stress, and successful recovery from trauma (Lalonde 2007). As Ali (2009) argues, Indigenous Peoples possess a tenacity stronger than all the negative forces levied against them.

THE RISE OF NEO-LIBERAL ECONOMIC PHILOSOPHY

Counteracting the thrust of the Truth and Reconciliation Commission is the existing ideology of economic practice. Neo-liberalism involves the linkage of responsibility and marginalization. Responsibility is acknowledged through the belief that each person has a moral duty to participate in the labour force and maintain that involvement over extended periods of time (e.g., ages twenty-four to sixty-five). However, neo-liberalism also ensures that the allocation of income is not equal. In neo-liberalism, distributing resources differently allows the wealthy to secure new privileges and develops new ways of marginalizing minority groups. Through cuts in social expenditures by the state, the privatization of services, tax incentives, and the deregulation of activities, the philosophy of neo-liberalism shapes the opportunities for individuals to participate in the labour force as well as the rewards that they receive for that participation. In the end, government intervention is reduced, and a new relationship between individuals and the state is posited. For example, individual solutions are presented regarding access to the market and capital so that individual decisions can be made, thus reinforcing the tenets of neo-liberalism.

As Rose (1996, 57) points out, neo-liberalism supports individuals actively responsible for themselves, and they are to meet their national obligations by fulfilling themselves within their communities. Thus, neo-liberalism makes individuals responsible through their individual choices both for themselves and for those to whom they owe allegiance. However, individuals can achieve their personal or moral worth only by participating in the capitalist system because that is not only the "correct" but also the "right" decision. Individuals who do not participate in the capitalist system are viewed as undertaking inappropriate behaviour and thus not fulfilling their responsibility to support the nation. Moreover, the decision not to participate in the capitalist system is defined as a "free choice" and thus again suggests that the individual has voluntarily chosen not to contribute to the welfare of the state and its citizens. Consequently, individuals who do not participate in the capitalist system deserve little support from the government and only philanthropic support from the private sector.

Polzer and Power (2016, 15) argue that neo-liberal ideology transforms demands for social change and greater autonomy into privatized solutions. It also makes the individual responsible to support the capitalist state, and those who refuse to cooperate are defined as not useful or responsible. This in turn legitimizes their marginalization in and exclusion from the state and private sector corporate activities. In turn, those individuals who contribute to the labour force and support the capitalist system are elevated to the status of good citizens and appropriately rewarded for their behaviour. Those who cannot or will not participate in the capitalist system are considered "drains" on society and need to be punished for not participating. They are subject to surveillance and control since they are viewed as problem individuals. Overall, exclusion restructures welfare state programs, implicitly supports other forms of discrimination (e.g., sexism, racism, other phobias), and in turn disenfranchises and marginalizes groups through the enactment of laws.

The individual's right to a modest living through economic involvement in the labour force has been diverted by discussions of the individual's responsibility for actions in the dimensions of labour, education, and health. Today the focus is on the individual's responsibility to ensure health, labour force involvement, and management of risks in life. As Polzer and Power (2016) point out, individuals are now viewed as consumers in society rather than recipients of care and social entitlements. As such, they are supposed to take on the duty by which they utilize their free choices and informed decisions.

At the same time, there is inadequate access to business capital for Indigenous communities. They have been unable to develop the business infrastructure required to accommodate their purchasing needs. The federal government policy on Indigenous capital is problematic. The government holds Indigenous capital for both welfare and development initiatives, and accumulated finances are held in a "trust fund" and invested in government bonds. Hence, it is estimated that over $100 million a year is held by the government and not released to community business ventures. On receiving a request from an Indigenous community, before funds are released, the government subjects the project to a series of bureaucratic procedures before it is approved, generally taking between one and five years. The government has not shown any leadership in helping Indigenous Peoples in the area of business development. The current policy on encouraging economic development of Indigenous communities focuses on decision-making, assessment, and communication.

There is a belief that involvement in the economic aspects of Canadian life can be achieved by carefully limiting an individual's risk activities. The new ideological perspectives have been constructed through discourses in the media and educational institutions. In short, in the language of neo-liberalism, citizens are to "govern" themselves through freedom of choice, self-responsibility, and maximization of life chances. Individuals are often informed through many outlets that they can ensure their involvement in the labour force and obtain well-paying jobs. As Polzer and Power (2016) indicate, this individualistic ideology resonates deeply with the tenets of capitalism. Economic involvement in the labour force is predominantly couched as an obligatory and lifelong pursuit of the individual. Individuals who do not enter and maintain a presence in the labour force are not recognized as worthy citizens. The impact of such a philosophy on marginal groups such as Indigenous people is clear. However, it is also important to understand the role of the government in the support of marginalized people.

THE RIGHTS RECOGNITION FRAMEWORK

The issue of reconciliation and the role of Indigenous Peoples in decision-making and governance have long been discussed. The current Liberal government has stated that all relations with Indigenous Peoples will be based upon the recognition of Aboriginal Rights via a new Aboriginal Rights framework that has been proposed but remains in its infancy. The outline (ten principles) of this new framework is now public and will be discussed in both Indigenous and non-Indigenous communities before it becomes final. The government claims that the new framework will establish certainty regarding Aboriginal Rights and give clarity to the private sector for economic development.

Even though Aboriginal Rights are entrenched in the Constitution, the government reacts in an adversarial manner when a First Nation raises a collective right, demanding that the First Nation "prove it." Previous governments did not recognize or affirm Aboriginal Rights. As the minister of justice noted in 2018, Aboriginal Rights have been denied, policies put in place, and programs implemented without Indigenous input or consideration. The *Indian Act*, the building of residential schools, the dispossession of Indigenous Peoples from their lands, and the failure to implement agreements made in treaties have all demonstrated the government's denial of Aboriginal Rights. If Indigenous communities that contest the state do not accede to its wishes, then the state uses its coercive powers to force laws on those groups that do not cooperate. However, the new Liberal government wants to build trust with Indigenous Peoples and reposition the existing relationship with them to be one of "problem solvers" rather than to turn to the courts for the resolution of issues. The new framework will focus on how rights are to be respected and do away with the government's insistence on the "extinguishment" of rights when agreements are signed. In addition, the National Reconciliation Council has been established as a working group of ministers to review laws and policies related to Indigenous Peoples and the principles of the government of Canada's relationship with them.

To achieve a final rights recognition document, the government established twenty exploratory tables (now called recognition of rights and self-determination negotiation tables). They are non-binding discussions regarding national policy on Indigenous self-government and sovereignty rights, breathing new life into section 35 of the Constitution. In addition, they are developing new terms for land claims and self-government processes that will guide comprehensive claims. The government claims that it is a visionary process that will lead to co-development and shared ideas about self-determination and treaties, the ultimate goals of Indigenous Peoples in Canadian society. To date, however, no one knows what is being discussed at these tables (Diabo 2018a). Critics of this process point out that the new policies that the government wants to enact have several non-negotiable core mandates—such as third-party interests, incorporation, taxation, and types of governance—before the discussions start. Others note that the Supreme Court has ruled that Indigenous Peoples hold underlying title to lands based upon their prior occupation to assertions of crown sovereignty and settlement (Diabo 2018a) and thus wonder why these issues are being debated. Put another way, why is the burden of proof for title on First Nations and not the provincial crown? Critics argue that a new policy that recognizes and affirms Aboriginal Title and Indigenous laws and jurisdiction in the planning and management of lands and resources is required.

Other critics of the framework for rights and the tables argue that they comprise a rights-denying approach rather than a rights-affirming approach (Palmater 2017a). Diabo (2018a) notes that, even though a working group of ministers has been established, it operates in secret and only involves government agencies. Moreover, the ten principles released had no prior consultation with Chiefs, Indigenous leaders, or Indigenous communities before they were made public (Diabo 2018b). Critics also note that the approach will do away with the *Indian Act* by forcing First Nations into a form of self-government that will suppress Indigenous self-determination (King and Pasternak 2018). They go on to argue that, though labelled as new and transformative, the approach is reflective of an older and largely discredited strategy. Moreover, the framework does not address the issues of land restitution and treaty obligations (Palmater 2018b). Opponents of the new framework argue that it will transfer administrative responsibility for service delivery to First Nations but not change the federal, provincial, or territorial powers regarding Indigenous Peoples. In addition, the framework does not deal with broad issues integral to Indigenous Peoples such as self-government and land rights. It does address the issue of certainty to ensure clarity and predictability for non-Indigenous corporate investments (Green and Starblanket 2018). As such, the framework will weaken the link between Aboriginal Rights and the fiduciary duty of the government. The "new" approach does not deviate from the existing authority of the government, does not change the power dynamics of discussions, and thus entrenches the authority of government institutions (Palmater 2018b). Critics also note that Indigenous people who object to the process will be coerced to conform to it or be defined as dissidents or criminals. However, Manual and Derrickson (2015) argue that repression by the government does not extinguish resistance but simply makes it go underground.

The framework makes no mention of the UNDRIP, which states that Indigenous Peoples retain rights to unceded lands and resources as well as the right of "free, prior and informed consent" to the appropriation of their lands (Diabo 2018c). The UNDRIP focuses on the right of self-determination and allows decolonization to take place. It grants a space for Indigenous Peoples to express their political, cultural, and social identities. Decolonization involves a transitional process, but it requires that policies and institutions restore Indigenous ways of knowing and Indigenous ways of relating to Traditional Territories.

As such, decolonization requires the renegotiation of power and dispossession and the emergence of new forms of government and engagement (Strelein and Tran 2013). Opponents of the process and the proposed policy argue that the framework will maintain the status quo and is misleading Indigenous people about its transformational nature. Palmater (2017b) argues that the government's claim to engage in nation-to-nation dialogue seems to begin and end with the AFN and ignores any partnership with Aboriginal and Treaty Rights holders themselves. In the end, the framework will result in a narrow vision of Indigenous jurisdiction over lands, resources, and self-determination (King and Pasternak 2018).

If Indigenous Peoples are to trust the government, it needs to ensure more transparent communications when dealing with them. In addition, the government needs to understand the dilemmas that they face in all regions of Canada. Measures need to be taken to improve the socio-economic conditions of Indigenous Peoples. Currently, the biggest challenge is to mitigate the negative impacts of development on Indigenous Peoples' Traditional Territories, and this concern is reflected in the United Nations Declaration on the Rights of Indigenous Peoples. Many Canadians are aware that there are numerous obstacles to realizing the rights of Indigenous Peoples. From language to land, from poverty to participation, Indigenous Peoples continue to face discrimination, exploitation, and disproportionate impacts of neo-liberalism. As Moore (2010) cogently notes, the goal of Indigenous Peoples is to build structural and legal protections to keep them from being subjected to future injustices. It remains to be seen how Canadians will demonstrate equity, fairness, and justice in their dealings with Indigenous Peoples.

As Indigenous Peoples move forward, they are trying to build new institutions and industries as well as to create, through education, a new ethos and reclaim the spirit and human capacity of their communities. They are creating a mix of tradition and modernity to bring about a cultural match between economic and social institutions in their communities. Indigenous leaders insist that institutions created in Indigenous communities be allowed to control the lives of their members and incorporate their cultural values. However, culture does not equal the creation of wealth in communities. In the end, Indigenous Peoples want to establish autonomy-producing institutions rather than dependency-producing institutions (Watt-Cloutier 2015).

ACKNOWLEDGEMENTS

This book has been a labour of love for the past four years, and that has meant a constant updating of material (and sometimes a revising of arguments). I am indebted to a number of colleagues who have provided me with those materials to keep me current and others who have challenged my assessments of various issues: Dr. Michael Lickers, Dr. Marie Delorme, Line Laplante, and Dr. Jacqueline Quinless. I would also like to thank David Laidlaw and Monique Passelac-Ross, who gave much time and thought to questions that I took to them. Other colleagues who have given of their time and attention to issues raised in the book over the years are Shawna Cunningham, Lorna Crowshoe, Suzanne McCloud, and Dr. Cash Ahenakew. Their support has immeasurably enhanced the quality of the book.

 The process of bringing this book to print began with contact with Karen Clark, Scholarly Acquisitions Editor at the University of Regina Press, and her support has been unwavering. I am grateful for the talent and effort of the editorial team at the press, including Kelly Laycock, Managing Editor, and Duncan Campbell, Art Director. Finally, I would like to thank Dallas Harrison for his careful editing and for challenging me to be clear in my writing. His contribution has been exceptional and ensures the reader's understanding of the material presented.

REFERENCES

ARTICLES, CHAPTERS, BOOKS

Abdelal, R., Y. Herrera, A. Johnston, and R. McDermott. 2009. "Definition, Conceptualization, and Measurement Alternatives." In *Measuring Identity*, edited by R. Abdelal, Y. Herrera, A. Johnston, and R. McDermott, 165–97. New York: Cambridge University Press.

Aboriginal Affairs and Northern Development Canada (AANDC). 2015. *Aboriginal Affairs and Northern Development Canada and Canadian Polar Commission: 2015–16 Report on Plans and Priorities*. Ottawa: Minister of Aboriginal Affairs and Northern Development.

Alcantara, C. 2003. "Individual Property Rights on Canadian Indian Reserves: The Historical Emergence and Jurisprudence of Certificates of Possession." *Canadian Journal of Native Studies* 23, no. 2: 391–424.

———. 2013. *Negotiating the Deal*. Toronto: University of Toronto Press.

Alfred, T. 2008. *Peace, Power, Righteousness: An Indigenous Manifesto*. 2nd ed. Don Mills, ON: Oxford University Press.

———. 2009. "Colonialism and State Dependency." *Journal de la santé autochtone* 5, no. 3: 42–60.

———. 2011. "Colonial Stains on Our Existence." In *Racism, Colonialism, and Indigeneity in Canada*, edited by M. Cannon and L. Sunseri, 123–47. Oxford: Oxford University Press.

———. 2013. *Wasase: Indigenous Pathways of Action and Freedom*. Toronto: University of Toronto Press.

Alfred, T., and J. Corntassel. 2005. "Being Indigenous: Resurgences against Contemporary Colonialism." *Government and Opposition* 40: 597–614.

———. 2011. "Being Indigenous: Resurgences against Contemporary Colonialism." In *Racism, Colonialism, and Indigeneity in Canada*, edited by M. Cannon and L. Sunseri, 125–47. Oxford: Oxford University Press.

Ali, S. 2009. *Mining, the Environment, and Indigenous Development Conflicts*. Tucson: University of Arizona Press.

Allodi-Ross, F. 2017. "Who Calls the Shots? Balancing Individual and Collective Interests in the Assertion of Aboriginal and Treaty Harvesting Rights." In *The Right Relationship: Reimagining the Implementation of Historical Treaties*, edited by J. Borrows and M. Coyle, 149–63. Toronto: University of Toronto Press.

Alvarez, A. 2014. *Native America and the Question of Genocide*. Baltimore: Rowman and Littlefield.

Anastakis, D., M.-H. Kelm, and S. Morton. 2017. "New Approaches to Indigenous History." *Canadian Historical Review* 98: 60–63.

Anaya, J. 2014. *Report of the Special Rapporteur on the Rights of Indigenous Peoples*. New York: United Nations Human Rights Council.

Anderson, C. 2014. *Métis Race, Recognition, and the Struggle for Indigenous Peoplehood*. Vancouver: UBC Press.

Anderson, K., and R. Innes, eds. 2015. *Indigenous Men and Masculinities*. Winnipeg: University of Manitoba Press.

Anderson, M., and C. Robertson. 2015. *Seeing Red*. Winnipeg: University of Manitoba Press.

Angel, N. 2012. "Before Truth: The Labors of Testimony and the Canadian Truth and Reconciliation Commission." *Culture, Theory, and Critique* 53, no. 2: 199–214.

Anuik, J. 2018. "Language, Place, and Kinship Ties: Past and Present Necessities for Metis Education." In *Roots of Entanglements: Essays in the History of Native-Newcomer Relations*, edited by M. Rutherdale, P. Lackenbauer, and K. Abel 209–29. Toronto: University of Toronto Press.

Ariss, R., and J. Cutfeet. 2012. *Keeping the Land*. Halifax: Fernwood.

Asch, M. 2002. "From *Terra Nullius* to Affirmation: Reconciling Aboriginal Rights with the Canadian Constitution." *Canadian Journal of Law and Society* 17: 23–39.

———. 2014. *On Being Here to Stay*. Toronto: University of Toronto Press.

Asch, M., J. Borrows, and J. Tully. 2018. *Resurgence and Reconciliation: Settler Relations and Earth Teachings*. Toronto: University of Toronto Press.

Axtell, J. 1981. *The European and the Indian*. New York: Oxford University Press.

Backhouse, C. 2001. "'Race' Definition Run Amuck: 'Slaying the Dragon of Eskimo Status' before the Supreme Court of Canada, 1939." In *Law,

History, Colonialism: The Reach of Empire, edited by D. Kirby and C. Coleborne, 75–101. Manchester: Manchester University Press.

Balfour, L. 2014. "Framing Redress after 9/11: Protest, Reconciliation, and Canada's War on Terror against Indigenous Peoples." *Canadian Journal of Native Studies* 34, no. 1: 25–40.

Barkan, E. 2000. *The Guilt of Nations: Restitution and Negotiating Historical Injustices*. New York: Norton.

Barker, A. 2012. "Locating Settler Colonialism." *Journal of Colonialism and Colonial History* 1: 1–20.

Beaton, R. 2018. "De Facto and de Jure Crown Sovereignty: Reconciliation and Legitimation at the Supreme Court of Canada." *Constitutional Forum Constitutionnel* 26, no. 4: 18–47.

Belanger, Y. 2014. *Ways of Knowing: An Introduction to Native Studies in Canada*. 2nd ed. Toronto: Nelson Education.

Bell, A. 2014. *Relating Indigenous and Settler Identities*. London: Palgrave Macmillan.

Bell, C. 1995. "Métis Constitutional Rights in Section 35(1)." *Alberta Law Review* 36: 180–217.

Benjamin, C. 2014. *Indian School Road: Legacies of the Shubenacadie Residential Schools*. Toronto: Nimbus.

Bianchi, E. 2001. "First Nations Government Act: A New and Improved Assimilation Policy." Unpublished paper. https://www.kairoscanda.org.

Black, J. 2014. *Contesting History: Narratives of Public History*. London: Bloomsbury.

Blackstock, M. 2013. "Blue Ecology: A Cross-Cultural Ecological Vision for Freshwater." In *Aboriginal Peoples and Forest Lands in Canada*, edited by D. Tindall, R. Trosper, and P. Perreault, 114–36. Vancouver: UBC Press.

Bland, D. 2014. *Time Bomb: Canada and the First Nations*. Toronto: Dundurn Books.

Blaut, J. 1993. *The Colonizer's Model of the World: Geographical Diffusionism and Eurocentric History*. New York: Guilford Press.

Bonesteel, S. 2006. *Canada's Relationship with Inuit: A History of Policy and Program Development*. Ottawa: Indian and Northern Affairs Canada.

Borrows, J. 2002. *Recovering Canada: The Resurgence of Indigenous Law*. Toronto: University of Toronto Press.

———. 2003. "Crown and Aboriginal Occupations of the Land: A History and Comparison." Paper commissioned by the Ipperwash Inquiry.

———. 2005. "Crown and Aboriginal Occupations of Land: A History and Comparison." https://www.attorneygeneral.jus.gov.on.ca/inquiries/ipperwash/policy_part/research/pdf/History_of_Occupations_Borrows.pdf.

—. 2010a. *Canada's Indigenous Constitution*. Toronto: University of Toronto Press.

—. 2010b. *Drawing Out Laws: A Spirit's Guide*. Toronto: University of Toronto Press.

—. 2013. "Aboriginal and Treaty Rights and Violence against Women." *Osgoode Hall Law Journal* 50: 699–736.

—. 2016. "Legislation and Indigenous Self-Determination in Canada and the United States." In *From Recognition to Reconciliation: Essays on the Constitutional Entrenchment of Aboriginal and Treaty Rights*, edited by P. Macklem and D. Sanderson, 42–59. Toronto: University of Toronto Press.

—. 2017a. "Changing Historical Frameworks." *Canadian Historical Review* 98: 114–35.

—. 2017b. "Canada's Colonial Constitution." In *The Right Relationship: Reimagining the Implementation of Historical Treaties*, edited by J. Borrows and M. Coyle, 17–38. Toronto: University of Toronto Press.

—. 2018. "Earth-Bound: Indigenous Resurgence and Environmental Reconciliation." In *Resurgence and Reconciliation: Settler Relations and Earth Teachings*, edited by M. Asch, J. Borrows, and J. Tully, 49–64. Toronto: University of Toronto Press.

—. 2019. *Law's Indigenous Ethic*. Toronto: University of Toronto Press.

Borrows, J., and M. Coyle, eds. 2017. *The Right Relationship: Reimagining the Implementation of Historical Treaties*. Toronto: University of Toronto Press.

Bradford, T. 2012. *Prophetic Identities: Indigenous Missionaries on British Colonial Frontiers, 1850–1875*. Vancouver: UBC Press.

Brady, M., and J. Kelly. 2017. *We Interrupt This Program*. Vancouver: UBC Press.

Brannigan, A. 2013. *Beyond the Banality of Evil*. Toronto: Oxford University Press.

Brewer, M. 2010. "Social Identity Complexity and Acceptance of Diversity." In *The Psychology of Social and Cultural Diversity*, edited by R. Crisp, 46–67. Chichester, UK: Blackwell.

Bryant, R. 2016. "The State of the Crown-Aboriginal Fiduciary Relationship: The Case for an Aboriginal Veto." In *From Recognition to Reconciliation: Essays on the Constitutional Entrenchment of Aboriginal and Treaty Rights*, edited by P. Macklem and D. Sanderson, 223–36. Toronto: University of Toronto Press.

Buckley, H. 1993. *From Wooden Ploughs to Welfare: Why Indian Policy Failed in the Prairie Provinces*. Montreal and Kingston: McGill-Queen's University Press.

Bumsted, J., L. Kuffert, and M. Cucharme, eds. 2011. *Interpreting Canada's Past*. 4th ed. Toronto: Oxford University Press.

Butera, F., J. Levine, and J.-P. Vernet. 2009. "Influence without Credit: How Successful Minorities Respond to Social Cryptoamnesia." In *Coping with Minority Status*, edited by F. Butera and J. Levine, 311–32. New York: Cambridge University Press.

Butt, E., and M. Hurley. 2006. *Specific Claims in Canada*. Ottawa: Law and Government Division.

Cairns, A. 2005. *First Nations and the Canadian State: In Search of Coexistence*. Kingston: Queen's University, Institute of Intergovernmental Relations.

———. 2006. *First Nations and the Canadian State*. Kingston: Queen's University, Institute of Intergovernmental Relations.

Cajete, G. 1994. *Look to the Mountain: An Ecology of Indigenous Education*. Santa Fe: Kivaki Press.

Capitaine, B., and K. Vanthuyne, eds. 2017. *Power through Testimony*. Vancouver: UBC Press.

Cardinal, H. 1969. *The Unjust Society*. Edmonton: Hurtig.

Carey, M. 2008. "Whitefellas and Wadjulas: Anti-Colonial Constructions of the Non-Aboriginal Self." PhD diss., Murdoch University, Australia.

Carson, W.G. 1979. "The Conventionalization of Early Factory Crime." *International Journal for the Sociology of Law* 7: 123–57.

Chartrand, L. 2018. "Uncertain Accommodation: Aboriginal Identity and Group Rights in the Supreme Court of Canada." BC *Studies* 22: 182–83.

Chartrand, P., ed. 2002. *Who Are Canada's Aboriginal Peoples: Recognition, Definition, and Jurisdiction*. Saskatoon: Purich.

Chisholm, B. 2013. "Early Occupation and Forest Resource Use in Prehistoric British Columbia." In *Aboriginal Peoples and Forest Lands in Canada*, edited by D. Tindall, R. Trosper, and P. Perreault, 234–56. Vancouver: UBC Press.

Clatworthy, S. 2005. *Indian Registration, Membership, and Population: Change in First Nations Communities*. Winnipeg: Four Directions Project Consultants.

Coates, K. 2015. *#Idle No More and the Remaking of Canada*. Regina: University of Regina Press.

———. 2018. "Reclaiming History through the Courts: Aboriginal Rights, the Marshall Decision, and Maritime History." In *Roots of Entanglements: Essays in the History of Native-Newcomer Relations*, edited by M. Rutherdale, P. Lackenbauer, and K. Abel, 187–219. Toronto: University of Toronto Press.

Coates, K., and B. Crowley. 2013. *New Beginnings: How Canada's Natural Resource Wealth Could Re-Shape Relations with Aboriginal People.* Toronto: MacDonald-Laurier Institute.

Cornell, S. 2013. "The Harvard Project on American Indian Economic Development and Its Application to Canadian Business." Presentation at Simon Fraser University, Burnaby, October 2.

Cornell, S., and J. Kalt, eds. 1992. *What Tribes Can Do?* Cambridge, MA: Harvard University, American Indian Studies Center.

Corntassel, J. 2008. "Towards Sustainable Self-Determination: Rethinking the Contemporary Indigenous Rights Discourse." *Alternatives* 33: 104–08.

———. 2012. "Re-Envisioning Resurgence: Indigenous Pathways to Decolonization and Sustainable Self-Determination." *Decolonization: Indigeneity, Education, and Society* 1, no. 1: 86–101.

———. 2018. *Everyday Acts of Resurgence.* Olympia, WA: Daykeeper Press.

Coulthard, G. 2007. "Subjects of Empire: Indigenous Peoples and the 'Politics of Recognition' in Canada." *Contemporary Political Theory* 6: 437–60.

———. 2014. *Red Skin, White Masks: Rejecting Active Decolonization.* Minneapolis: University of Minnesota Press.

Coyle, M. 2005. *Addressing Aboriginal Land and Treaty Rights in Ontario: An Analysis of the Past Policies and Options for the Future.* https://www.attorneygeneral.jus.gov.on.ca/inquiries/ipperwash/policy_part/research/pdf/History_of _Occupations_Coyle.pdf.

———. 2008. "Respect for Treaty Rights in Ontario: The Law of the Land?" *Ottawa Law Review* 39, no. 2: 45–69.

———. 2017. "As Long as the Sun Shines: Recognizing that Treaties Were Intended to Last." In *The Right Relationship: Reimagining the Implementation of Historical Treaties*, edited by J. Borrows and M. Coyle, 39–69. Toronto: University of Toronto Press.

Crosby, A., and J. Monaghan. 2018. *Policing Indigenous Movements.* Halifax: Fernwood.

Culhane, D. 1998. *The Pleasure of the Crown: Anthropology, Law, and First Nations.* Vancouver: Talon Books.

Daniel, R. 1981. *History of Native Claims Processes in Canada: 1967–1979.* Ottawa: Department of Indian and Northern Affairs.

Daschuk, J. 2013. *Clearing the Plains: Disease, Politics of Starvation, and the Loss of Aboriginal Life.* Regina: University of Regina Press.

Davin, N. 1879. *Report on Industrial Schools for Indians and Half Breeds.* Ottawa: Department of the Interior.

Day, S., and J. Green. 2010. "Indian Act Remedy Bill C-3 Is Flawed." *Rabble*, May 21, B5–7.

de Greiff, P. 2008. "The Role of Apologies in National Reconciliation Processes: On Making Trustworthy Institutions Trusted." In *The Age of Apology: Facing Up to the Past*, edited by M. Gibney, 120–36. Philadelphia: University of Pennsylvania Press.

Dewar, B. 2009. "Nunavut and the Nunavut Land Claims Agreement: An Unresolved Relationship." *Policy Options* 30. https://policyoptions.irpp.org/magazines/Canadas-water-challenges/Nunavut-and-the-nunavut-land-claims-agreement-an-unresolved-relationship.

Dewsbury, J., and P. Cloke. 2009. "Spiritual Landscapes: Existence, Performance, and Imminence." *Social and Cultural Geography* 10, no. 6: 67–84.

Diabo, R. 2012. "Harper Launches Major First Nations Termination Plan: As Negotiating Tables Legitimize Canada's Colonialism." *Rabble*, November 9. https://intercontinentalcry.org/harper-launches-major-first-nations-termination-plan-as-negotiating-tables-legitimize-canada-colonialism/.

———. 2018a. "UNDRIP: Lands, Territories, and Resources and the Indigenous Forests in Canada." Paper presented at the NAFA National Meeting on Indigenous Forest Certainty, Gatineau, March 8.

———. 2018b. "UNDRIP, FPIC, and Hijack Indigenous Self-Determination." Paper presented at Empowering Our Future, Free, Prior, Informed Consent Conference, Blue Mountains, ON, October 25.

———. 2018c. "Stopping the Liberal Assault on Our Rights." *Indigenous Policy Journal* 29, no. 1: 24–29.

Dickason, O. 1992. *Canada's First Nations: A History of the Founding Peoples from Earliest Times*. Toronto: McClelland and Stewart.

———. 2002. *Canada's First Nations*. Toronto: Oxford University Press.

Dickason, O., and M. Calder. 2006. *A Concise History of Canada's First Nations*. Don Mills, ON: Oxford University Press.

Dickason, O., and W. Newbigging. 2015. *A Concise History of Canada's First Nations*. 3rd ed. Toronto: Oxford University Press.

Dixon, E. 1999. "The First Colonization of North America." In *Bones, Boats, and Bison: Archeology and the First Colonization of Western North America*, edited by E. Dixon, 19–43. Albuquerque: University of New Mexico Press.

Dobbin, M. 1981. *The One-and-a-Half Men*. Vancouver: New Star Books.

Dobyns, H. 1966. "Estimating Aboriginal American Population: An Appraisal of Techniques with a New Hemisphere Estimate." *Current Anthropology* 7: 395–416.

Doerfler, J. 2015. *Those Who Belong*. Winnipeg: University of Manitoba Press.

Doxtator, D. 2011. "The Idea of Indianness and Once upon a Time: The Role of Indians in History." In *Racism, Colonialism, and Indigeneity in Canada*, edited by M. Cannon and L. Sunseri, 67–98. Oxford: Oxford University Press.

Dunbar-Ortiz, R. 2006. "The First Decade of Indigenous Peoples at the United Nations." *Peace and Change* 31, no. 1: 58–74.

———. 2014. *An Indigenous Peoples' History of the United States*. Boston: Beacon Press.

Duncan, S. 1913. *General Instructions to Indian Agents in Canada*. Ottawa: Department of Indian Affairs.

Dussart, F., and S. Poirier, eds. 2017. *Entangled Territorialities*. Toronto: University of Toronto Press.

Duthu, B. 2013. *Shadow Nations: Tribal Sovereignty and the Limits of Legal Pluralism*. New York: Oxford University Press.

Dyck, N. 1991. *What Is the Indian Problem? Tutelage and Resistance in Canadian Indian Administration*. St. John's: Memorial University, Institute of Social and Economic Research.

Elsey, C. 2013. *The Poetics of Land and Identity among BC Indigenous Peoples*. Halifax: Fernwood.

Ennab, F. 2010. "Rupturing the Myth of the Peaceful Western Canadian Frontier." MA thesis, Department of Sociology, University of Manitoba.

Ens, G. 1996. *Homeland to Hinterland: The Changing Worlds of the Red River Métis in the 19th Century*. Toronto: University of Toronto Press.

Erickson, L. 2005. "Constructed and Contested Truths: Aboriginal Suicide, Law, and Colonialism in the Canadian West(s), 1823–1927." *Canadian Historical Review* 86: 595–618.

Espeland, W. 2001. "Bureaucrats and Indians in a Contemporary Colonial Encounter." *Law and Social Inquiry* 26: 403–33.

Eyeford, D. 2013. "Forging Partnerships, Building Relationships." Report prepared for the prime minister.

Fenge, T., and P. Quassa. 2009. "Negotiating and Implementing the Nunavut Land Claims Agreement." *Policy Options* 30. https://policyoptions.irpp.org/magazines/canadas-water-challenges/negotiating-and-implementing-the-nnavt-land-claims-agreement/.

Fisher, R. 1977. *Contact and Conflict: Indian-European Relations in British Columbia, 1774–1890*. Vancouver: UBC Press.

Fixico, D. 2013. *Indian Resilience and Rebuilding: Indigenous Nations in the Modern American West*. Tucson: University of Arizona Press.

Flanagan, T. 1991. *Métis Lands in Manitoba*. Calgary: University of Calgary Press.

———. 2009. "Resource Industries and Security Issues in Northern Alberta." Paper prepared for the Canadian Defense and Foreign Affairs Institute.
———. 2019. *The Wealth of First Nations*. Vancouver: Fraser Institute.
Flanagan, T., C. Alcantara, and A. Dressay. 2010. *Beyond the Indian Act*. Montreal and Kingston: McGill-Queen's University Press.
Fleras, A. 2011. "Reclaiming Aboriginality: From Mainstream Media Representations to Aboriginal Self-Representation." In *Visions of the Heart: Canadian Aboriginal Issues*, 3rd ed., edited by D. Long and O. Dickason, 189–212. Don Mills, ON: Oxford University Press.
Foster, H. 2018. "One Good Thing: Law and Elevator Etiquette in the Indian Territories." In *Roots of Entanglements: Essays in the History of Native-Newcomer Relations*, edited by M. Rutherdale, P. Lackenbauer, and K. Abel, 289–312. Toronto: University of Toronto Press.
Foster, H., B. Berger, and A. Buck, eds. 2008. *The Grand Experiment: Laws and Legal Culture in British Settler Societies*. Vancouver: UBC Press.
Frideres, J., and R. Gadacz. 2011. *Aboriginal Peoples in Canada*. 9th ed. Toronto: Prentice Hall–Pearson.
Furniss, E. 1999. *The Burden of History: Colonialism and the Frontier Myth in a Rural Canadian Community*. Vancouver: UBC Press.
Gagnon, A. 2014. *Minority Nations in the Age of Uncertainty: New Paths to National Emancipation and Empowerment*. Toronto: University of Toronto Press.
Gallagher, B. 2012. *Resource Rulers: Fortune and Folly on Canada's Road to Resources*. Waterloo, ON: Bill Gallagher.
Gaudry, A., and D. Lorenz. 2018. "Indigenization as Inclusion, Reconciliation, and Decolonization: Navigating the Different Visions for Indigenizing the Canadian Academy." *AlterNative* 14, no. 3: 218–27.
Gehl, L. 2017. *Claiming Anishinaabe: Decolonizing the Human Spirit*. Regina: University of Regina Press.
Gilbert, J. 2006. *Indigenous Peoples' Land Rights under International Law: From Victims to Actors*. New York: Transnational Publishers.
Girvan, R. 2010. *Who Speaks for the River?* Toronto: Fitzhenry and Whiteside.
Globe and Mail. 2017. https://www.theglobeandmail.com/opinion/editorials/indigenous-peoples-and-the-need-for-a-way-forward-made-in-canada/article34568640/.
Gordon, I. 2009. *A People on the Move: The Métis of the Western Plains*. Victoria: Heritage House.
Government of Alberta. 2013. *Government of Alberta's Policy on Consultation with First Nations on Land and Natural Resource Management*. Edmonton: Aboriginal Relations.

Government of Canada. 1981. *In All Fairness: A Native Claims Policy*. Ottawa: Indian and Northern Affairs Canada.

———. 1982. *Outstanding Business: A Native Claims Policy—Specific Claims*. Ottawa: Indian and Northern Affairs Canada.

———. 1986. *Comprehensive Land Claims Policy*. Ottawa: Indian and Northern Affairs Canada.

———. 1997. *Gathering Strength—Canada's Aboriginal Action Plan*. Ottawa: Indian Affairs and Northern Development.

———. 2006. *Contracting Policy Notice 2006-4: Addition of Two Comprehensive Land Claims Agreements to the Information Contained in CPN 1997-8*. Ottawa: Treasury Board of Canada.

———. 2007. *Specific Claims: Justice at Last: Specific Claims Action Plan 2007*. Ottawa: Indian and Northern Affairs Canada.

———. 2018. *Status of Specific Claims in Canada*. Ottawa: Aboriginal Affairs and Northern Development Canada.

Graben, S., and M. Mehaffey. 2017. "Negotiating Self-Government Over and Over and Over Again." In *The Right Relationship: Reimagining the Implementation of Historical Treaties*, edited by J. Borrows and M. Coyle, 164–86. Toronto: University of Toronto Press.

Grammond, S., I. Lanntagne, and N. Gagne. 2016. "Non-Status Indigenous Groups in Canadian Courts: Practical and Legal Difficulties in Seeking Recognition." In *From Recognition to Reconciliation: Essays on the Constitutional Entrenchment of Aboriginal and Treaty Rights*, edited by P. Macklem and D. Sanderson, 259–84. Toronto: University of Toronto Press.

Gray, L. 2011. *First Nations 101: Tons of Stuff You Need to Know about First Nations People*. Vancouver: Adaawx Publishing.

Graziadei, M. 2009. "Legal Transplants and the Frontiers of Legal Knowledge." *Theoretical Inquiries in Law: Legal Histories of Transplantation* 10: 723–43.

Green, J., and G. Starblanket. 2018. "Recognition of Rights or Termination of Rights Framework?" APTN *National News*, August 2.

Greenwood, M., S. de Leeuw, N. Lindsay, and C. Reading, eds. 2015. *Determinants of Indigenous Peoples' Health in Canada*. Toronto: Canadian Scholars' Press.

Griffith, J. 2018. *Words Have a Past*. Toronto: University of Toronto Press.

Guha, R. 1997. *Dominance without Hegemony: History and Power in Colonial India*. Cambridge, MA: Harvard University Press.

Guimond, E. 2003. "Fuzzy Definitions and Population Explosion: Changing Identities of Aboriginal Groups in Canada." In *Not Strangers in These*

Parts: Urban Aboriginal Peoples, edited by D. Newhouse and E. Peters, 35–50. Ottawa: Policy Research Initiative.

Hankard, M. 2014. "The Indian Status Card as Regulator of Traditional Healer Access." *Canadian Journal of Native Studies* 34, no. 1: 73–86.

Harding, P. 2006. "Historical Representations of Aboriginal People in the Canadian Media." *Discourse and Society* 17: 205–25.

Harding, R. 2005. "The Media, Aboriginal People, and Common Sense." *Canadian Journal of Native Studies* 25: 311–35.

Hare, J. 2018. *Learning from the Land*. Vancouver: UBC Press.

Haring, S. 2005. "There Seemed to Be No Recognized Law: Canadian Law and the Prairie First Nations." In *Laws and Societies in the Canadian Prairie West 1670–1940*, edited by L. Knafla and J. Swainger, 85–105. Vancouver: UBC Press.

Harland, F. 2017. "Taking the Aboriginal Perspective Seriously." *Indigenous Law Review* 14, no. 1: 1–30. https://ilj.law.utoronto.ca/sites/ilj.law.utoronto.ca/files/users/enrightp/ILJ14_Fraser_Harland.pdf.

Harring, S. 1998. *White Man's Law: Native People in Nineteenth-Century Canadian Jurisprudence*. Toronto: University of Toronto Press.

Harrison, J. 1985. *Métis: People between Two Worlds*. Calgary: Glenbow-Alberta Institute; Vancouver: Douglas and McIntyre.

Healy, B., and L. Smith. 2018. *Voices from the Field*. Prince George, BC: National Collaborating Centre for Aboriginal Health.

Healy, S. 2013. "Constructing a Legal Land System that Supports Economic Development for the Métis in Alberta." *Journal of Aboriginal Economic Development* 2, no. 1: 18–23.

Hedican, E. 2014. "Eurocentrism in Aboriginal Studies: A Review of Issues and Conceptual Problems." *Canadian Journal of Native Studies* 34, no. 1: 87–110.

Helin, C. 2008. *Dances with Dependency: Out of Poverty through Self-Reliance*. Wood Lands, CA: Ravencrest.

Henderson, J. 1997. "Interpreting *Sui Generis* Treaties." *Alberta Law Review* 36: 46–97.

———. 2009. "Dialogical Governance: A Method of Constitutional Governance." *Saskatchewan Law Review* 72: 167–98.

Henry, R., C. Tait, and STR8 UP. 2016. "Creating Ethical Research Partnerships: Relational Accountability in Action." *Engaged Scholar Journal* 2, no. 1: 183–204.

Hoffecker, J., and S. Elias. 2007. *Human Ecology of Beringia*. New York: Elsevier Press.

Hoffecker, J., S. Elias, and D. O'Rourke. 2014. "Out of Beringia?" *Science* 28: 970–80.

Holen, S., et al. 2017. "A 130,000-Year-Old Archaeological Site in Southern California, USA." *Nature* 544: 479–83.
Huel, R. 1996. *Proclaiming the Gospel to the Indians and the Métis.* Edmonton: University of Alberta Press.
Hurley, M. 2000. "Aboriginal Title: The Supreme Court of Canada Decision in *Delgamuukw v. B.C.*" Background Paper 459E.
Imai, S. 2007. *The Structure of the Indian Act: Accountability in Governance.* Ottawa: National Centre for First Nations Governance.
——. 2019. *Annotated Aboriginal Law: The Constitution, Legislation, Treaties, and Supreme Court of Canada Case Summaries 2019.* Toronto: Carswell.
INAC. 1986. *Land Management.* https://www.aadnc-aandc.gc.ca/eng/1100100010002/1100100010021.
Ing, R. 2017. Correspondence with the author.
Innes, R. 2013. *Elder Brother and the Law of the People.* Winnipeg: University of Manitoba Press.
Innis, H. 1999. *The Fur Trade in Canada: An Introduction to Canadian Economic History.* Toronto: University of Toronto Press.
Isaac, T. 2004. *Aboriginal Law: Commentary, Cases, and Materials.* 3rd ed. Saskatoon: Purich.
——. 2013. *Aboriginal Title.* Saskatoon: Native Law Centre, University of Saskatchewan.
Isaac, T., and K. Annis. 2013. *Treaty Rights in the Historic Treaties of Canada.* Saskatoon: Native Law Centre, University of Saskatchewan.
Jacobs, B. 2014. Correspondence with the author.
Jai, J. 2017. "Bargains Made in Bad Times." In *The Right Relationship: Reimagining the Implementation of Historical Treaties*, edited by J. Borrows and M. Coyle, 105–48. Toronto: University of Toronto Press.
Jordan-Fenton, C., and M. Pokiak-Fenton. 2010. *Fatty Legs: A True Story.* Montreal: Annick Press.
Jorgensen, M., ed. 2007. *Rebuilding Native Nations: Strategies for Governance and Development.* Tucson: University of Arizona Press.
Joseph, B. 2018. *21 Things You May Not Know about the Indian Act: Helping Canadians Make Reconciliation with Indigenous Peoples a Reality.* Toronto: Indigenous Relations Press.
Keith, J. 2015. "The Totalizing Nature of the Canadian State: Modern Treaties in the Era of Recognition." *Canadian Journal of Native Studies* 35, no. 1: 45–67.
Kelly, F. 2015. "Reconciling Sovereignties: Combining Traditional Law and Contemporary Western Law to See Truth and Reconciliation." Public lecture, McGill Faculty of Law, Moot Court, September 21.

Kelm, M.-E., and K. Smith. 2018. *Talking Back to the Indian Act*. Toronto: University of Toronto Press.

Kenny, G. 2015. *Indians Do It*. Winnipeg: University of Manitoba Press.

Kermoal, N., and I. Altamirano-Jimenez, eds. 2016. *Living on the Land: Indigenous Women*. Edmonton: Athabasca University Press.

Ketilson, L. 2014. "Partnering to Finance Enterprise Development in the Aboriginal Social Economy." *Canadian Public Policy* 40: 39–49.

King, H., and S. Pasternak. 2018. *Canada's Emerging Indigenous Rights Framework: A Critical Analysis*. Toronto: Yellowhead Institute.

Knowles, E., and B. Lowery. 2012. "Meritocracy, Self-Concerns, and Whites' Denial of Racial Inequity." *Self and Identity* 11: 202–22.

Krasowski, S. 2019. *No Surrender: The Land Remains Indigenous*. Regina: University of Regina Press.

Kroskrity, P., and M. Field, eds. 2009. *Native American Ideologies*. Tucson: University of Arizona Press.

Kulchyski, P. 1994. *Unjust Relations: Aboriginal Rights in Canadian Courts*. Toronto: Oxford University Press.

———. 2006. *Like the Sound of a Drum: Aboriginal Cultural Politics in Denendeh and Nunavut*. Winnipeg: University of Manitoba Press.

Laidlaw, D. 2019. "The Challenges in Using Aboriginal Traditional Knowledge in the Courts." In *Environment in the Courtroom*, edited by A. Ingelson, 606–33. Calgary: University of Calgary Press.

Laidlaw, D., and M. Passelac-Ross. 2014. *Alberta First Nations Consultation and Accommodation Handbook*. Calgary: University of Calgary, Canadian Institute of Resources Law.

Lalonde, C. 2007. "Identity Formation and Cultural Resilience in Aboriginal Communities." Unpublished paper.

LaRocque, E. 2010. *When the Other Is Me: Native Resistance Discourse 1850–1990*. Winnipeg: University of Manitoba Press.

Lawrence, B. 2004. *Real Indians and Others: Mixed-Blood Urban Native Peoples and Indigenous Nationhood*. Lincoln: University of Nebraska Press.

———. 2011. "Rewriting Histories of the Land: Colonization and Indigenous Resistance in Canada." In *Racism, Colonialism, and Indigeneity in Canada*, edited by M. Cannon and L. Sunseri, 45–78. Oxford: Oxford University Press.

———. 2012. *Fractured Homeland*. Vancouver: UBC Press.

Leclair, J. 2006. "Federal Constitutionalism and Aboriginal Difference." *Queen's Law Journal* 31: 521–35.

Leddy, L. 2017. "Intersections of Indigenous and Environmental History in Canada." *Canadian Historical Review* 98: 83–95.

Leigh, D. 2009. "Colonialism, Gender, and the Family in North America: For a Gendered Analysis of Indigenous Struggles." *Studies in Ethnicity and Nationalism* 9: 70–88.

Lemont, E. 2006. *American Indian Constitutional Reform and the Rebuilding of Native Nations.* Cambridge, MA: Harvard University, American Indian Studies Center.

Levy, J. 2000. "Aboriginal Citizenship." *Australasian Journal* 78, no. 3: 418–21.

Lewis, J. 2000. "Ancient Values, New Technology: Emerging Methods for Integrating Cultural Values in Forest Management." MA thesis, University of British Columbia.

Lewis, J., and S. Sheppard. 2013. "First Nations' Spiritual Conceptions of Forests and Forest Management." In *Aboriginal Peoples and Forest Lands in Canada*, edited by D. Tindall, R. Trosper, and P. Perreault, 289–324. Vancouver: UBC Press.

Little Bear, L. 2009. "Jagged Worldviews Colliding." In *Reclaiming Indigenous Voices and Visions*, edited by M. Battiste, 78–85. Vancouver: UBC Press.

Longstaffe, M. 2017. "Indigenous Women as Newspaper Representations." *Canadian Historical Review* 98: 230–60.

Loppie, S. 2014. *Aboriginal Experiences with Racism and Its Impact.* Prince George, BC: National Collaborating Centre for Aboriginal Health.

Lutz, J. 2008. *Makuk: A New History of Aboriginal-White Relations.* Vancouver: UBC Press.

Lyons, O. 2008. "Listening to Natural Law." In *Original Instructions: Indigenous Teachings for a Sustainable Future*, edited by M.K. Nelson, 45–67. Rochester, VT: Bear and Company.

Macdougall, B. 2010. *One of the Family: Métis Culture in Nineteenth-Century Northwestern Saskatchewan.* Vancouver: UBC Press.

———. 2017. "Space and Place within Aboriginal Epistemological Traditions." *Canadian Historical Review* 98: 64–82.

MacEwan, G. 1984. *Report of the MacEwan Joint Metis-Government Committee to Review the Metis Betterment Act and Regulations.* Edmonton: Alberta Municipal Affairs.

MacKinnon, S. 2015. *Decolonizing Employment.* Winnipeg: University of Manitoba Press.

Macklem, P. 2001. *Indigenous Difference and the Constitution of Canada.* Toronto: University of Toronto Press.

———. 2016. "Indigenous-Canadian Relations and the 'Ethos of Legal Pluralism." In *From Recognition to Reconciliation: Essays on the Constitutional Entrenchment of Aboriginal and Treaty Rights*, edited by P. Macklem and D. Sanderson, 257–79. Toronto: University of Toronto Press.

Macklem, P., and D. Sanderson. 2016. *From Recognition to Reconciliation: Essays on the Constitutional Entrenchment of Aboriginal and Treaty Rights*. Toronto: University of Toronto Press.

MacNeil, M. 2018. "Doctrine of Laches in Canada." In *Encyclopedia of Canadian Laws*. https://lawi.ca/category/de/page/2/.

Manual, A., and R. Derrickson. 2015. *Unsettling Canada*. Toronto: Between the Lines.

Martin-McGuire, P. 1999. "The Importance of the Land: Treaty Land Entitlement and Self-Government in Saskatchewan." In *Aboriginal Self-Government in Canada: Current Trends*, edited by J. Hylton, 98–125. Saskatoon: Purich.

Maybury-Lewis, D., T. Macdonald, and B. Maybury-Lewis, eds. 2009. *Manifest Destinies and Indigenous Peoples*. Cambridge, MA: Harvard University Press.

McBride, J. 2010. *Are There Lessons from the "Harvard Project on American Indian Economic Development" that Could Be Applied to Urban Aboriginal Economic Development in Canadian Centres?* Vancouver: Embree and McBride Consulting.

McCallum, M. 2015. *Indigenous Women, Work, and History: 1940–1980*. Winnipeg: University of Manitoba Press.

———. 2017. "Starvation, Experimentation, Segregation, and Trauma: Words for Reading." *Canadian Historical Review* 98: 96–117.

McHugh, R. 2016. "A Common Law Biography of Section 35." In *From Recognition to Reconciliation: Essays on the Constitutional Entrenchment of Aboriginal and Treaty Rights*, edited by P. Macklem and D. Sanderson, 137–63. Toronto: University of Toronto Press.

McNeil, K. 2007. *The Jurisdiction of Inherent Right Aboriginal Governments*. Ottawa: National Centre for First Nations Governance.

———. 2013. "Aboriginal Title in Canada: Site-Specific or Territorial?" *All Papers* Paper 19. http://digitalcommons.osgoode.yorku.ca/all_papers/19.

———. 2016. "The Absolute Theory of Crown Unity in Canada and Its Relevance to Indigenous Claims." *Review of Constitutional Studies* 20, no. 1: 1–28.

———. 2017. "Indigenous Rights Litigation, Legal History, and the Role of Experts." In *The Right Relationship: Reimagining the Implementation of Historical Treaties*, edited by J. Borrows and M. Coyle, 70–104. Toronto: University of Toronto Press.

———. 2018. "Indigenous and Crown Sovereignty in Canada." In *Resurgence and Reconciliation: Settler Relations and Earth Teachings*, edited by M. Asch, J. Borrows, and J. Tully, 293–314. Toronto: University of Toronto Press.

Merryman, J., and R. Perez-Perdomo. 2007. *The Civil Law Tradition: An Introduction to the Legal Systems of Europe and Latin America*. Stanford, CA: Stanford University Press.

Métis Nation of Alberta. 2009. *Policy Guidelines Regarding the Duty to Consult and Accommodate Métis Aboriginal Rights and Interests in Alberta*. Edmonton: Métis Nation of Alberta.

———. 2017. *Memorandum of Understanding to Advance Reconciliation with the Government of Canada*. Ottawa: Indigenous and Northern Affairs.

Miller, J.R. 1989. *Skyscrapers Hide the Heavens: A History of Indian-White Relations in Canada*. Toronto: University of Toronto Press.

———. 2000. *Skyscrapers Hide the Heavens: A History of Indian-White Relations in Canada*. 2nd ed. Toronto: University of Toronto Press.

———. 2009. *Compact, Contract, Covenant: Aboriginal Treaty-Making in Canada*. Toronto: University of Toronto Press.

Milne, D. 1995. *Report of the Task Force on Aboriginal Issues*. Moncton: Aboriginal Affairs New Brunswick.

Moffett, R. 1982. "Furrows of Stone: Race Politics and the Alberta Métis Land Question, 1932–1936." MA thesis, Simon Fraser University.

Monchalin, L. 2016. *The Colonial Problem*. Toronto: University of Toronto Press.

Moore, M. 2010. "Indigenous Peoples and Political Legitimacy." In *Between Consenting Peoples*, edited by J. Webber and R. Macleod, 143–63. Vancouver: UBC Press.

Moore, M., A. Turcotte, and J. Winter. 2014. *Aboriginal-Canadians and Energy Literacy: A Survey of Opinions and Thoughts on Energy*. Calgary: University of Calgary School of Public Policy.

Morin, J.-P. 2018. *Solemn Words and Foundational Documents*. Toronto: University of Toronto Press.

Mosby, I. 2013. "Administering Colonial Science: Nutrition Research and Human Biomedical Experimentation in Aboriginal Communities and Residential Schools, 1942–1952." *Histoire sociale/Social History* 46, no. 1: 145–72.

Moss, W., and E. Gardner-O'Toole. 1991. *Aboriginal People: History of Discriminatory Laws*. http://publications.gc.ca/Collection-R/LoPBdP/BP/bp175-e.htm.

National Aboriginal Law Section, Canadian Bar Association. 2010. *Bill C-3—Gender Equity in Indian Registration Act*. Ottawa: Canadian Bar Association.

National Inquiry into Missing and Murdered Indigenous Women and Girls. 2019. *Reclaiming Power and Place: The Final Report of the National Inquiry into Missing and Murdered Indigenous Women and Girls*. Vols. 1a and 1b. Ottawa.

Nettelbeck, A., R. Smandych, L. Knafla, and R. Roster. 2016. *Fragile Settlements*. Vancouver: UBC Press.

Neu, D., and R. Therrien. 2002. *Accounting for Genocide: Canada's Bureaucratic Assault on Aboriginal People*. Black Point, NS: Fernwood.

Newhouse, D. 2004. "Indigenous Knowledge in a Multicultural World." *Native Studies Review* 15: 67–84.

———. 2009. *The Duty to Consult: New Relationships with Aboriginal People*. Saskatoon: Purich.

Newman, B. 2016. "Consultation and Economic Reconciliation." In *From Recognition to Reconciliation: Essays on the Constitutional Entrenchment of Aboriginal and Treaty Rights*, edited by P. Macklem and D. Sanderson, 207–22. Toronto: University of Toronto Press.

Newman, D. 2014. *Revisiting the Duty to Consult Aboriginal Peoples*. Saskatoon: Purich.

Nicholl, F. 2004. *Goodspeed: How Different It Was: Canadians at the Time of Confederation*. Toronto: Dundurn.

Niezen, R. 2013. *Truth and Indignation: Canada's Truth and Reconciliation Commission*. Toronto: University of Toronto Press.

Nnaemeka, E. 2017. "Uncertain Accommodation: Aboriginal Identity and Group Rights in the Supreme Court of Canada." *Review of Constitutional Studies* 22, no. 2: 429–33.

Nobles, M. 2008. *The Politics of Official Apologies*. New York: Cambridge University Press.

O'Brien, K. 2018. *Petitioning for Land*. New York: Bloomsbury Academic.

O'Connor, L., M. O'Neil, L. Dolha, and J. Ada. 2010. *Dark Legacy*. Vancouver: Totem Pole Books.

Palmater, P. 2011a. "Stretched Beyond Human Limits: Death by Poverty in First Nations." *Canadian Review of Social Policy* 65: 112–28.

———. 2011b. *Beyond Blood: Rethinking Indigenous Identity*. Saskatoon: Purich.

———. 2012. "Updated Bill C-3-Gender Equity in Indian Registration Act." http://www.pampalmater.com.updated-bill-c-3-gender-equity-in-indian-registration-act.

———. 2014. *Indian Status: Why Lynn Gehl's Court Challenge Matters*. https://www.cbc.ca/news/indigenous/Indian-status-why-lynn-gehl-s-court-challenge-matters-1.2806534.

———. 2015. *Indigenous Nationhood: Empowering Grassroots Citizens*. Halifax: Fernwood.

———. 2017a. "Nation to Nation Relations Need Repeal of Paternalistic Laws." *Lawyer's Daily*, April 17. https://www.thelawyersdaily.ca/articles/2889/

nation-to-nation-relations-need-repeal-of-paternalistic-laws-pamela-palmater.

———. 2017b. "Bill s-3: An Act to Amend the Indian Act." Presented to the Senate Standing Committee on Aboriginal Affairs.

———. 2018a. "The Indigenous Right to Say No." *Lawyer's Daily*, October 12. Nationtalk.ca/story/the-indigenous-right-to-say-no-pamela-palmater-the-lawyers-daily.

———. 2018b. "Trudeau's Dance of Deception on Indigenous Rights." *Lawyer's Daily*, February 26. https://indigenousnationhood.blogspot.com/2018/02/trudeaus-dance-of-deception-on.html.

Panagos, D. 2017. *Uncertain Accommodation: Aboriginal Identity*. Vancouver: UBC Press.

Passelac-Ross, M., and V. Potes. 2007. "Crown Consultation with Aboriginal Peoples in Oil Sands Development: Is It Adequate, Is It Legal?" Canadian Institute for Resources and Law, University of Calgary, occasional paper.

Penner, K. 1983. *Indian Self-Government*. Ottawa: Indian Affairs and Northern Development.

Polzer, J., and E. Power, eds. 2016. *Neoliberal Governance and Health*. Montreal and Kingston: McGill-Queen's University Press.

Ponting, J.R. 1986. *Arduous Journey: Canadian Indians and Decolonization*. Toronto: McClelland and Stewart.

Public Policy Forum. 2014. *Realizing the Potential: Global Perspectives on Indigenous Economic Development*. Ottawa: Public Policy Forum.

Purich, D. 1986. *Our Land: Native Rights in Canada*. Saskatoon: University of Saskatchewan.

Randall, W. 2011. "Greater Rights for Métis Settlements in Alberta?" Unpublished manuscript.

Ray, A. 1974. *Indians in the Fur Trade: Their Role as Trappers, Hunters, and Middlemen in the Lands Southwest of Hudson Bay, 1660–1870*. Toronto: University of Toronto Press.

———. 1982. "Reflections on Fur Trade Social History and Métis History in Canada." *American Indian Quarterly* 6: 91–107.

———. 2011. *Telling It to the Judge*. Montreal and Kingston: McGill-Queen's University Press.

———. 2016. *Aboriginal Rights Claims and the Making and Remaking of History*. Montreal and Kingston: McGill-Queen's University Press.

Razack, S. 2002. *Race, Space, and the Law: Unmapping a White Settler Society*. Toronto: Between the Lines.

Reading, C. 2013. *Understanding Racism*. Prince George, BC: National Collaborating Centre for Aboriginal Health.

Redmond, L. 1996. "Diverse Native American Perspectives on the Use of Sacred Areas on Public Lands." In *Nature and the Human Spirit: Toward an Expanded Land Management Ethic*, edited by B. Driver, 34–56. Edmonton: Venture Publishing.

Regan, P. 2010. *Unsettling the Settler Within: Indian Residential Schools, Truth Telling, and Reconciliation in Canada*. Vancouver: UBC Press.

Reilly, J. 2014. *The Myths of First Nation Equality and Judicial Independence in Canada*. Calgary: Rocky Mountain Books.

Richter, D. 2001. *Facing East from Indian Country: A Native History of Early America*. Cambridge, MA: Harvard University Press.

Roach, K. 1992. "Aboriginal Peoples and the Law: Remedies for Violations of Aboriginal Rights." *Manitoba Law Journal* 21: 478–507.

Robertson, D. 2012. *Sugar Falls: A Residential School*. Winnipeg: Portage and Main Press.

Rose, N. 1996. "Governing 'Advanced' Liberal Democracies." In *Foucault and Political Reason: Liberalism, Neo-Liberalism and Rationalities of Government*, edited by A. Barry, T. Osborne, and N. Rose, 37–65. Chicago: University of Chicago Press.

Rotman, L. 1997. *Parallel Paths: Fiduciary Doctrine and the Crown-Native Relationship in Canada*. Toronto: University of Toronto Press.

Royal Commission on Aboriginal Peoples. 1996a. *Looking Forward, Looking Back*. Vol. 1 of the Report of the Royal Commission on Aboriginal Peoples. Ottawa: Supply and Services Canada.

———. 1996b. *Restructuring the Relationship*. Vol. 2 of the Report of the Royal Commission on Aboriginal Peoples. Ottawa: Supply and Services Canada.

Rutherdale, M. 2018. "Alaska Highway Nurses and DEW Line Doctors: Medical Encounters in Northern Canadian Indigenous Communities." In *Roots of Entanglements: Essays in the History of Native-Newcomer Relations*, edited by M. Rutherdale, P. Lackenbauer, and K. Abel, 159–77. Toronto: University of Toronto Press.

Rutherdale, M., P. Lackenbauer, and K. Abel. 2018. *Roots of Entanglements: Essays in the History of Native-Newcomer Relations*. Toronto: University of Toronto Press.

Sanderson, D. 2016. "Overlapping Consensus, Legislative Reform, and the Indian Act." In *From Recognition to Reconciliation: Essays on the Constitutional Entrenchment of Aboriginal and Treaty Rights*, edited by P. Macklem and D. Sanderson, 320–56. Toronto: University of Toronto Press.

Satzewich, V. 1997. "Indian Agents and the 'Indian Problem' in Canada in 1946: Reconsidering the Theory of Coercive Tutelage." *Canadian Journal of Native Studies* 17, no. 2: 227–57.

Sawchuk, J., P. Sawchuk, and T. Ferguson. 1981. *Métis Land Rights in Alberta: A Political History*. Edmonton: Métis Association of Alberta.

Sellars, B. 2012. *They Called Me Number One: Secrets and Survival at an Indian Residential School*. Vancouver: Talon Books.

Shih, M., D. Sanchez, and G. Ho. 2010. "Costs and Benefits of Switching among Multiple Social Identities." In *The Psychology of Social and Cultural Diversity*, edited by R. Crisp, 67–98. Chichester, UK: Blackwell.

Shore, R. 2017. "Heiltsuk First Nation Village among Oldest in North America." https://warriorpublications.wordpress.com/2017/03/29/heiltsuk-first-nation-village-among-oldest-in-north-america-archeologists/.

Shreve, B. 2017. "Frontiers and Perspectives." *Tribal College* 28, no. 3: 1–5.

Simpson, A. 2014. *Mohawk Interruptus: Political Life across the Borders of Settler States*. Durham, NC: Duke University Press.

———. 2017. *As We Have Always Done*. Minneapolis: University of Minnesota Press.

Simpson, A., and A. Smith, eds. 2014. *Theorizing Native Studies*. Durham, NC: Duke University Press.

Simpson, L., ed. 2008. *Lighting the Eighth Fire: The Liberation, Resurgence, and Protection of Indigenous Nations*. Winnipeg: Arbeiter Ring.

———. 2011. *Dancing on Our Turtle's Back: Stories of Nishnaabeg Recreation, Resurgence, and a New Emergence*. Winnipeg: Arbeiter Ring.

Slade, H., and A. Lombard. 2015. *Specific Claims Tribunal Canada: Five-Year Review*. Ottawa: Supply and Services.

Slattery, B. 2016. "The Generative Structure of Aboriginal Rights." In *From Recognition to Reconciliation: Essays on the Constitutional Entrenchment of Aboriginal and Treaty Rights*, edited by P. Macklem and D. Sanderson, 100–36. Toronto: University of Toronto Press.

Smith, K. 2014. *Strange Visitors: Documents in Indigenous-Settler Relations in Canada*. Toronto: University of Toronto Press.

Specific Claims Research Centre. N.d. *Where History Meets Justice*. https://www.specific-claims.ca/faq.php.

Statistics Canada. 2013. "Aboriginal Peoples in Canada: First Nations People, Métis, and Inuit." Ottawa: Minister of Industry.

———. 2016. https://www.150.statcan.gc.ca/n1/daily-quotidien/171025/t001a-eng.htm.

———. 2017. Aboriginal Peoples Highlight Tables, 2016 Census. https://www12.statcan.gc.ca/census-recensement/2016/dp-pd/hit-fst/abo-aut/Table.cfm?Lang=Eng&T=101&S=99&O=A.

Steckley, J., and B. Cummins. 2008. *Full Circle: Canada's First Nations*. Toronto: Pearson.

Stevenson, M. 2013. "Treaty Daze: Reflections on Negotiating Treaty Relationships under the BC Treaty Process." In *Aboriginal Peoples and Forest Lands in Canada*, edited by D. Tindall, R. Trosper, and P. Perreault, 118–45. Vancouver: UBC Press.

Strelein, L., and T. Tran. 2013. "Building Indigenous Governance from Native Title: Moving Away from 'Fitting in' to Creating a Decolonized Space." *Review of Constitutional Studies* 18: 19–38.

Suzack, C. 2017. *Indigenous Women's Writing*. Toronto: University of Toronto Press.

Swaminathan, N. 2014. "Destination Americas." *Archaeology*. https://www.archaeology.org/issues/145-1409/features/2367-peopling-the-americas-paradigm.

Teillet, J. 2013. *Métis Law in Canada*. Vancouver: Pape Salter Teillet.

Tilbury, F. 2000. "'What's in a Name?' Wadjula Self-Labelling and the Process of Reconciliation." *Balayi: Culture, Law, and Colonialism* 1, no. 2: 73–78.

Trees, K. 1998. "Narrative and Co-Existence: Mediating between Indigenous and Non-Indigenous Stories." PhD diss., Murdoch University.

Trigger, B. 1986. "The Historians' Indian: Native Americans in Canadian Historical Writing from Charlevoix to the Present." *Canadian Historical Review* 67, no. 3: 315–42.

Tuck, E., and K. Yang. 2012. "Decolonization Is Not a Metaphor." *Decolonization: Indigeneity, Education & Society* 1, no. 1: 1–40.

Tully, J. 2000. "The Struggles of Indigenous Peoples for and of Freedom." In *Political Theory and the Rights of Indigenous Peoples*, edited by D. Ivison, P. Patton, and W. Sanders, 36–59. Cambridge, UK: Cambridge University Press.

United Nations. 2007. *United Nations Declaration on the Rights of Indigenous Peoples*. New York: United Nations.

United Nations Environment. 2019. *Global Environment Outlook 6: Healthy Planet, Healthy People*. Cambridge, UK: Cambridge University Press.

Varcoe, C. 2011. *Harms and Benefits: Collecting Ethnicity Data in a Clinical Context*. Michael Smith Foundation for Health Research. http://www.ciqss.umontreal.ca/Docs/SSDE/pdf/Varcoe.pdf.

Vasey, D. 2011. "Opposing Fortress North America: Tar Sands Development and Indigenous Resistance." *Ecosocialism Canada*, September 12. https://ecosocialism.ca/2011/09/opposing-fortress-north-america-tar-sands-development-and-indigenous-resistance/.

Veracini, L. 2011. "On Settlerness." *Borderlands* 10, no. 1. www.borderlands.net.au/vol10no1_2011/veracini_settlerness.pdf.

———. 2013a. "Isopolitics, Deep Colonizing, Settler Colonialism." *Interventions: International Journal of Postcolonial Studies* 13, no. 2: 171–89.

———. 2013b. "Settler Colonialism: Career of a Concept." *Journal of Imperial and Commonwealth History* 41, no. 3: 313–33.

Victor, W. 2012. "Xexa:ls and the Power of Transformation: The Sto:lo, Good Governance and Self-Determination." PhD diss., Simon Fraser University.

Waiser, B. 2018. "They Have Suffered the Most: First Nations and the Aftermath of the 1885 North-West Rebellion." In *Roots of Entanglements: Essays in the History of Native-Newcomer Relations*, edited by M. Rutherdale, P. Lackenbauer, and K. Abel, 233–58. Toronto: University of Toronto Press.

Waldram, J., A. Herring, and K. Young. 2006. *Aboriginal Health in Canada: Historical, Cultural, and Epidemiological Perspectives*. Toronto: University of Toronto Press.

Wallace, R. 2013. *Merging Fires: Grassroots Peacebuilding between Indigenous and Non-Indigenous Peoples*. Halifax: Fernwood.

Walters, M. 2017a. "Rights and Remedies within Common Law and Indigenous Legal Traditions." In *The Right Relationship: Reimagining the Implementation of Historical Treaties*, edited by J. Borrows and M. Coyle, 187–207. Toronto: University of Toronto Press.

———. 2017b. "Judicial Recognition of Indigenous Legal Traditions: *Connolly v. Woolrich*." *Review of Constitutional Studies* 22, no. 3: 347–77.

Warry, W. 2007. *Ending Denial: Understanding Aboriginal Issues*. Toronto: University of Toronto Press.

Watt-Cloutier, S. 2015. *The Right to Be Cold*. Toronto: Penguin.

Webber, J., and C. Macleod, eds. 2010. *Between Consenting Peoples*. Vancouver: UBC Press.

White, K. 2016. "We Want Doors Opened, Not Slammed Shut." MA thesis, University of Saskatchewan.

Widdowson, F., and A. Howard. 2008. *Disrobing the Aboriginal Industry: The Deception behind Indigenous Cultural Preservation*. Montreal and Kingston: McGill-Queen's University Press.

Wilkes, R. 2004. "First Nation Politics: Deprivation, Resources, and Participation in Collective Action." *Sociological Inquiry* 74: 45–67.

Wilkes, R., and T. Ibrahim. 2013. "Timber: Direct Action over Forests and Beyond." In *Aboriginal Peoples and Forest Lands in Canada*, edited by D. Tindall, R. Trosper, and P. Perreault, 234–59. Vancouver: UBC Press.

Wilson, S. 2001. "What Is an Indigenous Research Methodology?" *Canadian Journal of Native Education* 25: 78–89.

Wilson-Raybould, J. 2018. "The Recognition and Implementation of Rights Framework Talk." Speech to the Business Council of British Columbia, Vancouver, April 13.

Wolfe, P. 2006. "Settler Colonialism and the Elimination of the Native." *Journal of Genocide Research* 8: 387–409.

Woolford, A. 2005. *Between Justice and Certainty: Treaty Making in British Columbia*. Vancouver: UBC Press.

———. 2009. "Ontological Destruction: Genocide and Canadian Aboriginal Peoples." *Genocide Studies and Prevention* 4, no. 1: 81–97.

———. 2015. *This Benevolent Experiment: Indigenous Boarding Schools, Genocide, and Redress in Canada and the United States*. Winnipeg: University of Manitoba Press.

Wright, J. 2006. "A History of the Native People of Canada: 10,000–1,000 BC." Mercury Series, Archaeological Paper 152, Canadian Museum of Civilization.

York, G. 1989. *The Dispossessed: Life and Death in Native Canada*. Toronto: Lester and Orpen Dennys.

Younging, G. 2018. *Elements of Indigenous Style: A Guide for Writing by and about Indigenous Peoples*. Edmonton: Brush Education.

LEGAL CASES

Alberta (Aboriginal Affairs and Northern Development) v Cunningham, 2011 SCC 37

Behn v Moulton Contracting Ltd., 2013 SCC 26

Calder v Attorney-General of British Columbia, [1973] SCR 313, [1973] 4 WWR 1

Campbell v British Columbia (Attorney General), 2000 BCSC 1123

Canada v Kitselas First Nation (2014), 460 NR 185 (FCA)

Cardinal v Attorney General of Alberta, [1974] SCR 695, [1973] 6 WWR 205

Chartrand v The Queen, 2015 TCC 298

Connolly v Woolrich (1867), 17 RJRQ 75

Corbiere v Canada (Minister of Indian and Northern Affairs), [1999] 2 SCR 203

Daniels v Canada (Minister of Indian Affairs and Northern Development), 2013 FC 6

Daniels v Canada (Minister of Indian Affairs and Northern Development), 2016 SCC 12

Delgamuukw v British Columbia, [1997] 3 SCR 1010

Deschenaux v Canada (Attorney General), 2015 QCCS 3555

Gehl v Canada (Attorney General), 2017 ONCA 319

Grassy Narrows First Nation v Ontario (Natural Resources), 2014 SCC 48
Guerin v The Queen, [1984] 2 SCR 335
Haida Nation v British Columbia (Minister of Forests), 2004 SCC 73
Hamlet of Baker Lake v Canada (Indian Affairs and Northern Development) (1979), [1980] 1 FC 518
Manitoba Métis Federation Inc. v Canada (Attorney General), 2013 SCC 14
McIvor v Canada (Registrar of Indian and Northern Affairs), 2009 BCCA 153
McIvor v The Registrar, Indian and Northern Affairs, 2007 BCSC 26
Mikisew Cree First Nation v Canada (Minister of Canadian Heritage), 2005 SCC 69
Mitchell v Minister of National Revenue, 2001 SCC 33
Peavine Metis Settlement v Alberta (Minister of Aboriginal Affairs and Northern Development), 2007 ABQB 517
Quebec c Corneau, 2015 QCCS 482
The Queen v Nowegijick, [1983] 1 SCR 29, 144 DLR (3d) 193
R v Badger, [1996] 1 SCR 771, [1996] 4 WWR 457
R v Beer, 2012 MBPC 45
R v Belhumeur, 2007 SKPC 114
R v Bernard, 2005 SCC 43
R v Blais, 2003 SCC 44
R v Dick, [1985] 2 SCR 309, 22 CCC (3d) 129
R v Gladstone, [1996] 2 SCR 723, [1996] 9 WWR 149
R v Goodon, 2008 MBPC 59
R v Gray, 2006 SCC 54
R v Horseman, [1990] 1 SCR 901, [1990] 4 WWR 97
R v Laviolette, 2005 SKPC 70
R v Marshall (1999), [1999] 3 SCR 456, 177 DLR (4th) 513
R v Marshall, [1999] 3 SCR 533, 179 DLR (4th) 193
R v Marshall, 2005 SCC 43
R v Pamajewon, [1996] 2 SCR 821, 138 DLR (4th) 204
R v Powley, 2003 SCC 43
R v Sappier, 2006 SCC 54
R v Simon, [1985] 2 SCR 387, 24 DLR (4th) 390
R v Sioui, [1990] 1 SCR 1025, 70 DLR (4th) 427
R v Sparrow, [1990] 1 SCR 1075, [1990] 4 WWR 410
R v Syliboy (1928), [1929] 1 DLR 307
R v Van der Peet, [1996] 2 SCR 507, 137 DLR (4th) 289
R v White and Bob (1965), 52 DLR (2d) 481
Ross River Dena Council Band v Canada, 2002 SCC 54

Sandra Lovelace v Canada, Communication No. 24/1977: Canada 30/07/81, UN Doc CCPR/C/13/D/24/1977

St. Catharines Milling and Lumber Company v The Queen, (1887) 13 SCR 577

Taku River Tlingit First Nation v British Columbia (Project Assessment Director), 2004 SCC 74

Tsilhqot'in Nation v British Columbia, 2014 SCC 44

INDEX

2SLGBTQQIA people, violence facing, 256

Abenaki People, 17
Aboriginal Affairs and Northern Development Canada, 12, 241
Aboriginality, definition, 224
Aboriginal Human Resource Council, 249
Aboriginal Peoples
   "civilizing" of, 18–22, 48, 62, 67, 74–77, 183
   definition, xix, xxii, 27–28, 169
Aboriginal Rights, 1
   changes to, 2, 27–28, 134–35, 225
   comprehensive claims, 134–35, 139–42, 148–51, 185. See also comprehensive claims
   definition, xix, xxi, 28, 155–58, 171–77, 217, 229, 238
   extinguishment of, 32, 62, 115, 123, 140–42, 200, 209–10
   framework, 270–74
   history of, 160–71, 186–92
   ignorance of, 20, 61, 95–96, 118–19, 170, 183
   infringement of, 137, 149, 159, 170–77, 192–96, 221–24, 252
   land, 66, 95–96, 104, 117, 128, 158. See also land claims
   limitations on, 157, 176–78, 215–17
   negotiation of, 202–4, 212, 247–49, 258, 260–64
   settler criteria of, 36, 103–5, 159, 171–73, 182–83, 193
agriculture, 258
   barriers to, 82–83, 162, 166
   Indigenous, 73, 83
   settler, 9, 48, 61–62, 72–73, 117, 123–24
Alberta, 158, 206–7
   Assembly of Grand Chiefs, 215
   colonial renaming, 39
   Court of Appeal, 243
   duty to consult, 214–18, 222
   Indigenous population in, 46, 254
   land negotiations, 146, 148, 213, 222
   Métis recognition, 34, 49, 128, 131–32, 179, 181, 240–45
   Wildlife Act, 206–8

Alberta (Aboriginal Affairs and Northern Development) v Cunningham, 241, 299
Alberta Indian Investment Corporation, 254
Alcantara, Christopher, 261
Alfonso v, 21
Alfred, Taiaiake, 20
Algonquin People, 17
Ali, Saleem, 267
Anglican missionaries, 6
Anishinaabe First Nation, xxi, 39, 64–66
    Aboriginal title, 163–64, 197, 205
    "half-breed adhesion," 117–18
Anishinabek, 13
apprehension of children, state, 9
Ariss, Rachel, 119
Assembly of First Nations, xxv, 44, 230, 237, 259, 273
    Confederacy of Nations, 238
    Council of Elders, 239
    Council of Women, 239
    Council of Youth, 239
    Executive Committee, 238–39
    First Nations-in-Assembly, 238, 240
    roles of, 239–40
assimilation, 38, 40, 83, 227, 232, 261
    crown policies, 5, 123–24, 149–50, 193, 198, 203
    Indian Act, xxiv, 20–21, 25, 47–49
Assiniboine People, 17
Atlantic provinces, 38, 47, 122, 165, 197
Attawapiskat reserve, 71

Badger, Wayne, 206–7
Baffin Land Inuit, 17
Baker Lake Inuit, 158–59
Balfour, Lindsay, 54
band councils
    definition, xix, xx
    duties, 157, 162, 234–37, 253
    elections, 235–36
    federal monitoring of, 71
bands, First Nations, 191, 220
    definition, xx
    membership criteria, 43–44, 231
Beaver People, 17
Bella Bella People, 17
Bella Coola People, 17
Beothuk People, 17
Beringia (land bridge) theory, 14–15
Behn v Moulton Contracting Ltd., 156, 299
Bill c-3. See *Gender Equity in Indian Registration Act*
Bill c-31, xx, xxv, 42–43, 60. See also *Act to Amend the Indian Act*
Bill c-38. See omnibus bills
Bill c-45. See omnibus bills
Bill of Rights, 168, 170
Bill s-3, xxvi, 43
Blackfoot People, 17
Black, Jeremy, 55
blockades, Indigenous-led, 109–11
Blood People, 17
"blood quantum," 37, 40, 44, 48, 231, 236, 243
Borrows, John, 25–26, 96–99, 109–11, 197, 222–25, 255, 262
Brannigan, Augustine, 8
Britain, 120
    citizenship, 46
    colonial exploration, 18–21, 153, 197
    constitutional change, 154–55
    Indigenous relations, 65, 116–17, 120, 156, 204, 250

law, application of, 8, 59, 76–78,
    92, 188, 257–58
  see also crown, the; Royal
    Proclamation
British Columbia, 63, 95, 165, 142,
    188
  Court of Appeal cases, 163, 209,
    212–14, 220
  fishing rights in, 190–91, 192
  hunting rights in, 199, 206
  Indigenous population in, 15, 46,
    100, 110–11, 146, 181, 244, 263
  land rights, 126, 131–36, 158, 172,
    198, 209–13, 220–23
  place renaming, 39
  Supreme Court, 208, 212, 218
British Columbia Treaty
    Commission, 138
British North America Act, xxiv, 161,
    163
"Brown Paper," xxv, 167
Bryant, Michael, 194

*Calder v British Columbia (Attorney
    General)*, xxv, 2, 66, 199, 218
  precedence of, 42, 134–36, 150,
    157–58, 170–71, 187, 249
Caledonia, Ontario, 54, 109
Campbell v British Columbia, 218,
    299
Canada–Métis Nation Accord, 133
Canada v Kitselas First Nation, 259,
    299
Canadian Council for Aboriginal
    Business, 249
capitalism, 9
  Indigenous participation in,
    77–82, 250, 257, 268–69
  settler expansion and, 68–69,
    86, 202

values of, 21–24, 58, 70–73,
    100–1, 186, 189, 270
Cardinal, Harold, 167
*Cardinal v Attorney General of
    Alberta*, 222, 299
Caribou Inuit, 17
Carrier (Dakelh) Sekani People, 17,
    263
Cartier, Jacques, 23, 137
Cayuga People, 17
certificate of location/possession,
    157
Charter of Rights and Freedoms, 93,
    100, 120, 137, 163, 195, 236
  Aboriginal and Treaty Rights,
    159, 167–71, 185, 190–92
  section 35: 130, 193, 224
Chartrand v The Queen, 222, 299
Cheyenne People, 17
Chiefs' Committee on Claims, 146
Chinook People, 17
Chipewyan People, 17
Chippewas, 205
Christianity
  Catholic missionaries, 6, 18
  in colonization, xi, 23
  forced conversion, 5–6, 21, 62,
    80
  work, views of, 72
churches, 72, 158
  genocide, role in, 5–6, 76
  rationalism, 90
  state collaboration, 6–7
Clatworthy, Stewart, 43
Coates, Ken, 55
colonialism
  continuation of, 23–24, 187–89,
    203, 222, 225
  dismantling of, 255–56
  early, xx, xxiii, 122, 193

colonialism *(continued)*
  genocidal policies, 3, 5, 8, 21, 78, 209, 231, 235
  history of, 53–57, 183, 196, 235
  imposition of norms, 16, 18–20, 59, 81, 115, 257–58
  influence of, 62, 85–86, 153,
  institutional systems and, 9, 66–67, 103–5, 196–98
  land claiming, 22, 72–76, 99–100, 109, 116–18, 158–60
  resistance to, 2, 66, 250, 262
  types of, 58–59
  See also settler colonialism
colonization, 1, 16
  beliefs and myths of, 20–24, 60, 72
  criminal acts, 5, 8–9, 54
  deep colonizing. *See* deep colonizing
  effects of, 27, 85–86, 223, 232
  isopolity. *See* isopolity
  legal-social system, 18–26, 58–59
  resistance to, 253, 255, 257–60, 272–73. *See also* decolonization
  strategies, 20–21, 77. *See also* subordination, peaceable
common law, British
  application of, 20, 23, 157, 211
  Indigenous law versus, 95, 136, 151
  Indigenous Rights in, 150, 157, 168, 171
communities, Indigenous
  attributes of, 228–29, 232–34
  colonization, effects on, 235
  decision-making in, 235–37
  diversity among, 231–35
  economic development, 267–70
  elections, 235–36
  elites in, 77, 234–35
  surveillance of, 235, 237, 269
Comox People, 17
comprehensive (land) claims, xxi, 2, 196, 228
  amendments to, 116, 137
  growth in, 12, 136, 138–39, 200
  models of, 140, 142–43
  process of, 25, 70–71, 133–36, 140, 147, 199–202, 271
Confederation, 161
Congress of Aboriginal Peoples, xxv, 37, 181–82, 230–31, 244–45
Connolly v Woolrich, 97, 299
Conservative government, 23, 54, 130, 144, 215, 233, 252–53, 256, 264
Constitution Act, 1867, 36, 161, 163–65, 167
Constitution Act, 1982, xx, xxii, 129–30, 136, 154–59, 167–70, 206, 241, 260
  Aboriginal recognition, 27–29, 119, 158, 172, 181, 185–87, 225, 228–29
  breach of, 189–92, 195–96, 270–71
  section 35: 35–37, 137, 158, 177–79, 202–3, 209–12, 265
Constitution of Alberta Amendment Act, 1990, 132, 241
constitutional change, 154, 157–58, 170, 253
Copper Inuit, 17
Corbiere v Canada (Minister of Indian and Northern Affairs), 236, 299
Corntassel, Jeff, 20

corporations, 52–54, 72, 78–79, 86, 90, 235
　certainty for, 140, 202, 263–64, 270
　lack of trust in, 233–34, 268
　rights of, 59, 70, 215, 272
Coulthard, Glen, 25, 58, 189, 203
courts
　Aboriginal Rights, 186–96, 209–10, 215–17, 221–25
　Aboriginal Title test, 210–211
　capitalist ideology, 189, 202–3
　decision-making approach, 171, 189–93, 199–204, 206–13, 219–25
　duty to consult, xxvi, 185, 211–18, 264–65
　government versus, 186–89, 195–96, 199, 212, 220–24, 258–65
　Indigenous use of, 170, 188, 223–24
　Supreme, *see* Supreme Court of Canada
　tort law, use of, 95, 171, 182, 188, 193, 222–24, 260
　treaties, 196–99, 201–10, 212–15, 222–24
Coyle, Michael, 255, 260, 262
creation stories. *See* stories
Cree, xxi, 39, 254
　legal system involvement, 97, 212, 265, 300
　origin story, 13, 15, 106–7
　treaties, 136, 206
Criminal Code, 93, 156, 173, 175
Crow People, 17
crown, the, xxii, 98–99, 151, 202
　abdication of role, 10–11, 19–20, 61, 64–66, 186–87, 216, 241

alienation, Indigenous, 3–5, 51–54, 88, 98, 188–90, 205, 234
fiduciary responsibility, 19, 129–43, 160, 173, 213–14, 218–22, 259, 265. *See also* duty to consult
hegemonic control of, 4, 18, 44, 70–71, 198, 228
Indigeneity and, 27–37, 40, 42, 49, 153–57, 176–77, 232
land, control of, 87, 95–96, 104, 108, 163–65, 195–98
negotiations with, 12, 115–30, 147–48, 159, 180–83, 217–22
sovereignty, 8, 97, 103, 151, 171–72, 209–13, 225, 271
Crown-Indigenous Relations and Northern Affairs Canada, xxvi, 12, 30, 142, 161, 167
crown land, xx, xxii, 65, 108–9, 164–65, 194, 204, 207, 214
Crown Lands and Forests Act, 97, 194
Crown Lands Protection Act, xxiv
cryptoamnesia, 60
culture, Indigenous, 39, 175
　land-based, 95, 101, 106–7, 255
　resilience, 3, 78, 131, 267
　settler structures versus, 24–26, 67–68, 81, 104, 182–84, 193, 257–58
　vibrancy, 62, 67
Cutfeet, John, 119

Daniels v Canada (2013), 36–37, 299
Daniels v Canada (2016), xxvi, 131, 181, 299
Daschuk, James, 124
Davin Report, 6

decolonization, 1, 253–58, 272–73
deep colonizing, 59–60
Delgamuukw v British Columbia, xxv, 2, 95, 105, 138, 172, 174, 208
Dene People, 17
Dene Tha People, 17
Descartes, René, 90
Deschenaux v Canada, 42–43, 299
Dewar, Barry, 149
discrimination
    freedom from, 168
    gender, 40, 42–43, 156, 163
    government, 52, 166, 229
    in the *Indian Act*, xx, xxvi, 42–43, 48, 60
    individualized, 85
    labour market, 84–85, 166; *see also* stereotypes; work
    Métis-focused, 34, 131
    systemic, xxvi, 8, 85, 225, 253–56, 269, 273
disease, 18, 86, 124
    water-borne, 83
disenfranchisement, 5, 116–17, 269
doctrine of discovery, 21
Doerfler, Jill, 44
Dominion Lands Act, 35, 154
Douglas, James, 199
Douglas Treaties, xxiv, 63
duty to consult,
    changes to, 2, 264–65
    land claims, 171, 243
    power struggles with, xxvi, 189, 194–95, 211–18, 220, 222

Eagle Lake First Nation, 175
economy, traditional Indigenous, 81–83
economy, wage, 76
    disparities in, 4–5, 84
    Indigenous participation in, 3, 78–82
    See also work
education, 49, 166
    forced, 6, 32, 80
    Indigenous control of, 111, 148, 156, 239–40, 247, 252, 266–67, 273
    lack of, 3, 79, 82m 86
    Western systems of, xiv, 41, 76, 83, 94, 235, 267, 269
    See also residential schools
eels, selling of, 204
Elders, 237–38
    importance of, 82, 87, 96, 239, 248
    oral testimony of, 105, 187, 207
Elias, Scott, 14
Elsey, Christine J., 87, 100, 102, 104, 106
enfranchisement, xxiv, xxv
    involuntary, 41, 162, 166
    removal of Indian status, 40–41, 47–48
    See also disenfranchisement; *Gradual Enfranchisement Act*
English settlers, xxiii, 18–19, 58, 65, 75, 104. *See also* Britain; common law
treaty negotiation, 119, 205, 228
Enlightenment, Age of, xiv, 21, 81, 89–92, 101
Enoch Cree First Nation, 254
environmental protection, 106, 112, 140, 253, 255
Environmental Protection Act, 253
Environment, Department of the, 149
Erie People, 17

Eurocentrism, 78, 83
  institutional, 2, 9, 18–26, 92, 96, 104, 112–13
  land use, 97–100, 102. See also *terra nullius*
  settler ideologies, 60–62, 90, 228, 257–58
Ewing Commission, 132, 179, 241
Eyeford, Douglas, 234

famine, 124, 126
Federal Court of Appeal, 37, 220, 259
federal government, 23–26, 55–57, 143
  abdication of role, xxvi, 12, 164, 170–72, 186, 209–10, 231–33
  adversarial position of, 95–99, 139–43, 150–51, 228–30, 250–52, 259, 270
  control of, 1–4, 83–86, 135–38, 154, 166–67, 202–3, 257–59
  courts versus the, 186–89, 195–96, 199, 212, 220–24, 258–65
  differential treatment, communities', 232, 234, 259
  disregard for Indigenous Peoples, 19–22, 53–55, 60–64, 213, 230–34, 260–62
  genocidal policies, 5–6, 48–49, 66, 78–86, 150–51, 229, 233
  Indigenous distrust of, 88, 147, 231–35, 249–50, 253–61, 272–73
  Indigenous identification, 26–49, 85, 130–33, 154–60, 167, 173
  land negotiations, 74–75, 103–5, 109–13, 128–29. See also *terra nullius*
  legislative interpretation, 66, 120–24, 165–66, 257–58
  monitoring of communities, 44, 59, 69–71, 74, 80, 161–62, 230, 235, 237
  residential schools, 6–8
  topographical maps, 73–75, 104
  treaties. *See* treaties
  See also duty to consult; *Indian Act*; land claims
federalism, constitutional, 223–24, 229
Finance, Department of, 149
financial compensation, xxi, 103, 140, 145–47, 166, 195, 209, 220, 223
First Nations,
  definition, xx, 37–38, 42–45, 74, 160
  population, 18, 45–49, 53, 62, 65, 115–16
First Nations Bank of Canada, 254
First Nations Land Management Act, 252, 263–64
Fisheries Act, 78, 190–92, 204
fishing, 60, 72–73, 107, 140, 232
  barriers to, 83–84, 207–8, 215
  commercial, 83–84, 191–92, 208
  licences, 80, 204
  rights, 99, 117–18, 122, 137, 190–92, 213–15, 221
Flathead People, 17
Fort St. John Band, 131, 198
Foster, Hamar, 20, 57
French, the, xxiii, 18, 65, 67, 117
  colonial exploration, 58, 76, 104, 160, 188
  legal system of, 9, 19, 23, 116, 196–97, 250
frontier myth, 75

funding, 235, 269
    incoherence, 3, 25–26, 135, 230
    lack of, 86, 142, 146, 259. See also social services
fur trade, xxiii, 6, 18, 58, 64, 81, 116, 130–31, 162, 258

gambling, 155, 173–75
Gathering Strength—Canada's Aboriginal Action Plan, 121–22
Gehl v Canada (Attorney General), 40–42
Gender Equity in Indian Registration Act (Bill C-3), xxvi, 42–43
gender inequity, 40, 163, 239
    colonial, 156, 234
    "paternity rule," xxv, xxvi, 41–43, 254
genocide, Indigenous, 5, 18, 76, 256
George III, 65, 160
Gitxsan People, 17, 64, 172, 187, 208–9
    Reconciliation Agreement, 210
glaciers, prehistoric, 14
government, *see* federal government; provincial government
Gradual Enfranchisement Act, xxiv, 47–48
Grassy Narrows First Nation v Ontario (Natural Resources), 151, 223, 299
Gray, Darrell, 194
Great Law of Peace, 196
Great Peace Treaty, xxiii
Gros Venture People, 17
grounded normativity, 189
Guerin v The Queen, xxv, 171, 219, 300
Guha, Ranajit, 78
Gwichin People, 17

Haida Nation, 3, 212
Haida Nation v British Columbia (Minister of Forests), xxvi, 2, 212, 300
Haisla People, 17
Hamlet of Baker Lake v Canada (Indian Affairs and Northern Development), 158–59, 192, 300
Han People, 17
Harland, Fraser, 95
Harper, Stephen, 23, 54, 130
Haudenosaunee,
    Confederacy, 196
    Sky Woman, 13, 15, 106
health care, 148
    lack of, 3
Heiltsuk Nation, 15, 100
Henderson, James, 119
history, 112, 151
    colonial retelling of, xiv, 18–19, 56–57, 61–62, 67
    denial of, 23–24, 54, 119, 150
    factors in understanding, 56, 61–65, 85–86
    Indigenous telling of, 55, 57, 61–62, 64, 105–9, 265
    legal documentation, 56–57, 61–66
    oral, xxii, 100, 143, 207
    pre-, 13–16
Hobbes, Thomas, 21–22
Hoffecker, John, 14
Honouring the Truth, Reconciling for the Future (TRC), 266
Horseman, Bert, 207–8
Hudson Bay, xxiii, 29
Hudson's Bay Company, xxiii, 124, 155–56
hunting, 72–73, 99, 122, 198–99, 213
    commercial, 149, 206, 208, 215, 242

Métis, 33, 131, 179–80, 242, 244
rights, xxvi, 60, 84, 107, 117, 149, 170, 206–8, 221
Huron People, xxiv, 17, 117, 137

Ibrahim, Tamara, 108
Idle No More, 249, 255–56
Igloolik Inuit, 17
imperialism, 20
incarceration, Indigenous, 3, 110
Indian
    definition, xx, xxv, 32, 85, 163, 169
    identification, 27, 29–30, 34–49, 55–56, 241, 243
    name changes, 39–40, 75–76, 104
    "problem" 3–4, 24, 51–52, 62, 68, 73–74, 85–86
    See also Non-Status (Indian); Status (Indian); Treaty Indians
Indian Act
    of 1876: xxiv, 40, 48, 74, 78, 161–62, 166, 254
    of 1951: xxv, 9, 29, 32, 66, 162, 165–67, 177
    assimilation. *See* assimilation
    colonization, 18–26, 58–59, 78, 84
    definition, xx
    discrimination. *See* discrimination
    federal control through, 25, 43–44, 66, 103, 166–67, 222, 270, 272
    Indigenous law. *See* law, Indigenous
    property rights, 157–58, 161–62, 178
    registry, 29–30, 40, 42–44
    reserves. *See* reserves
    residential schools. *See* residential schools
    restrictions of, 69–70, 83–84, 234–37
    revisions of, xxiv–xxvi, 29, 32, 40–43, 66, 161–63, 177, 253
    taxation, 84, 177–78
    See also Non-Status (Indian); Status (Indian); Treaty Indians
Indian Affairs, Department of, 47, 143, 146
    control of, 3, 23, 40–44, 79, 134, 166–67, 200, 254
    creation of, xxiv
    jurisdiction, 29, 71, 157–58, 162, 235, 237, 253, 264
    See also Indian and Northern Affairs Canada
Indian Lands Act, xxiv, 164
Indian and Northern Affairs Canada, xxv, 143, 236
Indian Specific Claims Commission, 138, 143–44, 146, 199
Indigenization, 267
Indigenous Bar Association, 249
Indigenous and Northern Affairs Canada, xxi, xxvi, 12, 30
Indigenous Peoples,
    alienation, 4, 19, 24, 42, 56–60, 95–96, 228, 251–52, 273
    consent, "free, prior and informed," 150, 205, 215, 228, 264–66, 272
    culture. *See* culture, Indigenous
    definition of, xxi, 27–28, 73–74
    demographics, 18, 44–47, 82, 115
    epistemologies, 58, 87, 89, 91–92, 96

Indigenous Peoples (continued)
  erasure, 10, 42, 54, 56–60
  extinguishment of rights. See Aboriginal Rights
  identification, 26–49, 55, 85, 130–33, 154–60, 167, 173
  marginalization, 24, 33–35, 76–77, 86, 166–67, 267–70
  ontologies, 58, 87, 89, 91–92, 96, 100–1, 123
  personhood, 6, 8, 19–24, 119, 234
  resistance movements, xxiv, 7–9, 32, 54, 109, 126, 189, 255–58, 272. See also political activism
  sovereignty. See sovereignty, Indigenous
  treaties, views on, 64–65, 98, 118–19, 122–24, 148–49, 186, 197, 205
Indigenous Services Canada, xxvi, 12, 161, 167
Indigenous Traditional Knowledge, 91, 248
individualism, 9, 20, 24, 68, 72–75, 81, 101
  autonomy, 93–96, 268–70
inequity, systemic, 228, 253
  gender. See gender inequity
  privilege. See privilege
  with settlers, 59–60, 77–79, 112, 151
  socio-economic, 4–5, 94, 166, 263–64
  See also power imbalance
infrastructure, 132
  lack of, 86, 269
Innu Peoples, xxi, 17
Interior Salish People, 106
Interpretation Act, 252
Inuit, 58, 161, 228
  definition, xxi, xxv, 28, 32, 49
  identification, 28–32, 44–46
  land negotiations, 158–59
  organizations, 245–49
  regional districts, 31, 138
  relocation of, 136
Inuit Circumpolar Council of Canada, 249
Inuit Relations Secretariat, 30
Inuvialuit, xxi–xxii, 32, 142, 245–46, 249
  Final Agreement, xxv
  Regional Corporation, 246
  See also *Western Arctic Claims Settlement Act*
Inuvialuit Claims Settlement Act, xxv
Ipperwash, 109
isinglass, 60
isopolity, 59–60

Jai, Julie, 115–16, 150
James Bay Cree, 17
James Bay and Northern Quebec Agreement, 135–36, 247
Jesuit missionaries, 6
job creation, 139
José de Acosta, Fray, 14
Justice, Department of, 23, 128, 134–35, 142–45, 149, 195, 200–2, 252–54

Kaska People, 17
Kativik regional government, 247
Keith, Jennifer, 70, 203
Kelm, Mary-Ellen, 56, 250
Kitselas First Nation, 259
Kiyawasew, Leroy, 206–7
Ktunaxa Nation, 100
Kutenai People, 17

labour. *See* work
Labrador Inuit, 17
Labrador Inuit Association, 247–48
Labrador Inuit Land Claims
 Agreement, 247
Lake Okanagan People, 17
land, 66, 70, 75, 118, 122–23, 132,
 140, 189
 acquisition of, 22, 32, 47, 62,
  118–19, 127–32, 169, 197–98,
  205
 capitalist view of, 9–10, 22–24,
  68–70, 99–100, 189
 commodification of, 58, 69, 88,
  98–101, 189
 dispossession, 5, 23–25, 96–100,
  126–28, 147, 223, 257, 270
 fee simple title, 100, 132, 157,
  219–20, 233
 importance of, 1, 10, 69, 87–92,
  95, 98–109, 170, 189
 Indigenous identity and, 87, 99,
  101–3, 105–9, 189
 mapping of, 73–75, 104
 ownership of, 2, 18–19, 25, 58–59,
  85–87, 96, 101–11, 197, 202
 spirituality and, 95–102, 105–13,
  123–24, 189, 237
 stewardship of, 88, 101, 108–9,
  112, 123, 156
 surrender of, 19, 64–74, 84,
  109–19, 157, 164–65, 253, 258,
  262
 treaties. *See* treaties
 See also political activism;
  terra nullius; Traditional
  Territories
land claims
 classes of, xxi, 133
 costs, 135–36, 139–40, 147
 doctrine of laches, 128–29, 135,
  139
 establishment of, 99–105, 113
 Gitxsan-Wet'suet'en, 64, 187,
  208–10
 growth of, 12
 Inuit, 29–30, 32, 247, 249
 legislation, 104, 134–42, 170–71,
  271
 settlement, factors of, 261–62
 state litigation, 11–12, 113, 128,
  148–49, 222, 247, 258, 261
 treaties and, 29–30, 32, 63–64,
  139–50, 169, 196–203
 See also comprehensive
  claims; specific claims; title,
  Aboriginal
law, Indigenous, 129, 173, 262–63
 Aboriginal law versus, 94–95
 composition of, 20, 255
 epistemologies, 94–96, 151, 255
 ignorance of, 19–20, 42, 95–98,
  105–12, 155, 175, 193, 225
 land, relationship to, 98–113
 restorative justice, 95, 188, 229
 as "tradition," 97–98
law, international, 10, 147
Lawrence, Bonita, 255
law, Western
 autonomy of, 9–10, 47–49
 coerciveness of, 12, 59–60,
  77–78, 96, 108–9, 150
 composition of, 20, 62–64, 96,
  113, 258–60
 critiques of, 103, 108–9, 182, 193,
  258–65
 epistemologies, 87–89, 92–94,
  98–99, 151, 255
 imposition of, 19–20, 40–42, 57,
  76, 98, 150–51, 222

law, Western *(continued)*
   "on the face" interpretation, 56, 204, 209
Lewis, John, 100
Liberal government, 12, 130, 157–58, 167, 253, 256, 264
liberalism, 20, 23, 77–78, 101, 154, 229
   neo-, 53, 267–69, 273
Lillooet People, 17
Lil'wat Nation, 110–11
Locke, John, 21–22, 73
logging, 9, 18, 80, 110–13, 117, 163, 204, 220, 258
   expansion, xxiii, 105
   See also timber
Lougheed, Peter, 132, 158
Lovelace, Sandra, 42, 60, 300
Lutz, John Sutton, 59, 68, 77, 79, 86

Macklem, Patrick, 9–10, 183
Mahican People, 17
Maliseet People, 17, 194
Manitoba, 39, 180
   Indigenous population in, 3, 45–47
   Métis, 127–31, 181, 241, 244
   missionaries, 6
   treaties, 142, 148
   See also Red River Settlement
Manitoba Act, 35, 116, 120, 126–30, 168, 228, 241
Manitoba Métis, 127–28, 241
   court case, 128–30, 300
Marshall, Donald, 204
Massachuset People, 17
Matsqui (Sto:lo Nation), 263
McEachern, Allan, 208–9
McIvor case, xxvi, 42, 163, 300

McNeil, Kent, 150
media, 44, 239
   on Indigenous people, 20, 51–55, 61, 71, 269
Membertou First Nation, 254
Menomini People, 17
meritocracy, valuing, 4–5
Merryman, John, 94
Métis, 222
   discrimination, 34, 130–31, 228
   identification, 32–38, 44–46, 181–82
   land issues, 118, 126–30
   Nation, xxi–xxii, 34, 36, 131, 181, 245
   official recognition, *see* Alberta
   organizations, 131, 240–45
   Rights, 33, 131, 178–81, 242, 244
   scrip, receiving, 32, 35, 126–30
   settlement areas, 33, 35, 38, 130–33
Métis General Council, 132, 242
Métis National Council, xxv, 37, 131, 133, 181, 230
   federal representation, 245
   governance of, 243–44
Métis Population Betterment Act, 132, 179, 241
Métis Settlements Accord, 132
Métis Settlements Act, 2000, 241–44
Métis Settlements Appeal Tribunal, 242
Miami People, 17
Michel First Nation, 198
migration theories, prehistoric, 14–16
Mi'kmaq, 17, 97, 122, 138
   Treaty of 1752: 117, 120
   Treaty Rights, 198, 204

Missing and Murdered Indigenous
    Women and Girls Commission,
    256
missionaries, xxiii, 6–7, 18, 64.
    See also Anglican missionaries;
    Christianity; Jesuit missionaries
Mississaugas, 205
*Mitchell v Minister of National
    Revenue*, 193
Methodist missionaries, 6
*Mikisew Cree First Nation v Minister
    of Canadian Heritage*, 212–13,
    265, 300
mining, 9, 59, 117, 164, 213–14
moditional economy, 79–80
Mohawk (Kanien'keha:ka), 6, 17, 193
Monchalin, Lisa, xiv, 24, 53–54, 188
Montagnais People, 17
Moore, Margaret, 116, 229, 273
Morin, Jean-Pierre, 151
Mount Currie Band, 110
Mulroney, Brian, 154
Musqueam Band, 137, 190, 219–20

National Centre for Truth and
    Reconciliation, 266
National Indian Brotherhood, xxv,
    44, 237
National Indian Council, 237
National Inuit Youth Council, 249
National Reconciliation Council, 271
nation-to-nation relationship, 120,
    181, 197–98, 224, 253, 273
nation-state
    building the, 19–20, 56, 268
    policies of, 24–25
Native Council of Canada, xxv,
    244–45
Native Women's Association of
    Canada, xxv, 230

Natural Resources Transfer Act,
    xxiv, 77, 128, 165
    Treaty Rights, 64, 131–32,
    148–49, 204, 207–8
Natural Resources Transfer
    Agreement, 206
Netsilik Inuit, 17
Neutral People, 17
New Brunswick, 34, 46, 194
Newfoundland and Labrador,
    xxi, 32, 46, 126, 142. See also
    Labrador Inuit Association
Newman, Dwight, 189
Nez Perce People, 17
Nisga'a, xxv, 17, 136, 158, 187–88,
    218, 235
    Final Agreement, 138
    See also *Calder v British
        Columbia*
Nitinat People, 17
Nolin, Joseph, 197
non-Indigenous people, 113, 171, 255
    beliefs about Indigenous people,
        20–24, 54–61, 79, 84–85,
        229–30. See also meritocracy;
        stereotypes
    colonial interactions, 24, 58–59,
        62, 64, 85–86, 98, 117
    conflict resolution with, 224,
        229–30, 251–58, 266, 270–72
    economic exchange values,
        67–69, 70–85, 88–90, 98–100,
        112, 139, 162
    ignorance of, 5, 44, 87, 109–11,
        231, 273
    Indigenous inequity with, 4, 51,
        64, 166, 168, 222–23
    legal perceptions, 19, 62–66, 95,
        109, 153–60, 182–88
    privilege of, 25, 83–85, 96, 166

non-Indigenous people *(continued)*
  on treaties, 121–22, 186, 203
  victimization, 54, 131–32
  See also colonialism; English settlers; French, the; law, Western; reconciliation; Western culture
Non-Status (Indian), 28, 36, 132, 237, 245
  definition, xx, xxii, 44
  legal debate, 40–42, 171, 181–82,
  population of, 47–48
North Airline, 254
Northwest Territories, 39, 126
  Indigenous population in, xxi, 32, 34, 45–47, 131, 181
  land claims, 133, 142
Nova Scotia, 46, 122, 198, 254
Numbered Treaties, xxiv, 126, 128, 142, 170, 196, 262
  different understanding of, 122–23, 148–51, 215, 228
  negative impact of, 115–19, 202–3, 258
Nunangat, xxii, 32, 36, 245
Nunatsiavut, xxii, 32, 245
  self-government, 247–49
Nunavik, 30, 32, 245
  Makivik Corporation, 247
  self-government. *See* Kativik regional government
Nunavut, xxii, 138, 245
  Indigenous population in, 32, 46
  land claims, 29–30, 32, 142
  Legislative Assembly, 248
Nunavut Land Claims Agreement, 29–30, 248
Nunavut Tunngavik Incorporated, 248–49
Nuu'Cha'Nulth People, 17

Odawa People, 17
Office of Native Claims, 134–36, 199
oil and gas industry, 52, 113, 232, 243
  Indigenous communities and, 217, 234, 246
Ojibwa People, 17
Oka Crisis, xxv, 109
Ominayak, Ernest, 206–7
omnibus bills, 252–53
Oneida People, 17
Onondaga People, 17
Ontario, 66, 244
  court cases, 41, 151, 223
  Indigenous population in, 45–47, 49, 131, 181
  protests in, 54
  residential school, 6
  treaties, 117, 151, 163–64, 205
organizations, Indigenous.
  See political organizations, Indigenous; social organizations, Indigenous
O'Rourke, Dennis, 14
Osoyoos First Nation, 254

Palmater, Pamela, 52, 273
Panagos, Dimitrios, 224
papal bulls, 18, 20–21, 23
Papaschase First Nation, 198
Parliament, 27, 71, 170, 246, 249, 264–65
  Aboriginal Rights, 118, 154–56, 183, 196, 222, 252
  colonialism, 23–24, 96
  courts versus, 186–89, 195–96, 199, 212, 220–24, 258–65
  gender discrimination, 43, 163
  Indian Act, 29, 49
  land claims, 134, 163, 165
Passamaquoddy People, 17

Passelac-Ross, Monique, 216
Pauktuutit Inuit Women of Canada, 249
Paulette Caveat case, xxv
Peace Hills Trust, 254
Pearson, Lester B., 134
Peavine Métis Settlement v Alberta, 222, 300
Peigan People, 17
Penner Report, 251
Penobscot People, 17
Perez-Perdomo, Rogelio, 94
petitions. *See* political activism
Phelan, Michael, 36, 181
pipelines, 88, 224, 253
Plains Cree, 17
political activism, Indigenous, 166–67, 254–55
    civil disobedience, 109, 182
    government ignorance of, 8, 42
    petitions, 2, 8, 44, 66, 76
    seen as security threat, 54, 230
    See also Idle No More
political organizations, Indigenous, 230, 238, 249
    discrediting of, 11
    See also social organizations, Indigenous
Polzer, Jessica, 268–70
Pope Alexander VI, 21
Pope Nicolas V, 21
Portugal, colonial exploration, 21
positivism, 19, 89
Potawatomi People, 17
Potes, Veronica, 216
Potlatches, 61, 167
poverty, Indigenous, 3, 9, 52, 167, 273
Power, Elaine, 268–70
power imbalance, 143, 233
    colonial, 58–62, 74, 77–78, 149–50

    corporate, 53, 86, 234
    crown versus Indigenous, 12, 96, 104–8, 115, 154, 172, 217, 252, 260–65
    legal, 37, 63–64, 94, 183, 218–19, 222
    rectifying, 247, 250–51, 255–58, 262–63, 273
    state coercion, 25, 70, 130–31, 166, 196, 259, 261, 270–72
    treaties, 115–19, 197, 203
Prime Minister's Office, 53, 149
privilege, 82, 259, 267
    male, 78
    white, 5
Privy Council, 62, 66, 163–64, 188, 218
property, 74–75, 178, 257
    certificate of possession, 157
    communal, 99, 107, 113, 156–57, 172, 220
    laws, 47, 161, 171, 218
    private, 18, 58–59, 68, 76, 81
    rights, 22, 61–62, 73, 93, 156–57, 163, 209, 220
provincial/territorial governments, xix, 26, 76–77, 82–84, 163–65, 254
    child apprehension, 7, 9
    federal government versus, 48–49, 145, 191, 218, 221–24, 262, 271
    ignorance of Indigenous concerns, 26, 57, 63, 130, 240–44, 265, 272
    Indigenous populations in, 34, 45–47, 96, 180–82, 209–17, 266
    jurisdiction, 25, 132, 154–58, 168, 177–80, 198–99
    land claims and, 63–66, 108–11, 136, 139–40, 149–51

Quebec, 126
  Indigenous population in, 46–47, 231, 244, 247, 254
  Indigenous women, xxvi, 42–43
  jurisdiction, 29
  land claims, 135, 142, 146, 165, 197
  Métis, 34, 38
  northern, xxv, 133
Quebec Inuit, 17
The Queen v Nowegijick, 177–78, 300

Raft, the (Cree origin story), 13, 15, 106–7
rationalism, rise of, 21–22, 68, 75, 81, 90–91, 101, 104
Ray, Arthur J., 19, 61, 63, 67, 126, 143, 187, 223
Razack, Sherene, 257
reconciliation, 187, 225, 255–56
  calls to action, 251–52, 264, 266–67
  government failure, 4, 151, 196, 216, 253–55, 259, 270
  Métis, 130, 133
  treaties, 202, 210
  See also Truth and Reconciliation Commission
Red River Settlement, 34, 37–38, 126–28, 131, 243
Red Sucker Lake, 39
Regan, Paulette, 4, 57
relational knowledge, 91, 260
relocation, forced, 3, 76, 96, 136, 162, 198, 267
reserves, xxii, 147, 198, 213, 224, 259
  conditions on, 71, 83, 167, 234
  creation of, 21, 74–75, 83, 104, 122–23, 134, 205
  government relocation of, xxii, 84, 111–12, 219, 253
  off of, xxii, 44, 166, 177–78, 181, 236, 245
  population on, 47, 110, 231
  regulation of, 9, 70, 119, 126, 162–66, 175–78, 263–64
  Status Indians and, 47, 157
Residential School Compensation Act, xxvi
residential schools, xxiv
  forced attendance, 6–7
  investigation of, 265–66
  policies of, 5–7, 82, 166, 270
  resistance to, 7–8
resources, 108, 232–33
  Aboriginal Rights to, 108–10, 133, 200–3, 209, 271–73
  comprehensive claims, 139–40, 242
  exploitation of, 21, 111–12, 117, 139, 214, 257, 267
  management, xx, 140, 195, 246
  settler approach to, 9, 21–25, 58, 73, 81, 110, 231
  state control of, 70, 96–99, 163–65, 259
  See also Natural Resources Transfer Act
Revenue Canada, 12, 178, 193, 222
Riel, Louis, 38
  resistance movement, xxiv, 32, 34, 126
Roach, Kent, 261
Robinson-Huron Treaty, xxiv, 117, 197
Robinson-Superior Treaties, xxiv, 117, 197
Robinson, William, 117–18
Rose, Nikolas, 268
Ross River Dena Council Band v Canada, 150, 300

Royal Commission on Aboriginal
  Peoples, xxv, 35, 109, 112, 251
Royal Proclamation, xxiii, 135, 150,
  168–69, 194, 197–99, 211, 222–23
  land rights, 65, 103, 117, 155–60,
  218, 249
Rupert's Land, xxiii, 118, 126,
  155–56
Rupert's Land Order, 150
R v Badger, 186, 206, 215, 300
R v Beer, 181, 300
R v Belhumeur, 180, 300
R v Bernard, 204, 300
R v Blais, 128, 300
R v Dick, 222–23, 300
R v Goodon, 181, 300
R v Gray, 194, 300
R v Horseman, 63–64, 149, 207, 300
R v Laviolette, 180, 300
R v Marshall, 121, 137–38, 204
R v Powley, xxvi, 35–37, 129, 131,
  228, 244, 300
  test, 179–80
R v Sappier, 194, 300
R v Simon, 97, 204, 300
R v Sioui, 137, 204, 300
R v Sparrow, xxv, 2, 137, 160,
  171–72, 190–92, 195, 300
R v Syliboy, 97, 120, 198, 300
R v Van der Peet, 95, 121, 179–80,
  192–94, 300
  test, 172–75, 192
R v White and Bob, 177, 300

Saalequun community, 199
Salish Peoples, 17, 198
Samson Cree, 254
Sanderson, Douglas, 25–26
Sappier, Dale, 194
Saskatchewan, 148, 180, 244
  Indigenous population in, 34,
    45–47, 131, 179, 241
  land claims, 145–46
  Métis Act, 241
  missionaries, 6
Sauk Fox People, 17
Saulteaux (Anishinaabe), 17, 64–66,
  197
Sayisi Dene, 3
science, privileging of, 20, 23,
  89–90, 92
scrip. *See* Métis
Second World War, xxv, 165–66, 249
self-determination, 55, 111, 202
  petitions, 2
  strategies, 231, 257, 262–63
  suppression of, 272–73
  systemic change, 228–29, 238,
    271
self-government, Indigenous, 235,
  254, 262–63
  definition, xix
  Inuit, 247–48
  land claims and, 147–48, 202–3,
    241
  legislative power distribution,
    154, 218, 263, 272
  negotiation of, 12, 140, 142, 182,
    218, 229–31, 252, 272
  right to, 154–56, 175, 209, 244,
    271
Senate, Canadian, 252, 264
settler colonialism, 5
  attributes, 58–60
  denial of, 10, 19, 23–24
  ideologies, 257–58
  See also colonialism;
    colonization
Seven Years War, xxiii, 65, 160–61
Shawanaga First Nation, 175

Shoshone People, 17
Siksika First Nation, 39, 44, 75–76
Sioux People, 17
Six Nations, 6–7
smallpox, 3
Smith, Keith D., 56, 250
social media, Indigenous use of, 249–50
social organizations, Indigenous
   community differences, 231–32
   local Chief and council, 77, 235–37
   Métis Settlement Council, 242–43. *See also* Métis General Council
   national, 237–240, 243–45, 248–49. *See also* Assembly of First Nations; Métis National Council
   non-political, 229
   political goals of, 228–29, 251
   regional, 245–48
   self-government. *See* self-government, Indigenous
   spiritual, 237
   the state, critiques of, 228–29
   surveillance of, 71, 230, 235
   temporary, 230
   under-resourcing of, 230
   See also communities, Indigenous
social services, 133, 146
   apprehension of children, state, 9
   Indigenous delivery of, 240, 244, 247–48
   state provision, 25–26, 83, 86, 268
Songish People (Lekwungen People), 17
sovereignty
   crown, 8, 97, 103, 151, 171–72, 209–13, 225, 271

   Indigenous, xxiv, 19–20, 55, 103, 147, 155, 182, 255, 271
   settler, 58, 75, 116, 118, 133, 154–55, 257
   territorial, xxiv, 23, 61–62, 160, 164, 210–11
   treaties and, 119, 124, 147, 202
Spain, colonial exploration, 18–19, 21
Sparrow, Ronald, 190–92. *See also* *R v Sparrow*
Specific Claims Resolution Act, 143
Specific Claims Tribunal, 146
   Act, 200, 259
   See also Chief's Committee on Claims
specific (land) claims, xxi, xxv, 133, 142
   compensation, 146–47
   new policies for, 136, 143–44, 199
   resolution of, 144, 146, 150–51, 200, 259
   summary of, 145
   tribunal decision-making, 144, 146, 200, 259
Squamish Salish People, 17
Status (Indian), 161, 177, 193, 206
   band status versus, 43–44, 236
   definition, xx, xxii, 35–36
   gaining/losing, 27, 32, 47–49, 162
   legal debate, 40–44, 47–48, 157
   organizational representation, 237–38, 245
   population, 46–47
St. Catharines Milling and Lumber Company v Regina, 66, 163–65, 188, 218, 301
stereotypes, 58, 62, 67, 73–74, 81, 83, 85–86, 166
Stevenson, Mark, 113

Sto:lo First Nation, 192, 263
stories
    creation, 13, 15–16, 99, 101, 106–7
    Indigenous history, 18–19, 55, 87–88, 100–5, 187, 239
    types of, 106–8
subordination, 21, 59, 68, 81, 115, 195
    peaceable, 76–80, 86, 224
Sundances, 61, 70, 167, 237
Supreme Court of Canada, 153–60,
    decisions, xxv, 42, 61, 100, 138, 163, 183, 236, 250
    duty to consult, xxvi, 185, 211–18, 264–65
    Indian Act, 29, 60
    Indigenous Rights, 135–37, 149–51, 171–77, 186–96, 221–25, 261
    on Métis, xxvi, 35–37, 116, 129–30, 133, 179–81, 241
    oral testimony, 105, 187, 266–67
    ruling power, 27, 189, 209–11, 220, 222, 228, 271
    on treaties, 120–21, 137, 143, 148, 186, 197–98, 203–8
    Van der Peet test, 172–75, 179, 193. See also *R v Van der Peet*
Suzack, Cheryl, 100
Swampy Cree, 17

Tagish People, 17
Tahltan People, 17
Taku River Tlingit First Nation v British Columbia, 213, 301
Tamanawas dances, 167
Tapiriit Kanatami, xxv, 230, 248–49
Teillet, Jean, 32, 119–20, 148
terra nullius, 19
    colonization, 21, 23, 62, 73, 116
    land claims, 103

treaties, 115, 265
Teslin People, 17
Thompson People, 17
timber, 254
    cutting unlicensed, 194, 204
    unlawful possession of, 204
title, Aboriginal, 218, 223, 238
    "burden" on crown, 19, 156–61, 209
    changes to, 2, 211–13, 271
    criteria for, 103, 138, 151, 155, 172–73, 182, 210
    definition, xix–xxi, 28, 220–21
    Métis, 32, 132
    resource ownership, 139
    test for, 210–11
    treaties, 123, 163–65, 197, 260
    unaddressed, 133–36, 139, 142–43, 146, 187–88, 208–9
Tlicho Agreement, 138
Tlingit People, 17
Tobacco People, 17
Traditional Territories, 27, 103, 206–7, 220, 224
    as cultural heritage, 100, 105–6, 108, 189, 272–73
    loss of, 88, 109–10, 133, 164, 203
    occupation of, 35, 73, 113, 160, 187–88
    right to, 95, 103, 117, 197–98, 213–14, 250
trapping, 242
    colonial, 6
    commercial, 208, 215
    Indigenous, 60–61, 72–73, 81, 84, 213
    rights, xix, xxi, 117, 198, 207–8, 215, 221
Treasury Board, 134
treaties, xxi, 130, 147, 186, 271–73

treaties *(continued)*
   areas with no, 63, 110, 133–35. *See also* Treaty Land Entitlement
   colonization, 10, 59, 98, 103
   disenfranchisement. *See* disenfranchisement
   exploitation through, 104, 108, 115, 118–19, 122–24, 252, 254–55
   federal government and, 103, 117–27, 132–33, 144–51, 163–65, 259
   historical, 125, 163–65, 183, 196–202, 254, 258, 270
   interpretation of, 63–65, 119–24, 137, 143, 177–78, 228
   land cession, 122, 147–49
   Métis, 32, 116
   modern, 2, 25, 70, 133, 139–43, 148, 196, 202–11, 235
   Numbered, xxiv, 115–19, 122–28, 148, 151, 170, 215, 228, 262
   oral promises versus, 119, 205–6
   payments, 39–40, 47, 117
   Peace and Friendship, xxiii, 115–18, 122, 147, 170, 196, 228, 258
   periods of, 115, 147
   process of, 117–19, 126, 148–51, 186, 238
   re-examination of, 147–48
   rights, 118, 136, 148–51, 158–59, 168–72, 188–91, 196–215, 260
Treaty of 1752: 97, 117, 120, 198
Treaty of 1760: 122, 137–38, 204
Treaty Indian, 206
   definition, xxii, 45, 48–49
   Non-, 48–49
Treaty Land Entitlement, 134, 144–45
   Framework Agreement, 145

Treaty of Niagara, 194, 197, 222–23
tribal councils, xxii, 263
Trigger, Bruce G., 57
Trudeau, Pierre, 154
Truth and Reconciliation Commission, xxvi, 251, 265–67
Tsetsaut People, 17
Tsilhqot'in Nation v British Columbia, xxvi, 2, 95–96, 138, 151, 172, 210, 265, 301
   Aboriginal Title case study, 220–23
Tsilhqot'in People, 17
Tsuut'ina People, 17
Tutchone People, 17
Tully, James, 255
Two Axe Early, Mary, 60
Two Row Wampum Belt (*Kamien'Kehaka Kaswentha*), 197

United Nations, 27, 42, 147, 238, 265
United Nations Declaration on the Rights of Indigenous Peoples (UNDRIP), xxvi, 138, 250, 252, 264, 273
universal rights, 20, 23

Van der Peet, Dorothy, 192–94
Veracini, Lorenzo, 59
violence,
   Indigenous women and girls, 240, 256
   state-sanctioned, 8–9
Vuntut Gwitchin, 254

Walters, Mark, 261
Waswanipi Cree, 254
water, 140
   government regulations, 73, 83, 132

lack of potable, 83, 252
protection of, 53, 69, 99, 107
Western Arctic Claims Settlement Act, 246
Western culture, 117–18
  autonomy in, 93
  epistemologies, 87, 89, 92–94, 102–3, 151
  ideologies, 257–58
  imposition of, 16, 18, 60–62, 203, 222
  ontologies, 87, 89, 261
  values, 21–25, 72, 255
  See also education; law, Western
Wet'suet'en Nation, 64, 187, 208–9
  Reconciliation Agreement, 210
White Paper (1969), xxv, 157, 167
Wilkes, Rima, 108
Williamson, Paul, 218
Williams Treaty, 205
women and girls, Indigenous, 97, 238, 240, 249
  discrimination against, xx, xxvi, 78, 156, 234
  legal struggles, 41–43, 47–48, 60, 100
  Missing and Murdered (MMIWG), 240, 256
  See also gender inequity
Woodland Cree, 17
work
  cross-cultural exchange, 22, 67–73, 76
  enframement, 77–80
  "ethic," 60–61, 72–73
  labour force participation, 267–70
  labour pools, 79, 81–86
  See also job creation

Xeni Gwet'in v British Columbia. See *Tsilhqot'in Nation v British Columbia*

Yukon, 34, 45, 46, 138, 142, 254

ABOUT THE AUTHOR

James Frideres is the author of *Aboriginal Peoples in Canada* and *First Nations in the 21st Century*. He was the co-editor of *Canadian Ethnic Studies* for over two decades as well as for the *International Journal for Aboriginal Policy*. He taught at the University of Calgary and was the director of the International Indigenous Studies program for nearly a decade. He is currently professor emeritus and lives in Calgary.

www.ingramcontent.com/pod-product-compliance
Lightning Source LLC
Chambersburg PA
CBHW030432300426
44112CB00009B/957